Doniphan's Epic March

MODERN WAR STUDIES

DONIPHAN'S EPIC MARCH

The 1st Missouri Volunteers in the Mexican War

Joseph G. Dawson III

University Press of Kansas

Published by the University Press of Kansas (Lawrence, Kansas 66049), which was organized by the Kansas Board of Regents and is operated and funded by Emporia State University, Fort Hays State University, Kansas State University, Pittsburg State University, the University of Kansas, and Wichita State University

Library of Congress Cataloging-in-Publication Data

Dawson, Joseph G., 1945–
Doniphan's epic march : the 1st Missouri Volunteers in the Mexican War / Joseph G. Dawson III.
p. cm. — (Modern war studies)
Includes bibliographical references and index.
ISBN 0-7006-0956-3 (alk. paper)
1. United States. Army. Missouri Infantry Regiment, 1st (1846–1847) 2. Mexican War, 1846–1848—Regimental histories. 3. Doniphan, Alexander William. 4. Mexican War, 1846–1848—Campaigns. I. Title. II. Series.
E409.5.M58D39 1999
973.7'478—dc21 98-55515

British Library Cataloguing in Publication Data is available.

Printed in the United States of America

10 9 8 7 6 5 4 3 2 1

The paper used in this publication meets the minimum requirements of the American National Standard for Permanence of Paper for Printed Library Materials Z39.48-1984.

To Ashley Lois Dawson,
who found her own connections to
Liberty, Missouri

CONTENTS

ILLUSTRATIONS

ACKNOWLEDGMENTS

Major Thomas Tyree Smith, U.S. Army, intrepid traveler to Chihuahua, provided several research suggestions for this project. His tactical observations about the Sacramento battlefield were crucial to improving my understanding of that engagement. His maps also present geographic perspectives of Doniphan's marches and battles. Working with Major Smith, an author and editor himself, is a classic example of the professor learning from his student.

Grateful acknowledgment is hereby made to Señor Alberto Delgado of Colonia Granjas, Sacramento, Chihuahua, Mexico, for taking Major Smith and me across the Sacramento battlefield, for responding patiently to our many questions, and for being gracious and cordial to strangers from Los Estados Unidos.

My home away from home has been with Mark and Gay Leutbecker of Arlington, Virginia. With good humor and patience they have made room for me many times on my research trips to Washington, D.C., in my pursuit of Colonel Doniphan and other denizens of the nineteenth century. Their hospitality has meant so much to me over the years, and I thank them for all of their support.

Librarians and archivists have rendered much assistance. Michael Musick, archivist at the National Archives, Washington, D.C., deserves special mention for locating needle-in-the-haystack documents and answering numerous questions concerning research. As many other researchers will attest, Mr. Musick is a treasure. Ms. Kenette Harder of the Curry Library at William Jewell College, Liberty, Missouri, guided me to documents in the archives there. On two visits to the campus of the University of Missouri, librarians and archivists were exceptionally considerate at the Joint Collection of the University of Missouri, Columbia–Western Historical Manuscript Collection and the State Historical

Society of Missouri. The staff of the Missouri Historical Society, St. Louis, brought out documents and pointed out local history publications in their collections. Richard Salmon and other archivists at the Missouri State Archives in Jefferson City were courteous and thoughtful, locating documents and providing microfilms. Meg Carpenter and the staff in the Interlibrary Loan Office at Sterling C. Evans Library of Texas A&M University responded to my many requests for hard-to-find items. John Paul Fullerton of the Government Documents Division at Evans Library was also quite helpful.

Others deserve my gratitude. Douglas C. McChristian of the National Park Service discussed U.S. military firearms. T. Michael Parrish sent books and citations to other sources. Henry C. Schmidt patiently provided alternate translations of Mexican sources. Robert E. May shared his vast knowledge of American filibusters, in particular Captain Philip Thompson. George C. Rable offered sound advice and boundless assistance over the years. Thomas E. Schott made numerous suggestions on matters of style. Charles E. Brooks and Frank J. Wetta rendered thoughtful comments on selected chapters. Brian M. Linn and Kurt H. Hackemer gave computer assistance that was most appreciated. Colonel Doniphan Carter kindly provided me with a copy of a daguerreotype of Alexander W. Doniphan, made in 1847. Robert P. Wettemann helpfully located references I had not tracked down.

I am pleased to acknowledge the assistance to this project provided by a research travel grant from the Military Studies Institute at Texas A&M.

Thanks to R.J.Q. Adams, colleague and friend, for his vital encouragement.

I am grateful for permission to use material that appeared in "American Civil-Military Relations and Military Government: The Service of Colonel Alexander Doniphan in the Mexican War," *Armed Forces & Society* 22 (Summer 1996) (a version of chapter 4) and "American Xenophon, American Hero: Alexander Doniphan's Homecoming from the Mexican-American War as a Hallmark of Patriotic Fervor," *Military History of the West* 27 (Spring 1997) (a version of chapter 9). In each case, chapters in the book have been revised and vary in some ways from those articles.

Doniphan's Epic March

Colonel Alexander W. Doniphan before the campaign. (From Hughes, *Doniphan's Expedition* [1847]; courtesy of the Kansas Historical Society)

PROLOGUE

Two Tall Men: A Legendary Meeting

Missourians liked to tell the story that in February 1861 President-elect Abraham Lincoln met an American legend. Standing six feet, four inches tall and noticeable in any crowd, Lincoln stepped forward to shake hands with Alexander William Doniphan, who matched Lincoln's height in an era when the average American man stood about five feet, five inches.

Lincoln's gnarled hand grasped Doniphan's. "And this is the Colonel Doniphan who made the wonderful march from Santa Fé to Monterey against both the Indians and the Mexicans." The gangly Illinoisan paused for a moment. "Now, colonel, permit me to say you are the only man connected with any great military enterprise who ever came up in his looks to my expectations."[1]

Doniphan's accomplishments in the war between the United States and Mexico propelled him to national prominence, making him well known to Lincoln and his contemporaries. This is a study of Doniphan and the campaign of his volunteer regiment in the war with Mexico. That war raised controversies among Americans in the 1840s and has raised debates among historians since. A small-town lawyer from Missouri, untutored in military affairs, Doniphan enlisted as a private in June 1846 and soon was elected the colonel of the 1st Regiment of Missouri Mounted Volunteers, a unit of about eight hundred soldiers. The colonel knew exactly why the war was being fought. His purpose was clear: to protect Texas (admitted to the United States only a few months earlier, in December 1845), gain control of additional Mexican lands, such as New Mexico, and broaden the reach of democracy across the continent to California. It is sometimes said that people take action for two reasons: their public or ostensible goal and their private or real motive. In Doniphan's case, the two were the same. He believed in America's Manifest Destiny—national expansion of the United States by the grace of God.

For Doniphan and many of his fellow citizen-soldiers from Missouri, the war was a triumph of American republicanism. The Missourians enlisted for several reasons. They shared Doniphan's nationalism and support for Manifest Destiny, believing that America was already a great country and one that should be greater still. Some enlistees expressed excitement about the prospect of war and volunteered for military service; they considered travel and adventure in exotic locales a welcome chance to drop their daily routines and responsibilities, leave families and jobs, and find out for themselves what the danger of war might be like. These volunteers also shared an ethnocentric egotism, assuming that American arms would triumph and that Mexico's military would prove unequal to the task of defending its borders.

A few of the volunteers may have dreamed of covering themselves in enough glory to make them heroes, leading to fame, fortune, and political success. The less fanciful were well aware that after previous wars—the American Revolution and the War of 1812—the U.S. government had awarded a bounty of land to veterans. Thus, an act of Congress might arrange such a land bounty again. An economic motive—real estate, a farm of their own—also impelled some men to volunteer.[2]

Sincere idealists in the ranks believed that their service would promote the ideals of a republican government and representative democracy, which many nineteenth-century Americans worshiped as if it were a religion. By capturing New Mexico and thus providing a base for the campaign to take California, the Missourians would expand the area of democracy and America would grow in wealth and domain. Often a combination of these motives applied to most of those who enlisted in Doniphan's regiment for twelve months of service during 1846–1847. Some found adventure and returned home; others died and were buried in the nation they came to conquer.

On the American side, the war was one of long marches. Several commanders led units from points in the United States on attacks into Mexico. Initially under the command of Colonel Stephen W. Kearny, Doniphan led his Missourians for long marches through deserts and across mountains. Lack of water, poor food, and hardship became the volunteers' daily routine for hundreds of miles. The Missourians not only fought against Mexico's soldiers but also struggled against the land of Mexico itself. Overcoming the rugged terrain was a part of the story that seemed more understandable than defeating military forces more than twice the size of the one Doniphan commanded. The status of the Mexican army units Doniphan fought and their inability to turn back his invasion, combined with the Mexicans' recurring disappointments against nearly every contingent of American soldiers they battled, indicated much about Mexican nationalism in the 1840s.

Standing in Missouri, Doniphan could see on a map that he had a long way to go before fighting any Mexicans. President James K. Polk designated a Regular Army officer, Colonel Kearny, to lead the grandiosely styled "Army of the West," composed of Doniphan's regiment, plus some four hundred other volunteers and three hundred Regular U.S. Army soldiers, on an invasion of Mexico. Most of them rode on horseback from the frontier post of Fort Leavenworth, just west of Doniphan's hometown of Liberty, Missouri, down the Santa Fe Trail to attack the Mexican state of New Mexico, hundreds of miles away.

Marching to Santa Fe turned out to be only the first stage in an adventure covering thousands of miles, making Doniphan a principal officer in one of multiple American invasions of Mexico in 1846–1847 and a leader in one of the longest military marches in history. All told during their military service, Doniphan's men not only covered more than five thousand dangerous miles across land and water but also made strategic contributions to the American war effort. The colonel and his regiment were instrumental in the capture of the state of New Mexico in August 1846; six months later they diverted Mexican soldiers from Santa Anna's army at the Battle of Buena Vista (La Angostura) and fought them outside Chihuahua City.

Supported by his regiment, Doniphan achieved remarkable success as a combat commander, winning two engagements against Mexican forces larger than his own. Although he received good advice from Regular Army officers, Doniphan appeared to be "a natural soldier," for whom the military was second nature. His contemporaries rated him as one of the best American regimental commanders of a war in which several colonels achieved fame in their own states. The service of the successful colonels, Doniphan's especially, confirmed the American expectation that because its Regular Army was small, during wartime civilians would step forward to become military officers.

Besides his battlefield victories and extraordinary marches, Doniphan proved exceptional in two other ways. First, his experience as an attorney led to his making another important contribution to America's territorial expansion: he supervised the first American military government administering conquered enemy lands. In Santa Fe, Doniphan became de facto military governor of the province he helped capture. Second, the colonel worked in remarkable cooperation with Regular U.S. Army officers during a war when the relationship between most other volunteers and regulars was strained or sour. Taking all these things into account, and more than any other volunteer colonel, Doniphan rose to heroic stature across America by war's end.

Independent since 1783, the United States was sixty-three years old in 1846, and Doniphan's countrymen wanted to believe that his military success said something about the depth of their nation's pool of leaders and about America's magnificent accomplishments as well as its glorious prospects for the future. The war created several American popular heroes, including General Zachary Taylor, nicknamed Old Rough and Ready, frontiersman Ben McCulloch, whose exploits helped make the Texas Rangers famous, and Colonel John C. Frémont, hailed as the Pathfinder of the West. While these military men rated highly as American heroes, journalists and speechmakers awarded Doniphan an unusual complimentary sobriquet. They called him the American Xenophon, a military commander equal to or greater than Xenophon, the renowned ancient Greek military commander who, about 400 B.C., led Greek soldiers on their own long march across Asia Minor during a war against Persia. The United States in the 1840s was expansionist, belligerent, proud, and dynamic. Comparing Doniphan to Xenophon not only paid tribute to the colonel; it was one of several ways that writers and politicians indicated to Americans that their country should be compared favorably to the ancient Greeks.

In 1847 the Philadelphia *North American* expressed the view that a "history of Col. Doniphan's expedition would form a volume of rare interest and . . . military adventure."[3] The following narrative describes how Doniphan and his regiment of volunteers became agents of Manifest Destiny, making major contributions to America's westward expansion and to the American war effort. Analyzing Doniphan's military experience and the successes of his expedition helps to arrive at some conclusions about how America won its first overseas war and how Mexico lost half of its dominion. Widely praised in the 1840s, the American Xenophon and his regiment of volunteer citizen-soldiers prosecuted the war that changed forever the national outlook of both Mexico and the United States. Ironically for Doniphan, satisfying the urge for national expansion helped to plant one of the seeds of the American Civil War.

CHAPTER ONE

Going Off to War

Alexander William Doniphan embodied one of the most important expectations of Americans in the nineteenth century: in time of war, citizens would become soldiers. This expectation grew out of a tradition of the legendary "minutemen" of the American Revolution, those local colonial militia units that turned out on short notice to defend their town or county and, later, the intrepid volunteers from several states fighting under General Andrew Jackson against the British at the Battle of New Orleans in the War of 1812. Sixty years after contributing to victory in the Revolution and thirty years after Old Hickory's astounding victory over British regulars in Louisiana, however, militias in most states were moribund. Intent on limiting national military expenditures, and not entirely trusting professional soldiers, the U.S. Congress approved funds for only a small standing army. At the outbreak of war with Mexico, America needed more military units. Congress soon approved enlisting some new Regulars, but U.S. leaders put aside the militia, relying mostly on a variable of the citizen-soldier concept tried in the War of 1812, calling for individual men to volunteer to serve in new state regiments for one year. Doniphan was one of thousands of such volunteers in 1846.[1]

Americans also relied on the certainty that exceptional individuals, sometimes called "natural soldiers," would lead men into battle. As Alexis de Tocqueville, who toured America in 1831, phrased it, the army of a democracy "allows extraordinary men to rise above the common level."[2] Those leaders would be elected or appointed as officers for the new volunteer regiments. Americans knew, of course, that these talented commanders would include men with prior military service but that novices also would show their ability for soldiering. And some believed that soldiering, even as an officer, was an avocation requiring dedication, patriotism, and luck but not much special knowledge. Several volunteer commanders, including Doniphan, had little or no military experience before the Mexican-American War, but he stood out as the best and most famous of the volunteer colonels—the one his contemporaries called "American Xenophon."

Doniphan's background was probably Irish, and the family name originally may have been Donovan. Some relatives told stories about forebears in either Spain or Scotland, but most Doniphans in America claimed an Irish ancestor who arrived in Virginia around 1670. Alexander's father, Joseph, was born in King George County, Virginia, about 1760. Joseph Doniphan served in the rebel militia at the beginning of the American Revolution, but the prospect of new land lured him westward to Kentucky. Family tradition held that Joseph Doniphan returned to Virginia for further service in the Revolutionary cause.[3]

After marrying Ann Smith in 1785, Joseph decided to move to Kentucky about five years later. Finding a likely spot along the Ohio River, the couple located in Mason County, near the town of Maysville, sixty miles southeast of Cincinnati, Ohio. Over the years, Joseph Doniphan's crops and investments prospered. By 1813, he had served as sheriff of Mason County and accumulated a substantial estate, including eighteen slaves, making him a local dignitary. Alexander William, the tenth and last of Joseph's children, was born on July 9, 1808. Upon his father's death in 1813, the youngest child, called "Will" by family and friends, inherited part of the farm and one slave. Raising Will proved a challenge to his widowed mother. She arranged for him to live with an older brother, George, and his wife, Mary Ann Marshall Doniphan, in another Ohio River town, Augusta, Kentucky, in Bracken County, about twenty miles northwest of Maysville. Doniphan later recalled the deep impression made by the town's enthusiastic Irish schoolmaster, Richard Keene. The teacher drilled him at arithmetic and introduced him to poetry, demanding his young pupil's attention to the poems' meter and verbal nuances.[4]

In 1822 Doniphan matriculated at Augusta College, a recently established Methodist Episcopal academy; four years later he graduated with honors. Setting his sights on becoming an attorney, the young man was aware that there were few law schools in America in the 1820s. Like most aspirants of the time, he sought out a practicing attorney to assist while studying the books in his office before taking the state bar examination. For nearly three years Doniphan read law in the office of Martin Marshall, father of his sister-in-law and nephew of the great jurist John Marshall, chief justice of the U.S. Supreme Court. Martin Marshall also completed the young man's education by encouraging him to read works of history and literature. Drawing upon this preparation, Doniphan passed the Kentucky bar examination in 1829 and then, like his father, looked west for new prospects.[5]

Doniphan moved to St. Louis in 1830. Part of Thomas Jefferson's marvelous Louisiana Purchase of 1803, Missouri provided a base for the flourishing western fur trade; St. Louis investors coordinated expeditions to the West and purchased individual trappers' pelts and hides, then sold them to be made into hats and coats. By 1820 Missouri's population had grown to more than sixty thousand residents, one-sixth of whom were African-American slaves. Many of the settlers migrated from upper South states such as Kentucky, Tennessee, and Virginia. The territory qualified for statehood, but its request for admission to the Union as a slave state had caused controversy. Eventually, members of Congress arranged the Missouri Compromise: the district of Maine, then a part of Massachusetts, was admitted as a free state, while Missouri entered as a slave state in 1821, but no new slave states would be admitted above Missouri's southern boundary of 36°30′ north latitude. While lead mines operated in Washington County, in eastern Missouri, and small factories of various kinds in St. Louis employed German-speaking immigrants, most Missourians involved themselves in some aspect of agriculture. Enterprises ranged from large plantations using slave labor to grow commercial crops, such as hemp and tobacco, to modest and small farms raising a variety of foodstuffs and livestock produced for local sale. By the time Doniphan arrived, businessmen had developed an overland trade along the Santa Fe Trail, across the unorganized federal territory between Independence, Missouri, and Santa Fe, capital of Mexico's northern state of Nuevo México (New Mexico).[6]

Passing the Missouri bar examination but finding many lawyers already practicing in St. Louis, Doniphan headed west again. First opening a law office in Lexington, in 1833 he finally hung out his shingle in tiny Liberty, a village of only three hundred people close to the state's western boundary. Even Liberty already had another energetic young lawyer, David Rice Atchison, also recently transplanted from Kentucky. Both men were slave owners and supported the legal status of the institution of slavery, but they differed on other aspects of politics. Atchison became one of Missouri's prominent Democrats—the party that dominated most of the state—and Doniphan joined the opposition Whigs. The two young attorneys enjoyed a jousting repartee and decided to share a law office. They developed a lasting friendship.[7]

In the early years of his law practice, Doniphan took on all sorts of clients but gradually established credentials as a persuasive advocate in criminal law, especially as a defense attorney in capital cases. Speaking on behalf of his clients required him to travel through several counties, and he became a familiar face on the judicial circuit in western Missouri. A man of Doniphan's height towered over most other people and impressed everyone he met. His weight of more than two hundreds pounds was distributed evenly on a lanky frame. He brushed thick brown hair away from his face, letting it fall to his ears. His high, broad forehead evinced intelligence to many in the nineteenth century. Pensive, probing eyes added to his scholastic demeanor. Doniphan spoke in a commanding voice through sharply etched lips. Witnesses, judges, juries, attorneys, and courtroom visitors recognized him as an exceptional public speaker in an era that prized oratory. Hearing Doniphan's persuasive arguments in court, one of his contemporaries characterized him as an "absolute master at the bar."[8]

During the 1830s, income from his legal fees allowed Doniphan to make investments, increasing his stature in Liberty and Clay County. He bought hundreds of acres of land as well as acquiring town lots. Rather than speculating on the country land by reselling it, he usually leased it to farmers to provide more income. Buying property in a border area near the Missouri River known as the Platte District, he championed its annexation into the state of Missouri. Such diligence made him successful but not wealthy.[9]

Seeking mastery of matters beyond the courtroom, in 1836 Doniphan ran for public office. Campaigning as a Whig from Clay County, he won a two-year term to the house of representatives in the Missouri General Assembly. Created to oppose President Andrew Jackson, the Whig party was led by Daniel Webster of Massachusetts and Henry Clay, favorite son of Doniphan's home state of Kentucky. The Whigs advocated both individual opportunity and an active federal government that would maintain a national bank, build "internal improvements"—federal construction projects such as interstate roads and canals—and set a tariff high enough to protect new American industries competing with inexpensive foreign-made goods. Although Jackson's Democrats dominated Missouri, Clay County was a Whig bastion. In the General Assembly, Doniphan marked out his areas of interest. He endorsed a bill to establish the University of Missouri in December 1836. Doniphan voted with a unanimous house in January 1837 to prohibit antislavery literature from entering the state. As a member of the Judiciary Committee, he worked with other legislators to support the Platte Purchase, adding to Missouri's western counties land where he had made investments. Hoping to boost the state's economy, Doniphan called for chartering a state bank and a railroad company, and found common ground with an influential Democrat, John C. Thornton of Clay County. During Doniphan's first term of service in the state legislature, he also supported organizing at least one county, Caldwell, that would be reserved for settlers belonging to a controversial religious group, the Mormons.[10]

Doniphan and Atchison seldom turned down a client, and since 1833 they had represented members of the Mormon Church, officially known as the Church of Jesus Christ of Latter-day Saints, who had settled in western Missouri. Admirably industrious on their farms and jobs, Mormons were also zealous disciples for their church. The Saints proselytized their neighbors, including seeking converts among Indian tribes, preaching from their own *Book of Mormon*, a gospel they considered holy scripture to be placed next to the Bible. Describing an ancient Christian settlement in North America and yielding revelations originally in a mysterious unknown language before being printed in English, *The Book of Mormon* was distrusted, or at least viewed with skepticism, by non-Mormons. Mormons' criticisms of slavery also made them anathema to numerous Missourians, who considered the institution to be necessary for the social and economic well-being of the state. The Mormons' beliefs combined to make others uncomfortable around the Saints. Some lawyers would not represent Mormons, but among Doniphan's earliest court victories had been cases on their behalf, and they paid well for his competent counsel.[11]

Meanwhile, Doniphan used his political connections and found another way to promote his career. After serving for several years as a private in the Missouri state militia and although he was a Whig, he sought an appointment as a brigadier general from Democratic governor Lilburn W. Boggs. Receiving such a commission carried risks, as became evident when disputes between Mormons and other settlers erupted into violence, the so-called Mormon War of 1838.[12]

During the 1830s, misunderstandings and altercations had accumulated between Mormons and other Missourians in the western counties, and those opposing the Saints banded together when members of the controversial church established themselves beyond their haven of Caldwell County. Assailants burned Mormon businesses, assaulted individual Mormons, and, after forcing them out of Jackson County, intended to drive them out of the state. In self-defense the Mormons organized their own militia-style companies. Blaming the "war" on the Mormons, their opponents called on Governor Boggs to suppress the unrest. Boggs mobilized hundreds of militiamen, including General Doniphan and David Atchison, who was also a general. Of course, the two generals knew many of the Mormons, some of whom had been their clients.

Although he held no brief for their religion, Doniphan believed that the Mormons deserved fair treatment under the guarantees of the U.S. Constitution, especially to practice freedom of religion as permitted by the First Amendment.[13]

Dissatisfaction with the Mormons focused on one of their leaders, the prophet Joseph Smith, founder of the church and the man who had translated *The Book of Mormon*. A judge signed a warrant for Smith's arrest. In late October militia from several localities converged on Caldwell County, following Governor Boggs's harshly worded order to exterminate or expel the Mormons from Missouri. The war reached its nadir when undisciplined militia murdered eighteen Mormons in the village of Haun's Mill on October 30 and others surrounded the Mormon settlement of Far West. Major General Samuel Lucas of the state militia wanted to burn down Far West and execute Joseph Smith. Serving as presiding judge, Lucas arranged for Smith to face a militia court-martial on trumped-up charges of treason, anticipating a guilty verdict and a death sentence. Supported by some determined militiamen from Clay County, Doniphan rejected Lucas's illegal action. At a crucial moment in the crisis, on November 2 Doniphan refused Lucas's orders to shoot Smith and six other Mormons, averting a tragedy and winning the Mormons' lasting devotion. Some disgruntled Missourians harbored long-lasting enmity against the Mormons, but many others recognized that Doniphan had stood resolutely for due process and the rights of the accused.[14]

More well known than ever before, Doniphan returned to politics a few months after the Mormon War. Having sat out one legislative term, he was reelected to the General Assembly by a comfortable margin in 1840, even as the national Whig ticket and the Whig candidate for Congress lost in western Missouri. During his second term in Jefferson City, Doniphan served again on the house Judiciary Committee and paid particular attention to banking legislation and reform. In 1844 he ran a losing race for presidential elector as a Whig supporting the party's nominee, Henry Clay, opposed by a young Democratic attorney, Willard P. Hall.[15]

On the eve of the Mexican War, Doniphan had emerged as a major figure in Missouri's political and social life. On December 21, 1837, he had married Elizabeth Jane Thornton, an attractive young woman from Clay County who was twelve years younger than he. Jane was the daughter of John Thornton, the collegial senior Democrat in the state legislature. Jane Thornton was an excellent match for the rising lawyer. Also married in the same ceremony were one of Jane's sisters and Doniphan's close friend Oliver P. Moss, who was also a native of Maysville, Kentucky. Will and Jane had two sons, John, born in 1838, and Alexander Jr., born in 1840. Developing a prosperous law practice, establishing a family, owning a home, farmland, and investment properties, winning two elections to the state legislature, and holding the rank of brigadier general in the Missouri militia all redounded to Doniphan's credit and made him a leading figure in the state.[16]

Along with thousands of other Americans in 1845, Doniphan supported Manifest Destiny, a widely held civic faith cutting across party lines that the United States would expand across the continent, acquiring land all the way to the Pacific Ocean. Writing in the *Democratic Review,* editor John L. O'Sullivan had spawned the term, endorsing the annexation of Texas and declaring it America's "manifest destiny to overspread the continent allotted by Providence for the free development of our yearly multiplying millions." Unapologetic nationalists devoted to Manifest Destiny, most Democrats and a minority of Whigs, believed it was God's will for the United States to encompass all of North America, asserting that adding more land would be both good for the country and good for the growth of democracy. O'Sullivan's phrase caught America's fancy, but the idea was not new. Jefferson's purchase of Louisiana in 1803, followed by the purchase of Florida from Spain in 1819, stimulated dreams of more additions. To many Americans, the concept of a growing nation was like pollen in springtime: it was everywhere in the air.[17]

Manifest Destiny sparked controversy during the presidential election of 1844. Many Democrats, including the party's eventual nominee, James K. Polk of Tennessee, reinvigorated debate over annexing Texas, acquiring much of the Oregon country, then jointly occupied with Great Britain, and buying some of Mexico's northern provinces. Waxing hot and cold over bringing Texas into the Union, Senator Henry Clay of Kentucky, nominee of the Whig party, concluded that annexing Texas would lead to war with Mexico. Although some Northern Whigs active in commerce favored national expansion, other Northern and Southern Whigs opposed Manifest Destiny, the former concerned over slavery expansion and the latter fearing the consequences of a war with Mexico, England, or both. Polk won comfortably in the electoral college (170 to Clay's 105), but the margin was narrow in the popular vote (1,337,000 to Clay's 1,299,000). Close though it was, Polk's victory added momentum to expansionism, and he intended to fulfill his promises.[18]

In the election Polk had carried Missouri, with its strong Democratic party. But unlike many other fellow Whigs who had voted for Henry Clay, Doniphan's nationalism led him to adamantly favor expansion even by the use of military force. Holding that view on this controversial national issue, he stood in stark contrast to his party's leaders from both sections, such as Henry Clay, Daniel Webster, William Seward of New York, and Alexander Stephens of Georgia. Those Whig stalwarts foresaw the likelihood of gradual American expansion to the west, even adding Texas, but they preferred diplomacy to force. Doniphan understood the explosiveness of the Texas question. Belying what appeared to be an otherwise moderate persona, he wanted Texas brought into the Union, was willing to fight a war to gain the new state, and happily bore the label "annexationist." For Doniphan, it was illogical for Mexico to claim that Texas was still its province ten years after the revolution that had created the Lone Star Republic. Going to war against Mexico represented a significant personal effort to annex more land for the United States. As a citizen-colonel, Doniphan would become one of the primary agents of Manifest Destiny.[19]

As tensions mounted between Mexico and the United States, and expecting war to break out at any time, in September 1845 Doniphan was one of many Americans writing Secretary of War William L. Marcy, volunteering for field duty. Along with his friend Henry Routt, Doniphan specified that "a portion of the patriotic citizens of the Western frontier Counties of Missouri have formed themselves into a mounted Regiment and . . . have requested . . . to offer their services to the President of the United States for any Service their Country may require in Connexion [*sic*] with the anticipated war with Mexico." It was Doniphan and Routt's "decided opinion that the Government will not be able to employ more efficient troops for that Service—they [the volunteers] have been all horsemen from their infancy, and having been repeatedly engaged in frontier warfare with the Indians." Eager to enter military service, Doniphan and Routt assured Secretary Marcy that the Missourians' "patriotic zeal for the success of this war will be second to no part of the American people as they all are and always have been warm friends of Texas and zealous for her annexation." The Missourians pledged to "be efficient soldiers in repelling the predatory and guerrilla excursions by which Mexico will doubtless harass the frontier [boundary] of the State of Texas."[20]

Doniphan and his friends knew about the debates over the boundaries of that frontier. Mexicans reminded all who would listen that the Nueces River had formed the boundary between Texas and the province of Tamaulipas to the south. Even one of Missouri's newspapers, the Columbia *Statesman*, recognized that the Nueces River, not the Rio Grande, had been the southern boundary of Texas. And everyone acknowledged that the commercial center of Santa Fe, about thirty miles *east* of the Rio Grande, was in Mexico's province of New Mexico. After Texans, or "Texians" or "Texicans," as they sometimes called themselves, demanded that General Antonio Lopez de Santa Anna sign a treaty ending the Texas Revolution in 1836, they asserted a bold claim to the Rio Grande (known to Mexicans as the Río Bravo del Norte) as the boundary of their new republic. By asserting this claim, the Texans wanted the Rio Grande to be not only their southern boundary but their western border as well. The long river also snaked far northward into New Mexico, and if Texans validated their claim to the Rio Grande boundary, Santa Fe would be a Texas city.[21]

While Britain, France, and other nations approved of the Rio Grande boundary when they extended diplomatic recognition to the Texas Republic, the dispute over control of Santa Fe flared as an important corollary issue. As a devoted Whig who "worshipped Clay as no man but him was ever worshipped by his followers," Doniphan must have seen the irony in his annexationist views on Texas and New Mexico. They matched those of Clay's nemesis, Andrew Jackson, who as a general and U.S. president had coveted Santa Fe along with Florida and Texas.[22]

Viewed from a strategic perspective after the Texas Revolution, Santa Fe marked the northeastern outpost of the Mexican nation, and it had served both Spain and Mexico as a trading center. Neither the Spanish nor the Mexicans developed good communications between Mexico City and Santa Fe. Dispatching military replacements and supplies, collecting taxes and delivering mail all had been neglected. The Spanish discouraged intrusions by curious Americans, but after gaining its independence in 1821 Mexico opened legal trade with the United States. During the 1830s, commerce increased between Santa Fe and Missouri. Adventuresome American entrepreneurs drove wagons loaded with tools, firearms, and other manufactured goods down one thousand risky miles of the Santa Fe Trail. Some courted more danger, and more profits, transporting goods farther south to Ciudad Chihuahua, capital of the Mexican state of Chihuahua. Buying hardy Mexican mules, the traders returned to Independence, Missouri, bearing silver bullion, silver coins, furs, and other items. Only about two hundred of the Mexican army's twenty-nine thousand regular soldiers were stationed in Santa Fe. The regulars were supplemented by around one thousand militia, some of whom had experience fighting New Mexico's several Indian tribes. Frontier and provincial defense rested mainly with local forces. As a result of chronic shortfalls in New Mexico's tax collections and lack of appropriations from the national government, those citizen-soldiers were ill equipped and sporadically paid. Santa Fe's commerce with the Americans boosted New Mexico's economy, including the collection of customs' fees, but also made the city an attractive target for American expansion.[23]

Texans had mounted expeditions to capture Santa Fe. In 1841 a small "army" of about three hundred exhausted Texans staggered through the desert and into New Mexico unfit for combat. A few Mexican troops easily rounded them up and threw them in prison. Altogether, three Texan invasions of New Mexico met with ignominious failure, even against the weak Mexican defenses. If the Texans learned anything from these expeditions, it was that the Mexicans, like the Spanish before them, posted only a small garrison in Santa Fe. Meanwhile, the Mexicans observed that the city possessed strong natural defenses—unforgiving deserts and rugged mountains that hindered invaders. But there were distances to consider. Santa Fe stood about 1,400 miles from Mexico City, 650 miles from Chihuahua City, and 400 miles from El Paso del Norte (modern Juárez). Santa Fe lay 1,200 miles from Missouri. In response to a major invasion, it was debatable if Mexican reinforcements or American invaders would reach Santa Fe first. Based on their opinion of Mexico's fruitless attempts to retake Texas, some Americans concluded that Mexico could never dispatch substantial military forces to respond to U.S. invasions of New Mexico and California or to mount strong counterattacks to regain those provinces if they fell.[24]

In addition to capturing a commercial prize, Doniphan and his friends wanted to take Santa Fe to penalize Mexico for its treatment of Texans taken prisoner on the Mier Expedition. One of Doniphan's neighbors included the punishment meted out to the Texans at Mier as among "the insults and wrongs which had been repeatedly heaped on American citizens" by Mexicans during the 1830s and 1840s. In 1842 a small force of some three hundred Texans, seeking to retaliate for a Mexican attack on San Antonio, hastily crossed the Rio Grande near the Mexican village of Mier. After a sharp skirmish, with casualties on both sides, the surrounded Texans surrendered and hoped for the best. To discourage such belligerent ventures in the future, the Mexicans intended to make an example of the Texan raiders. The Mexican commander called for the Texans to draw lots by picking white or black beans from a gourd. Black beans meant death, and the process literally decimated the Texans—one of every ten drew a black bean and was shot. The rest were incarcerated in one of Mexico's most notorious prisons.[25]

From 1836 to 1845 clashes, such as the one at Mier, intensified bitterness on both sides. Mexico never officially acknowledged Texas independence or accepted the Rio Grande as the boundary of Texas. Although they attacked and captured San Antonio, the Mexicans could neither hold the city nor mount military expeditions capable of controlling all of the province. In 1845 José Herrera gained the presidency on a platform of reconquering Texas, proclaiming that the reconquest was the only way to uphold national honor. Some Mexicans believed that renewed military effort would yet bring Texas back under control of the central government.[26]

Before Mexico could recover Texas, Doniphan and other Americans sought to annex it and confirm the claim of the Rio Grande boundary. They supported President John Tyler's proposed treaty of annexation, but it failed to gain the votes of two-thirds of the U.S. Senate. Tyler then persuaded Congress to support an extraordinary joint resolution to annex Texas. Tyler signed the measure on March 1, 1845.[27]

Many Americans endorsed the Texans' claim of the Rio Grande boundary both to the south and west, even if Frank Edwards, a Missourian soon to enlist as a soldier, recognized that they had been unable "to subjugate the more northern part of their territory," and everyone knew that Santa Fe remained "in possession and under the dominion of the Mexican government." Only at this eleventh hour, working with a British diplomat, some desperate Mexican officials agreed to recognize Texas independence in order to block annexation, but that change in Mexican policy came too late. Thus, even before President Polk took office on March 4, 1845, Tyler's annexation scheme had created a furor in Mexico that would lead directly to war.[28]

Another reason impelling American interest in Texas was the prospect of British meddling. Although Britain had recognized Texas independence, some Americans suspected that the English did so only to increase their commercial influence in the republic. Most Americans, even those leery of annexing Texas, concluded that keeping Texas independent and out of the Union was to England's advantage. Behind the scenes, British diplomats and their French counterparts had been working to persuade Mexico to recognize Texas independence. In return, Mexico would receive Anglo-French trade benefits and guarantees to keep Texas from becoming part of the United States.[29]

The slavery question complicated matters further. Slavery had been abolished in the British Empire during the 1830s. Should British businesses achieve dominance in Texas, many Southerners feared that the English might use their economic leverage to abolish slavery there. Deep South politicians, of course, feared a roadblock to slavery's expansion toward the Pacific, and some proslavery annexationists seized on those fears. They marshaled their bitter opposition against Clay in 1844, because he would not endorse immediate annexation, and then rushed to pass John Tyler's joint annexation resolution. Making Texas a state seemed to solve these problems. Annexation expanded the United States westward, removed any chance of British economic dominance or abolitionist interference in that region, and also added a new slave state to the Union.[30]

Manifest Destiny also drew American eyes toward the Pacific Coast, an area where John O'Sullivan worried about the "hostile interference" of Europeans in North America, especially about England's steps to control Oregon. Of course,

Americans recognized that so long as the British held Canada, they had a direct interest in North American affairs from the Atlantic to the Pacific. But English claims in the Oregon country—from the boundary of Russian America (Alaska) at 54°40′ south to the Columbia River—seemed excessive. Moreover, Britain wanted to cancel the long-standing agreement of joint occupation of the region with the United States. Adding most of Oregon to Canada, England would leave America only a window on the Pacific Coast. Undoubtedly, many Americans, including President Polk, wanted all of Oregon for the United States. In the winter of 1845–1846, Polk and the Democrats used the catchy slogan "54°40′ or fight!"—implying that war would come if America did not get all of Oregon. Eventually, diplomacy replaced saber-rattling in April 1846. British and American diplomats agreed to divide Oregon between them by a simple extension of the forty-ninth parallel, and a treaty confirmed this equitable compromise in June. The most ardent American annexationists, including Polk, were not satisfied, but many Americans noted the symmetry of solution. They also understood that it removed the likelihood of war between England and the United States at the same time that America was on the verge of war with Mexico.[31]

Simultaneously, American, British, and Mexican interests all converged in California. The United States obviously coveted the Mexican state of Alta California (Upper California), though dreams of Manifest Destiny could be shattered if England interfered there. But once again British intentions were not clear. It was well known that British investors held Mexican bonds as well as commercial notes that were overdue. On behalf of its citizens, the United States lodged various claims for debts against Mexico, but would the English intervene to force payment of debts Mexico owed to British businesses? British control of California would have vastly increased English imperial influence in North America. Or, acting as arbitrators, English diplomats could assure Mexico's retention of California, preventing the United States from acquiring the province. That scenario could permit England to take California from Mexico later. Americans, of course, resented any British steps to arbitrate relations between them and Mexico. In hindsight, Britain's taking California seemed unlikely or even far-fetched, but such a possibility played a part in the thinking of President Polk and other Americans in the 1840s, prompting the president to revive the Monroe Doctrine during his annual message to Congress in December 1845.[32]

After all, European interest in the Western Hemisphere was not without recent precedent. France had intervened in Mexico in 1838, the so-called Pastry War, a conflict brought on by Mexico's failure to pay its debts to French investors. Eventually France stationed twenty-six of its navy ships in the Gulf of Mexico, landed soldiers at Veracruz and elsewhere on the Gulf Coast, and easily forced

Mexico to pay the debts. Mexican legislators and newspaper editors, aware of the sizable sums spent on the Mexican army over the years, were outraged by the fiasco of the Pastry War. The embarrassing affair had tarnished Mexican sovereignty and exposed its vulnerability to foreign invasion. And France, which suffered no financial or political penalty for the intervention of 1838, might intervene again at any time.

By the 1840s, rumors spread of Anglo-French diplomatic intrigues involving California. On October 20, 1842, responding to an unfounded rumor that Britain was going to annex California, U.S. Navy Commodore Thomas ap Catesby Jones landed a force of sailors and marines at Monterey. Jones withdrew the next day, but his ill-timed incursion led Mexico to make a gesture to strengthen its defenses in California. Supported by editorials in Mexico City's newspapers, the minister of war, Pedro García Conde, wrote a plan for expeditionary units to reinforce California's garrisons in 1845. García Conde's intent was laudable, but his execution was deficient. The Expedicíon a las Californias never left the Valley of Mexico. Many Americans agreed with former president Andrew Jackson: before Mexico could be given another chance to reinforce its northern posts, the United States should obtain California for itself, if only to prevent Britain from blocking American access to the Pacific Ocean.[33]

Other American attitudes contributed to the pressure for war in 1846. Many American volunteer soldiers, including Doniphan and other Missourians, believed that they fought for more than just land. Fighting Mexico meant protecting democracy in Texas, and annexing other Mexican states meant expanding democracy to other parts of North America. A nationalistic poet, Walt Whitman, sounded a similar altruistic theme, as did William Franklin, one of Doniphan's Missouri volunteers. Franklin rejoiced that American soldiers would bring democracy to the residents of Santa Fe and break "the Chains of Tyranny, & set them free from the hands of their oppressors." In Franklin's opinion, "The American eagle seemed to spread his broad pinions, and westward bear the principles of republican government." Jessup W. Scott, writing in *DeBow's Review*, later asserted that the trans-Mississippi West had become "the great centre. It is the body of the American eagle whose wings are on the two oceans."[34]

As war approached, both Mexico and the United States marshaled potent symbols to inspire their people. "All parties were united in one common cause for the vindication of the national honor," wrote John Hughes, a schoolteacher from Clay County, Missouri. Resorting to force of arms, Hughes continued, men of both nations would "defend the rights and honor of their country; to redress her wrongs and avenge her insults." Numerous insults begged for vengeance. Mexicans, Texans, and Americans all harbored ill feelings about the recurring raids across the Rio Grande. Both sides bristled over misunderstandings and grievances regarding crediting diplomats, the sincerity of negotiations, and blatant U.S. intentions to acquire California.[35]

Ready for war, the Missourians stressed noble purposes for fighting, imparting nobility to their soldiers. Oliver P. Moss, Doniphan's brother-in-law, praised Missouri volunteers as "men of a higher type, with nobler and truer principles than can be found in Armies generally. The reason is obvious, they fight for their country's honor, not for [individual] gain or plunder." Isaac George, a carpenter from Lafayette County, Missouri, contended that "the honor of their country" was a primary motivating factor for the Missourians. Of course the American flag received lavish praise. Seeing the Stars and Stripes reminded William Franklin that similar flags, carried by his victorious forefathers, had "floated gallantly in the bitter days of the [American] revolution." No one would think of betraying this gallant heritage. "For ceartainly [*sic*] the blood that flowed in '76 in the veins of our foreparents have descended to the sons, & daughters of '46." Likewise, John Hughes, soon to enlist as a private soldier, concluded that he and his fellow volunteers felt the "same noble impulses and the same quenchless love of freedom, which animated the breast of our ancestors of '76, and caught inspiration from the memory of their achievements."[36]

Americans were united in recalling the Spirit of '76, but their divisions became obvious when the issue of slavery entered the debate over the coming of war. Arguments over slavery had blocked the annexation of Texas during the 1830s. By 1846 some, including many Whigs, opposed war and the addition of any new territories that would be suitable for plantation agriculture. Doniphan, a slave owner since childhood, supported the right of slaveholders to take their property into the territories. For its part, when it became an independent republic, Mexico officially had prohibited slavery, and some Mexican leaders were uncomfortable about how the United States perpetuated the institution and allowed it to expand. Doniphan and many Missourians believed that slavery was a mainstay of American economic and social life, but few of them dwelled on the institution's tragic aspects. Slavery violated both the humanity of the individual slave and the concept of individualism, denying slaves freedom of movement and expression and a means to earn their own way in life. A growing number of Northerners believed that slavery was degrading, harsh, and greedy—a system of personal and economic exploitation. The longer America permitted the institution of slavery to exist, the more controversial it became.[37]

Alert to the increasing divisiveness that slavery was causing in the United States, Mexicans hoped that sharp disagreements between Northerners and Southerners would prevent annexation of Mexican lands. Mexican politicians followed the debates over Texas annexation and applauded when Daniel Webster postulated that "there must be some limit to the extent of our [American] territory, if we would make our institutions permanent." For Webster and many other Northerners, concern over slavery's expansion was a vital issue that needed to be resolved by limiting the institution's growth and restricting it to states where it already existed.[38]

Yet another element played a part in the approach to war. Contemporary remarks clearly demonstrated the paternalism and racial attitudes of Anglo-Americans and Missourians toward Mexico and Mexicans. By the 1840s, in speeches and newspaper columns, Americans stereotyped Mexico's population as the inferior stock resulting from many decades of combinations of Indians and Europeans. Anti-Indian and anti-Mexican attitudes were widespread in the United States, and, according to Sam Houston, "the Mexicans are no better than the Indians." If war came with Mexico, in the opinion of James Buchanan, a Pennsylvanian serving as Polk's secretary of state, the "Anglo-Saxon blood could never be subdued by anything that claimed Mexican origin." Knowing of this biased attitude, some critics of the annexationists questioned their sincerity about expanding democracy and contended that such a high-sounding goal merely justified taking lands from a neighboring nation on the grounds of racial superiority. Responding to such critics, Francis Lieber, one of America's notable legal scholars of the nineteenth century, hoped that the United States would take California because he believed that the Mexicans were "a half-civilized race," one unable to make worthwhile use of such land. On the other hand, a minority of those opposing the war approached the crisis by looking through their own racial perspective. Various opponents of war and annexation were motivated by concern about adding lands inhabited by large numbers of Indians and Mexicans to the United States, and about how difficult it would be to assimilate these groups into American life.[39]

Doniphan and other Missourians shared the racial sentiments representative of the United States. One exposition sharply captures their point of view. Richard S. Elliott of St. Louis, a federal Indian agent soon to serve as an American volunteer officer with Doniphan, described what he considered "the general sentiment" of his acquaintances "that the Mexicans were a half-barbarous set any way, and had no business to send their greasy and ragged soldiers over the Rio Grande, into a territory always owned by them but constructively conquered by the Texans who were the advanced guard of our [American] superior civilization." An equally strong opinion came from Isaac George from Lafayette County, who ranted: "Virtue, honesty, honor, piety, religion, patriotism, generosity, and reputation were to them [Mexicans] pompous and unmeaning terms."

On the other hand, George continued, "Vice, fraud, deceit, treachery, theft, plunder, murder and assassination, stalked abroad [in Mexico] in open daylight. . . . Such was the moral and social system in Mexico." Therefore, many of the Missouri volunteer soldiers and other Americans strongly held such racial attitudes, which no doubt played a part in motivating their actions for war.[40]

On May 11, 1846, President Polk delivered his war message to Congress. By then the president knew that American and Mexican mounted troops had fought a skirmish on April 25 north of the Rio Grande, but the details were still uncertain. Two days after receiving Polk's message, the U.S. House of Representatives voted for a declaration of war against the Republic of Mexico. The vote was overwhelming, with 174 in favor of war and only 14 opposed; it was notable that twenty congressmen abstained. Indicating the widespread support for war across America, the following day the Senate had acted in similar fashion, voting for war by a margin of 40 to 2, with only two senators abstaining. Anticipating the vote, the St. Louis *Reveille*'s bellicose headlines blared "WAR! WAR! To Arms! To Arms!" The *Reveille* called out to prospective soldiers: "Young men . . . now is your chance! Mexico! California!"[41]

From the Mexican point of view, U.S. troops landing on the Texas coast in July 1845 and marching overland from Louisiana in 1846 constituted acts of war. In March 1845, to protest the impending annexation of Texas, Juan N. Almonte, the Mexican minister in Washington, already had broken diplomatic relations with the United States, withdrawing his credentials and leaving Washington. On April 23, 1846, President Mariano Paredes of Mexico announced that a state of "defensive war" existed between Mexico and the United States. In the nineteenth century, breaking diplomatic relations often was interpreted to mean that war was imminent, even if no one could be sure what Mexico meant by a "defensive war." If Mexico was intent on reclaiming Texas after it had been annexed by the United States, then a war was sure to result. Upon learning of the official votes for war by the U.S. Congress, the Mexican Congress responded by reiterating the declaration of a defensive war on June 16.[42]

The U.S. Congress already had approved a call for raising thousands of volunteer soldiers, endorsing a plan for recruiting fifty thousand volunteers for one year of national service, with various quotas being assigned to several Southern and western states, including Missouri. Responding immediately, Doniphan and his friend Henry Routt, on behalf of some of their fellow Missourians, wrote to Secretary of War Marcy, "again tender[ing] their Services to the Government."

Already on record as favoring America's acquisition of Texas and the Rio Grande boundary of the new state, this time the Missourians recommended a new element of strategy. They deemed "it not arrogating too much . . . to suggest to your honor the propriety of *sending a force to the provinces of New Mexico & Chihuahua.*" Filled with confidence, the two anticipated that their "services would be invaluable as many of us are intimately acquainted with that Country." Sensing Santa Fe's vulnerability and intent on upholding Texas's Rio Grande boundary, Doniphan and his fellow Missourians pledged to defend "our rights and *maintain them the whole length of the Rio Grande.*" It was soon clear that Doniphan's personal objectives dovetailed precisely with those of President Polk.[43]

Doniphan and his fellow Missouri volunteer soldiers expected to fight the Mexican army. Both nations assigned the same missions to their regular military forces, including protecting settlers against Indian attacks and providing for defense against foreign threats. The standing armies of the two nations displayed some similarities. Neither Mexico nor the United States established national military training camps. Mexican department commanders and regimental colonels were responsible for training, while colonels of each U.S. Army regiment (a standard outfit of about one thousand soldiers) held a similar responsibility. Both armies lacked a general staff for making long-range plans and a war college for developing senior commanders. Each nation operated its own military academy, enrolling under two hundred cadets, for training and educating lieutenants, the lowest-ranking officers in their army.[44] There the similarities ended, and the two military establishments displayed numerous contrasts.

Permanent units of the Mexican army that Doniphan might encounter presented, at least on paper, a formidable presence in 1846. Mexico's army appeared to have satisfied Antoine Henri de Jomini's admonition that "the first means of encouraging the [national] military spirit is to invest the army with all possible social and public consideration." During the 1840s, Mexico's army numbered between 20,000 and 30,000 regular soldiers, drawing from a total national population of around seven million. In 1846, 29,300 officially served on active duty, divided as follows: 17,900 infantry, 9,600 cavalry, and 1,800 artillerists. Although Waddy Thompson, the U.S. minister to Mexico, contended that the actual enrollment was less than half of the official count, the Mexican army included several reputable units. According to Brantz Mayer, the secretary of the American legation in Mexico City, the cavalry was widely held to be the "most effective arm of the Mexican service." During the Texas Revolution, Texans admitted that the Mexicans' mounted regiments were excellent. The cavalry's reputation and quality remained high in 1846, and selected units of foot soldiers also turned out well.[45]

On the other hand, Mexico's military organization displayed numerous deficiencies. Some Mexicans enlisted in the army, but most soldiers were conscripted for six-year terms. Vagrants, criminals, peons, and Indians were forced into service to meet military quotas. Authorities took draftees from towns and fields, sometimes chaining new soldiers together to prevent desertion. To one American observer it appeared that "the drilling of these men is constant and severe," but, like soldiers in any army, Mexico's enlisted men could fight well when given good leadership, training, and weapons. Regiments usually were raised and served within a group of provinces designated a military department; there were nine such departments in 1845. A general commanded the forces of each department and exerted great political, social, and economic influence over the provinces. Opening the way for fraud, Mexican policy called for each department commander to provide muster rolls listing his soldiers to the War Department in Mexico City. According to the muster rolls, the War Department sent money for pay, clothing, and subsistence to the department commander, who paid his soldiers, purchased supplies, and constructed and repaired military posts. Sometimes the generals' muster rolls carried the names of soldiers who had died, deserted, or been discharged, and department commanders could withhold pay from their soldiers and spend military funds for their personal use. Desertion was rife in the Mexican army, but because commanders juggled their muster books, it was impossible to obtain an accurate count of troops on active duty. Much of Mexico's military funding, consuming more than half of the national budget in the 1840s, had been squandered.[46]

While some department commanders engaged in questionable practices, other Mexican officers that Doniphan would engage fulfilled their duties in a professional manner. By 1846 several senior Mexican army officers had been serving for more than fifteen years, and numerous officers, ranging from lieutenant to general, were dedicated and patriotic. But many Americans shared Brantz Mayer's lack of respect toward Mexican officers because of "the irregular manner in which persons arrive[d] at command and the want of soldierlike education and discipline" among some commanders. Aware of the army's extraordinary influence, some Mexican politicians obtained military commissions only to elevate their personal status, not to become professional officers. Waddy Thompson commented, "They have more than two hundred generals, most of them without commands," leaving the impression among Americans that many Mexican officers were inexperienced novices or ineffectual political appointees not obligated to serve with their units. Holding ranks gained through patronage rather than merit, many Mexican officers lacked training or basic military skills and were not well prepared to lead soldiers into battle.[47]

Each country supplemented its regular army with units of citizen-soldiers. Mexico divided these supplements into two groups, the National Guard and *activos*, activated militia units, usually led by regular army officers. In 1838 the Mexican militia supposedly enrolled some twenty-seven thousand men—workers from farms, mines, and cities—but by 1846 their numbers were reduced, perhaps by half. The National Guard enlisted a few thousand more. National Guardsmen received haphazard training and sporadic deliveries of supplies, but most of the militia were indifferently armed, untrained, and unpaid. Therefore, the reliability in a battle of Mexico's citizen-soldiers was questionable.[48]

The American state militias were also in woeful condition, one reason some Mexicans were confident that their forces could contend with the U.S. military. In national emergencies the U.S. government could call state militia units into service for national defense. The American state militias were made up of white men aged eighteen to forty-five. Units varied sharply from state to state in number and training as well as in quality of arms and equipment, and in 1846 around twenty-five thousand militiamen were available. Good militia units existed, but most local companies were worthless. Mexican politicians, military officers, and newspaper editors recalled the poor showing of the American militia against British forces during the War of 1812. Then some state governors refused to respond to President James Madison's call for sending militia units into national service. In campaigns along the Canadian border, other militia units defied direct orders to invade British Canada. Moreover, in the years since 1815, several states abolished compulsory militia service. Accordingly, based on the small size of the U.S. Army in 1846 and the demonstrable inadequacies of both the army and the American militia in the War of 1812, Mexican leaders were justified in believing that the United States would have difficulty in mounting offensives against Mexico.[49]

As a result of the disappointing performance by militiamen during the War of 1812, many U.S. political and military leaders no longer cared to rely on them for wartime service. In 1846, Missouri's governor, Democrat John C. Edwards, clearly stated his opinion about "the character of our militia system. This is found to be utterly useless. The system is a subject of ridicule and burlesque" because too many militiamen rejected taking "any serious preparation to defend their country"; they "refuse[d] to learn" about military matters and instead turned militia meetings into social events. As an alternative, American leaders took the approach of creating from scratch several new state volunteer regiments to serve for one year. Alexander Doniphan joined one of these new volunteer regiments, but the number and quality of such units remained to be seen, as those enlisting in the volunteer regiments would be coming from the same pool of men who either already served in state militias or could have enlisted in them. Some of the volunteer regiments were armed by the states, but Americans also counted on their War Department to store and control thousands of extra weapons and supplies of ammunition in arsenals around the United States that might be issued to volunteers.[50]

Many Mexicans and some Americans failed to appreciate the combination of America's military capabilities in 1846. The small Regular U.S. Army was supported by good logistics and quality artillery units. The United States raised and outfitted thousands of new volunteer soldiers in a few weeks. In contrast to Mexico's tiny navy, soon dissolved, the professional U.S. Navy was able to transport troops and blockade Mexico's coasts. These attributes combined to mean that the United States possessed considerable potential to send military forces beyond its borders.[51]

In summary, systemic problems in Mexico during the 1840s prevented Mexican civilian and military leaders from overcoming their army's deficiencies. Mexico's chaotic fiscal circumstances, bordering on bankruptcy, contributed to military weakness. Despite spending sizable sums of money on its army during the 1830s and 1840s, creating several reputable units, and having several good commanders, the Mexican army was staffed by inadequate officers who had distributed supplies and forces in such a way that the army could not defend more than half of its country. One of the maxims of Napoleon Bonaparte may be applied to Mexico's war crisis in 1846: "It is very difficult for a nation to create an army when it has not already a body of officers and non-commissioned officers to serve as a nucleus, and *a system of military organization*."[52]

Unfortunately for Mexico, its military organization reflected the weakness of Mexican nationalism. Rivalry between the Catholic Church on the one hand and secular leaders, both political and military, on the other created discord in the heart of the nation. In 1846 Mexico had been independent for only twenty-five years, and much of the nation's population had not developed an allegiance to the national government. Political factionalism undermined national unity, and one's loyalty to province or region sometimes took priority over loyalty to Mexico itself. After the Texas Revolution, separatist unrest had broken out in the state of Tabasco, and secessionists in the state of Yucatán announced that the province had seceded, requiring the army to reassert the authority of the national government. Presidios in the northern states of Upper California and

New Mexico had fallen into disrepair, and their garrisons were absent or understrength. Travelers in the north risked attacks by Indians or bandits. Depredations by Indian tribes, such as Apaches in Sonora and Pimería Alta (the southern portion of modern Arizona) and Navajos in New Mexico, discouraged settlement in those provinces. From Upper California to Yucatán, peons and Indians spoke little Spanish, had not converted to Catholicism, were unfamiliar with republican procedures, and had little sense of national allegiance. Mexico's leaders were aware of these many problems but hoped that nationalists would unite during the wartime emergency with the United States. Some may even have considered that war and the threat of invasion would inspire a burst of nationalistic spirit.[53]

Viewing the crisis from another perspective, some Mexicans hoped for the best because prominent Americans from both parties publicly opposed the war. Such opposition might undermine support for the war and bring about an armistice before Mexico lost its lands. Doniphan had no patience with the war's opponents. They included former vice president and U.S. senator John C. Calhoun of South Carolina, the most significant voice of America's slaveholders. During a long career in politics, Calhoun had been in both the Democratic and Whig parties. Now a dissident Democrat, Calhoun believed that as a result of the war the United States would annex territories filled with Catholics and Mexicans, a populace that would be difficult for the United States to assimilate, and he would refuse to support American citizenship for Mexicans. Significant Southern Whigs, all slave owners, also denounced the war, among them John Crittenden of Kentucky, Alexander H. Stephens and John Barrien of Georgia, and Henry Clay, presidential nominee of the Whig party in 1844. Concerned that the war might be used to expand slavery, or believing that Polk's conduct of the war was unconstitutional, several Northern Whigs also criticized the war, including Charles Sumner, George Ashmun, Joseph Grinnell, Charles Hudson, Daniel P. King, and John Davis, all from Massachusetts; George Evans and Luther Severance, both of Maine; Joshua R. Giddings, Thomas Corwin, Joseph M. Root, Columbus Delano, Daniel R. Tilden, Joseph Vance, and Robert C. Schenck, all of Ohio; and Richard W. Thompson of Indiana. Former president John Quincy Adams, then serving as a member of the House of Representatives from Massachusetts, emphasized that in his view the war was unconstitutional. Along similar lines, noted jurist Francis Lieber eventually decided that, although the United States might gain from the conflict, it was "an unjust war." Albert

Gallatin, a Democrat who had served as secretary of the treasury, decried increased military expenditures and joined those condemning the war.[54]

Other opponents came from among writers and intellectuals. In a work of satirical verse, *The Biglow Papers,* first published anonymously in 1846, James Russell Lowell railed against the war, especially because he believed it would bring about the expansion of slavery. In his treatise "Resistance to Civil Government," later retitled "The Duty of Civil Disobedience," essayist Henry David Thoreau contended that the war was wrong, both because it appeared designed to encourage slavery's expansion and also because it seemed to erupt as a result of a mass mania—Manifest Destiny. Much the individualist, Thoreau was skeptical of a crusade, unless it should be a crusade to end slavery. Other opponents of the war included noted newspaperman Horace Greeley of the New York *Tribune,* poets William Ellery Channing, Henry Wadsworth Longfellow and John Greenleaf Whittier, theologian Theodore Parker, and abolitionist Wendell Phillips.[55]

Criticisms aside, in the spring of 1846 surges of patriotism swept over both Mexico and the United States. In New Mexico, Governor Manuel Armijo had already called for militia to prepare for duty, and the state-run newspaper condemned the U.S. annexation of Texas.[56] Across their country, Mexicans demonstrated admirable patriotism and willingness to defend their nation. Mexicans could claim, with justification, that it was not just or moral for the United States to demand negotiations for the sale of any part of Mexico, no matter how distant from Mexico City or how lightly populated the lands were. Looking to the future, Mexican nationalists rejected the sale or secession of any states, since the loss of any provinces now might mean the loss of more later. Disregarding logic, many Mexican leaders insisted that Texas was still a Mexican province; they rejected U.S. annexation of Texas and asserted that the movement of American soldiers from Louisiana into Texas amounted to an encroachment on Mexican land. On the other hand, Mexicans logically refused to sell California, especially since the amount offered was insultingly small for a region of such potential. By that time it was too late to deflate the crisis by calling for trilateral negotiations involving Great Britain and the United States to settle issues over Texas that had been unresolved for a decade.

Mexico would have to go to war to block U.S. expansionism. The United States and Mexico were about the same size, and the war was fought over which nation would control much of North America. At stake were all of the potential resources between Santa Fe and San Francisco and the ports of California. The two nations confirmed attitudes that meant they were on a collision course:

Mexico had no interest in selling its provinces that the United States was determined to possess.[57]

Many Americans, including Alexander Doniphan, believed in American Manifest Destiny and supported annexing Texas and acquiring New Mexico and California. Numerous Americans asserted that the United States could use the lands, especially seacoasts and harbors, more effectively than Mexico. Many Mexicans believed just as strongly that their nation was destined for greatness. But to achieve that greatness Mexico had to regain control of Texas as well as hold the provinces of Upper California and New Mexico—the "national patrimony"—the places for the nation to develop in the future. Looking at the map differently, William Marcy, the U.S. secretary of war, wrote to General Zachary Taylor, claiming that "the War is represented, on their [Mexico's] part, as one of 'national existence' as if it was our wish to destroy the Mexican Nation!" Denying any intent to destroy Mexico, Marcy indicated, however, that it would please the United States if certain Mexican "departments or states" were to secede and "to declare their independence of the Central Government of Mexico," thus weakening Mexico even more. Marcy indicated that the coming military campaigns might inspire Mexican states, such as Tabasco and Yucatán, to push for independence while the central government fought its war with the United States. Knowing that Texas already had seceded and two other states threatened to secede, belligerent Americans questioned the strength and nationalism of Mexico.[58]

According to one writer, "War is a dispute about the measurement of power." Other analysts have contended that "*perceptions* of relative [military] effectiveness are themselves a major factor in conducting war and keeping the peace." Some on both sides in the 1840s maintained that a victory by the United States over Mexico could have been predicted. They asserted that Mexico's army was inadequate, and its government inept and insolvent. Others, especially Mexicans, pointed to America's small army, weak militia, and military embarrassments in the War of 1812. For many in 1846, the only way to measure the power of Mexico and the United States was on the battlefield. In other words, while some Mexicans and some Americans believed they could see disaster looming for one nation or the other, most could agree neither on how to measure the belligerents' strengths nor on what the outcome of a Mexican-American War would be. Going to war would decide the geographic configuration of the two countries and much about their future as well. By helping to create and by serving in one of the new volunteer regiments that was given important strategic objectives, Alexander Doniphan intended to contribute to what he believed would be the future national greatness of the United States.[59]

CHAPTER TWO

Assembly at Fort Leavenworth

Responding to President Polk's call for troops, on May 15 Missouri's governor, John Edwards, issued a proclamation urging Missourians to support the war against Mexico. In ringing tones, Edwards called out: "Our [American] frontier is in danger. The Mexicans invade our [U.S.] territory. . . . [O]ur army is menaced by superior numbers. . . . *Twelve Hundred Volunteers Are Required from Missouri.*" The governor reiterated the notion that "every good citizen will [want] to procure by arms redress for the attempt to prevent the United States from asserting her claims *within her own territory* [to the border of Texas]." Those men who "enter the service promptly," the governor continued, and those "who reach the seat of war at an early period, may be employed in active and hard service." Edwards concluded on a cautionary note, contrary to any taproom talk dismissing the Mexicans' capabilities: "Be prepared to fight. Expect no light work. A brave soldier has no reason to underrate his adversary."[1]

Promoting Missouri's contribution to the war effort and looking across party lines, Governor Edwards called on Alexander Doniphan and Sterling Price, a leading Democrat, to recruit volunteers. A Virginian, Price had moved to Missouri in 1830, taking up residence in Chariton County, in the north-central part of the state. There Price prospered in agriculture and business investments, served in the legislature and the militia, and was elected to the U.S. House of Representatives. Doniphan promptly responded to the governor's call, sending messages to acquaintances in Missouri's western counties and making speeches on behalf of enlistment. Federal authorities expected each state volunteer to "provide himself with [such basics as] a good horse, which will pass inspection at Fort Leavenworth; a Spanish saddle; a saddle blanket; halter; bridle; good Mackinaw blanket; and saddle-bags." Neophyte soldiers also had to provide themselves with an overcoat; the army would issue such necessities as weapons, ammunition, and canteens.[2]

Missouri's reaction to the declaration of war and the calls for volunteers pleased Doniphan. The famous French traveler in America, Alexis de Tocqueville, had postulated a few years earlier that "there are two things which a democratic people will always find very difficult—to begin a war and to end it." In 1846, however, Doniphan felt that the level of American "patriotism was at fever heat." Volunteer companies sprang up throughout the state's belt of central counties. Though some of the volunteers hoped for government bounties or land grants, there were no guarantees of such awards. In Doniphan's view, "the generous promptings of an uncalculating patriotism" spurred most men to enlist. That the service would be only for one year also helped. Doniphan noted that "the volunteer becomes a soldier for a limited period, and, when the emergency is past, he resumes the ordinary avocations of life." Others agreed with him. "The War created much excitement in this region [western Missouri]," observed Waldo Johnson, a young Democratic lawyer from Independence, who was "anxious 'to see the elephant'"—to find out what combat was like. Richard S. Elliott, an Indian agent and a volunteer lieutenant from St. Louis, remembered the air being "full of patriotism." Responding to their "patriotic impulses," the enlistees saw themselves as "Alexanders in uniform, each ready to conquer a world if he could only get the right kind of chance." Frank Edwards, an unemployed man soon enlisted as an artillery private, concluded that "the young men of all classes were eager to go—indeed, it became a question who must be left [behind]." John Hughes, a schoolteacher in Liberty, recounted that "every man [who enlisted] feels that he is . . . the citizen of the MODEL REPUBLIC." Coming together as a part of the concept of recruiting new volunteer regiments instead of using already established state militia units, individual companies of high-spirited recruits from several Missouri counties prepared to report to federal military authorities. The United States had used volunteer regiments in the War of 1812 and in Florida during the Seminole War, and now national volunteering would be tested on a larger scale.[3]

Enlistees coming together for the 1st Regiment of Missouri Mounted Volunteers joined one of thirty American regiments raised during May, June, and July 1846 following President Polk's initial call. Regiments contained several companies and varied in strength from around five hundred to more than eight hundred men. In addition to Missouri, the president asked several other Southern and midwestern states to enlist volunteers during those early months of the war, including Louisiana, Texas, Maryland (along with the District of Columbia), Alabama, Mississippi, Arkansas, Tennessee, Kentucky, Illinois, Indiana, and

Ohio. During the course of the war, sixty-three men would serve as volunteer colonels leading regiments freshly raised for wartime service, some specifically for one year of duty, others for the duration of the war, which, by the time they were recruited, often amounted to about one year. Some states responding to Polk's initial call raised more troops, and other states also sent regiments, including Michigan, Massachusetts, Pennsylvania, South Carolina, North Carolina, Virginia, and Georgia. Eventually, more than seventy-three thousand Americans signed up as volunteer soldiers during the war. Some served only a few months, but eighteen thousand were one-year men and more than thirty-three thousand enlisted "for the war." While many served, few fought in a battle.[4]

On June 6, 1846, less than a month after writing Secretary of War Marcy and offering to serve, Doniphan, his brother-in-law, Captain Oliver Moss, and more than one hundred other volunteers of Company C from Clay County presented themselves for duty. The soldiers in Company C averaged twenty-four years of age. Although there were several teenagers mixed in, most of the men in the regiment were in their twenties. Moss was thirty-three, typical of the other captains, most of whom were in their midthirties. One by one, the other companies arrived, each also enrolling over one hundred men. From Jackson County, Captain David Waldo, a merchant in the Santa Fe trade, led Company A. Lafayette County sent Company B under Captain William P. Walton, a farmer who had settled in Missouri from Virginia in 1826. Volunteers from Franklin County, mostly from the towns of Union and Washington, came in Company E under Captain John D. Stevenson (age twenty-six), a native Virginian who had set up a law office in Union in 1842. Mosby Monroe Parsons, a lawyer from Jefferson City who moved to Missouri from Virginia in 1835, commanded Company F from Cole County. Congreve Jackson, a veteran of the Second Seminole War who owned a large farm and several slaves, led Company G of Howard County. Many of the new soldiers disembarked at the steamboat landing on the Missouri River and then made their way four hundred yards to one of America's most important military posts, Fort Leavenworth, located in unorganized territory west of the Missouri state boundary. At that place Doniphan and his fellow enlistees began the brief transition designed to change their outlook from civilians into soldiers.[5]

Established by the army as a cantonment in 1827 and officially designated a fort in 1832, Leavenworth was both impressive but something less than a number of the volunteers might have expected. No wooden palisades lined the fort's perimeter, but sturdy blockhouses guarded each corner of a twenty-acre-square parade ground. On the eastern lateral, two imposing brick barracks, each two stories high with wide porches, gave an air of permanence and decorum to the

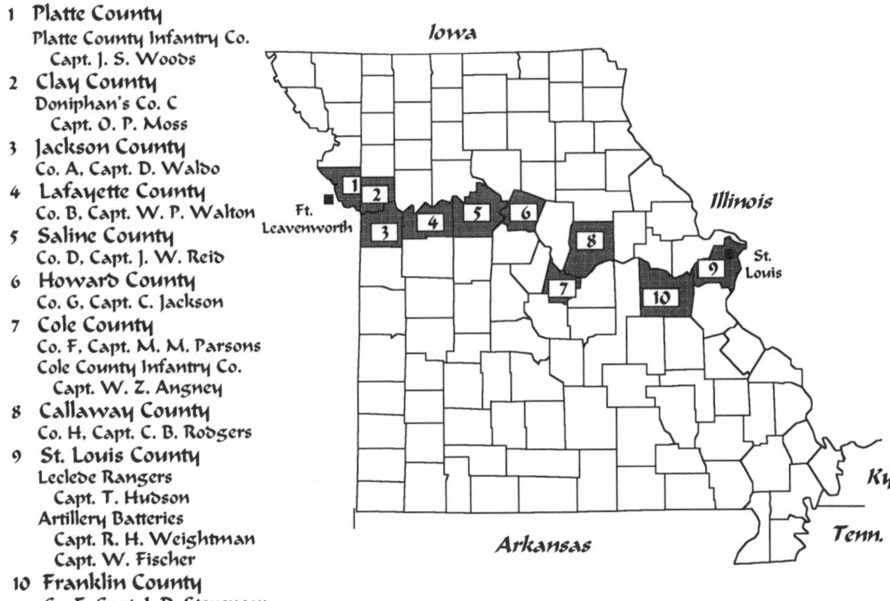

Missouri county units in Doniphan's regiment. (Original rendering by T. T. Smith, 1998)

post. Regular army enlisted men lived in the barracks. Married officers and their families occupied a row of handsome brick quarters lining the northern side of the square. Commissary and quartermaster buildings lay to the northeast. Scattered brick and wood frame structures dotted the western side of the fort: an arsenal, bachelor officers' quarters, and houses for a few civilians employed at the post. Log stables ran all along the fort's southern edge, with a log guardhouse a short distance away. Off the southwest corner of the fort, separated from the barracks and houses, stood a large brick hospital building, featuring wide wraparound porticoes. It provided the place for soldiers to recuperate from wounds, disease, or injuries. Well beyond the hospital, soldiers tended more than one thousand acres of farmland, growing food for the garrison and its livestock. And due west of the post stretched some three hundred acres of drill fields, spotted with tufts of grass, "a beautiful space," as one newspaper reporter described it. During the next three weeks Doniphan and the 1st Missouri Volunteers spent many hours on those drill fields, learning the basics of soldiering according to the U.S. Army.[6]

In the meantime, the new soldiers faced a dozen tasks, everything from setting up designated camping sites and making arrangements for rations to preparing to draw weapons. The regiment's companies arrived over a period of several days before being officially mustered into federal service. A Regular U.S. Army captain, James Allen of the 1st Dragoons, swore them in for one year. The volunteers already had met the Regular officers who would be in charge of training. Even as the companies got settled in at the fort, twenty-nine additional volunteers stepped forward to enlist in the regiment. They were distributed among the companies, including the St. Louis cavalry and artillery units arriving later. As the men of the regiment had prepared to give their oath, the Columbia *Statesman* reckoned that "the State of Missouri will be honorably represented wherever they may be called upon to do duty."[7]

From the volunteers' point of view, a top priority was electing senior officers for the 1st Regiment of Missouri Mounted Volunteers. This election was important: the colonel who would lead the regiment also would be second in command on the expedition to New Mexico, outranked only by the senior Regular Army officer in charge. Secretary of War Marcy corresponded with governors of several states about matters pertaining to raising troops, emphasizing to Governor Edwards, among others, that it was a matter "of extreme importance" that the officers be "judiciously selected." Besides the colonel, his chief subordinates, the lieutenant colonel and the major, had to be chosen. Out of more than eight hundred volunteers in the regiment, four serious contestants, all considered well qualified, presented themselves for election. Naturally, Private Doniphan indicated that he would run for colonel. Some hoped that Private John W. Price, a long-term Missouri resident, would win that post, and Price offered strong competition. A former militia general, Price had held the rank of volunteer colonel and led Missouri troops during the Second Seminole War, but without much success. Price owned four slaves and engaged in agriculture in Clay County.[8]

Two men originally from Pennsylvania contended for the spot of lieutenant colonel. One was Private William Gilpin, thirty-one years old, who enlisted in Company A from Jackson County. Flamboyant and well connected politically, Gilpin boasted friendships with rich and important patrons, including Thomas Hart Benton, a leading Democrat and one of Missouri's U.S. senators, and Benton's son-in-law, John C. Frémont, the famous western explorer. Following his graduation from the University of Pennsylvania in 1833, Gilpin was appointed to West Point but attended for only a few months before leaving to study law. Subsequently, his political friends arranged for a commission in the army. As a first lieutenant in the 2nd Dragoons from 1836 to 1838, Gilpin served as a recruiting officer in Missouri and then engaged in field duty in Florida during the Second Seminole War. Deciding to seek business opportunities in Missouri, he resigned from the army. Among his pursuits, Gilpin operated a newspaper, served as clerk of the Missouri House of Representatives, guarded a wagon train on the Santa Fe Trail in 1843, and explored the Oregon country. An ardent nationalist and advocate of Manifest Destiny, Gilpin was well known to most of the enlistees in the regiment. The other candidate for lieutenant colonel was Private Charles F. Ruff, in Doniphan's own Company C. Like Gilpin, Ruff also had gained an appointment to the Military Academy from Pennsylvania in 1834, but unlike him, Ruff had earned his commission by graduating in the West Point Class of 1838, ranking forty-fourth of forty-five cadets. Ruff also served with the dragoons, but his tour of duty lasted four years. In 1842 he resigned to read law, eventually hanging out his shingle in Liberty, Doniphan's hometown. In keeping with the American volunteer tradition, all of the officer-candidates were men with established reputations and whose accomplishments and education were known to most of the men in the regiment.[9]

On June 18 the volunteers anticipated casting their votes. Each of the candidates addressed the regiment's assembled companies. Drawing upon his recognition from the Mormon War as well as his years in the state legislature and having persuasively addressed many juries, Doniphan excelled at public oratory and his speech was well received. On the other hand, a saucy volunteer heckled Price when he mentioned his service in Florida, taunting him that "it would have been better to keep that fact a secret." Doniphan won the election for colonel over Price by a wide margin, perhaps around 500 to 350. Although disappointed, Price continued to serve in the regiment during the coming campaign.[10]

America's volunteer colonels may be subdivided in several ways. One subgroup, not including Doniphan, comprised fifteen men who had held a commission in the Regular U.S. Army, served in uniform, and then turned to civilian pursuits. Eleven of the state colonels were graduates of the U.S. Military Academy, two were former students at the Academy who had not graduated, and two had received direct commissions from civilian life. During the war some former Regulars who distinguished themselves as colonels were Jefferson Davis of Mississippi, William McKee of Kentucky, George Hughes of the District of Columbia, and Ward Burnett of New York. The former Regulars formed a pool of educated citizens familiar with military matters, and most provided capable leadership when they returned to military service. But the uneven burden on the Southern and midwestern states to raise troops, combined with politics and personalities, meant that men other than former Regulars would serve as regimental commanders. Moreover, a widespread American attitude held that employing volunteer officers who had little or no military training was still an appropriate and necessary way to obtain leaders for wartime service.[11]

Another subgroup of volunteer colonels—forty-eight officers—possessed no Regular service, but about one-third of them, and Doniphan fit into this category, had held appointments in their state's militia. Militia service put their names before the public and may have reflected patriotism, but it was just as likely to indicate political connections and ambitions as military knowledge or proficiency. Turning their lack of formal military training into republican virtue, some future colonels played upon the widespread antipathy toward the Regular Army, perceived by many to be elitist. Indeed, wartime military service in 1846 linked expectations of republican citizenship with an inherent dislike of standing armies.[12]

Most regimental commanders, like Doniphan, were in their thirties and drew upon their county or state recognition to get elected colonel. Volunteer regimental commanders averaged thirty-seven years of age; at thirty-eight, Doniphan was slightly older than the average. In an era when few Americans attended college, a place in society was accorded those who had a college education. Like Doniphan, half of the colonels had attended or graduated from college. Several, including Doniphan, gained further recognition through the legal profession and politics. More than twenty were lawyers and had served in one or both branches of their state's legislature. Thirty-eight colonels (60 percent) served with Southern regiments and twenty-five (40 percent) with Northern regiments. As a colonel from a slave state, Doniphan was in the majority. A few—only eight—had won elections to Congress as well.[13]

As a Whig, Doniphan was in the minority of those holding the rank of volunteer colonel during the Mexican War. Working politics to the advantage of his party, President Polk appointed only Democrats to be volunteer generals. By election or appointment, Polk's party also dominated the state colonelcies, with twenty-six Democrats and ten probable Democrats, for thirty-six of the sixty-three men who served in the rank of colonel.[14] High-profile Democrats who were colonels included four infantry officers, Jefferson Davis, 1st Mississippi; Caleb Cushing, 1st Massachusetts; Joseph Lane, 2nd Indiana; and Jonathan Stevenson, 1st New York; and two cavalry or mounted officers, Archibald Yell, 1st Arkansas; and Sterling Price, 2nd Missouri. Besides Doniphan, twelve other Whigs were colonels and four more were probably Whigs, giving the party notable representation in quality, if not in quantity, among the regimental commanders. Among other prominent Whig colonels, all infantry officers, were William Campbell, 1st Tennessee; William McKee, 2nd Kentucky; Albert Sidney

Johnston, Johnston's Texas Regiment; Charles Clark, 2nd Mississippi; Balie Peyton, 5th Louisiana; and John J. Hardin and Edward Baker, leading the 1st and 4th Illinois regiments, respectively. Most of the Whig colonels came from the slave states.[15]

In the next election, a close contest for the lieutenant colonelcy of the 1st Missouri demonstrated some animosity toward Charles Ruff, the graduate of the Military Academy. Although Gilpin also had matriculated at West Point and served in a dragoon regiment, the Regular officers of dragoons at Leavenworth lobbied for Ruff, while the volunteers divided almost equally between the two. In the voting Ruff defeated Gilpin for the lieutenant colonelcy by a margin of only two votes. In short order, the position of major went to William Gilpin by unanimous consent, though others had indicated they wished to be considered. Doniphan had known Gilpin since they met in the Missouri legislature in 1840, and the colonel had favored him as his top subordinate. Relations between Doniphan and Ruff seemed cool after the election. For his part, Colonel Stephen Watts Kearny, commanding officer of the 1st Dragoons at Fort Leavenworth, stressed to all the newly elected officers and the other volunteers "the necessity of being prompt and energetic in the performance of their several duties. Not a moment should be lost in preparing themselves and their respective commands for the arduous service which will be required of them."[16]

Colonel Kearny was one of the best senior officers in the U.S. Army. Kearny had entered the army as a lieutenant in 1812, gained combat experience, and later earned exemplary marks as an infantry officer during the 1820s. He was promoted to lieutenant colonel of dragoons in 1833 and to colonel commanding the 1st Dragoons in 1836. Known as fair and honest, Kearny deserved his reputation as a "strict disciplinarian" and stickler for detail. His intelligent, expressive eyes seemed to pierce subordinates when he addressed them. As Doniphan's tutor and mentor as well as the commanding officer of the "Army of the West," Kearny exerted a positive influence on Doniphan's military service, though the Missouri colonel came to his regiment already displaying several qualities of leadership. In public, Kearny set a high standard of soldierly qualities and provided practical advice to Doniphan, but he always delivered it with courtesy. Privately the two discussed the war in general, prospects for the campaign, and unit organization. Doniphan acknowledged studying a book on French dragoon tactics that Kearny provided him. The two officers shared mutual respect: Doniphan described Kearny as a "gallant and accomplished soldier," and the dragoon fully appreciated his subordinate's potential. Their relationship exemplified cooperation in a war replete with many instances of friction, hostility, and distrust between Regulars and volunteers.[17]

Responsibilities for issuing arms and equipment rested with Colonel Kearny. Most of the volunteers owned firearms, and some brought various shotguns, pistols, and revolvers with them to Fort Leavenworth, but the army planned to issue government weapons to the 1st Missouri Regiment. Recently adopted by the War Department, the standard-issue shoulder weapon of the U.S. Army was the Model 1842 percussion musket. Distinguished from its predecessors by a new percussion cap-firing mechanism, more reliable than flintlocks in damp conditions, the Model 1842 was a smoothbore, muzzle-loading, single-shot piece that fired a heavy .69 caliber lead ball, sometimes supplemented with buckshot. Soldiers called the combination "buck and ball." The range of the Model 1842 was less than one hundred yards, being accurate to only about fifty yards, even in the hands of experienced infantrymen. Except for the reliability of the percussion cap, in other respects, such as length and weight (about five feet long and weighing about nine pounds), the Model 1842 was the most recent in a long line of smoothbore muskets modified over the years. All of these were based on the British army's "Brown Bess" or Tower musket, a design familiar to European soldiers and colonists before and during the American Revolution. The Brown Bess was a single-shot flintlock weapon with counterparts in all of Europe's armies. Many Mexican soldiers in the 1840s carried some version of the Brown Bess. In fact, by the time of the Mexican-American War several U.S. Army units had not turned in their flintlocks for a percussion model, and American soldiers in several Regular units carried flintlock muskets into battle.[18]

Under the pressures of wartime, the army had no surplus Model 1842 muskets to issue to volunteer units, but it was prepared to issue other weapons, including rifles, depending on stocks available at various posts or arsenals. Ordnance officers held several different shoulder weapons at Fort Leavenworth in the spring of 1846. A majority of volunteers could have expected to be armed with older model flintlock muskets, but the 1st Missouri received rifles instead of smoothbores.[19]

Some of Doniphan's men, perhaps a majority of the regiment, carried Hall's rifles. For instance, all of the soldiers in Captain John Stevenson's Company E from Franklin County were so equipped. Lieutenant George Gibson of the Platte County infantry company later relished the memory of having a Hall's rifle and remarked that one was also carried by a friend. Private Marcellus Edwards later recalled that "the two cavalry companies [D, under Captain John Reid, and F, Captain Mosby Parsons] exchange[d] their yagers [Mississippi rifles] for patent breech carbines, which are very handy to load." The Hall's was one of the most innovative weapons of the first half of the nineteenth century. First patented in 1819 and approved for federal use in 1827, the original Hall's rifle was a .52

caliber flintlock used by the Marine Corps. Between 1842 and 1844 the federal arsenal at Harpers Ferry, Virginia, manufactured three thousand modified Hall's rifles with percussion caps, on an order from the War Department. The Hall's sported a breech-loading system, distinguished by a remarkable lever action. Pulling down a lever near the trigger guard pushed the breechblock up, revealing an aperture into which a soldier fed powder and a single round of ammunition. Returning the lever to its original position brought the breechblock flush with the stock, and the rifle was ready to fire a single shot. Accurate to about 250 yards, the Hall's gave soldiers a distinct advantage in range over opponents carrying any standard smoothbore musket. Like many early model breech-loaders, however, the Hall's suffered from gas leakage at the breech. After several discharges of the weapon, hot gas sometimes escaped from the breech, very distracting to the soldier firing it.[20]

Colonel Doniphan and other veterans of the regiment wrote of being armed with some sort of *rifles,* not smoothbore muskets, but did not indicate which kind of rifles they carried. According to one soldier serving in Captain Thomas Hudson's mounted company, they had been issued the so-called Mississippi Rifle. Officially the U.S. Model 1841, the "Mississippi Rifle" was a muzzle-loading, percussion cap, .54 caliber rifled weapon, four feet in length, with a range of 300 yards. Made famous by Colonel Jefferson Davis and his 1st Mississippi Volunteer Infantry Regiment, the "Mississippi Rifle" became one of the most popular of all shoulder weapons used by volunteers during the war because of its range, sturdiness, and reliability.[21]

Before Doniphan's election, other units vital to the formation of the "Army of the West" had arrived at Fort Leavenworth. Bearing a silk flag sewn by the ladies of St. Louis and with the cheers of the city's citizens still ringing in their ears, the Leclede Rangers, a volunteer cavalry company over one hundred strong, departed their city on June 7 and paraded into Leavenworth a few days later, proudly wearing uniforms of their own design. Captain Thomas Hudson, supported by his lieutenant, Richard S. Elliott, commanded the Rangers. Hudson, a thirty-two-year-old attorney, had been born in Davidson County, Tennessee, in 1814. Arriving in St. Louis in 1835, he established a law practice, landed the appointment as city attorney, and was elected to the city council in 1840. In 1842 he won a seat in the lower house of the Missouri General Assembly. Formerly a Pennsylvania journalist, Elliott had moved west, taking a federal post as a subagent for Indian affairs. On May 28 the Rangers had chosen Hudson to be captain by acclamation, and Elliott won second in command by a wide margin. Neither had any prior military experience.[22]

The proficiency of the batteries of Major Meriwether Lewis Clark's artillery battalion, also raised in St. Louis, came to rival Regular artillerists. Outfitted in blue uniforms trimmed with red, modeled after those worn by Regular Army artillery units, Clark's cannoneers acknowledged that their gun drill was due to more than enthusiasm. The son of William Clark, of the famed Lewis and Clark Expedition, Major Clark was a graduate in the West Point Class of 1830, ranking twenty-third of forty-two cadets. He had served on active duty in the infantry, participating in the Black Hawk War, before resigning his commission in 1833 and settling in St. Louis. There he made his living as an architect and civil engineer; he also served a term in the state legislature beginning in 1836. Clark's half sister was married to Colonel Kearny. A District of Columbia native, Captain Richard H. Weightman, one of the battery commanders, had graduated from the University of Virginia and then attended West Point from 1835 to 1837 but did not complete his studies there. Weightman had practiced law in Washington and moved to Missouri, arriving in St. Louis around 1842. The other battery commander, Captain Woldemar Fischer, was a popular German-American grocer instrumental in recruiting others from that ethnic group to serve in the battalion. Fischer was born in Saxony and served as a junior officer in the Prussian army before immigrating to America in 1834. Despite his military background, Fischer seemed to have difficulty getting his battery to drill as well as Weightman's. The guns and artillerists of Weightman's battery proved instrumental in the success of the expedition.[23]

As the coming campaign demonstrated, the education and experience of West Pointers would be vital to supplement the enthusiasm and lack of experience of the regiment's citizen-soldiers. Most volunteer officers on the expedition were capable, competent, cooperative, and energetic. Doniphan was first among those who acknowledged his debt of gratitude to such sterling subordinates. "Like most other volunteer commands we had some officers who had graduated [from West Point], and some who had been [t]here for several years [as cadets]," the colonel recalled. "To the training received from these sources I attribute much of the efficiency of the column." He generously noted that the regiment reaped the benefit of "the skill and attainments of those who had been more fortunate in their early military educations" and could apply that education to the training of their fellow Missourians. As regimental commander, Doniphan could not afford to let "false pride, nor a wanton recklessness of the lives of the soldiers" block him "from applying to officers of inferior rank for such information as I needed." Untutored volunteer, West Point graduate with a few years of service, or experienced Regular, all contributed their advice to the colonel.[24]

With the preliminaries finished, Kearny turned to the serious business of training the volunteers. Doniphan's regiment would be trained as dragoons, soldiers who usually rode horses to their objective and then dismounted for combat. Sometimes, of course, dragoons fought while mounted. Suited to be instructors, officers and noncommissioned officers from Kearny's regiment were assigned to train the volunteer companies. Depending on when they arrived at the fort, most companies received between two and three weeks of tactical drills. Having only a few days to work with the volunteers, Colonel Kearny put aside practicing for parades and focused his drills on the army's tactical formations. Hours of drill introduced the volunteers to the meaning of orders that would be issued on the battlefield, moving in formation, preparing them to fight both mounted and dismounted. Kearny believed that learning the combat formations and understanding standard orders would instill some discipline into the volunteers. Like other Regulars, Kearny knew the importance of unit cohesion and discipline on the battlefield in order for soldiers to be the commander's effective instruments. Not surprisingly, the volunteers balked at emulating their Regular counterparts too closely. Already familiar with firearms and horsemanship, some citizen-soldiers failed "to understand why they should be drilled before they take up the line of march," even if what the professional soldiers were trying to teach was for the volunteers' own good.[25]

According to Lieutenant Elliott of the Leclede Rangers, their training officer, Lieutenant Andrew Jackson Smith of the 1st Dragoons, displayed an "inexhaustible patience" while instructing the Rangers in "the 'School of the Trooper.'" Covering such matters as designating which soldiers would be horse-holders and which would form line of battle, Lieutenant Smith imparted his knowledge of tactical drill, but he seldom cracked a smile, no matter what high jinks the volunteers perpetrated. Elliott claimed that he and the Rangers caught on quickly to the drills, but that Doniphan's regiment made much slower progress. Elliott also chided Doniphan's men for, unlike the Rangers, they had no uniforms. Other officers of the 1st Dragoons were more understanding. Lieutenant Abraham Johnston saw little difference between the Rangers and Doniphan's men. "To equip and put in fighting order fifteen hundred volunteers, all of whom (even the officers) being ignorant of their duties," Johnston said, "is a task requiring a large stock of patience."[26]

Under pressure from Washington to get his units into shape and move out as soon as possible, Kearny worked during June "to harmonize all the elements here assembled," putting the volunteer companies through two stringent series of daily drills held at 5:00 A.M. and 4:00 P.M. Each session usually lasted for two hours. After the morning drills, the men curried their horses and then went to breakfast, consisting of plain fare of fat pork or tough beef, "sour loaf bread," and weak coffee, "made by cooks who had . . . learned . . . exactly how many grains

Brigadier General Stephen Watts Kearny. (Courtesy of the Museum of New Mexico, negative no. 7605)

it took to color a pint of water," recalled Private Marcellus Edwards of Company D of Saline County. Loading wagons, packing equipment, gathering fodder for draft animals, and policing the stables took up the volunteers' time until the afternoon drill. "Industriously drilling" under the eyes of the dragoons' officers, Doniphan's men began to make progress in responding to the orders and learning the tactical evolutions, including "march by sections of four, the sabre exercises, the charge, the rally, and other cavalry tactics." Kearny also included formal inspections of weapons, horses, and equipment between mounted drills.[27]

The hoofbeats of hundreds of horses trampled the grass on the fort's parade ground and on the drill field, "Campus Martis" the volunteers called it, a corruption of the Latin phrase "Campus Martius," a field for military exercises. After a few days the riders churned up clouds of powdery dust, which settled over both sweating volunteers and horses. Poking fun at Doniphan's men, Lieutenant Elliott related that "there are some rich scenes and specimens of horsemanship, when the sabres are used." Regulation equipment for dragoons, the sabers looked imposing, but most of the volunteers considered them a "great annoyance" rather than vital weaponry. Private John Hughes acknowledged, however, that Kearny's insistence on constant "martial exercises . . . doubtless proved subsequently to be of the most essential service."[28]

Even Elliott had to admire the enthusiasm of Doniphan's men. "They march around the parade [ground], waving their flags, and giving vent most lustily to their patriotism." Captain Fischer's high-spirited company of German-Americans, decked out in their own uniforms of gray coats and matching pants with a yellow stripe down the seam, added to the din by belting out German songs. Unmoved by such displays of enthusiasm, Kearny "looked very grave," no doubt wondering what kind of soldiers these volunteers were going to make. Governor Edwards, who considered the Missourians "hunters—marksmen, who know how to handle and keep their guns in order—men inured to toil, fatigue, hardships, and all sorts of privations in life—men anxious to enter the service, and ready to march to the Pacific, or anywhere else they may be commanded to go," might be forgiven his enthusiasm. Watching their daily training, Colonel Kearny concluded that the troops were still "*very raw*," in his opinion. But he did not show it. Even "with onerous and vexatious duties pressing upon him—with many scenes passing around him which must offend his sense of military propriety—with many intrusions upon his busiest hours, and a thousand questions, suggestions, &c, thoughtlessly if not improperly made to him—he is still 'calm as a summer's morning,' apparently as unruffled as if nothing but the ordinary business of the garrison were going on." Kearny's stoic determination paid off. Near the end of June Elliott reported that "the discipline is yet very imperfect but it is improving," and Private Hughes complimented the Regulars on their "kindly and most gentlemanly manner" during their training.[29]

Late arrivals joining the expedition had no chance to be exposed to even a few days of tactical drills. Two supplementary infantry companies assembled in Weston, Missouri, on the morning of June 28. A Regular Army officer officially mustered them into federal service later that day at Fort Leavenworth, an aggregate of 145 officers and enlisted men. A lawyer from Jefferson City, William Z. Angney, led Company A from Cole County, and Captain William S. Murphy commanded Company B from Platte County. The army issued rifles to the late arrivals, and Kearny plugged them into the marching order so hastily that they were unable to receive the standard federally issued equipment given to other volunteers at Fort Leavenworth. Instead, Kearny required the sutlers accompanying the troops to issue such items as blankets and shirts on the march.[30]

Before the campaign began, crowds of Missouri civilians praised their volunteer soldiers, bolstering the civic pride they had for enlisting. As the various units had made their way to Fort Leavenworth, going through several small towns, the populace turned out to cheer them. In Jefferson City, the state capital, local and state leaders had presented flags and refreshments to units bound for war. Enthusiastic citizens handed a silk scroll embossed with the words "Missouri River to the Rio Grande!" to Captain Angney and Lieutenant Lucian J. Eastin. Crowds thronged the streets and docks of Jefferson City to hail the soldiers "who are faithful representatives of the martial spirit which now animates the State."[31]

During the week before the Army of the West began departing, contingents of well-wishers from St. Louis and other Missouri towns showed up at Leavenworth, offering encouragement in the form of flags, food, and hurrahs. On June 23 "a large delegation of ladies from Clay [County]" gave their men a national flag to carry in the campaign, and one of the women delegates made a sincere speech calling for the volunteers "'to sustain the honor of our common country, and to redress the indignities offered to its flag'"—a reference to Mexico's supposed slights toward the United States during the previous months. Seeking to inspire the recruits and expressing heartfelt patriotism of the day, the lady went on to say: "'In presenting to you this token of our regard and esteem, we wish you to remember that some of us have sons, some brothers, and all of us either friends or relatives among you, and that we would rather hear of your falling in honorable warfare, than to see you return sullied with crime, or disgraced by cowardice. We trust, then that your conduct in all circumstances, will be worthy [of] the noble, intelligent and patriotic nation whose cause you have so generously volunteered to defend [and] let your motto be: 'Death before Dishonor.'" Sewn into the fabric of the flag were words that linked religion and state, "The

Love of Country Is the Love of God." Encouraged to the "gallant discharge of duty," Private John Hughes and the other volunteers "were . . . prepared to breast every storm of adversity, by the remembrance of the dear pledges of affection they left behind them; their mothers, their sisters, their young brides, their aged fathers, who, they knew would receive them with outstretched arms, if they returned triumphant from many a well contested field with the laurels of victory; but who, they were equally certain, would frown with indignation upon him who, in the hour of battle, would desert the flag of his country." One mother later admonished her son by alluding to the ancient Greeks. According to Marcellus Edwards, one of the son's companions, "She felt like the Spartan mother who presented a shield to her boy as he was going to battle and said: 'Return with it or return upon it.'" Although grim, the lad's send-off indicated wholehearted support for the war effort from his family. The volunteers had no doubt that their friends and families planned to pay attention to their behavior as soldiers and that they held high expectations for success of the regiment.[32]

Hometown newspapers provided another link with the folks back home. Two volunteers, Private John Hughes, of Company C, and Lieutenant Richard Elliott, of the Leclede Rangers, writing under the nom de plume "John Brown," arranged to submit reports about the expedition to the Liberty *Weekly Tribune* and the St. Louis *Reveille*, respectively. A third member of the regiment, Lieutenant Lucian Eastin, of Captain Angney's infantry company from Cole County, may have made a similar arrangement; his reports later appeared in the Jefferson City *Weekly Inquirer*. Lieutenant Christian Kribben, of Captain Fischer's battery, wrote several letters to the St. Louis *Daily Republican*, using the signature "bb." The rank and file of the regiment soon learned about newspaper reporters among them. Naturally, this influenced their attitudes and outlooks as soldiers. How they comported themselves on the battlefield would be described to everyone's friends and family. Even though four "reporters" on an expedition of more than one thousand men seems like a token number, nineteenth-century newspapers typically reprinted stories from their competitors. Stories showing up first in the *Tribune*, the *Inquirer*, and the *Reveille* would reach a wide audience covering most of Missouri and even papers in other states.[33]

While the volunteers waved their new flags and reveled in the patriotic speeches, their brief training drew to a close, and Regular officers on Kearny's competent staff attended to the details of what the expedition needed for its campaign. Major Thomas Swords and Captain William McKissack, quartermaster and assistant quartermaster, respectively, took care of the numerous details of supplies. Lieutenant William N. Grier, commissary officer, arranged for the soldiers' food. Captain Henry S. Turner, Kearny's assistant adjutant general, handled paperwork, including official enrollment documents and numerous messages. Four Regular Army Topographical Engineers provided expertise in terrain analysis and mapping along the route. They included First Lieutenant William H. Emory, First Lieutenant William H. Warner, Second Lieutenant James W. Abert, and Brevet Second Lieutenant William G. Peck.[34]

Various tallies differed in regard to how the soldiers were divided among the several units of the Army of the West. They were apportioned approximately as follows: some 300 Regulars of the 1st Dragoons in five companies and Kearny's staff; 856 men of Doniphan's 1st Missouri Mounted Regiment; Clark's battalion of artillery, 250 men ready to deploy sixteen cannon (twelve 6-pounders and four 12-pounders); the two companies of volunteer infantry from St. Louis, 145 soldiers; and the Leclede Rangers under Captain Hudson, 107 riders, making a total of 1,358 volunteers, for a complement of 1,658 officers, noncommissioned officers and enlisted men. But the expedition numbered far more than that. Kearny arranged to have fifty mounted Delaware and Shawnee Indians to serve as scouts and interpreters. Furthermore, unspecified hundreds of civilian teamsters and merchants also supported the soldiers. Some were private businessmen and their employees willing to risk the passage to Santa Fe for personal profit. To drive the government supply wagons, some of which were newly built with green lumber, Kearny hired more teamsters, some of whom were experienced drivers who had made trips down to Santa Fe; others were youngsters out for adventure. Armed with a variety of weapons, most were capable of contributing in any combat against Indians or Mexicans. Finally, a few of the Missourians brought along about a dozen African-American slaves to act as cooks and servants. Bringing their slaves were Captain John W. Reid, a lawyer from Jefferson City commanding Company D, and Lieutenant John B. Duncan of Callaway County's Company H, under Captain Charles B. Rodgers, a veteran of the Second Seminole War. Lieutenant Gibson mentioned two "servants" and one unidentified black teamster. Altogether the expedition comprised 1,556 wagons pulled by 3,658 mules and 14,904 oxen, and brought along an additional 459 horses, truly a prodigious number of draft animals. Not counting the horses of the 1st Missouri Regiment or its supporting artillery, this amounted to nearly one wagon and eleven draft animals for each soldier on the expedition. When the Army of the West staged out of Fort Leavenworth it probably included more than 3,000 men and 20,000 animals. As Kearny's senior commissary officer, Major Swords, concluded, "The distance of the scene of operations from this, the nearest point [Fort Leavenworth] from which supplies can be sent, is nearly 1,000 miles and the nature of the country over which they have to be carried without settlements of any kind will make this an arduous and expensive operation."[35]

Considering the ambitious, belligerent strategy of the United States, Kearny's Army of the West, of which Doniphan's volunteer regiment constituted the biggest segment, played a significant role. Indeed, it was to carry out an integral part of President Polk's national strategy. Strategy may be defined several ways, but a definition by an English writer is instructive: "the art of distributing and applying the military means to fulfill the ends of [national] policy."[36]

On May 14, 1846, Polk told Secretary Marcy and General Winfield Scott that "the first movement should be to march a competent force into the Northern Provinces [of Mexico] and seize and hold them until peace was made." Breathtaking in its scope, Polk's strategy relied on less than half of the small U.S. Regular Army (totaling only about 8,500 men), hastily gathered volunteer units, like the 1st Missouri Regiment, and squadrons of the U.S. Navy already standing off of Mexico's shores, both the coast of California and in the Gulf of Mexico. Acting through the War Department, Polk ordered one army contingent (Kearny's, with Doniphan as second in command) to invade Mexico and capture Santa Fe. Then Kearny would take his Regulars and move across hundreds of miles of northern Mexico to complete the conquest of another province, California, while the 2nd Missouri Mounted Volunteer Regiment (under Colonel Sterling Price) reinforced Santa Fe. The U.S. Navy's contribution to the plan included a squadron of nine ships (seven warships and two transport vessels), under Commodore John D. Sloat, operating off of California. Transporting one company of artillerists (about 100 men) and coordinating with other U.S. forces, the naval squadron would land marines and sailors to supplement the army units' takeover of California. The president wanted additional forces dispatched to the Pacific Coast as soon as possible, but the initial invasion of California sent in less than 1,000 effectives, including about 300 sailors and marines; Captain John C. Frémont with 160 riflemen; Kearny with 300 dragoons; and the artillery company delivered by the navy. The supplemental units turned out to be Colonel Jonathan Stevenson's 1st New York Volunteer Regiment (understrength at only 500 men) and the volunteer Mormon Battalion (350 men) led by a Regular dragoon officer, Captain Philip St. George Cooke. As it turned out, Kearny decided to take only 88 dragoons with him to the coast, reducing the number of Regular soldiers deployed there. Meanwhile, Brigadier General Zachary Taylor, with another force numbering between three and 4,000 Regular soldiers, planned to patrol along the Rio Grande, thus asserting American control over Texas, the province still claimed by Mexico. Polk's strategy assumed that if American military forces guarded the Rio Grande and occupied key spots in New Mexico and California, Mexico would have no choice but to concede defeat. It was a brazen plan: Polk proposed to achieve his goals in Texas, New

Mexico, and California by using less than half of the Regular U.S. Army, a few ships of the U.S. Navy, and fewer than 3,000 volunteer soldiers.[37]

The objectives assigned to Colonel Kearny and, should any accident befall him, to Colonel Doniphan reflected the remarkable hubris of President Polk and the audacious reach of United States under the concept of Manifest Destiny. On May 16 the president explained to the full cabinet at the White House that his "plan to march an army of 2,000 men on Santa Fé and near 4,000 men on Chihuahua [mostly state volunteers, under John E. Wool, a Regular Army general] and at once conquer the Northern Provinces." Kearny's Army of the West, only 1,658 soldiers, supplemented by a few hundred civilian teamsters and merchants, was ordered to capture Santa Fe and place the province of New Mexico under the control of the United States. Kearny was also charged to protect some 400 American merchants engaged in trade down the Santa Fe Trail. By carrying out these orders, Kearny would capture for the United States the most important commercial center between the Mississippi River and the Pacific Coast. Taking Santa Fe would be the first step in gaining possession of all of the Mexican province of New Mexico. Possessing New Mexico would be the necessary preliminary stage before approaching the next ambitious objective assigned to Kearny: leading a U.S. military force westward through the Mexican province of Sonora, near Pimería Alta (part of modern Arizona) to invade Alta California, Mexico's northernmost province extending up to the Oregon country. Even if Mexico failed to defend Upper California with regular soldiers, to attack and capture a large state with only a few hundred soldiers was certainly one of the boldest parts of Polk's remarkable strategic scheme.[38]

The plan included provisions for other contingencies. Kearny packed various presents to be given to the Indian tribes he would encounter in New Mexico. The War Department expected Kearny to bring these tribes into some alliance or comity with the United States. Finally, a Catholic priest was assigned to the expedition to pacify the fears of the Mexicans concerning American discrimination against the Catholic religion in the area that Kearny was out to conquer. Freedom of religion would continue to be the official policy of the United States, and Kearny was enjoined from any action that would disquiet Mexican Catholics.[39]

Studying the plans and operations of America's invasion forces, First Lieutenant Roswell S. Ripley, a Regular Army officer who wrote a book evaluating the American war effort, tended to emphasize the accomplishments of Regulars and slight those of volunteers. Later complimenting "the speedy organization of the force and the celerity of the march from Fort Leavenworth to Santa Fé," Ripley generously termed those accomplishments "remarkable." Of course, much of the credit for mounting and moving the expedition rested with another Regular, Colonel Kearny. But Ripley also contended that "the expedition had little to do with the great questions of the war," apparently meaning the largest battles between the principal Mexican and American armies, including those in northern Mexico and on the road to Mexico City, failing to acknowledge that the Army of the West sought to fulfill Polk's strategic design of conquering New Mexico. Ripley admitted that his view was influenced by the fact that Kearny's expedition "was small," and he briefly acknowledged that the "marches were regulated by the nature of the route and of the territory against which it was directed."[40]

On active duty for only four years when the war started, Ripley overlooked a number of factors about the exigencies of war, Polk's strategy, and the role of Kearny's expedition. First, Ripley, who was from well-watered Ohio, did not appreciate the difficulties of anyone, even a modest military force the size of Kearny's and Doniphan's, trekking across more than eight hundred miles of semiarid land. Furthermore, Ripley underplayed the potential response by Mexican forces opposing American soldiers in New Mexico and California. Additionally, Ripley failed to note the strategic role of Kearny and Doniphan, both the need to gain a base of operations in New Mexico, from which Kearny could strike into California, and the potential of Doniphan's offensive move deeper into northern Mexico, which would support Kearny and also any other American expeditionary force between the Rio Grande and Monterrey.[41]

Polk's plan and the officers implementing it assumed that Mexico could not correct military weaknesses in its northern provinces. To most Americans, some of whom were familiar with Mexico after years of trade down the Santa Fe Trail, it seemed unlikely that Mexico could raise battle-worthy local militias to supplement the small regular garrison in Santa Fe. It also seemed unlikely that the Mexicans could dispatch significant reinforcements from Mexico City, or from Chihuahua, and send them northward in time to protect New Mexico.[42]

In contrast to these assumptions, even before the Army of the West departed, rumors had reached Fort Leavenworth about the Mexican dispositions. Unconfirmed reports placed some five thousand Mexican defenders preparing to meet the invading Americans in the vicinity of Santa Fe. Most Americans discounted such reports. For example, General Winfield Scott anticipated that "undisciplined as Kearny's army may be, the opposing Mexicans will be equally so; and physically and morally, every two Americans may safely be considered as, at least, equal to three Mexicans." Scott contended that Kearny and Doniphan would not encounter a Mexican force even as strong as twenty-five hundred, much less have it adequately armed and equipped. Furthermore, the Americans relied heavily on the element of surprise. This did not mean that Mexico would be caught completely unaware by U.S. invasions of New Mexico and California, but that those American invasions would be mounted and conducted too swiftly for the Mexicans to raise a satisfactory defense.[43]

Enthralled with the prospect of conquest, many Americans failed to acknowledge that the American forces invading Mexico's northern provinces could be rejected or defeated by one or a combination of factors. Colonels Kearny and Doniphan, however, certainly were aware of such contingencies. Although confident, they recognized that luck could influence the outcome of the campaign.

Doniphan, a novice at formal military operations, already knew that happenstance played a part in anyone's life. While Doniphan respected religion, he was not a church member. His faith in some supreme being or higher force was apparently a general notion rather than one following a specific Protestant denomination and certainly not the more rigid strictures of the Catholic Church. In war the unexpected—luck, fate, or fortune—whatever one might call it, could seem magnified and become the factor that tipped the balance at a crucial time. Presidents, cabinet secretaries, generals, and Regular officers could plan or critique a campaign in a book, but actually carrying out such designs could turn out quite differently.[44]

One means of highlighting the difference between war on paper and real war is by using the concept of "friction," meaning the variety of unpredictable contingencies interacting in such a way to make it impossible to forecast the outcome of individual battles and war itself. Elements of battle, sometimes overlooked, misunderstood, or ignored, especially by civilians, include the presence of danger and its effects on those involved. Danger, and the looming elements of uncertainty and chance, tend to affect the behavior of officers and soldiers on campaign. Therefore, numerous unpredictable elements mean that war could never be turned into a series of basic formulas to yield predictable results time after time.[45]

Caught up in nationalistic excitement, most civilians gave no indication they had considered the ways that various elements could combine to create "friction," delaying or disrupting military operations. For example, the progress of the Army of the West could be slowed by unexpected bad weather. Logistical problems could result from losing food and other supplies to storms or enemy raids. Soldiers could drown in flooding rivers. Crossing deserts raised the prospects of water shortages; both men and animals could suffer severely from the heat. Prairie fires could panic horses and burn supply wagons. Moving through mountains, even in summer, meant the possibility of freezing temperatures and icy conditions. And then there was disease. Measles, cholera, fevers, and especially dysentery haunted army camps in the nineteenth century and could cripple an army on the march.

Kearny knew and Doniphan learned that any of these factors could affect their army before the enemy acted to block their way. As for the enemy, the two colonels needed accurate information about his strength, locations, and intentions. Lieutenant Ripley seemed almost to dismiss the possibility of the Americans suffering reverses in battle, but of course it was a real possibility. Mexican defenders could fight the Americans to a draw or, worse, inflict a defeat on them. If the Army of the West lost significant percentages of its soldiers or supplies in battle, it would have to retreat.

Another dangerous possibility existed. Without fighting a formal battle, the Mexicans could drive off or kill large numbers of the expedition's draft animals or burn its wagons and supplies in hit-and-run raids. Indians might do the same things. Serious losses incurred due to raids could also produce an embarrassing retreat by Kearny and Doniphan, requiring President Polk to mount another expedition or ruining his strategy for capturing two of Mexico's northern provinces.[46]

Among the most important and least appreciated aspects of friction relates to a commander overcoming the inertia of his own force—its unwillingness or reluctance to move and reach the commander's objectives. Among other things, cooperation among officers, especially subordinate commanders, was vital. Evidence of friction in American military history included lack of cooperation and lack of mutual respect between Regular Army officers and volunteer officers. There were no guarantees that things would be any different for the Army of the West.[47]

Near the end of June, pushed by government leaders in Washington, Kearny decided the expedition should set out. Some of the volunteers had only three weeks of training under Kearny's supervision, and others received much less, but he began designating the marching order for the expedition's units. These included detaching Captain Hudson's Leclede Rangers from service with Doniphan's regiment and assigning it to the 1st Dragoons. This assignment confirmed several of the Rangers in their conviction that the St. Louis company was better than any unit in the 1st Missouri. It also fostered the subsequent haughtiness by the Rangers, though Lieutenant Elliott of the Rangers conceded that "Doniphan and his regiment were a hard lot to scare. They did not know what fear meant. Not pretty soldiers for show, perhaps, but first-class for service." The expedition's initial objective lay six hundred miles distant from Fort Leavenworth across American territory—Bent's Fort, a privately owned, fortified trading post

"THE VOLUNTEER." (From Hughes, *Doniphan's Expedition* [1847]; courtesy of the Museum of New Mexico, negative no. 171106)

famous throughout the West. There Kearny and Doniphan planned to replenish their soldiers' supplies before invading Mexico and seizing their strategic target of Santa Fe.[48]

Only a matter of weeks before, few in Mexico and some in America would not have believed that Kearny and Doniphan could have recruited and equipped such an expeditionary force and had it ready to deploy. More difficult for anyone to predict was the expedition's combination of elements: well-motivated soldiers armed with rifles, led by capable officers, and supported by an artillery battalion. To the delight of many Americans, the 1st Missouri Regiment gave the impression that it contained a marvelous cross section of Missouri society: "There might be seen under arms, in the ranks the lawyer, the doctor, the professor, the student, the legislator, the farmer, the mechanic, and artisans of every description, all united as a band of brothers to defend the rights and honor of their country." To the great satisfaction of those skeptical about America's need for a professional army, Doniphan and his subordinate officers proved that the reservoir of leaders in the United States was deep. Raising this regiment indicated much about the military organization and martial potential of the United States. To fulfill that potential, Kearny proposed to advance across inhospitable dry plains at a rate of about 20 miles per day. At that rate, it would take Kearny and Doniphan forty-three days to travel the 850 miles between Fort Leavenworth and Santa Fe. Allowing for three or four days of rest would mean a journey of forty-six or forty-seven days. It was an ambitious plan, complementing President Polk's ambitious strategic reach.[49]

A few days before the Missourians set out, the St. Louis *Reveille* rendered a partial summary of their goals. "This expedition is no mere holiday affair—for show and display. It is no pleasure trip. . . . It is a serious *demonstration upon a Province* occupied by the enemy, undertaken for the protection of American *commerce,* American lives and American *honor.* Its object is the protection of that commerce, those lives, and that honor, [using] *the strong arm of military power.*" Some questions would remain unanswered until the Army of the West actually invaded Mexico. The expedition's officers and soldiers were uncertain if they could reach Santa Fe ready for combat before the Mexicans either raised defensive forces or dispatched reinforcements to the city. They were unsure what sort of Mexican defenses would confront them near Santa Fe or whether Mexican forces might venture to meet them on U.S. territory. Providing a cheer to send off its neighbors, the newspaper of Fayette, Missouri, wished "Success to the Missourians!"[50]

CHAPTER THREE

Down the Santa Fe Trail to Invade Mexico

Marching across the Great Plains introduced Colonel Doniphan to wartime operations away from the friendly confines of a well-supplied fort and distant from the hospitality of his home state. Americans considered it unlikely that Mexicans would encroach onto U.S. territory and, though the conditions on the Santa Fe Trail proved to be grueling, moving from Leavenworth to the Mexican border allowed the new colonel to gain practical experience leading his regiment. Furthermore, he observed how Colonel Kearny managed what was, by American standards, a sizable military field force. On June 26 four of Doniphan's companies under Lieutenant Colonel Charles Ruff left Fort Leavenworth, and Kearny planned to send two more volunteer companies (E and H) out on the trail on June 28 under Major William Gilpin. Doniphan, with another detachment, intended to leave on June 27, move forward rapidly to overtake the other companies, and "concentrate his Regiment near the 'Crossing of the Arkansas'" River, according to Kearny's order.[1]

Based on his own experience crossing the Plains the previous year and the advice of other plainsmen, Colonel Kearny believed it necessary to stagger the departure times for units of the Army of the West in order not to draw too heavily on the limited availability of water and grass on the Santa Fe Trail. Previously, the colonel had ordered two detachments of Regulars to forge ahead of the volunteers. One group of seven soldiers escorted George T. Howard, a businessman familiar with Santa Fe and the Trail, and the other included two companies of dragoons under Captain Benjamin D. Moore, soon supplemented by another company, led by Second Lieutenant Patrick Noble. Moore sought to locate and stop Albert Speyer, leader of a civilian wagon train suspected of carrying guns and military stores consigned to the Mexican authorities in Santa Fe. On

Army of the West crossing the Plains. (Drawing by Kenneth Chapman, from Twitchell, *History of the Military Occupation of the Territory of New Mexico* [1909]; courtesy of the Museum of New Mexico, negative no. 163234)

June 15 Kearny ordered the lead supply element of the main column to move out, one hundred wagons and eight hundred cattle. The cattle would be used to supplement barrels of salted pork and game hunted on the march. On June 22 companies A and D of the 1st Missouri Regiment, under Captain John Reid, left Fort Leavenworth. Gaining the protection of the army, merchants driving more than four hundred wagons left at different times and took parallel paths or followed in the wake of the expedition.[2]

Captain Thomas Hudson and the Leclede Rangers departed Fort Leavenworth on June 29 at 1:00 P.M. Pulled by mules or oxen, dozens of military supply wagons squealed into motion. Hudson's company displayed "excellent spirits," according to Lieutenant Richard Elliott of the Rangers. In fact, morale was high among all the units of the Army of the West, pictured by one of the volunteers as "full of ardor, full of spirit, full of generous enthusiasm, burning for the battle field, and panting for the rewards of honorable victory." Colonel Kearny, his staff, Major Meriwether Clark's artillery battalion, and the infantry battalion left the fort the next day. One of the artillery battery commanders, Captain Richard Weightman, was too ill to travel but caught up to the expedition later. Among the infantry talk covered many topics, including the possibility that the war might end before they got to Mexico, meaning they would be back in Missouri before Christmas. Others pronounced that they would have to fight for sure and

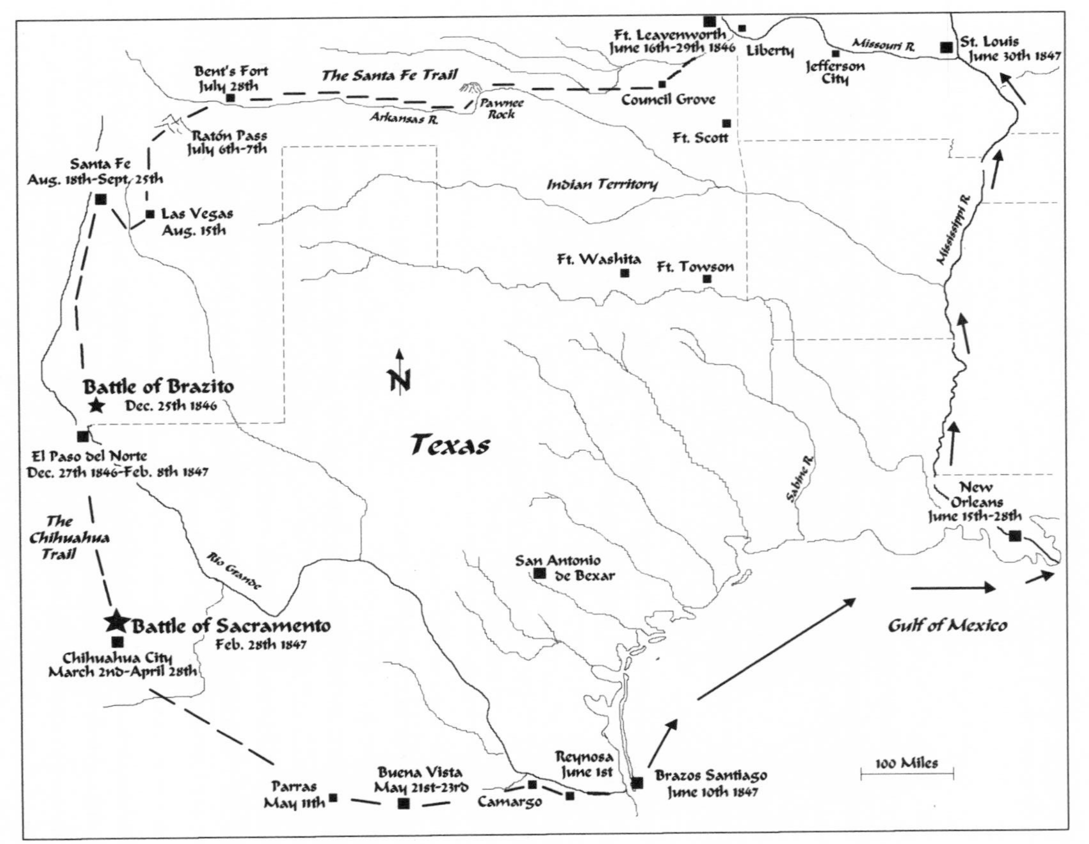

Doniphan's march. (T. T. Smith, 1998)

would be gone for the full year of their enlistment. Morning and evening bugle calls confirmed that they were "soldiers under military law . . . and on their way to fight the battles of their country." A detachment of two additional companies of the 1st Dragoons, led by Captain Edwin V. Sumner and Captain Philip St. George Cooke, brought up the rear on July 6.[3]

Even before reaching the juncture with the Santa Fe Trail, Lieutenant Colonel Charles Ruff's contingent of volunteers, including companies B, C, F, and G of the 1st Missouri Regiment, encountered a remarkable natural obstacle. A daunting two-hundred-foot limestone outcropping stopped their progress. Trying to go around the "bluff" would have taken them miles out of their way. Using a practical solution, the Missourians decided to tie ropes to their wagons and pull them up the ledge. Ruff assigned one hundred of his men to pull up the wagons, then to lower them down the other side.[4]

This sequence of departures meant that the expedition's contingents were strung out over the prairie leading to the Santa Fe Trail. In 1846 the Trail was already famous. Although many settlers had made the trek, that did not mean the progress of Kearny's expedition should have been taken for granted. Some Americans might have pictured the Trail as a smooth and easy route. Supporting those notions, one soldier said that the Trail was "as plainly marked as any highway," and another recorded an idyllic image: "The boundless plains, lying in the ridges of wavy green not unlike the ocean, seemed to unite with the heavens in the distant horizon." An infantry officer used a similar metaphor: "We . . . passed through the most beautiful country I ever beheld. . . . The tall grass would be ruffled by the gentle breeze until you imagine it was the rising waves of the ocean." One of the artillerymen called it "one of the most beautiful sights in nature to see a puff of wind sweep over these grassy plains, turning the glistening sides of the grass to the sun, and seeming to spread a stream of light along the surface of the wave-like expanse."[5]

Soon, however, comments of distress and observations of adversity offset the rosy first impressions of the expedition's early days on the march. Several of Doniphan's detachments strayed off course within a dozen miles from Fort Leavenworth, costing them an extra day or two of travel to get reoriented. Officers came to rivers "too deep to ford," uneven roadways that resulted in broken wagon axles, and muddy creeks with water unfit to drink. At several spots, boggy quicksands near river crossings and the soft prairie allowed "wagons [to] sink to their beds in the sand. . . . When this happens, their loads have to be . . . packed out [and reloaded] piece by piece." The most detailed chronicler of the expedition, Private John Hughes, indicated that the miles between Fort Leavenworth and picking up the Santa Fe Trail included "many deep ravines, and creeks with high and rugged banks. . . . The banks must be dug down, the asperities leveled, bridges built, and roads constructed, before the wagons could pass. All this required time and labor." Hughes depicted other discouraging factors: "The heat was often excessive; the grass was tall and rank; and the earth in many places so soft that the heavily loaded wagons would sink almost up to the axle upon the level prairie. The men were frequently compelled to dismount and drag them from the mire with their hands. The mules and other animals being mostly unused to the harness, often became refractory and balky. Numbers of wagons daily broke down." Dragging heavily loaded wagons, several of the oxen grew so tired they refused to walk; some dropped dead in their tracks. Soldiers pushed or pulled or prodded the recalcitrant beasts. Crossing streams required attaching ropes to wagons and having the soldiers "act the part of horses" to pull the heavy loads up the opposite bank. Similar scenes were repeated among the artillerymen. Their horses reluctantly pulled the weight of the cannons and caissons, and the soldiers added their backs to the effort. From time to time, horses broke their legs or necks slipping down embankments, depriving the expedition of valuable draft animals.[6]

Although the Santa Fe Trail was known to travelers, the passage across the Plains was not an easy one for the Army of the West. It was not a foregone conclusion that the expedition would reach Bent's Fort intact and ready for battle. To achieve that goal would take determined soldiers, dedicated leaders, and a certain measure of luck to overcome the many natural obstacles that lay ahead, as well as any Mexican resistance that might be encountered.[7]

Kearny had decided that the army must move as rapidly as possible—to average more than twenty miles a day—to stay on the dry Plains for as few weeks as possible and to attack Santa Fe as quickly as it could. Near the beginning of the march one volunteer noted that Kearny was "just strict enough to keep us all in order, but not in the least oppressive. He is, however, fond of rapid marching, and keeps us at it steadily. Yesterday, for example, we made thirty miles, and expect to make twenty-five tomorrow." After four weeks on the prairie, however, the demands began to tell on the soldiers' morale, and cursing the officers, including Doniphan, Kearny, and Ruff, was a major daily entertainment for the enlisted men.[8]

After only a few days of marching, the volunteers found much to complain about. The infantry, naturally, complained of sore feet. "Their feet were blistered by their long and almost incredible marches. The ground was often marked with blood in their foot-prints." Doniphan's mounted volunteers griped about sore legs and backsides from being in their saddles for sixteen or more hours a day. It was summer, and all complained about the heat and not having enough good water. They sometimes came to stagnant pools or muddy creeks, and wished for one good clear spring like the one with water "as cold as ice" they passed only a few miles from Fort Leavenworth. Carrying extra canteens, outriders paralleled the detachments, looking for water; if they found some, they filled the canteens and returned to share it with their fellows. Stopping at the occasional pond, the soldiers stirred up swarms of mosquitoes when they bent over to take a drink. The Missourians always kept their eyes out for any wild game close to the line of march. They shot deer, turkeys, and rabbits, but the amount of game varied greatly on the trek.[9]

Day by day the soldiers traced their progress by the water features they crossed. They went from one creek to the next stream, sometimes finding them dry, and from the Osage River to the Neosho River, where Captain Weightman caught up with his battery near Council Grove, site of the council between the Osage tribe and federal Indian commissioners in 1825, and a key stopping point for settlers' trains.[10] Private Jacob Robinson observed that the grove was "about a mile wide, composed of good timber, oak and walnut, having on its west side a fine stream, with steep banks near 50 feet in height." Private Hughes recalled that the stream contained "the finest and most delicious water." According to Kearny's plan, units arrived and departed Council Grove at staggered times. For example, Colonel Ruff's detachment reached Council Grove on July 5 and Lieutenant Gibson and the infantry companies arrived on July 8. The first to arrive found an abundance of wild cherries and picked the bushes clean. The trees at Council Grove, reputed to be the last large stand on the Santa Fe Trail, provided wood for wagon repairs, such as split boards, cracked wagon tongues, and broken axles. There were several of those. The officers in charge of each contingent arranged for repairs at the blacksmith's shop.[11]

Some of the volunteers thought the going had been rough enough on the stretch up to Council Grove. Having been introduced to the hazards of Plains travel by the time they reached the Grove, fainthearted settlers could turn back, knowing where and how to return to the settlements. The soldiers serving with Doniphan had no such option. Ahead stretched a march to Santa Fe about the same length as that of Napoleon's line of communications from his base in Poland to Moscow during the Russian campaign of 1812. The country through which the Army of the West would pass was without towns or farms and contained little water. One of the soldiers considered "how discouraging the first sight of these immense plains is to one who has read the numerous glowing accounts of them! [They were] only covered with a short poor grass in some parts, and, in others, producing nothing but a dry bushy plant or wild sage; they may be travelled over for miles and miles, without your finding bush or tree to obstruct or break the view." Kearny worried that soldiers might start grass fires, ruining the little natural fodder available on the march, and therefore issued orders to make sure that all campfires were carefully extinguished each morning. Of course, in the weeks to come Kearny could not have prevented enemy soldiers or agents, had any ventured into U.S. territory, from setting such fires. Not appearing to be too concerned by the miles the expedition would travel or the conditions of the trail, Private Hughes concluded that so far, at least, most of the "frolicsome" volunteers had displayed the "greatest good humor and most cheerful flow of [high] spirits."[12]

Government contract wagons carried food for the expedition, and merchants offered various products for sale, but there was a problem with distribution. On some days the wagons fell behind or the detachments camped apart from the merchants, leaving the soldiers to fend for themselves and, as one of them put it, "to *feast* or *famish* by turns," depending on where the wagons halted. The expedition's leaders expected buffalo and deer to be available in numbers sufficient to keep the army partially supplied, and a sergeant of dragoons related that good hunting meant the soldiers ate well on some days. Detachment commanders often sent riders ahead or back to wagons requesting assistance. For example, on July 9 Doniphan dispatched a galloper to Ruff, and, though short of food himself, he set aside four barrels of supplies (two of flour and two of pork) for the colonel. From time to time the soldiers slaughtered a cow, but Kearny did not want to deplete the herd too quickly, so salted pork forked from barrels was a standard item on the morning and evening menus in most companies. The volunteers and dragoons supplemented their meals with anything available. They picked wild berries and plums from plants growing by some of the streams and caught fish swimming in them, hunted buffalo, deer, rabbits, and turkeys, and purchased canned foods from the merchants; sardines were a particular favorite.[13]

After departing Council Grove the soldiers had to adjust to cooking without wood. The typical substitute was dried buffalo manure, called "prairie fuel" or "buffalo chips." Private Robinson thought that it "burns as well as charcoal." Lieutenant George Gibson, a lawyer from Weston, Missouri, gave his opinion: "The smell of the smoke is not agreeable, and some rather than use it went without cooking. But to men hungry and fatigued, as most of us were, there was nothing repulsive, and we soon became used to it." One soldier decided that liberally shaking pepper on any meat cooked over buffalo chips helped to offset some of the pungent "ammoniacal [*sic*] odor," but by contrast another concluded that the prairie fuel seemed "to impart a peculiar, [but] pleasant flavor to meat broiled on its smothering heat." On most days between Council Grove and

Bent's Fort the typical unit of the Army of the West lived on half rations—half the normal allotment the U.S. Army expected to issue to soldiers for their daily fare—but sometimes they were cut to one-third rations. Half rations amounted to about half a pound of flour and less than half a pound of meat per day, and the commissary sparingly doled out other items such as coffee, sugar, rice, beans, salt, and pepper.[14]

The weather on the Plains varied sharply from day to day: sudden thunderstorms drenched the soldiers while on the march; an all-day rain soaked through their clothes and meant going to their sleeping rolls wet, with no fires and no hot food at the end of the day. Torrential rains at night turned campsites into pools. During such a storm one soldier found himself "surrounded by water. It was running thro [*sic*] the tent like a perfect sluice." Gusty winds blew down tents, permitting the rain to soak unprotected clothes and supplies. One volunteer recalled waking up "wet, chilled, and without even wood to cook breakfast." Heavy storms during the day sometimes prompted an early halt. Many of the soldiers carried canteens of liquor, refilling them from the stock of sutlers or merchants, and, night or day, several eased their discomfort with draughts of whiskey. The sudden rains seemed to offer a cooling respite from the relentless heat, on many days rising above ninety-five degrees Fahrenheit, as indicated on thermometers carried by the soldiers. Well out on the Plains, the detachments would be met by "blasts of heated air, so hot as to scorch the skin and make it exceedingly difficult to breathe," just like standing before "a blast from a furnace," one said. Another likened it to "a perfect sirocco, blinding from its severity and blistering where it touched."[15]

Shimmering in the heated distance, mirages beckoned, especially the "deceptive phenomenon of the water mirage." A soldier elaborated: "About a mile distant from us appeared a crystal lake, studded with numerous islands, so perfectly defined that no one could imagine it to be any thing else than a real lake. . . . As we advanced, the water apparently receded, and at the same time became more extensive, until . . . when we came there [to where the image had been], it was nothing but the same level prairie, covered with the like grass, and destitute of ridges, water and trees." The expanse of prairie and occasional hills combined with the sunshine to play other tricks on the soldiers' eyes and brains: what appeared to be a town, even a city, shimmered in the distance; one soldier thought he "could plainly distinguish gilded domes of churches and roofs of houses," but when they reached the site he found only "huge sand-hills, entirely destitute of vegetation."[16]

During the second week in July, at the crossing of the Little Arkansas River, an astounding plague of gnats and mosquitoes covered Doniphan and his soldiers. They swatted at swarms of mosquitoes, but the thick cloud of gnats "got into the nostrils, eyes, and ears, creating a singularly pricking sensation, and making our horses almost frantic with pain." The men enjoyed a bath in the river, although a short distance away the prairie was littered with "bones, skulls, and carcasses of animals in every state of decay," a grim reminder of the difficult path they traveled. As night fell on July 11, near a stream called Cow Creek, Doniphan joined his contingent with Ruff's, bringing together six of the eight companies of the 1st Missouri Regiment.[17]

Doniphan and his men neared the Arkansas River on July 12 desperate for water. A stripe of green on the horizon—the sight of trees up ahead—created a rush. "Horse and man ran involuntarily into the river, and simultaneously slaked their burning thirst," one volunteer recalled the scene. Arriving at the same place a few hours after the colonel, Lieutenant Gibson relished the "ponds and muddy water, which the company gladly drank. . . . Sunset was magnificent, the air balmy, and all the company enjoyed it, bathing, smoking, writing, cooking, laughing, and talking." The men appreciated the water all the more when they realized that the next major water source was the Pawnee Fork, some thirty-seven miles away.[18]

On July 13 Doniphan approached one of the notable landmarks on the Santa Fe Trail, Pawnee Rock, a thirty-foot sandstone monolith approximately three hundred miles from Fort Leavenworth. Many passersby, including Indians, Anglos, and Mexicans, had carved their names on the stone. Near Pawnee Rock the Missourians were treated to an amazing display—many thousands of buffalo. Private Jacob Robinson of Company D described "one of the grandest sights ever beheld. Far over the plain . . . was one vast herd of buffaloes. . . . Every acre was covered, until in the dim distance the prairie became one black mass, from which there was no opening, and extending to the horizon. Every man was astonished." An artilleryman from St. Louis contemplated the herd that "resembled a shadow cast upon the earth from a black cloud as it passes across the sun." For a few moments, mouths agape, the volunteers sat on their horses as they felt the ground shake and watched the creatures run toward them. Then the soldiers recovered and, pulling out their rifles and pistols, took up a "close pursuit [with] guns firing from every quarter and fulalo [*sic*] falling in every direction." They killed about forty buffalo but also stampeded some of their unattended horses, prompting an understated remark from one of the volunteers: "The loud bellowing and tramping [of the buffalo], [and the] chasing, firing and shouting [of the soldiers] composed a scene of the greatest excitement."[19]

While some volunteers roasted their buffalo steaks, others bagged bountiful game, including turkeys and squirrels, drew water from the Pawnee Fork, and picked grapes and wild squash from vines. Improving the expedition's capability to supply itself were twenty-five army wagons with provisions, camped not far from Pawnee Rock. These were among the first wagons that Kearny had sent out from Fort Leavenworth. Doniphan and the volunteers appreciated Kearny's foresight. The Pawnee Fork was flooded, and two soldiers drowned on July 13 and 14 trying to cross, forcing the troops to pause until the waters receded. Lieutenant Gibson described his camp: "The whole bend of the river [was] strung with tents, horses, oxen, men, wagons, mules, etc., besides many traders and their caravans." Another soldier took pride in "our white tents pitched in regular form along the shore of the river." Members of the expedition dealt with merchants for all sorts of items—blankets, shirts, underwear, even exchanging worn oxen for a team of horses and adding another yoke of healthy oxen. In addition, soldiers drew rations from military supply wagons, including standard items of flour, coffee, sugar, and salt.[20]

Strengthened by buffalo meat and other provisions, the soldiers threw themselves into constructing a footbridge over the Pawnee Fork. On July 16 what they had built allowed Doniphan, Lieutenant Emory, other officers, and companies of soldiers to pass over to the far bank. Tying ropes to the horses, the soldiers guided the swimming animals across. The water was still too swift for the wagons to cross. The volunteers rigged more ropes, attached makeshift pontoon floats to the wagons, and pulled them through the current. When they set out again the next day, detachments marched on parallel paths. Stopping at a vantage point, Lieutenant Gibson looked back to survey "stragglers, wagons, oxen, beef cattle, etc., [stretching] as far as can be seen, both in front and rear, we had a column like the picture in the journey of the Israelites."[21]

At about this time Doniphan and Kearny, who had linked up with the regiment at the Pawnee Fork, engaged in a sharp disagreement about the 1st Missouri's discipline on the line of march. After enduring weeks of hot weather, thunderstorms, lack of water, short rations, broken wagons, and knowing it was unlikely for them to encounter any Mexican soldiers for several more days, the volunteers were straggling. Some rode solitaire or in pairs and trios, others bunched in small groups, and only a small number arranged themselves in a column of twos. Dissatisfied with the regiment's disposition, Kearny confronted Doniphan.

"Your men can never be soldiers, you indulge them too much & they will be utterly demoralized and unreliable unless you adopt more strict and soldier like discipline," the Regular officer lectured.

"We are 600 miles from any enemy—I fear more strict discipline would break down the men & horses. When the time comes for efficient action, you will find these men unflinching," the volunteer colonel responded.

Kearny fired a tart rejoinder: "Well, you will be held responsible for their efficiency."

Biting back a retort, Doniphan replied, "Certainly, I would not have accepted the command of men for whom I would not be responsible in any emergency." Viewing the matter of discipline with the eye of a professional soldier, Captain Henry Turner, Kearny's adjutant, agreed with his colonel: Doniphan's volunteers' "complaints are loud and long. The St. Louis companies bear up tolerably well, but Col. Doniphan's Regt. to a man is sick and tired of the business [of the long march]. But for the example set by the regulars, . . . the volunteers would not reach Santa Fe."[22]

Both colonels remembered their lively expression of opinions, but they may have been on edge because the army recently had tallied its first deaths. Until crossing the Pawnee Fork the expedition had been fortunate to have suffered no fatalities due to accident or illness, but the two soldiers (one of whom was identified as Private Arthur E. Hughes of the Leclede Rangers) who drowned in the Pawnee Fork were not the expedition's first casualties. Private Nehemiah Carson of Company G had died of a heart condition on July 13 and was buried near Pawnee Rock. Each day on the journey several soldiers were considered lame or sick enough to be placed in wagons. Some rode in the springless vehicles for days, getting bumped and bruised in the process. Many of the soldiers complained of stomach and digestive problems resulting from eating the salt pork, using inadequately cleaned cooking utensils, and drinking water of varying quality. It was common for the troops to partake of water "covered with green scum" or fouled by the passage of horses and wagons. At Pawnee Rock one of the expedition's surgeons discharged infantry Private Gustavus Sephert because of illness and sent him home with one of the returning supply wagons. Some soldiers complained about rattlesnake bites, but remarkably no one seemed to have died from the venom. There was no formal "sick call" each morning, but the surgeons made their rounds among the companies, treating a variety of maladies among both officers and enlisted men. Even Colonel Kearny was taken ill and had to ride in a wagon for a day, but Doniphan remained mounted and inspired the volunteers to push on.[23]

Near the Pawnee Fork crossing merchant George T. Howard sought out Kearny on July 17 to report on circumstances in Taos and possible Mexican defense of Santa Fe, creating "quite a sensation in [the] camp." Sent ahead at Kearny's request to ascertain the strength of Mexican defenses, Howard gave a report that seemed contradictory. According to the merchant, Mexican leaders were making preparations to resist the American invasion and had assembled, according to what he had heard, twenty-three hundred armed men in the vicinity of Santa Fe. On the other hand, Howard also gave his impression of the general populace, concluding that few among them would offer any resistance to the Army of the West. Picking up Howard's second point, Captain Turner, Kearny's adjutant, expressed the view that "everything [was] favorable to our object" of capturing Santa Fe. Soon Howard's estimate of twenty-three hundred armed Mexicans ballooned in rumors to more than ten thousand enemy soldiers ready to oppose the invaders. Most volunteers believed encountering such a strong force seemed improbable, and whatever the size of the opposing army, the prospect of adding more territory to the United States made the Missourians ready for a fight. Speaking for many, Lieutenant Gibson contended that "we expect to put our feet upon Mexican soil [south of the Arkansas River], which is soon destined to add to our already extended Union. There we shall leave our native soil until new acquisitions are made and the Stars and Stripes float in Santa Fé."[24]

Keeping along the north bank of the Arkansas River to remain in U.S. territory and have as much access to water as possible, the expedition proceeded twenty-five or sometimes thirty miles a day. The summer heat continued unabated, and one of the Regular officers looked out in vain "over the immense wastes in search of trees. Not one is to be seen." At one point, Colonel Ruff's battalion of four companies lost their patience with the former Regular officer when he stopped the column and demanded that they practice combat drill formations. Ruff showed that he was conscientious and had the right idea about drilling. But the volunteers' opposition to Ruff was so widespread that it "came near resulting in a total disregard of the order" to drill. The incident cost the regiment's lieutenant colonel much of his popularity. At another point, a plague of insects and creatures, including thousands of large grasshoppers, hundreds of chameleons, and hundreds of frogs, mystified and irritated the soldiers. Individualistic volunteers broke away from the line of march at a moment's notice, chasing down and killing selected choices from groups of buffalo and shooting rabbits for their dinners.[25]

On July 22 the lead element of the expedition drew within sight of Bent's Fort. Atop the main gate the soldiers could see the inspiring sight of a "huge United States flag flowing in the breeze." Reaching this important way station on the Plains, six hundred miles from Fort Leavenworth, raised the spirts of the volunteers. Doniphan and Kearny, with most of the 1st Missouri Regiment, including the artillery battalion, camped below the fort on July 28 and 29. Some

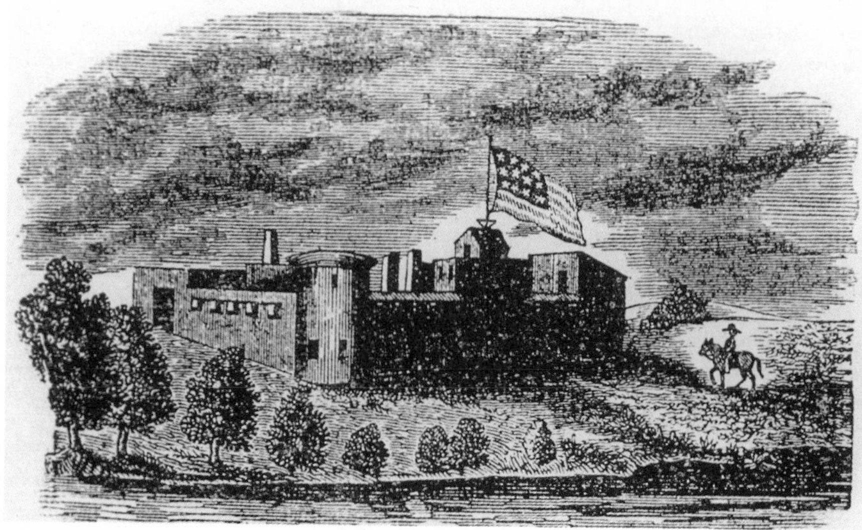

Old Fort Bent, Colorado. (From Hughes, *Doniphan's Expedition* [1847]; courtesy of the Museum of New Mexico, negative no. 171562)

companies actually set up tents on Mexican soil below the Arkansas River. Most of the merchants also arrived, among them Manuel Harmony and Samuel Owens.[26]

A self-contained community, Bent's Fort was intended to be an imposing structure, physically and symbolically. Obviously impressed, Private Hughes wrote, "The exterior of the walls of this fort, whose figure is that of an oblong square, are fifteen feet high and four feet thick. It is a hundred and eighty feet long and one hundred thirty-five feet wide." Established in 1833, the trading post welcomed all comers—traders, trappers, hunters, Indians, scouts, travelers, and military units. The post was owned and operated by two brothers, Charles and William Bent, and their partner Céran St. Vrain. Inside the fort travelers could pay for overnight accommodations with beds and entertain themselves at a billiard table. People had their choice of many kinds of foods and crafts and products for sale or barter, including tobacco and several types of alcoholic beverages as well as fresh eggs and milk, molasses, and vegetables. For a fee, those in need could purchase new wagons, replace wagon parts, and have their vehicles repaired. Officers of the Missouri regiment inspected and bought horses, mules, and oxen. The artillery batteries had been particularly hard hit; of their one hundred horses that began the journey, only forty were fit to continue; most of the rest would die on the way to Santa Fe. Replacements, including some mules, were arranged for the artillery battalion.[27]

Conflicting reports continued to come into the American camp about Mexican preparations in Santa Fe. Famous frontiersman Thomas "Broken Hand" Fitzpatrick brought intelligence from New Mexico. Confirming George Howard's information of two weeks earlier, Fitzpatrick reported that New Mexico's governor, Manuel Armijo, appeared to be readying the province's defenses and marshaling hundreds of men. Furthermore, on the outskirts of camp the expedition's pickets apprehended three Mexicans believed to be spies for Armijo. However, in his personal opinion, Fitzpatrick decided that the American expedition would encounter no fight near or in Santa Fe. Kearny's adjutant, Captain Turner, drew his own conclusion that reports from Fitzpatrick and Eugene (Eugenio) Leitensdorfer and other merchants who had come up from Santa Fe showed "that the reduction of the Province [of New Mexico] will be accomplished without bloodshed." Conflicting views were present among the volunteers. Lieutenant Christian Kribben, an attorney from St. Charles, Missouri, serving in Captain Fischer's artillery battery, sifted through the rumors and reasoned that combat was unlikely: "Apart from a few skirmishes in the mountain passes, we shall find little work to do this side of Santa Fé." On the other hand, in Lieutenant Gibson's opinion, "we all began to think we should have to fight" at Santa Fe. Another agreed, believing that at least some skirmishing was likely, but one of his fellows pointed out that, according to one rumor, of the five thousand Mexicans mustered at Santa Fe only one thousand had muskets, with the rest armed "with slings and stones."[28]

Not wanting to take anything for granted, Kearny sought ways to overawe the Mexican forces in New Mexico and undermine an effective defense of the province. First, on July 30 he had the three captured Mexican spies escorted around the expedition's sprawling camps, telling them to "take a good look" at the army. The leader of the spies seemed impressed, exclaiming, "My God! What is to become of our republic?" Then Kearny ordered them released and returned to Santa Fe, taking word of the specifics of the invading army—its size, arms, and equipment. Kearny hoped that the strength of his army would grow in the telling of the tale. The gaunt Missouri volunteers and few companies of Regular dragoons may have appeared intimidating. In Lieutenant Elliott's opinion, "So many horsemen *seem* to be more numerous than they really are." Though their camp may have appeared large to the Mexicans, their numbers were then clearly known to Mexican authorities by way of Albert Speyer and other traders who had reached Santa Fe. Second, Kearny asked Eugene Leitensdorfer, a merchant experienced in the New Mexico trade, to travel to Taos. He ordered Doniphan to pick twenty soldiers to guard the trader, who was carrying a proclamation from Kearny to the "Citizens of New Mexico." Kearny had also given copies of the proclamation to the three Mexican spies. Kearny proclaimed that his army (puffed as "a large military force") sought to bring the province under the control of the United States, "ameliorating the condition of the inhabitants," and giving the benefits of U.S. governance, including continuation of property rights and religious freedom. Pointedly, Kearny cautioned the Mexicans not to offer resistance to the American army.[29]

In addition to taking these steps, Kearny sent ahead an official letter, dated August 1, to Governor Manuel Armijo, worded in strong terms and boldly confirming Kearny's approach and intent. Carrying the letter on Kearny's behalf was Captain Philip St. George Cooke, a Regular officer in the 1st Dragoons with experience in New Mexico. In his letter Kearny held out the promise (and threat) that if there was no opposition on the part of the Mexicans, no reprisals would be forthcoming. In any case, Kearny told Armijo that he intended to take possession of New Mexico, according to the "annexation of Texas to the U.S., [based on the boundary of] the Rio Grande from its mouth to its source." Kearny also emphasized that additional U.S. forces were following behind the Army of the West, but even without them he asserted that they had "many more troops than sufficient to put down any opposition that you can possibly bring against us." Therefore, Kearny concluded that Armijo should "for the sake of humanity . . . submit to [your] fate."[30]

At Kearny's order, Cooke and twelve dragoons escorted James W. Magoffin, a merchant from Independence, Missouri, well known to Mexican political figures and business leaders in Santa Fe and Chihuahua City. In 1845 Magoffin appears to have met with U.S. senator Thomas Hart Benton (Democrat of Missouri) and President Polk in Washington and concluded that he could use his influence with the Mexicans to persuade them not to resist an American invasion—effectively negating the defense of the province. Perhaps Magoffin planned to offer bribes to Governor Armijo or other Mexican officials. Magoffin's exact plans were never confirmed, but Secretary of War William Marcy earlier had sent Kearny a letter endorsing the merchant as someone who "will give important information" about New Mexico and who had been "extensively engaged in trade in that [Chihuahua City] and other settlements of Mexico." Wanting other experienced advisers, Kearny also asked William Bent and half a dozen of his employees to come with him, drawing upon their knowledge of the countryside and proposing to use Bent's good offices and contacts among the Mexicans to convince them not to fight. By such letters and contacts Kearny sought to avoid combat and gain control of New Mexico by combining intimidation and promises of goodwill. He reported to Roger Jones, adjutant general of the U.S. Army: "It is impossible . . . to tell what opposition will be made to our entering New Mexico, but I at this time feel confident that our force is sufficient to overcome any that may be offered."[31]

While his messengers made their way south, Kearny and Doniphan looked to resupply the expedition and prepared to fight in case Kearny's blandishments and intrigues failed. On Doniphan's order, the volunteers turned their horses out to graze; some were picketed using eighteen-inch iron stakes attached to picket ropes. Soldiers set up a rotating guard mount on the herd. Then one of the freak events occurred that could have delayed the expedition or stopped it in its tracks. Some said that a pack of wolves prowled near the herd, or the horses may have been startled by the loud cracking sound produced when a limb snapped off a tree. Whatever the cause, on July 30 the volunteers witnessed "a scene of the wildest and most terrible confusion"—a major horse stampede. Several hundred, perhaps one thousand, of the expedition's horses bolted, running away for many miles before tiring and being rounded up. More than sixty were never found, and others were rendered useless by injuries suffered from being lashed by the iron picket stakes. The exact reason for the stampede was never determined, but the event pointed up the potential for a crippling loss of mobility of the entire mounted regiment if significant numbers of its horses had been stolen, driven off, or killed. Some of the lost animals were replaced from the stocks at Bent's Fort.[32]

The expedition had continued to suffer losses after crossing the Pawnee Fork and while it sojourned at Bent's Fort. Dozens of soldiers sought the attention of the physicians, and one of them, Augustus Leslie of Company C, had succumbed to some sort of lung illness on July 22. A Regular dragoon had died of a seizure two days later. After arriving at Bent's, Kearny and Doniphan decided they must leave some soldiers behind. Two volunteers were discharged from service for reasons of poor health. Furthermore, the commanders knew that a number of soldiers had complained about chronic diarrhea and fevers; more had other health problems. The officers concluded that twenty-one volunteers and several dragoons were too sick to travel, including Lieutenant Abert of the Topographical Engineers, who had been desperately ill for a week. Six soldiers soon died. The infirm were left at the fort in the care of one of Doniphan's regimental surgeons, Dr. Isaac Vaughn, and two volunteers acted as Vaughn's assistants, dropping about thirty men from the expedition.[33]

On August 1 the lead element of the Army of the West crossed the Arkansas River and invaded Mexico. A volunteer officer, Lieutenant James A. DeCourcy, took twenty volunteers to escort Eugene Leitensdorfer to Taos and check on any Mexican defenses. He would also meet with the Pueblo Indians, emphasizing that they should remain peaceful and not interfere with the expedition, "otherwise," Kearny promised, "they would be considered as enemies of the United States and treated accordingly." On August 2 Kearny and Doniphan assembled the regiment outside of Bent's Fort. Dozens of spectators—including Indian and Mexican women—watched the spectacle of the mounted invaders, their supply wagons, and the merchant train roll into Mexico. Kearny continued the practice of dividing his force to make the best use of any water and grass available as the expedition drew closer to the enemy.[34]

Meanwhile, Mexican leaders struggled with decisions over how the city of Santa Fe and the province of New Mexico might be defended. Governor Manuel Armijo was an experienced provincial administrator, having served as governor of New Mexico off and on since 1837. Under his orders, Mexican soldiers had imprisoned the exhausted Texans of the Santa Fe Expedition in 1841. Because of Armijo's diligent collecting of customs duties Josiah Gregg, an American merchant, called him "an ambitious and turbulent demagogue," but the governor displayed several qualities of personality and leadership while in office. He was clever, devious, beguiling, domineering, and always willing to benefit personally from the influence of his office, including the possibility of helping to arrange the sale of firearms to Apache Indians.[35]

As the American invading force drew nearer, Armijo, better than anyone, understood how few military resources he controlled. Years of haphazard attention to the militia and no regular army reinforcements any closer than Chihuahua City made Armijo doubt his own ability to raise forces adequate to block the U.S. invasion of New Mexico. As early as July 1 the governor had issued a call to arms to citizens of New Mexico and sent out a small group of scouts in an effort to see if the American invaders had set foot in Mexico. A few days later news arrived by way of Mexican businessmen who had traveled from Independence, Missouri, advising the governor that "a respectable body of the North American army was marching toward this department [New Mexico] to occupy it on orders of the United States." Upon receiving this vague but apparently reliable information, Armijo had only a few weeks to prepare in earnest. Leading citizens consulted with the governor, recommending that he consider appropriate steps to defend New Mexico.[36]

On August 1, at the time Kearny was sending his demand for surrender, a Mexican merchant reached Santa Fe with more specific intelligence: the North American invaders supposedly numbered five thousand men. It would have been logical for Armijo to be dismayed by this estimate of enemy strength. Nevertheless, he sent out messengers carrying copies of his proclamation exhorting Mexicans to resist the invasion, calling for displays of patriotism and reminding citizens to protect the honor of their families. Elsewhere in Mexico, fearing that the invading forces would be penetrating his province soon, the governor of Chihuahua had issued a proclamation similar to Armijo's and explained to the governor of Yucatán that rumor placed the invading army at six thousand soldiers.[37]

By the time Kearny's emissaries, Captain Cooke and James Magoffin, arrived in Santa Fe to discuss capitulation, Armijo's regulars and militia had been digging cannon redoubts and infantry firing positions at Apache Canyon, a natural defensive site through which the American invaders would pass. Armijo saw that the narrow canyon, not much wider than a single wagon, could be blocked by felling trees, halting the invaders and allowing defenders to place them under fire. It was unclear how many Mexican soldiers or militia Armijo actually posted at the canyon, but only a few hundred well-placed defenders would make fighting through the canyon a daunting prospect for the Americans. Armijo did not have to win the campaign in a single battle. If the Mexicans inflicted casualties and damaged or destroyed American wagons and supplies, the invasion would be weakened, perhaps crippled. Furthermore, when he met with Cooke and Magoffin, Armijo may have known, by way of the Mexicans Kearny had escorted around his camp, that the American expeditionary force numbered around fifteen hundred, not several thousand, although in his official report he later put American strength at "from three to four thousand men." Armijo and the two Americans met at the governor's palace, and the two emissaries urged him not to resist the American invasion. Armijo's contemporaries wondered if Cooke and Magoffin gave the governor something more than a persuasive presentation. Did some money change hands? Armijo knew that his few companies of regulars and several hundred ill-prepared New Mexico militia were available to bar the way of this latest Anglo invasion. But in contrast to the three hundred ragtag Texans who pretended to threaten Santa Fe in 1841, the Army of the West appeared ready for battle. The governor could only speculate what reprisals the Americans might take if they had to fight their way to Santa Fe.[38]

Putting up a brave front, Armijo rejected Kearny's call for surrender and turned to confer again with his officers and militia leaders. The governor heard those present voice their support for an active defense, but he was skeptical of the militia's capability to fight the Americans. Armijo may have already distributed all useful weapons from his arsenal, but he knew that the remaining muskets and ammunition, as the Americans soon found, were unserviceable. The meeting grew contentious, including an acrimonious exchange between Governor Armijo and Captain Dámaso Salazar. The meeting broke up and soon many of the militia dispersed, returning to their homes rather than face the invaders. Of course, Armijo recalled past militia musters and knew that they ran hot and cold when pursuing marauding Indians. If the governor aimed to defend his province, some militia support was crucial. Armijo had started defensive preparations at Apache Canyon, but now he no longer counted on the militia.[39]

After the Army of the West entered Mexico, the American colonels were aware of how the enemy, Indians, or natural elements might combine to disrupt or turn back their invasion. If the Mexicans had chosen to act, they could have ambushed any one of the separate American detachments, reducing the invaders' strength. Lieutenant Kribben decided that "a determined band of 500 men might have at least delayed our passage through [the mountains], perhaps destroyed our entire forces." Although they would damage their own resources in the process, enemy soldiers or agents could set grass fires, burning the scarce natural fodder on the line of march. Another specter haunted the American commanders. Acting independently, Indians could attack the expedition's contingents, destroying some of their supplies, driving off horses, or inflicting casualties. The Missourians had seen numerous signs of Indians on the Plains and had spoken to individuals from different tribes at Bent's Fort, but they never encountered a sizable force of Indians on U.S. territory. Furthermore, south of the Arkansas River, rough terrain, bad weather, and lack of water continued to take their toll on Doniphan's men and animals. The heat grew in ferocity, pushing the thermometer to 120 degrees Fahrenheit. Stinging dust blew into the faces of the soldiers, "causing soreness of the eyes and bleeding at the nose," as one of them remembered. After leaving Bent's Fort, Private Hughes was discouraged to see "parched earth [that] appeared as though it had not been refreshed by a shower since the days of Noah's flood." Exaggeration aside, two days away from Bent's Fort, the little available water was "muddy, bitter, [and] filthy." The landscape ahead was "dreary, sultry, desolate, [and] boundless solitude reigned as far as the eye could reach. . . . We suffered much from the heat, and thirst, and the driven sand—which filled our eyes, and nostrils, and mouths, almost to suffocation. Many of our animals perished in the desert. . . . The Roman army under Metellus, on its march through the deserts of Africa, never encountered more serious opposition from the elements than did our army in its passage over this American Sahara." On the same point, Lieutenant Emory noted that so many horses were wearing out and being left behind that the column was "followed by wolves."[40]

Soon the elements of nature seemed to oppose the American invasion of Mexico. Moving into the higher elevations, six or eight of the Americans' horses died every day on the way to Santa Fe. What water the soldiers found looked "filthy" and tasted "nauseating." The lack of good water put a dozen horses down; then another dozen collapsed, exhausted. Captain Henry Turner, Kearny's adjutant, related that since crossing into Mexico they had found "no grass for 4 days," and the quality of grass remained variable during the days to come. Turner also noted the amount and quality of water was so bad that "a change for the better must soon take place, or the army must be dismounted." The combination of high altitude, lack of water, and lack of fodder was killing the expedition's animals. Dozens of horses had died. To make matters worse, rocky trails discouraged their passage. For the wagons and caissons to move required the soldiers to use shovels and picks to widen the path, roll boulders out of the way, hammer apart large rocks, and chop down trees. Off in the distance the soldiers looked westward to see "Wah-to-Yah," an Indian phrase meaning the "breasts of the world"—the snowcapped Spanish Peaks—rugged, glorious mountains dwarfing Ruff's or Gilpin's Pennsylvania ridges and completely overwhelming Doniphan's Kentucky hills.[41]

On August 5, after a march of twenty-eight miles, the expedition's advance elements reached the Purgatorie River, where they found some fresh water and lucky soldiers snapped up additional treats of wild berries and plums. Everyone filled their canteens and water barrels. Ahead loomed the Ratón Pass, at an altitude of seventy-eight hundred feet above sea level at the Continental Divide, described by one civilian traveler as simply "a bed of rocks impassable for wagons," meaning more backbreaking work to get the wagons and caissons through. Kearny reached Ratón Pass on the sixth, followed by Doniphan and the others on the seventh. The Missourians had to attach ropes to wagons and, using soldiers as well as animals, pulled them up, then let them down the steep slopes of the pass. It came as no surprise that some wagon axles broke going over the rough ground; with no way to repair them, the soldiers left the wagons behind. The reward for their efforts: a grand view of the mountains but, more important, seeing the green valley, lined with flowers and abundant with grass, of the Río Colorado. Striking a note of avarice, Lieutenant Elliott of the Lecelde Rangers wondered if the area "was rich in gold and silver, and if so—how much?"[42]

On Sunday, August 9, Kearny wisely authorized a day of rest, but he saw it as an opportunity to do more than wash in the river and relax after the rough climb through the pass. Despite having replenished some supplies at Bent's Fort,

Kearny directed Doniphan to limit his men to half rations; a few days later he ordered a cutback to one-third. The army had to be kept as self-sufficient as possible until it reached Santa Fe. Soon the coffee and sugar were gone, but the soldiers supplemented their meager rations by hunting turkeys and antelope, and at least they again picked up wood for cook fires. The expedition now stood on Mexican soil, and contact with Mexican forces was more likely. Some of the dragoons had held tactical drills the day before, and Kearny wanted Doniphan to put his companies through combat drills, but he recalled Ruff's difficulties in holding a drill only two weeks before. Kearny decided to coax the drilling rather than order it.[43]

Drawing Doniphan into conversation, Kearny asked, "Colonel, would you rather have me present or not when you drill your regiment?"

The volunteer commander responded, "I do not suppose you can learn anything new. But I may learn much from your kindly criticism."[44]

It was this sort of cordial exchange, as well as the fortitude displayed daily by the volunteers, that prompted Lieutenant Emory to offer his opinion about "the excellent understanding which prevailed throughout between regulars and volunteers and the cheerfulness with which they came to each others' assistance. . . . The volunteers, . . . recently accustomed to the ease and comforts of smiling homes, bore up against fatigue, hunger and the vicissitudes of a long and tedious march, through unexplored regions, with a zeal, courage and devotion that would have graced time-worn veterans, and reflect the highest credit on their conduct as soldiers."[45]

All along the line of march the soldiers had told and retold jokes and lodged complaints, but there was little humor in their day-by-day passage over the rough country. On August 10 and 11, however, an incident occurred that allowed for levity but also was revealing of the Missourians' attitudes toward Mexicans. Lieutenant DeCourcy's returning patrol captured several Mexicans, and American scouts took others into custody; all were suspected of being spies. The dozen prisoners sat astride small donkeys, and the docile creatures and their unimposing riders, none of whom wore uniforms, "presented anything else but a warlike appearance," according to Lieutenant Gibson. Rather than be intimidated that Mexican scouts were snooping around the expedition, the American volunteers and dragoons poked fun at the captives' demeanor. Private Marcellus Edwards characterized the Mexicans as "laughable," and Lieutenant Emory concluded that the "diminutive asses" and their short riders "presented a ludicrous contrast by the side of the big men and horses of the first dragoons [*sic*]." Private Hughes reckoned that the volunteers were "more seriously annoyed by the *half-ration* experiment than the dread of Mexican armies." After allowing them to take a look at the gaunt American invaders, Kearny released all of the Mexicans, some of whom may have been Governor Armijo's scouts.[46]

The "donkey incident" had its serious side. The prisoners claimed that hundreds of Mexican militia had mustered in Santa Fe and that Pueblo and Ute Indians were planning to raid the American camps. Moreover, Eugene Leitensdorfer reported that the Pueblos did not appear to be friendly. Lieutenant DeCourcy returned to camp from his patrol saying that the Mexicans he spoke to reiterated "that there is some prospect of a fight." Lieutenant Gibson noted that "the probable force of the Mexicans is variously estimated, but we think we can meet any that will be brought against us." Kearny recognized the dangers. Each day he posted sentinels, sent out scouts, and told the volunteers to pay greater attention to security around camp.[47]

The possibility of contact with the enemy raised the spirits of some of the volunteers, who grumbled about short rations and losses caused by illness or accidents. Private Henry Moore of Company D had died of measles on August 8, and two other soldiers had died of illness a few days later. Reflecting a common attitude of many other nineteenth-century soldiers, in flowery terms Private Hughes explained what he saw as the difference between unanticipated, wasteful losses from disease and honorable casualties suffered in battle. He brooded over the expedition's discouragement due to their "numbers [being] diminished, not by the sword, but by disease. Almost every day some dragoon or volunteer, trader, [or] teamster, . . . actuated by a laudable desire to serve his country, found a grave on the solitary plains. To die in honorable warfare; to be struck down in the strife of battle; to perish on the field of honor; to sacrifice life for victory, is no hardship to the fallen brave. . . . But to see the gallant, the patriotic, the devoted soldier, sinking and wasting his energies under slow, sure progress of disease . . . fills the heart with melancholy."[48]

Calling upon his rhetorical skills, on August 12 Doniphan delivered a speech to boost the morale of his men. Talking to about half of the regiment camped at Ocate Creek, the colonel related how Kearny had sent a message warning "that from the best information he could gain we would have a battle in a few days." Therefore, Doniphan "strictly charged every man to keep his cartridges in a good condition and not fire one unnecessarily [for hunting], as two [days of] marches would in all probability bring us to the field of action." Private Marcellus Edwards believed this order was "cold comfort to men who never allow game of any kind to pass." Private Hughes paraphrased the balance of Doniphan's address. Stressing that the soldiers must recall "that their own honor, and the reputation of their State, demanded the . . . performance of [their] duty," the lawyer-colonel made his best case "that to retreat or surrender was a proposition that could not be considered." Doniphan concluded with a phrase he hoped would ring in the ears of his volunteers: "We must conquer or die, for defeat was annihilation."[49]

The arrival in camp of a Mexican merchant selling eight hundred pounds of flour compensated some for Doniphan's order prohibiting firing at game, but fresh reports described armed militia ready to defend Mexico against the invading expedition. Rumors abounded: Mexicans were stationed at mountain passes; militia units had gathered at Santa Fe; some three hundred regular dragoons from Chihuahua were marching to reinforce Santa Fe. Lieutenant Emory decided that "the advantages of ground and numbers will, no doubt, enable the Mexicans to make the fight interesting." The soldiers knew they were nearing a larger settlement: farms and crops, ranches and cattle gave the countryside "the semblance of civilization."[50]

Then on August 14 the expedition had its first official contact with Mexican authorities. Mounted on "small, spirited ponies," a Mexican lieutenant, accompanied by three enlisted dragoons, approached Kearny with a message from Governor Armijo, his reply to Kearny's letter of August 1. The Mexicans wore regulation uniforms of roundabout jackets with red piping and blue pants having a red stripe running down their length. The officer was "armed with a sabre, the others with carbines and lances [with eight-inch steel points], presenting a very respectable appearance." Lieutenant Gibson reported that the Mexican officer "informed us that he would give us battle at the village of [Las] Vegas, eight or nine miles ahead": Governor Armijo had rejected Kearny's call for surrender. Another volunteer pictured the lieutenant as asserting that if the Americans "gained possession of his [Mexico's] territory, it would be because he [Kearny] proved the strongest in the field."[51]

Lieutenants Abraham Johnston and Christian Kribben overheard remarks indicating that a large force of Mexicans, reported to number twelve thousand under Governor Armijo, would be deployed at a canyon fifteen miles east of Santa Fe, where "every effort would be made to oppose us." (Private Hughes recalled hearing about a prospective enemy force of two thousand, a more reasonable estimate.) Kearny reiterated to all of the expedition's units that combat might be in the offing. The Americans wondered what sorts of Mexican resistance might block their way, but, not knowing what the turn of events might produce, the soldiers of the Army of the West plunged ahead with enthusiasm.[52]

On the evening of August 14, the Missourians drew near to Las Vegas, a village of about three hundred persons and the place Doniphan called "the first Mexican town or settlement of any importance." Lieutenant Johnston described it as "an assemblage of mud houses covering a space of fifteen acres." Indicating a momentary lapse of confidence, Johnston noted that "the hills are covered with sheep and goats, so that we leave behind us now a certainty of not starving, even should reverses await us." Another soldier related one of several rumors passing through the regiment—one thousand Mexican lancers were reported in the vicinity, and the Americans should expect a skirmish. The expedition deployed in battle formation. A scout returned to reveal that no enemy soldiers, neither regulars nor militia, were in the vicinity.[53]

That evening Kearny requested that Doniphan step over to discuss some matters important to both of them. He informed Doniphan that Major Thomas Swords had arrived with a commission: Kearny had been promoted to the rank of brigadier general in the Regular Army. Doniphan "congratulated him & was glad to be the first who had the opportunity" to do so. Putting aside the commission, the general then brought up Doniphan's reputation as an attorney, remarking that part of their assignment in Mexico was "more the province of a lawyer than a military officer." Referring to official documents in front of him, Kearny confirmed that the U.S. government "designed holding at least New Mexico & California, besides Texas at the conclusion of the War." That step would entail "military occupation of this State [New Mexico, and to] administer the government as a military T[erritor]y—naturalise [*sic*] all the male citizens as he [Kearny] reached their respective localities—appoint officers, etc." Doniphan explained that he believed the term "naturalise" might be ill chosen, but he understood what the general meant. In effect, Kearny was indicating that he planned to place Doniphan in charge of a military government for New Mexico that would supervise Mexican civilians. For the first time American military officers would take responsibility for administering conquered lands, in this case a broad area that the officers expected would become United States territory and eventually states in the Union.[54]

Kearny appeared unsure of the legal steps to take, and Doniphan reinforced in him America's reliance on legal formalities. The colonel proposed that Mexicans be required to swear an oath "to obey our Constitution & laws & be true & faithful citizens," contingent on the idea that America was annexing New Mexico. Recommending another step, Doniphan suggested that the general elevate himself by standing on "the house top of the chief Alcaldes [*sic*] flat adobe roof" and give a public address to assemblies of Mexicans—"men, women, children & dogs"—calling for the men to swear the formal oath of allegiance to the United States. Kearny approved of the idea and used the procedure in the days to come.[55]

Leaving Kearny's tent, the two officers walked through the camp, discussing the various rumors concerning Mexican preparations to resist the expedition. Kearny was most concerned about potential enemy defenses at Apache Canyon, where reports placed a strong Mexican force of unspecified numbers, perhaps supported by artillery. Kearny described the canyon as "about a half mile long, very narrow & [having] perpendicular walls 1000 feet high with timber & stone fortifications or impediments . . . being rapidly constructed." Soliciting Doniphan's opinion, Kearny asked: "To flank it by another route will be ten miles or more out of a direct route—what do you say?"

Not giving the question more than a moment's reflection, Doniphan fired back a reply, indicating his lack of sophistication in military matters but showing his instinct for the situation at hand: "To produce a proper sense of fear an invading army should not flank or avoid any difficulty that can be swept away by a forward & prompt movement." According to the colonel, Kearny smiled at that response, saying it matched his own views: he had "determined to advance without hesitancy or delay." Next they took up the order of march and how they would engage the Mexicans. Doniphan pressed to allow his regiment to spearhead the expedition as it marched into the canyon. Kearny was skeptical that the volunteers were ready to lead the way, believing that the companies of Regular dragoons properly should go in first. Although Doniphan was disappointed, they left the arrangement with the dragoons as the advance element.[56]

At Kearny's request, Doniphan drafted a proclamation for the general to read to about 150 persons in the Las Vegas village square on August 15. Lieutenant Johnston watched as the general announced the new governance of the region from the rooftop of a house. Kearny required the town's mayor and militia officers to "take an oath of allegiance to the United States" and, after reappointing the town's mayor, emphasized that he must look to the general as governor. The general also promised that his soldiers would help to protect the villagers from depredations from Indians, a promise the villagers had heard from the Mexican government and one that the Americans were going to be hard-pressed to fulfill. Kearny's proclamation also reassured the Mexicans that U.S. forces would respect the Catholic religion. In the subsequent villages, such as San José and San Miguel, Kearny repeated the same proclamation, reappointed local officials, and demanded that they must now look to him as their leader. A man in San Miguel claimed that several hundred militia gathered up ahead were nervous and would run away if the Americans made a display by firing some of their cannon. No doubt Kearny and Doniphan hoped that the man was right.[57]

On August 16, near Apache Canyon, soldiers of the expedition captured the son of Mexico's Captain Dámaso Salazar. The young man revealed that Governor Armijo and Salazar had argued over New Mexico's defensive preparations.

General Kearny delivering a proclamation at Las Vegas, New Mexico. (Drawing by Kenneth Chapman, from Twitchell, *History of the Military Occupation of the Territory of New Mexico* [1909]; courtesy of the Museum of New Mexico, negative no. 163233)

Disagreements between the two leaders had divided and discouraged the Mexicans, causing numbers of militiamen to desert. As the Americans advanced into Apache Canyon, Lieutenant Elliott described how the expedition's companies crisply deployed. They found evidence of organized defenses having been prepared, but no Mexicans were there to oppose them.[58]

In the sequence of small towns, the Americans also got some answers about how the local populace might react to their invasion. At Tecolate, Hughes noted that "the inhabitants . . . willingly received us, and cheerfully took the oath of allegiance" to the U.S. government. The Mexicans sought opportunities to sell food to the American soldiers, who welcomed the chance to purchase such items as corn, chickens, milk, and fresh bread, although they thought that the high prices the Mexicans charged were outrageous. In an effort to keep friendly relations with the locals, Kearny insisted that the Mexicans be reimbursed for any damage to fences or crops and injuries to animals. Private Marcellus Edwards, among other soldiers, noted that not even "an ear of corn [was] pulled by any of our men unless the Mexican owner received a liberal compensation for it." More important, on August 17 the expedition encountered "three men from Santa Fe who report[ed] that [Governor] Armijo had fled to Albuquerque, that the Mexicans had left the canyon, and that all the regular troops had gone south." It was true; the way to Santa Fe lay open. Lieutenant Johnston sounded hopeful: "So here is the end of the campaign." At about 2:00 P.M. on the afternoon of August 18, the lead elements of the expedition topped a ridge a few miles from Santa Fe and the undefended city lay before them.[59]

Viewed at a distance, Santa Fe looked like a metropolis to the American soldiers who had been on the Santa Fe Trail since June and had crossed mountains and deserts to get there. Yet, some of the volunteers' descriptions indicated their initial disappointment with the place. The "narrow and crooked streets" lost their allure up close. One soldier believed that "the houses are all one story flat roof and built of sun dried bricks which give the whole town the appearance of an immense brick yard." To another Missourian the people of Santa Fe appeared "meanly clad, dirty and indolent." One of his companions summarized his views: the New Mexicans were "the filthyest [*sic*] looking people with a few exceptions I ever saw in any country[.] The town is badly laid out, [and] the streets narrow and dirty."[60]

Riding into the state capital in columns of four abreast, the Missourians reached the city's plaza at around 3:00 P.M., and Kearny immediately ordered the placement of a tall temporary flagpole; within minutes an American flag was flying at the top. Bugles sounded and cannons saluted the flag raising, signifying the first American conquest of foreign lands by military force. Overcoming natural obstacles and logistical problems, the Army of the West had completed part of President Polk's bold strategic plan.[61]

Mexico's defense of Santa Fe had failed on all counts. While Governor Armijo's supporters claimed that he had acted in the best interest of the city by not mounting a defense, his detractors had wanted some show of resistance, at least an act of defiance to assuage Mexican honor. Armijo's critics believed that a capable leader employing available regulars and inspiring the militia would have "fought the invaders, firing at them day and night. We would have managed to surprise them and seize their horses, to ambush them in the waterless deserts, to burn their pasturage, to take advantage of the almost inaccessable [*sic*] mountain passes which they had to cross." In response to such pleadings, Governor Armijo told George Ruxton, a former British army officer traveling in America, "They [his critics] don't know that I had but seventy-five men to fight three thousand. What could I do?" Armijo actually commanded two hundred regulars and an undetermined number of militia to go up against Kearny and Doniphan's sixteen hundred soldiers. The governor rejected any skirmishing, much less engaging in a battle, with the invaders, electing to retreat instead, and many Mexicans deplored his choice. Lieutenant Emory concluded that had Armijo "been possessed of the slightest qualifications as a general, he might have given us infinite trouble."[62]

After scouts notified him of the approach of Kearny and Doniphan, Armijo failed to formulate a sound defensive plan for New Mexico. The governor neither attempted to raid the Americans' supplies and drive off their horses nor inspired the militia to rally at Apache Canyon, acknowledged by the Americans to be an excellent natural defensive position. In the opinion of Lieutenant Abraham Johnston, "every inch of ground from the Ratón [Pass] to Santa Fe would have been disputed" if the Mexicans had been willing. Inflicting casualties on the American soldiers, killing or driving off their mounts and draft animals, and damaging their supplies, especially making a stand at Apache Canyon, presented Armijo with the opportunity to weaken the invading army or force it to retreat. By fleeing after a halfhearted attempt to fortify the canyon, Armijo left the Mexicans leaderless and lowered their morale. The governor of Chihuahua responded to word of the American invasion by sending a modest force of four hundred regular dragoons north on August 8. With such reinforcements added to his own regulars, Armijo could have given battle at Apache Canyon. Moving north at a brisk pace of around twenty-five miles per day, the Chihuahua dragoons had reached El Paso del Norte about the time the Army of the West captured Santa Fe.[63]

CHAPTER FOUR

Military Government in Santa Fe and the Indian Treaties

Marching in the successful campaign to capture Santa Fe, Doniphan fulfilled his personal goals of supporting the Rio Grande boundary and conquering lands that he hoped would be annexed to the United States. Newspapers in the United States printed positive stories about the capture of Santa Fe. For example, the Baltimore *Republican and Argus* and the Milwaukee *Sentinel* headlined "Santa Fe Taken Without Firing a Gun." The Richmond *Enquirer* heralded the "Fall of Santa Fe!" and gave lengthy coverage to the American takeover. The Baltimore *Sun* highlighted the "Flight of Gov. Armijo," and the Hartford *Times* related that the governor had "run away" rather than face Kearny's army. Striking a strategic note, the Washington *Daily Union* pointed out that Santa Fe was "an intermediate link in the chain of commercial communications between California and the United States" and concluded it was "impossible to calculate the importance of such an acquisition to the . . . intercommunication between the Pacific and the Gulf of Mexico." The Philadelphia *North American* speculated that Colonel Doniphan was expected to proceed to Chihuahua as soon as possible, while the New York *Tribune* instead indicated that Kearny would handle that phase of the campaign.[1]

To begin administering New Mexico, General Kearny assigned Doniphan tasks of civil affairs and military government, responsibilities unfamiliar to most U.S. Regular Army officers of the 1840s. Doniphan was a good lawyer, but before he invaded New Mexico he had no particular reason to take note of how army officers assisted the operation of government in the U.S. territories in the early 1800s. The army's constabulary experiences in the territories included protecting governors, patrolling public lands, negotiating with Indian tribes, collecting customs duties, and arresting persons charged with crimes. In these circum-

Santa Fe, sketch of the city as it appeared circa 1846–1847, from the 1848 report of Lieutenant James W. Abert. (Courtesy of the Museum of New Mexico, negative no. 10118)

stances, army officers acted to assist civil officials, not supersede them. For instance, Major General Andrew Jackson supervised New Orleans under martial law near the close of the War of 1812. His actions went to the edge of the line where civil authority ended and military dominance began, leaving some bitterness in his wake. On the other hand, Jackson held a one-year post as military governor of Florida in 1821. Not having to acknowledge an elected civil government in the former Spanish colony, General Jackson was in complete control.[2]

These limited examples of the army's experience with civil affairs and military government prior to the war with Mexico point up the differences between martial law and military government. Martial law is a *temporary* circumstance during or after the event of enemy attack or natural calamity in which military forces are called upon to act in concert with an *existing* civil government, one that may be disrupted and unable to function normally. Under such conditions, the military acts on the assumption that full civil governance will be restored in a short time—weeks or a few months at most—and military officers work closely with elected or appointed civil officials, assisting them in their duties and protecting them if local or state police forces are inadequate. Under those circumstances Jackson employed martial law in New Orleans in 1814–1815, for example. In contrast, military government may make use of local or state officials, but its power can override the civil government and is usually used in temporarily occupied enemy provinces or in conquered enemy lands that are expected to be annexed by the conquering nation. One authority concluded: "Martial law supports civil government; military government supplants it."[3]

In Doniphan's case, the invading U.S. expeditionary force supplanted the Mexican civil authorities in New Mexico. The Mexican governor had fled the state, leaving no one in his place. Kearny soon appointed a replacement for him and other civil officeholders, and their administration depended on American soldiers to protect them. In fact, after Kearny left New Mexico, Doniphan, as senior American military officer in the province, held extraordinary authority. He and a committee of citizen-soldiers were responsible for drafting the new territorial constitution and writing laws binding on all civil officials. General Kearny appointed those officials, but if they resigned, died in office, or were uncooperative, the senior army officer in the territory—Doniphan—could name their replacement, rather than holding an election. Therefore, the colonel's practical position was that of de facto military governor rather than a military officer enforcing martial law. Operating alongside Kearny, Doniphan was the first American military officer to establish U.S. governance over a conquered territory; after Kearny left New Mexico, Doniphan held responsibility for that government.[4]

Doniphan began by following Kearny's lead in civil affairs. On August 19, basing his authority on the orders Secretary of War William Marcy had given him three months earlier, Kearny took the first steps toward U.S. control of New Mexico. Using an interpreter, General Kearny read a formal proclamation in the plaza of Santa Fe: "New Mexicans, we have come amongst you to take possession of New Mexico, which we do in the name of the government of the United States." The general wanted to reassure his listeners that their religion would be respected: "Every man has a right to serve God according to his heart." In the same reassuring tone, Kearny stated that their property would be protected and that his "soldiers will take nothing from you but what they pay for." On the next point he was emphatic: "You are no longer Mexican subjects; *you are now become American citizens*, subject only to the laws of the United States. A change of government has taken place in New Mexico and you no longer owe allegiance to the Mexican government." Hoping that some continuity would be reassuring, Kearny expressed his "intention . . . to continue in office those by whom you have been governed, except the governor, and such other persons as I shall appoint to office by virtue of the authority vested in me." In this public forum, Kearny reminded his soldiers, Regulars and volunteers alike, that "humanity as well as policy requires that we should conciliate the inhabitants [of New Mexico] by kind and courteous treatment."[5]

Based on his impression of the Mexicans' response to his oratory, Kearny must have thought he was off on the right foot. The general rendered a hasty opinion of circumstances in New Mexico, informing his superiors in Washington that the people of Santa Fe were "tranquil & can easily be kept so." Giving no evidence of displeasure at the steps the general had taken, President Polk confided to his diary that Kearny "had proclaimed New Mexico to be a conquered province and part of the U[nited] States."[6]

Kearny took what he considered a conciliatory approach. Having no new orders to the contrary from the War Department, he proceeded on his authority as an army general in a conquered province to make a raft of appointments. First, he appointed a well-known and well-respected Anglo-American, Charles Bent, as acting civil governor. Involved in the fur trade since the 1820s, Bent had lived in Mexico for several years and married a Mexican woman. In partnership with his brother, William, and Céran St. Vrain, Bent operated the trading post at Bent's Fort. To support Bent, Kearny selected as officeholders other Anglo-Americans involved in the Santa Fe trade to fill the positions of U.S. attorney, territorial auditor, and territorial treasurer. In hopes of easing the transition to U.S. control, the general also appointed some Mexicans to office, as well as retaining local officials, such as alcaldes (mayors and town councilmen). Designated secretary to Governor Bent, Donaciano Vigil had been the military secretary to Governor Armijo; by collaborating with the new regime, Vigil held what amounted to the office of lieutenant governor and land registrar in the new territorial administration. Looking down the list of other offices, Kearny found places for a few other indigenous residents willing to cooperate with the Americans. For example, José Otero, a local merchant, accepted the chief judgeship on the territorial superior court, Tomás Rivera became collector of Santa Fe, and Francisco Sarracino and Miguel Roméro received lesser offices. Kearny explained to Adjutant General Roger Jones that he hoped by making such appointments, along with issuing announcements intended to keep the residents calm, he would "quiet the minds of the People, which are still a little excited by idle Rumors & Reports." Appointing some cooperative locals to office, and receiving their sworn public allegiance to the United States, became standard practice in subsequent U.S. military governments not only in California in the next two years but also following other U.S. military conquests later in the nineteenth century. After ordering a one-hundred-foot flagpole placed in the main square, and having the American flag run up, Kearny turned his attention to the time-consuming process of selecting soldiers and locating supplies for the trek to the Pacific. In the meantime, on August 31 the general confirmed that the burden of writing territorial laws and a constitution fell to Colonel Doniphan.[7]

Others were available to supervise the writing of these important legal documents shaping territorial government, and Kearny acknowledged that it was a "delicate & difficult task." Any one of several Regular army officers under his command might have drawn the job, but Doniphan, having substantive legal and legislative experience, was Kearny's natural choice. Otherwise, the general might have selected Charles Bent, whose title of "governor" implied that he was in charge of the territorial government, or the acting territorial U.S. attorney, also a civilian with legal expertise. Instead, Kearny created a confusing duality of a civilian governor who was actually subordinate to Colonel Doniphan, the military officer in charge of U.S. troops in New Mexico authorized to write territorial laws and to replace government officials. A St. Louis newspaper writer underscored that "this exercise of power [by Kearny and Doniphan] is novel and extraordinary, so far as the history and practice of our [U.S.] Government extends." Another journalist also understood the situation, cogently observing that "we presume the government of the country [New Mexico] will be *military* instead of civil, until a state of peace is brought about between the United States and Mexico.[8]

Actually, Doniphan confronted three demanding tasks in Santa Fe, and he dealt with them simultaneously. First, he (not Governor Bent or another civilian) would oversee the writing of a territorial constitution and set of laws for the captured province. Second, Doniphan (again, not Governor Bent) would negotiate treaties with the province's bellicose Indians, including the Navajos and Utes. And finally, on top of his responsibilities in military government, Doniphan also had to prepare his regiment for the next phase of its active service, an overland march down the Rio Grande toward El Paso del Norte, about 300 miles from Santa Fe, with the possibility of moving deeper into Mexico, south to Ciudad Chihuahua, an additional trek of 250 miles. Upon arriving at Chihuahua City, Kearny planned for the colonel to "report to Brig. General [John E.] Wool for duty." Mounting an expedition from San Antonio and acting on President Polk's orders, Wool would lead yet another invasion of Mexico with a modest force of three thousand men, mostly state volunteers. Wool was scheduled to commence his move south during September. Hedging his bets in regard to the peacefulness of Santa Fe, Kearny expected Doniphan to carry out his march south without Major Clark's artillery battalion. The cannons and artillerists would remain in Santa Fe to overawe the population and sustain the occupation forces, including the two infantry companies and the 2nd Regiment of Missouri Mounted Volunteers under Colonel Sterling Price, expected to arrive soon. Kearny's orders allowed some flexibility, however. If Doniphan needed artillery support, he could call for Clark to join him. Even before Kearny issued official marching orders to Doniphan, and indicating that continuing his own invasion was much on the colonel's mind, he told Private Waldo Johnson on August 24 that "a portion of the Mounted Volunteers now here [in Santa Fe] will be sent to El Passo [*sic*] *in a few days*."[9]

While his preparations to move south always drained his time, Doniphan's immediate priority pertained to legal matters. Several Anglo-Americans, including fellow volunteer soldiers, sat down with the colonel to write laws for New Mexico. General Kearny did not participate. Doniphan was assisted by Willard Hall and David Waldo. A private enrolled in Company C, Hall was a native Virginian who had resided in Missouri since 1840, a graduate of Yale College and a knowledgeable lawyer. Although Hall and Doniphan had opposed each other in politics, Hall's cordial personality and skill in the law prompted General Kearny to choose him for Doniphan's legal team. Captain of Company A, Waldo brought other valued qualities to the table. He had graduated from Transylvania College in Kentucky and settled in Missouri in 1826. Fluent in Spanish, Waldo made his money in the Santa Fe trade. Other team members included Governor Bent and the new U.S. territorial attorney, Francis P. "Frank" Blair Jr. Blair came from the prestigious political family that included members active in politics in Maryland as well as Missouri. Blair's father had been a partisan newspaper editor and adviser to President Andrew Jackson. Frank Blair had graduated from Princeton College and joined his brother Montgomery in a law practice for about two years in St. Louis before moving to New Mexico prior to the outbreak of the war.[10]

Pooling their knowledge, Doniphan's team worked diligently for three weeks to produce a set of laws and a territorial constitution. Naturally, they consulted the U.S. Constitution, but they also brought to bear what they knew about the state constitutions of Missouri and Louisiana as well as the laws of Kentucky and Texas. Doniphan related that "in addition to other duties, Willard P. Hall and myself are arranging the Government, &c, trying to get the machine in operation. It is a very arduous matter—the laws [of New Mexico] are all in Spanish, and every thing is done through an interpreter, and there is much in the laws conflicting with our [U.S.] Constitution to be altered."[11]

The team's labors yielded a booklet of more than one hundred pages, *Organic Law of the Territory of New Mexico*, printed in parallel columns of English and Spanish. This territorial framework was the first step in bringing a republican style of government to a colony administered by Spanish colonial bureaucrats and a state overseen by Mexico's combination of military-civil procedures. The booklet contained a territorial constitution, a bill of rights, election procedures and responsibilities of individual officeholders, and provisions for trial by jury and habeas corpus. All of these features reflected the outlook of representative democracy shared by Doniphan's legal team. During the territorial period, the governor served at the pleasure of the president of the United States. His authority extended to such matters as filling certain vacant offices, calling for new elections, granting pardons, and seeing that all laws were "faithfully executed." The governor was assisted by a territorial secretary, a sort of lieutenant governor. "The qualified voters of the several counties" would elect members of a bicameral general assembly. Those serving in the upper house, called the legislative council, had four-year terms; members of the lower chamber, the house of representatives, had two-year terms. The legislature would make or change laws for the territory, and nothing corresponded to the general assembly's function in Spanish or Mexican state governance. Specific provisions spelled out punishments for bribery of public officials, honoraria for legislators, operation of the general assembly, and maintaining journals for each of its houses. A territorial superior court of three judges provided a judicial forum for appeals from "inferior tribunals." The president would later appoint the judges, but Kearny established the court by choosing the first trio. Such a court was also absent in the Spanish and Mexican methods of governing states. Harkening back to America's Northwest Ordinance and a notable departure from Spanish or Mexican procedures, the *Organic Law* "encouraged" that "one or more schools be established in each village" and that "the poor shall be educated free of all charges."[12]

To ensure "that the GREAT and ESSENTIAL PRINCIPLES of LIBERTY and FREE GOVERNMENT" were "recognized and established," Doniphan's legal team attached a bill of rights to the territorial constitution. Emphasizing that "political power is vested in and belongs to the people," the bill of rights guaranteed peaceable assemblies, the right to petition the government, freedom of speech, freedom of religion, and separation of church and state. Paragraphs spelled out such matters as access to courts for "every person," protections for private property, and the rights of habeas corpus, due process, and a "speedy trial by a jury." Trial by jury was not part of either the Spanish or the Mexican legal system. Other paragraphs delineated protections against self-incrimination, double jeopardy, and "unreasonable searches and seizures." Looking to many practical day-to-day matters, the *Organic Law* provided for officeholders, such as clerks of court and constables, license fees, and punishments for various violations of the laws. Additional provisions covered dealing with creditors or suing for collecting debts, duties of jurors, and which parties in suits would pay court costs.[13]

Based on both their legal and their liberal educations, Doniphan's team enumerated an impressive list of idealistic provisions, but regarding slavery the New Mexico territorial constitution and laws were almost silent, despite the fact that the institution was obviously important in the constitutions of states that the drafters of the *Organic Law* used as guidelines. Avoiding the word "slavery" or some phrase such as "involuntary servitude," Doniphan and his cohorts indicated that in order to register each voter must be "a *free* male citizen" of the territory, that "all free male citizens" were eligible to vote, and that in addition to meeting age and residency requirements, any officeholder also had to be a "free male citizen." These phrases recognized that in the United States of 1846 some persons were not free.[14]

Ironically, the work of Doniphan's committee came to be called the "Kearny Code." Busy preparing for his march to California, Kearny only glanced over the lengthy legal compendium before endorsing it on September 22. In a letter to the adjutant general of the U.S. Army in Washington, Kearny accorded clear and gracious credit to the primary authors of the code: "I take great pleasure in stating that I am *entirely indebted* for these laws to Col. A. W. Doniphan, . . . who received much assistance from private Willard P. Hall." Three days after approving the code, and believing that he had "made the necessary military arrangements for maintaining . . . Peace & quiet now so happily existing," Kearny departed Santa Fe for California, leaving Doniphan in charge of military forces in New Mexico. Secretary of War Marcy, quite pleased with the legal work, informed General Zachary Taylor that the American "military occupation of the enemy's country" could be seen as a "blessing to the inhabitants in the vicinity" of Santa Fe. The Baltimore *Niles National Register* headlined a report on these military steps with the descriptive phrase "Americanizing Santa Fe," and the Richmond *Enquirer* supported the notion that American laws should follow the flag.[15]

The Kearny Code drawn up by Doniphan and his associates was the first such document used by an American military government in conquered territory. Kearny made an apt decision to call upon citizen-soldiers experienced in legal practice to write such laws. He could have assigned Regular officers to the task, but that would have taken them away from preparing for the march to California. As the expedition's senior officer, Kearny got the credit for approving the *Organic Law*.[16]

Some U.S. newspapers, however, questioned the propriety of a territorial constitution and laws issued by a military government. The St. Louis *Republican* was one of the most critical, contending, "We had supposed that some formalities were necessary before such wholesale annexations of territory could be made to the United States." To take such action, the *Republican* assumed that Kearny must have had "express instruction from the President." Other papers shared the *Republican*'s views, in some cases quoting from its story. The Detroit *Free*

Press doubted if Kearny had the authority to declare New Mexico a part of the United States so quickly, though obviously American forces had conquered the province. The Newark *Advertiser* worried that Kearny's "extraordinary stretch of power" was premature, and the Richmond *Enquirer* implied that Kearny had overstepped his bounds as a military commander in a conquered province, even if such a position was a novelty in the politics of the United States.[17]

In the days to come, leaders of the national government sparred over the propriety of military governments, Kearny's as well as others. Introducing resolutions and engaging in discussions over two days, members of the House of Representatives made it plain they believed the general had exceeded his powers. Led by Representative Garrett Davis, a Whig from Kentucky, some congressmen asserted that Kearny had taken actions that should have waited for congressional authorization and for official United States possession of New Mexico. On December 17 the House passed a resolution calling for President Polk to send over copies of all documents, proclamations, and orders pertaining to the actions of several senior military officers, including Kearny, "touching on the establishment of civil government in any portions of Mexico" captured by U.S. forces. Furthermore, the resolution requested that "the President inform this House whether he has approved and recognised [*sic*] any governments so established."[18]

From the executive branch, Secretary of War Marcy admonished Kearny (who by then had reached California) for his grandiose pronouncements. Although he had given Kearny the original elastic directions about what to do in conquered territory, Marcy informed the general that he had gone "beyond the line designated by the President" by conferring "upon the people [of New Mexico] Territory political rights under the Constitution of the United States." Privately, in his diary Polk recognized that Kearny "had misconceived the extent of his authority." Moreover, in a message to Congress, the president publicly qualified or objected to some of the steps Kearny had taken, ones that only a few weeks earlier had been deemed appropriate and necessary. The commander in chief indicated that Kearny should have announced only a temporary provisional government for New Mexico until diplomacy officially spelled out exactly what areas would be annexed by the United States. Specifically, the president backtracked on the matter of approving Kearny's enthusiastic pledge that the residents of the conquered region would automatically obtain political rights of U.S. citizens under the Constitution, temporarily leaving their status open to doubt.[19]

It should have come as no surprise to Kearny and Doniphan that setting up the first American military government in conquered enemy lands would be second-guessed by legal experts and Whigs in Congress. Trying out such complicated procedures for the first time revealed problems and required adjustments, especially under wartime conditions. Unanswered questions about the regime hung in the air. It remained to be seen how Mexicans and Indians in the province reacted to the American occupation. Especially important, the military government itself—the odd combination of civilian appointees, including Anglo-American residents and a few Mexicans, answering to the authority of a military officer—had to demonstrate that it could function. It could work smoothly only if peace prevailed. Any rebellion by the Mexicans would ruin the province's chances for expeditious assimilation into the Union and would lengthen the time under American military authority. Meanwhile, Indians of several tribes could be expected to protect their own interests and lands by attacking settlers. Undeterred Indian raids could discourage American settlement and delay by many months or years the territory's progress toward statehood under congressional guidelines. During the war and in its aftermath, the army could expect to continue supervising lands so recently gained by conquest. Critics of military government might have recalled that Florida, purchased by America from Spain in 1819, had remained a territory until 1845. Therefore, it was unrealistic to expect a rapid transition to statehood for New Mexico. However long it might take for New Mexico to become a state, Doniphan's draft of the Kearny Code formed the foundation for the territory's transition to democracy. The hurried efforts of a few days on the part of Doniphan and his committee produced worthwhile results.[20]

Meanwhile, having so many tasks calling for attention made Doniphan seem like a circus performer juggling several balls at once, but he had to address several issues dealing with the 1st Missouri Regiment itself. For example, his lieutenant colonel, Charles Ruff, applied to be recommissioned in the Regular Army. Official correspondence came through on September 17 for Captain Ruff to resume duty with the dragoons. The colonel did not appear sorry to lose Ruff; William Hayter said that the soldiers "cursed him" for being a stickler for regulations and too much the West Pointer. His departure meant that Doniphan had to arrange for an election to fill the vacancy. Doniphan fell ill with some unexplained malady, and Major Clark supervised the election. Captain Congreve Jackson of Company G, from Howard County, and Major William Gilpin announced as candidates and spoke earnestly to the volunteers. Jackson won the election, apparently demonstrating the Missourians' support of a volunteer (Jackson) over the more rigorous former West Pointer (Gilpin). Aside from personnel assignments, the colonel was concerned about the health of the regiment. Each day several soldiers presented themselves at sick call, and it was not unusual to have a dozen or more in a makeshift hospital during the weeks in Santa Fe. Doctors found that five others were too ill to continue the campaign and discharged them. Because of the resignations of Dr. George Penn and assistant surgeon Dr. Isaac P. Vaughn, new appointments were needed to the medical staff. Filling the gaps were Dr. T. M. Morton as surgeon and Dr. J. F. Morton and Dr. Moore as assistant surgeons.[21]

Another of Doniphan's concerns was the composition of Kearny's force bound for California. At first, Kearny considered the possibility of initiating the march to the Pacific as early as September 1. The general was unsure which units or individuals he would take, leaving Doniphan in doubt for more than a month about how many of his soldiers and which supporting units he might command in the weeks to come. For instance, Kearny was impressed with Private Willard Hall of Company C and decided to attach him to the troops bound for California. For a time it appeared that Captain Thomas Hudson and his Leclede Rangers would accompany Kearny. The captain proudly wrote home about this prospect and indicated that the Regular officers rated the Rangers as equal to "regular troops." Doniphan feared that he would lose more than the Rangers. The general authorized Hudson to recruit additional volunteers into a new company. Calling them the "California Rangers," Hudson drew together more than one hundred of the best Missouri soldiers into the new unit. Moreover, Kearny cast his eye on Clark's artillery battalion but eventually decided he would not take the guns, leaving them in Santa Fe, along with the infantry companies under Captains Angney and Woods, to support Colonel Sterling Price's 2nd Regiment of Missouri Mounted Volunteers. Kearny's decision to leave the artillery turned out to be quite important for Doniphan's campaign into Chihuahua. Expecting that Price would arrive soon, the general mulled over the idea of taking as many as half of Price's soldiers to California, but he eventually rejected that notion. By the end of September, shortly before his departure, Kearny finally decided that only Regular dragoons, plus a few individual exceptions, would march to the Pacific. Therefore, Doniphan, his adjutant, and all company officers of the 1st Missouri Regiment gave some of their attention to gathering supplies to march south to link up with Brigadier General John Wool, who was believed to be operating somewhere near Chihuahua City. Meanwhile, an article in the New Orleans *Picayune* indicated that the colonel's plans were public knowledge, or at least that speculation about his next objective was widespread. It would have been easy for Mexicans residing in New Orleans to relay such rumors about Doniphan's plans to Mexican authorities in Veracruz or Tampico.[22]

While Kearny speculated about which units he would take to California and dealt personally with Indian negotiations, he issued two orders that could be considered examples of questionable judgment. After he had been in New Mexico only a few weeks, the general specified that a company of Mexican militia would be raised for the defense of the territory, but only days later Kearny had second thoughts and canceled the order. Perhaps it was premature to begin putting large numbers of Mexicans under arms. In another order, however, the general authorized individual Mexicans to keep their weapons to protect themselves against Indian raids, allowing many Mexicans to remain armed. These weapons could be used for defense against Indians, but they also could be employed in a rebellion against the American occupation. In late November a Missouri soldier wrote back to St. Louis that "all things wear the appearance of profound peace, . . . but to a close observer, it is evident that it is all hypocrisy." The volunteer continued: "People conquered but yesterday could have no friendly feeling for the conquerors, who have taken possession of their country—changed its laws and appointed new officers, principally foreigners." Numerous rumors circulated in Santa Fe indicating that patriotic Mexicans might attempt to overthrow the American occupation.[23]

In order to strengthen the American hold on the province, Kearny had assigned Doniphan to supervise the construction of a fort to house part of the occupation garrison. Appropriately, Doniphan picked one of the Regular officers, Lieutenant William H. Emory of the Topographical Engineers, to attend to the daily duties of building "Fort Marcy," named in honor of the secretary of war. Emory drew plans for the fort on August 19, and construction began a few days later. Assisting Emory were First Lieutenant Jeremy F. Gilmer and Brevet Second Lieutenant William G. Peck, both Regular engineer officers. Assignments for labor details rotated among the companies of the 1st Missouri Regiment and the other volunteer units. Finding the rough manual labor distasteful, several of the soldiers went to sick call, where they received a dose of a "nauseous" elixir and decided they preferred doing construction work to taking the medicine. Emory also hired twenty Mexican masons, whose pay provided an infusion of cash into the local economy. Emory selected a site for the fort on a rise of ground some six hundred yards from the center of Santa Fe. The adobe structure, which took the form of an eight-pointed star with uneven sides, was completed in late September.[24]

Already an active trading center, Santa Fe bustled with extra commercial activity during the American occupation. Merchants and traders crowded the city, signing in at the Missouri House Hotel and other places with rooms to rent, making the town of six thousand people a "lively place." After the initial shock of the fall of the province, some residents welcomed the American soldiers. Stores, shops, taverns, and cantinas all attracted the Missouri soldiers. Street vendors hawked all manner of things to eat, including "melons, apples, plumbs [*sic*], apricots, peaches, pine nuts, bread, meat, cheese, [and] milk." Private John Hughes also reported that "the [Missouri] Traders are all here with their goods. Some of them have opened stores, . . . and . . . others are at some distance in the country grazing their stock, and awaiting permission to go on to Chihuahua." By early October several of the traders had packed up and moved south to El Paso del Norte.[25]

Some of the volunteers camped on the outskirts of town, where they found little for their horses to eat in what Lieutenant Richard Elliott called "a barren country." It was not any better in the city, where Private Daniel Hastings related that "corrals are strewed [*sic*] with dead animals producing a most unhealthy and disagreeable stench. . . . Thirty-five mules . . . starved to death in one corral within two days." Remaining animals chewed on wagon boards for nourishment, while dozens of crows feasted on the carcasses nearby. The lack of fodder meant it had to be transported from Bent's Fort. Soon enough, Doniphan sent some of his companies on patrols into the Indian country to alleviate overcrowding in Santa Fe, raise the visibility of the American occupation in the hinterland, and discourage the Indians from using violence to defend their lands. One Missourian left in the vicinity of the town, however, wrote home saying that "the variety of this city is not of that character to attract much attention." Another agreed, writing that "the novelty of Santa Fe is wearing off—it is growing dull and wearisome." The same soldier concluded, "Take Santa Fe all in all it presents no great inducements." And Captain Thomas Hudson decided there were few "attractions for a man of taste in this Country."[26]

Overall, the health of the expedition's soldiers was good, considering their uneven diet and variable water supply, but several volunteers complained of illnesses typical for those on campaign in a foreign land in the nineteenth century. Captain Hudson reported, "I have never before enjoyed my health so well. The climate here [in Santa Fe] is most delightful." But by the end of September thirty soldiers were in the expedition's makeshift hospital, and one, Benjamin Cockrell of Platte County, died there. Four weeks later things seemed worse, according to Private Hughes. Several volunteers were in poor health, and a number of other soldiers had died of various maladies. Hughes was appalled that "men become so callous and indifferent to the fate of their fellows that those who fall victims to disease are scarcely interred decently. Not a tear is shed, even by the relatives of the unfortunate deceased."[27]

After their hard weeks of marching on the trail from Fort Leavenworth, and not knowing how long their sojourn in Santa Fe would last, the Missouri volunteers made every effort to enjoy themselves. Excited and bursting with pride about their conquest of the city, the citizen-soldiers had rushed into the saloons on the evening of August 18, resulting in a rowdy night of celebration. Several of Kearny's Regulars from the 1st Dragoons had to remove them from the taverns. That first night appeared to set the tone for the weeks to come.[28]

Natural antagonisms between Mexicans under military occupation and the victorious Missouri volunteers strained relations during the occupation of Santa Fe. Some Americans displayed an obvious lack of respect for the Catholic faith and criticized the appearance that "priests hold full sway over the people." Others considered that Mexicans lacked proper morals and that Santa Fe itself was a den of iniquity. For instance, Private Daniel Hastings viewed the Mexicans as "ignorant, degraded, treacherous, and surprisingly deficient in point of morality." Hastings concluded his diatribe: "The [Mexican] men are indolent and fond of amusements such as dancing, music, gambling and cock-fighting. . . . Both sexes are generally great smokers." Appearing to confirm these attitudes, an article in the New Orleans *Daily Picayune* contended that the minds of Mexicans had "been withered and parched by lust and ungodly incest." In New Mexico, the *Picayune* postulated, "a gross sensuality predominates over all sense of shame," and the Mexicans were "destitute of principles of virtue." The paper quoted an unnamed American officer as saying that "the more of that country we annex to the United States the worse off we will be."[29]

Contemporary critics claimed that the Missouri volunteers' rowdy behavior in New Mexico pushed the Mexicans to oppose the American occupation. Of course, the Americans were using available troops for occupying New Mexico and California, and they happened to be volunteers rather than Regulars. Anticipating there might be trouble, on August 17 Kearny had ordered officers to assemble the volunteers and read aloud the paragraphs of the U.S. Army's *Articles of War* dealing with relations between soldiers and civilians. George Ruxton, a former English army officer traveling in the region, indicated the tone of Mexican opposition by writing, "Over all New Mexico that the most bitter feeling and most determined hostility existed against the Americans who, [were] not very anxious to conciliate the [Mexican] people, but by their bullying and overbearing demeanor toward them, have in a greater measure been the cause of this hatred." While the volunteers' belligerent attitudes may have antagonized some of the Mexicans, more than a month after the conquest Lieutenant Christian Kribben contended that the "tranquility and quietness prevade [*sic*] in every direction; all the natives, whether in good faith or not, seem thoroughly satisfied with the change of government." Kribben's views may have been sincere, but he overlooked the fact that many Mexicans would have opposed an American takeover and annexation of New Mexico even if the occupying soldiers were angelic.[30]

The Missourians were no angels, although according to Private John Hughes they were treating the residents of Santa Fe the same way they would treat the people of Philadelphia or St. Louis, but that it was really "no honor to conquer such a people." Nevertheless, any untoward action on the volunteers' part would be, in Hughes's opinion, a "disgrace of the American arms" as well as an "individual dishonor." Indeed, the volunteers did not want to alienate the locals but to enjoy themselves while they were in Santa Fe. Like Private Hastings, Hughes maintained that the "Mexicans had an inordinate passion for amusement and gambling," and, unfortunately, some of the Missourians were pleased to indulge in those same passions. Sergeant William Kennerly recalled that several of the volunteers sought out the "gambling establishment of *Señora* Barcelo," where a card game, monte, was the speciality and the senora herself the best dealer in the house. Hughes specified that every party always seemed to have "an abundance of the exhilarating vino or wine" on hand. Private Hastings also recounted that "alcohol is very abundant in Santa Fe, and notwithstanding the exorbitant prices attached to it, it is drunk to a great excess by many of our men, thereby producing frequent riots." As an alternative, high-toned form of entertainment, Lieutenant Elliott observed that some of the more sophisticated among the volunteers frequented a theater operated by Bernard Sorley, formerly of St. Louis.[31]

The women of Santa Fe were of great interest to the volunteers. Hughes related that "the Spanish ladies dress very gaudily . . . but with little taste"; striking a disappointing note, Hastings asserted that "the women with few exceptions are coarse and unattractive." However, Hastings admitted to looking forward to dancing with those exceptions. Sergeant Kennerly also enjoyed dancing with charming, dark-eyed senoritas, "who kept their red-heeled slippers tapping in perfect time to their castanets" and "cast sidelong glances from behind their fans."[32]

The good times the Missourians enjoyed degenerated nearly into disorder after the first six weeks of the American occupation. When Colonel Sterling Price's 2nd Missouri Regiment began arriving in late September, the city appeared to burst at the seams. Hughes related that Price's twelve hundred men were accompanied by "an immense train of baggage waggons [*sic*], [and] commissary teams," along with the five hundred men of the Mormon Battalion, placed under the command of a Regular Army officer, Captain Philip St. George Cooke. According to Hughes, this influx brought the capital "alive with a promiscuous throng of American soldiers, traders, visitors, stragglers, trappers, mountaineers, Mexicans, [and] Puebla [*sic*] Indians." Having two regiments of Missouri volunteers in Santa Fe was more than the city could stand, and by the end of September Doniphan assigned most of his men to duties in the countryside.[33]

Certainly, Kearny had wanted to maintain discipline among American troops in New Mexico, and Doniphan gave his full cooperation to that end. Serving on several courts-martial, Doniphan sometimes took the chair as president of the court, but the most serious cases that came to trial did not involve altercations between soldiers and Mexicans. For example, on August 19 he and other officers unanimously decided that Lieutenant James S. Oldham of Company A was guilty of "conduct subversive of good order and military discipline" by refusing Lieutenant Colonel Ruff's direct order to serve as officer of the guard at the camp at Galisteo Creek. Instead, Oldham took off and spent the night on the town in Santa Fe, though he said he was going to arrange supplies for his company. As punishment, Oldham was dismissed from the regiment and sent home. A more serious breach of discipline, but not one involving civilians, was on display in the trial of John Herkins of Company D. Doniphan's court convicted Herkins of "Mutinous Conduct," specifying that he had advanced with a drawn saber and threatened one of the expedition's Regular Army officers, Major Thomas Swords. Deciding that a standard punishment of six months at hard labor not be imposed, the court sentenced Herkins to stand before the paraded regiment, have the court's verdict read to his fellow soldiers, and be "drummed out of the service."[34]

The most serious case heard by any of the courts-martial, one chaired by Major Gilpin, came in the incident of Captain John Stevenson's fight with Private William Bray. The two men had argued, leaving their antagonisms unresolved. On September 17, drunk, disorderly, and armed with a knife, Bray set upon his company commander, apparently intending to kill him. Drawing his pistol, Stevenson defended himself and fired a shot, killing Bray instantly. According to John Hughes, Bray was a veteran of the War of 1812. Gilpin and the court heard the testimony of eleven witnesses before rendering their verdict. Evaluating the incident, General Kearny concluded that he "much regretted to see such a want of discipline & insubordination as exists in most of the companies of the Mo. Mounted Vols." Kearny admonished Doniphan and his regimental officers, but "particularly company commanders, [to] more closely attend to their duties and see that the men under them properly perform what is expected from Soldiers in the Service of the United States." The general expected more rigid discipline to be demonstrated in the future. He cautioned that the regiment was on the nation's service, and its officers were not "in the field . . . to make interest with those under their command so that they may secure their votes" in future political campaigns.[35]

Simultaneously trying to maintain discipline among his soldiers and drafting the territorial constitution and laws, Doniphan began carrying out the third part of his assignment under the de facto military government—dealing with Indians in New Mexico. Seated in offices at the "roomy and comfortable" governor's palace in Santa Fe, the colonel sought to emulate Kearny's "competent . . . diplomacy with the [Mexican] citizens and Indian tribes." Some of the Indians had sent representatives to meet with Kearny before his departure, offering flowery pledges of peace and friendship—the same sorts of words the Spanish and Mexicans had heard before. In mid-September, acting on Kearny's orders, Doniphan detached subordinate officers to command selected companies of volunteers and sent them out to treat with the tribes, including the Zunis, Apaches, "Eutaws" (Utes), and Navajos. Governor Bent estimated that New Mexico contained more than five thousand Apaches, some four thousand Utes, and seven thousand Navajos. The Navajos drew Doniphan's primary attention, but he had to contend with the others as well.[36]

Failing to stop Navajo raids on ranchers and travelers would undermine the Americans' newly established authority over the area, would undercut Kearny's personal pledge to protect the lives and property of New Mexicans, and could encourage Mexicans to resist the U.S. occupation. Indeed, astute Mexicans and Indians, especially the Navajos, already had begun to calculate the weakness of the U.S. military forces. Private John Hughes alertly noticed that the Mexicans (whom he sometimes called "Spaniards") were "becoming dissatisfied with the troops and I would not be surprised that we have some difficulty with them before spring." But the Indian raids also concerned the Americans. Lumping the tribes together, Hughes concluded that "the Indians are much more troublesome than the New Mexicans," and a fellow volunteer wrote to his hometown newspaper using almost the same words. Not surprisingly, none of the Americans appeared to see the circumstance from the tribes' viewpoints. Although Kearny had appointed or designated some state officeholders in an effort to forestall Mexican opposition to the Americans, Doniphan's forces faced two potential threats: a rebellion from Mexican civilians and Indian depredations.[37]

Negotiations with the Navajos proceeded fruitlessly, delaying the departure of the 1st Missouri Regiment for its march down the Rio Grande. Lack of a skilled translator contributed to anxiety on both sides and was a typical problem anytime Americans dealt with Indian tribes. The translators that Doniphan employed, including one of his aides, Thomas Caldwell, evidently offered partial or imprecise renditions of the Navajo point of view. Doniphan insisted that the Navajos end their attacks on ranches, freight wagons, and stagecoaches. The Navajos were reluctant to sign such an agreement. Warriors gained horses, sheep, and supplies, as well as establishing status and reputations for prowess, from such raids. Perhaps not quite understanding the design of the U.S. occupation, the Navajos also wanted to enlist the Americans as allies against the Mexicans. When the Navajos continued raiding and their leaders refused to appear for an important parley scheduled in late September, Kearny, who had been apprised of developments, sent a dispatch rider to Santa Fe with specific, ambitious orders: "Col. Doniphan . . . will march with his Regt. into the Navajoe [*sic*] Country. He will cause all of the Prisoners and all the Property they hold . . . to be given up. And he will require from them such security for their future good conduct as he may think ample and sufficient by taking hostages or otherwise." Private Hughes reported that the Navajos "sally forth and commit daily depredations upon the property of the *rancheros*. Honorable warfare with such an enemy is impossible." On the other hand, a captain of volunteers pictured the Navajos as "a warlike people . . . celebrated for their intelligence and good order. . . . They are handsome, well made, in every respect a highly civilized people, being, as a nation, of a higher order of beings than the mass of their neighbours [*sic*], the Mexicans."[38]

Based on Kearny's orders, Doniphan sent out several mounted contingents, directing his captains to inform the tribal leaders that he expected to promptly conclude formal negotiations in which the tribes would recognize U.S. authority. Moreover, the Indians would surrender all booty, animals, and captives taken since the Army of the West had arrived in New Mexico. After he had put his companies in motion, Doniphan offered an assessment to Secretary of War William Marcy that he would "bring the war to a close in 30 days"—and that his goal was to protect the Anglo and Mexican inhabitants of the territory. The colonel picked Ojo del Oso—Bear Spring—as the spot where the regiment's contingents would rendezvous. Replacing his companies on garrison duty were those of Colonel Sterling Price's 2nd Missouri Mounted Volunteers, but their arrival still did not give Doniphan enough soldiers to dominate all of the tribes. Even one of Kearny's staff officers, Quartermaster Captain William McKissack, cogently expressed the American viewpoint: "Col. Doniphan has received orders to proceed against the Navahoe [*sic*] Indians, who have been at war with the Mexicans for years & refuse to make peace. . . . Since our arrival in the country they have committed many depredations & will require severe punishment before they cease to molest the Inhabitants; but I fear another Florida [Seminole]

War if the Indians desire to protract it; as they live in the mountains impracticable for roads & can only be pursued slowly with pack mules for transporting stores, etc."[39]

While Captains Parsons and Reid and Lieutenant Colonel Jackson led companies to show the flag among the Navajos, Doniphan assigned his energetic regimental major, William Gilpin, to deal with the Utes. The major rode on a two-hundred-mile sweep into the countryside leading four companies of the 1st Missouri Regiment. Gilpin's negotiations with the Utes arranged for a council, attended by Doniphan, producing a treaty on October 15 that he hoped would be lasting. Chalking up what he considered a considerable step toward peace in the territory, the colonel then turned his attention to the Navajos.[40]

In late October and into November the patrolling and contacts with other tribes continued. Several inches of snow fell, and the Missouri volunteers and their horses suffered from the early onset of winter. Cold weather, inadequate food, and light clothing rendered many of the soldiers chilly, feverish, and perpetually hungry. A few died from these maladies, including G. W. Butler, Doniphan's adjutant. Morale suffered; persuading Indians to sign treaties was not why they had enlisted.[41]

After receiving reports about inconclusive parleys between his subordinates and Navajo bands, in early November Doniphan led three companies of volunteers toward the rendezvous, first stopping at Cubero, where Congreve Jackson was camped. Expecting to be joined by Captain David Waldo and other companies, the colonel and his men met some principal Navajo leaders and several hundred members of the tribe at Bear Spring on November 21, 1846. While it was a large gathering, it by no means represented the entire Navajo tribe. Most of the 1st Missouri Regiment assembled, probably surprised to see their colonel in his dress uniform.[42]

Speaking to the Navajos through his interpreter, Thomas Caldwell, Doniphan drew himself up to his full height of six feet, four inches, and delivered his demands, pausing for Caldwell to interpret. The colonel emphasized that "the United States had taken military possession of New Mexico" and that American law now applied to the province. The United States would "prosecute a war" against the tribe unless it behaved peacefully and agreed to a treaty.[43]

Not intimidated by either the colonel's menacing words or his regiment's patrols, one of the Navajo headmen, Zarcillos Largos, recounted and interpreted recent events. "Americans! you have a strange cause of war against the Navajos. We have waged war against the New Mexicans for several years. . . . You have lately commenced a war against the same people. You are powerful. You have great guns [cannons] and many brave soldiers. You have therefore conquered them." Zarcillos Largos expressed puzzlement: "You now turn upon us for attempting to do what you have done yourselves. We cannot see why you have cause of quarrel with us for fighting the New Mexicans on the west [of the territory] while you do the same thing on the east." The Navajo reminded Doniphan that he was "interfering in *our war*, [one] begun long before you got here." It might have seemed more logical for the Navajos and Americans to combine forces and conduct war against the Mexicans. Zarcillos Largos concluded: "*If New Mexico be really in your possession*, and it be the intention of your government to hold it, we will cease our depredations. . . . Let there be peace between us." Whatever misgivings they may have had about the nascent American administration of New Mexico, the assembled Navajo leaders signed the Treaty of Ojo del Oso on November 22, but Doniphan failed to appreciate that they could not sign for the whole tribe.[44]

Allowing his confidence to get the better of him, Doniphan overstated his case by writing Adjutant General Roger Jones that Ojo del Oso would be "a permanent treaty." The treaty specified that the Navajos would end raiding, return prisoners, and restore stolen property. Doniphan wanted to believe the Navajos understood that U.S. military forces would protect Mexicans as well as Anglo-Americans against Indian attacks in the future. While the colonel negotiated with the best of intentions, his treaty was never ratified by the U.S. Senate.[45]

In negotiating with the Navajos and other tribes, Doniphan had taken preliminary steps to carry out Kearny's orders, but his companies had been scattered and he could not bring the full weight of his regiment to bear against the tribes. Despite Zarcillos Largos's diplomatic words citing the Missourians' prowess, the Navajos remained unimpressed with Doniphan's volunteers, especially if they represented the might of the United States. Others also discounted the treaty. The New York *Evening Post* observed that "no one supposes that the Indians can be kept quiet." Lieutenant Richard Elliott, no friend of the colonel, was more emphatic, writing to the St. Louis *Reveille* that "Col. Doniphan's treaty has been much discussed. It is said to be very defective, and not likely to effect any very substantial peace." Even the colonel could have realized the treaty's deficiencies when two of his soldiers were ambushed and killed by Navajos on November 27.[46]

Doniphan's negotiations with the Indian tribes were well-intentioned but hurried. The demands of preparing his regiment for battle with the Mexican army distracted him from giving his complete attention to dealing with the Indians. As ordered, he had negotiated with belligerent elements of the population in New Mexico. Such negotiations with indigenous peoples became a standard administrative responsibility for leaders of all U.S. military governments in the future. Unfortunately for Americans, Mexicans, and Indians, Doniphan's Navajo treaty produced no long-lasting peace. Within days after Doniphan left New Mexico, Navajos, especially those not represented at Bear Spring, continued their attacks on vulnerable civilians.[47]

Among the most astute of Doniphan's contemporaries was Governor Charles Bent. Rendering his views on the Navajo treaty and the status of U.S. military actions in New Mexico, Bent sent a report to U.S. Secretary of State James Buchanan. Bent indicated that he had "but little ground to hope that it [the Navajo treaty] will be permanent." Recognizing that establishing New Mexico as a U.S. territory depended on military forces, Bent urged Buchanan to arrange for more American soldiers to be sent to Santa Fe. It appeared to the governor that the American volunteers were rowdy and unsuited for the purpose of occupying New Mexico; they failed to command the respect of either Indians or Mexicans. Bent had found the key to the U.S. takeover of New Mexico; he made a strong argument why U.S. Army Regulars should have been assigned to occupation duties, but the army was too small to take on all the tasks it needed to do. Doniphan's regiment could have remained in Santa Fe and its vicinity until more reinforcements arrived. Problems of discipline and logistics, especially inadequate supplies for men and horses and lack of appropriate quarters, would have continued if two regiments—volunteers or Regulars—had been posted in or near the capital. Bent had the right idea, but it would take years for the United States to properly garrison New Mexico.[48]

No one in the 1840s could call Doniphan's experiences textbook examples of military government because they were the earliest of their kind and predated the textbooks. In New Mexico the experiments by Kearny and Doniphan represented the U.S. Army's significant steps into the complicated field of civil-military relations. During the war with Mexico senior Regular Army officers, such as Kearny and Winfield Scott, had no reason to give a high priority to military government. Their main concerns naturally focused on enhancing logistics, evaluating enemy forces, deciding tactical deployments, and developing campaign plans. Anyway, involvement with such governments might last only a few weeks; the other concerns were perpetual. The War Department operated no office, staff section, or bureau responsible for civil-military relations. During the war, Regulars sometimes considered it prudent, or convenient, to select available volunteer officers with legal experience to supervise martial law or write new laws for conquered land. Having few officers to pick from, Kearny had selected Doniphan for legal duties; assigning some Regulars for civil-military relations, Scott also picked a volunteer officer, Major General John A. Quitman of Mississippi, for the difficult job of supervising Mexico City. Citizen-soldiers could handle some assignments without detracting from the careers of Regulars, although Scott knew by the time of the occupation of the capital that the United States was not going to annex Mexico City. Therefore, some aspects of military government were different in Mexico's capital than in New Mexico, a province the United States expected to keep.[49]

In the months to come, the U.S. Army continued to govern the new territories taken from Mexico. Due to the possibilities that Mexicans would rebel, military government would continue. Volunteers had mustered out, leaving Regulars to pick up the duty. In California Lieutenant Colonel Richard Mason became military governor, and Captain Henry W. Halleck contributed to the writing of the first California constitution. California's rapid settlement made it eligible for statehood in 1850, but problems in New Mexico meant that the army remained influential there for years to come. Regular officers such as Major John Washington, Major John Munroe, and Lieutenant Colonel Edwin Sumner drew assignments in New Mexico. In both territories officers operated ad hoc military governments, much like Doniphan's. Although the Regulars made no effort to duplicate Doniphan's procedures, they created governments using civilians—either appointed or elected—who answered to military officers.[50]

In 1846 the highest priority of the U.S. government was winning the war against Mexico, and the fact remained that President Polk's strategic reach stretched American military resources nearly to the breaking point. Polk not only needed soldiers to garrison Santa Fe, patrol New Mexico's hinterlands, and intimidate its Indian tribes. California had to be secured. If the Mexican government would not capitulate, Polk and Scott would consider mounting an expedition against central Mexico, invading at the coastal city of Veracruz. Meanwhile, both General Wool and Colonel Doniphan were expected to strike into the Mexican state of Chihuahua. In each theater of operations, the U.S. forces ran the risk of not meeting the operational goals assigned to them. In no place did the United States have the overwhelming numbers or resources preferred by invading or occupying armies, and nowhere had the Americans gained dominance over the territory they claimed to conquer. Volunteer Lieutenant Christian Kribben recognized the need for stronger American forces in Santa Fe within a few weeks of arriving in Mexico. To prevent the locals from becoming restless, Kribben stated, "Nothing but a strong armed force, sufficient for every contingency that may occur in support of a wise and humane civil government, administered by well known and popular men can insure lasting tranquility here [in Santa Fe]." Lieutenant Elliott agreed, writing that he had "no doubt that there prevails, among many of the New Mexicans, a very bitter feeling towards our Government and people." The same need applied to California for the remainder of 1846 and into 1847. In one of the few times that he failed to anticipate Mexican actions or misjudged their capabilities, Doniphan later concluded that "the services of so large a force [both his regiment and Price's, was] wholly unnecessary in that State [New Mexico]."[51]

Agreeing with Kearny's judgment that New Mexico was secure, given the difficulty of communications across the continent, and having received no new orders to the contrary, Colonel Doniphan decided his next step was to continue the campaign deeper into Mexico. Completing his assignments in New Mexico, Doniphan reorganized his staff and turned over responsibility for command in Santa Fe to Colonel Price. Although delays in negotiating with the Indians would have made it impossible for him to depart Santa Fe before December, the colonel of the 1st Missouri had been disappointed by "the want of provisions" as the regiment prepared to move south. Arrangements for the march to Chihuahua proceeded more slowly than any of the Missourians expected. Meanwhile, sketchy reports and unconfirmed rumors came in about General Wool; no one, officially or unofficially, confirmed the general's whereabouts. One of the Missouri merchants, "Major" Samuel C. Owens, wrote home with a bold prediction: "If Col. Doniphan marches his forces immediately against Chihuahua, he will win laurels to last . . . to all eternity." A Chicago journalist forecast: "It is the intention of Col. Doniphan to press on to Chihuahua with his command and not much resistance is anticipated." Like so many others, Owens and the Chicago writer seemed to discount or dismiss the defensive capabilities of the Mexican military. After weeks of preparations and distractions, Doniphan's first units began riding out of the Santa Fe area on December 14, 1846.[52]

CHAPTER FIVE

The Battle at Brazito

Doniphan now focused his attention on the prospects of leading his regiment in combat, as well as preparing for another overland march across rough country. Such exciting prospects offered the opportunity to contribute to the defense of Texas, support the American claim of the Rio Grande as the southern boundary of Texas, and perhaps gain more territory for the United States. Thus the personal interests of Doniphan and his soldiers matched the larger goals of American strategy. Beginning in late September, after being in Santa Fe for only a month, Doniphan had to devote some of his time to preparing for the next march. His objective was to reinforce the units of Brigadier General John Wool, who was thought to be operating in the state of Chihuahua. Doniphan's expectations of linking up with General Wool at Ciudad Chihuahua would influence the operations of American forces in northern Mexico in the months to come.[1]

In order to assist the colonel in the next phase of his campaign, General Kearny assigned three Regular Army officers to accompany Doniphan's column. It is not clear how precisely Kearny tried to define the roles these officers should play, but they offered technical and professional expertise to the volunteers—an extension of the guidance Regulars had given during the training days at Fort Leavenworth and the march from the fort to Santa Fe. How useful the Regulars would be depended on how skillfully they presented their advice and how willing the volunteers were to take it.

All three Regular advisers were graduates of the Military Academy. A veteran of eleven years in uniform and seconded from Kearny's 1st Dragoons, Captain Philip Thompson joined the Army of the West in Santa Fe on October 26, 1846, four months after his promotion to captain. The colonel and the captain had less than two months to work together before a battle was fought, but they seem to have gotten along well. In his official correspondence Doniphan cordially acknowledged Thompson's valuable assistance. On the other hand, First Lieutenant Charles F. Wooster, an artillery officer with nine years' service, had been assigned as an adviser to Doniphan's regiment on September 25. Their relationship is less clear, perhaps something between chilly and correct rather than cordial. In his own reports, Wooster appeared ready to claim accomplishments that no one else in the expedition mentioned or recognized. The actions and contributions of the youngest adviser, Second Lieutenant Bezaleel W. Armstrong, of the 2nd Dragoons, were given the least notice by participants in the campaign. Therefore, he seems to have played a minor part in the expedition. Most sources, with the exception of Wooster, indicated that Doniphan exercised the responsibilities for making decisions in the field for the regiment: if the Americans won, Doniphan would get the credit; if they were defeated, he would get the blame. He was the colonel.[2]

What made a good nineteenth-century regimental commander? More particularly, how to evaluate a colonel who was a citizen-soldier? Each colonel had much to do with shaping his regiment, especially if he took his job seriously. Furthermore, the colonel's personality also could play a significant part in the regiment's development. A good citizen colonel had to be fair but also solicitous of his men. The best volunteer commanders knew when to be familiar with their soldiers. Many colonels were well acquainted with their men before starting military service, and therefore they had to be selective about when to stand on ceremony. Doniphan was known either personally or by reputation to his soldiers. Any attempt at the puffery of rank would have been out of character, and his unpretentiousness heightened his popularity. One soldier remarked: "His great charm lies in his easy and kind manner. On the march he could not be distinguished from other soldiers, either by dress, or from his conversation." Another volunteer elaborated: Doniphan was the kind of "man who can familiarize himself with the poorest private, by some kind words, or ride among the troops, and make us forget that we were hungry or thirsty, by some pleasant converse, in our long and toilsome march; [moreover, he was] the [kind of] man who can forget his own personal safety in the hour of danger." In other words, Doniphan possessed the combination of physical presence and leadership instincts to lead by example and clearly projected his concern for the well-being of his soldiers.[3]

Successful colonels, including volunteers, possessed certain traits often associated with good military leadership in any age. Among these were courage; learning to evaluate terrain and enemy forces; developing some degree of technical military proficiency and the ability to make use of the advice of others who could impart technical knowledge; using language to inspire soldiers; and finally, sound health or above-average stamina. Doniphan acquired or displayed all of these traits except one. For a large, impressive-looking man, Doniphan had only satisfactory health. He suffered from recurring bouts of bronchitis, and eventually his health became worn down after many weeks on campaign.[4]

To put the 1st Missouri in order for its next march, Doniphan had some administrative changes to make among his regimental staff. Major G. M. Butler had died at Cuvarro in November, and the colonel needed a new adjutant to keep up with the regiment's paperwork and act as liaison with other officers. For the post Doniphan picked Lieutenant James A. DeCourcy from Company G. John Hinton had served as sergeant major but won the election as lieutenant to fill DeCourcy's vacancy in Company G. The colonel chose Private John Palmer of Company A to be the new sergeant major. Palmer held the rank less than a month before resigning, being replaced in early January by John T. Crenshaw, also of Company A.[5]

Needled by "considerable grumbling" among his soldiers, who did not want to continue their invasion of Mexico without taking along cannons, Doniphan decided before he left Santa Fe that some of the St. Louis artillery should accompany the column. The colonel considered it likely to meet some Mexican resistance to the south—rumors spread that the Mexicans had assembled three thousand men near El Paso del Norte. Therefore, he ordered Major Clark to prepare at least one battery of his battalion to follow on after the regiment as soon as it was able. The major responded affirmatively but explained that his remaining horses were "nearly starved to death"; mules already had replaced some of them. It would take several days to gather fresh horses in order to make his guns as "efficient" as possible. Clark promised to leave at "the very earliest moment" but estimated that he would not depart until Christmas. This exchange indicated that Colonel Doniphan decided having artillery on the expedition could be vital to its success. Moreover, having the artillery would bolster the regiment's morale. Displaying the self-confidence evident among the Missourians, one of the artillerymen predicted, "When we get to Doniphan, our force will be [numbered at] 1350, which I think [will be] equal to 3500 Mexicans."[6]

Not wanting to venture farther into Mexico by themselves, many American merchants sought the protection of Doniphan's column as it proceeded toward El Paso. Dozens of wagons and hundreds of merchants traveled with or near the column, the number varying at different points along the journey. Acting on his own, James Magoffin, one of the merchants having considerable experience in the Santa Fe–Chihuahua trade, had left Santa Fe on November 1. Supposing that he might try to relay information about El Paso and the status of Mexican troops back to Doniphan, the Mexican authorities arrested Magoffin and imprisoned him in Chihuahua.[7]

In Chihuahua City, Governor Ángel Trías Álvarez issued a call to arms, proclaiming the need to defend the state of Chihuahua against the "sacrilegious invaders of Mexico" who were advancing toward El Paso. Under the impression that General Kearny still led the invasion, Governor Trías admonished his citizens to "give a lesson to the pirates" and "to chastise the enemy" who would despoil Mexico. He trusted that Mexican soldiers would display the courage and discipline they had inherited from "the blood of the fathers of our Independence," and he assured them that they had the support of the people of the state of Chihuahua.[8]

On December 6, forging ahead of the rest of the regiment to seek information about enemy forces along the Rio Grande and perhaps linking up with General Wool's force, Lieutenant Colonel David D. Mitchell led a separate contingent of one hundred selected volunteers. On November 17 Colonel Sterling Price had authorized that Mitchell be detached from the 2nd Missouri Regiment of Mounted Volunteers to lead the reconnaissance. Born in Virginia in 1806, Mitchell had made his way to Missouri, worked for the American Fur Company, and served as federal superintendent of Indian affairs in St. Louis in the early 1840s.[9]

It seemed likely that Mitchell's special company might have the chance to engage the enemy first, sparking intense interest in the process of selecting the men for Mitchell's unit. Eventually, Doniphan agreed to allow Mitchell to accept ten volunteers from several of the companies, as well as a few men from the artillery batteries. Thus, Mitchell's composite outfit contained some of the hardiest and most adventurous men from the entire expedition. Accompanying Mitchell for a time was Captain Thompson, Doniphan's most trusted Regular adviser, and Captain Thomas Hudson, leader of the Leclede Rangers, the volunteer cavalry from St. Louis, and one of Doniphan's best officers. The new command, incorporating some of the Leclede Rangers and some of the men Kearny had considered taking to California (briefly dubbed the "California Rangers"), now called themselves the "Chihuahua Rangers." Ranging well south of Albuquerque, Mitchell's riders talked to villagers who reported that a strong Mexican force was moving northward from El Paso. Therefore, the Americans were aware that elements of the Mexican army could be on the march northward to meet them, but because similar reports of deployed Mexican units outside of Santa Fe had proved groundless, some of the Americans were naturally skeptical of the

Colonel Doniphan's army marching through the Jornada del Muerto, the "Journey of Death." (From Richardson's *Journal of William H. Richardson* [1848]; courtesy of the Museum of New Mexico, negative no. 171563)

latest raft of rumors. Giving the rumors greater credence than did some of his men, Mitchell decided not to chance an engagement against superior numbers. Thus Mitchell and his company retraced their steps and sought out Doniphan near Valverde.[10]

Meanwhile, with an early snow already indicating the onset of winter, Doniphan and his regiment faced La Jornada del Muerto, variously rendered by the Missourians as "the Journey of the Dead" or "the Journey of Death." Some said the journey was sixty miles, others said ninety; whatever the distance, the terrain was among the most forbidding the regiment crossed during its year of service. At other places along their march through Mexico, Doniphan's volunteers encountered other inhospitable *jornadas*, but this one ranked at the top of the list. The purpose in taking the *jornada* was to reduce the overall marching time south, and perhaps surprise the Mexicans by taking the more difficult route. Stretching from the volunteers' advance camp at Fray Christobal near the town of Valverde to the village of Doña Ana on the Rio Grande, La Jornada del Muerto was notorious among travelers because of the scarcity of water and wood. Therefore, these conditions dictated that once again the regiment would be divided to make the march. The soldiers planned to maintain a moderate pace for about sixteen hours per day until they were through the *jornada*. Doniphan approved this pace in order to traverse the *jornada* as rapidly as possible without wearing out the expedition's animals.[11]

On December 14 Major Gilpin set out with three hundred riders. He was followed by Lieutenant Colonel Congreve Jackson and two hundred men, departing on the sixteenth. On the night of the seventeenth, Mitchell's men found Doniphan's column, in camp at Fray Christobal, just below Valverde, and reported the rumors about Mexican forces awaiting them. The next morning Doniphan proceeded into the *jornada*, accompanied by Mitchell's special company and some four thousand sheep, brought along for food, with the remainder of the regiment strung out behind them.[12]

La Jornada del Muerto was a difficult passage. The temperature at night dropped below freezing, and a cutting wind chilled soldiers to the bone. Several men who had filled canteens with liquor before leaving the Santa Fe area claimed that a nip helped take the edge off of the cold nights. Some saw comrades tilting their canteens at various times during the day as well, and it was likely that several soldiers consumed alcohol daily so long as their private stock lasted. The volunteers had no hardwood for cook fires, but they tried to use substitutes, such as soapweed stalks, which burned quickly, providing brief, flaring light but little heat. For entertainment, while marching along at night soldiers set the stalks alight, and they "would blaze up like a flash of powder, and as quickly extinguish. . . . For miles the road was most brilliantly illuminated by sudden flashes of light, which lasted but for a moment, and then again all was dark." Some of the men ate beef jerky, corn cakes, or other food cooked before the march and fed ears of corn to their mounts. Others rejoiced when they found an isolated pool of water or feeble spring among the rocks and mesquite. More typically, one recalled that "we almost perished for [lack of] water."[13]

The regiment endured three days of the *jornada*'s difficult conditions before arriving near the Rio Grande, about sixty miles from El Paso, at the village of Doña Ana, referred to by one of the Missourians as "a small town, the most poorly constructed of any that" he had ever seen. On the other hand, the area was a well-watered spot with some grass for the animals. Another soldier recalled that Mexican merchants did a brisk business selling various wares to the soldiers and corn for the horses. By the time the entire regiment had assembled near Doña Ana on December 22, some of the Missouri volunteers had set up barricades of logs cut from a few trees along the river, just in case the Mexicans should attack. All of Doniphan's men delighted in having plenty of water and replenishing their supplies, including buying some more sheep to drive along with the column. At night nervous sentinels fired at what they thought were Mexican scouts, and the local residents reiterated the rumor of a substantial Mexican force assembled near El Paso. Doniphan sent Captain John Reid and his company to range ahead.[14]

During the entire march through Mexico, the Missouri volunteers were often rowdy in camp at night—typically "noisy and drinking," as one soldier recalled—and the gathering at Doña Ana was no exception. They must have presented quite a sight. In New Mexico many Missourians had acquired buckskins to replace worn-out shirts or pants; after trading with Mexicans or Indians, others were wearing serapes made from colorful blankets. George Ruxton, a former British officer traveling in North America, chanced upon the volunteers' camp at about that time and related the chaotic scene: "From the appearance no one would have imagined this to be a military encampment. The tents were in a line, but there all uniformity ceased. There were no regulations in force with regard to cleanliness. The camp was strewed [*sic*] with the bones of cattle slaughtered for its supply, and not the slightest attention was paid to keep it clear of other accumulations of filth. The men, unwashed and unshaven, were ragged and dirty, without uniforms and dressed as, and how, they pleased." Ruxton also deplored the fact that, rather than posting sentries, the volunteers "wandered about, listless and sickly looking, or were sitting in groups playing at cards, and swearing and cursing, even at the officers if they interfered to stop it." During the war, American volunteers often neglected to post sentries, but Ruxton's criticisms were justified. He concluded, "The almost total want of discipline was apparent in everything."[15]

As an upper-class Englishman and former British regular, Ruxton gave evidence of mixed emotions about the U.S. Regular Army. He asserted that "the American can never be made a [Regular] soldier; his constitution will not bear the restraint of [Regular Army] discipline, neither will his very mistaken notions about liberty allow him to subject himself to its [discipline's] necessary control." Thus, in America, where individualism reigned, the Regular "service is unpopular." At the same time, he conceded that West Point was "an admirable institution" and its graduates gallant officers, and "that on more than one occasion the steadiness of the small regular force . . . under their command, has saved the [U.S.] army from the most serious disasters." Then Ruxton observed that "the volunteering service, on the other hand, is eagerly sought, on occasions such as the present war with Mexico affords, by young men even of the most respectable classes, as, in this, discipline exists but in name, and they have privileges and rights, such as electing their own officers, &c., which they consider to be more consonant to their ideas of liberty and equality." While he concluded that the Americans' volunteer "system is palpably bad, as they have proved in this war"—

particularly that officers were "afraid to exact . . . either order or discipline" from volunteers—Ruxton finally admitted that "these very men [Doniphan's expedition], however, were full of fight as gamecocks." Despite their rowdiness and want of discipline, the noisy Missourians displayed more than empty bravado.[16]

Giving evidence of great confidence and high morale, and propelled by its success, the regiment resumed its march southward. Doniphan divided his command into two main segments, with some merchants accompanying each one. On December 23 the reconnaissance company under Captain Reid spotted Mexican scouts and killed two of them. This encounter indicated that the enemy was probably shadowing the column. Forewarned, Doniphan and his officers knew that a Mexican force could be nearby.[17]

Doniphan's first battle as an independent regimental commander came only about twenty-five miles short of the objective of his southward march—El Paso del Norte. Although the Missouri regiment had earlier marched across Mexican lands, it is important to recall that the continuation of Doniphan's expedition down the Rio Grande was one of several United States invasions of Mexico. The Missourians knew that on May 8–9 at Palo Alto and Resaca de la Palma, Brigadier General Zachary Taylor had won American victories to open the war. Subsequently, although the Missourians may not have known of Taylor's exact objectives, the general moved against Monterrey. Doniphan knew, however, that Brigadier General John E. Wool was supposed to be conducting operations in the vicinity of the Mexican towns of Monclova and Parras in the fall. Kearny had marched toward California, planning to coordinate with other U.S. land and naval forces attacking California in the winter of 1846–1847. Although not precisely coordinated, these invasions developed into a cordon offensive, sequential or almost simultaneous aggressive actions, stretching the Mexicans' defenses and resources and making it difficult for them to respond to each new incursion.

As Doniphan's regiment drew closer to El Paso del Norte, the colonel knew that the possibility of encountering Mexican defenders increased. Moving up from El Paso del Norte to meet this latest American invasion, Lieutenant Colonel Antonio Ponce de León[18] commanded Mexican forces numbering between eleven hundred and thirteen hundred. Colonel León sent out scouts to obtain information about the Missouri volunteers. In order not to deplete water, wood, and forage, Doniphan had dispersed his regiment in a long line of march. The volunteers displayed a relaxed attitude, appearing to devote more attention to chasing stray horses than watching for the enemy. A Mexican account claimed that the Americans moved with a lack of security, "which permitted Ponce to reconnoitre them to his satisfaction, and unobserved." However, Missouri scouts rode ahead of their column, and on Christmas Eve pickets killed two Mexican soldiers near the American camp, alerting the invaders that enemy forces were nearby. Furthermore, one of Doniphan's soldiers recollected that the colonel and other officers took their situation seriously enough to conduct a thorough inspection of the entire regiment on December 24, in case it should encounter Mexican troops.[19]

On December 25, after advancing about eighteen miles, Doniphan called a halt around 2:00 P.M. at a place called "Brazito," a "little arm" or old channel of the Rio Grande. The spot had good water and afforded a likely place to consolidate the regiment. Lieutenant Colonel Jackson and about half of the regiment were still some miles behind Doniphan's contingent. While some soldiers searched for firewood or hunted for rabbits, others began enjoying the holiday afternoon. Here and there card games began on spread blankets, and the colonel himself sat down to play a few hands of three-card loo, with the winner to receive a handsome stray horse thought to belong to a Mexican officer. Other soldiers dispersed in all directions looking for wood. Not wanting to be caught completely unaware, the colonel sent a few mounted scouts ahead of the column, although he neither posted sentinels outside of camp nor designated a company on alert in case the enemy should unexpectedly appear. Furthermore, he allowed his exuberant soldiers to fire off their rifles in honor of Christmas Day. Thus, Doniphan could be criticized for failing to maintain attention to camp security. One of his lieutenants may have overstated when he later exclaimed that "we were completely surprised."[20]

Colonel León ordered his soldiers to deploy into battle formation in an open area, "broken by small hills, resembling a potato patch . . . covered with thorn and other bushes." As they moved toward the Missourians' camp, the Mexicans created a considerable dust cloud. A volunteer officer—perhaps it was Major William Gilpin—drew Doniphan's attention to the dust, and they decided it must be the enemy. Telling his fellows they would have to resume the game later, "the colonel quickly sprang to his feet, threw down his cards, [and] grasped his sabre." Momentarily, scouts galloped into the campsite yelling that they had seen Mexican soldiers in combat formations.[21]

Doniphan began shouting a series of orders to prepare for his first battle. Other officers called to their men: "Fall into line!" "Get your horses!" "Throw away your wood!" "To arms, to arms!" Only about half of the regiment (around five hundred men) was present, with none of its supporting artillery, and the disorderly American camp was chaotic. Bugle notes sounded to rally the Missourians some distance from the camp. Although he could have tried to withdraw and consolidate his regiment at another location, Doniphan gave no indication of considering retreat. His men rushed helter-skelter, dropping firewood, grabbing their rifles, and forming into some semblance of a line of battle. Most were going to fight dismounted, but Captain Reid had assembled fewer than twenty mounted men and held them in readiness. Doniphan's decision to give battle against an enemy of undetermined strength and without his full regiment present is revealing. Doniphan and his men possessed unbounded self-assurance. As one American recalled, "Coolness and self-confidence pervaded our ranks. Laughing, talking, and jesting were common" along the Missourians' line of battle. They had received numerous reports of local Mexican militias preparing to fight at defenses in the vicinity of Santa Fe, but enemy resistance in New Mexico had failed to materialize. Aggressiveness combined with curiosity about their enemy made the Missourians eager to take the measure of the menacing Mexican force, whose composition, weapons, and leadership they did not know. Notwithstanding the lack of information about the enemy, a few hours earlier Lieutenant Gibson stated, "Our men are in fine spirits and confidently expect to be the victors."[22]

Starting from their own assembly point, distant about one-half mile, the Mexicans marched closer and the Americans noticed their impressive array. Infantry units, supported by a cannon, anchored the center of the Mexican line. Cavalry squadrons ranged on either wing. One Missouri soldier said that the Mexicans "drew up in good order. . . . Their cavalry [was] in bright scarlet coats with . . . snow white belts, carrying polished sabres and carbines and long lances, with red and green pennons." Another Missourian noted the "long, bold, beautiful front of the enemy," a sight that made his "blood flow chill." Dazzled, he watched "as they came abreast. Their beautiful steeds . . . prancing and tossing their heads to the sound of the bugles, the riders erect and firm in their seats, their red coats, high brazen helmets plumed with bear skin, and each armed with a carbine, lance, holsters, and sabre, were indeed worthy of admiration." A third volunteer was impressed by the enemy's "gallant and imposing appearance." As the Mexican battle line approached, an American lieutenant said that "their charge was a handsome one." Such anecdotes indicate that the U.S. soldiers were aware of their enemy's apparent quality and use of tactical drill; the key Mexican units were regulars, not rancheros or lightly armed militia.[23]

Before the combat came a kind of action deemed by some dramatic and by others comic-opera. In an effort to intimidate the Americans, Colonel León sent out a staff officer, Lieutenant Manuel Lara, riding a horse flecked with foam. Lara carried a distinctive swallow-tailed Black Flag, decorated with two skulls and sets of crossbones on one side, and the words "Libertad o' Muerte" (Liberty or Death) on the other. The lieutenant demanded that Doniphan discuss surrender or face battle with no quarter asked or given. Thomas Caldwell, a merchant

"MEXICAN LANCER." (From Frost, *History of Mexico and Its Wars* [1882]; courtesy of the Museum of New Mexico, negative no. 171107)

fluent in Spanish who acted as interpreter on Doniphan's behalf, met Lieutenant Lara less than one hundred yards from the American line. Caldwell rejected the cavalryman's demand that Doniphan present himself for parley or surrender.

"We shall break your ranks and take him," shouted Lieutenant Lara.

"Come and take him," Caldwell barked back, undaunted. "Charge and be damned."

"A curse upon you; prepare for a charge. We give no quarter and ask none," yelled Lara as he waved the Black Flag for emphasis. "There is no mercy for you and you will receive none." In conclusion, Lara warned, "Damned be he who first cries hold, enough."

Caldwell galloped back to the assembling American volunteers and "went up and down the line explaining to the men what was meant by a Black or Pirates [*sic*] Flag and screaming at the top of his voice, hurra [*sic*] for the American Stars and Stripes." Caldwell's words confirmed what most of the Missourians had already figured out: the gesture of waving a black flag emblazoned with skulls and bones meant that it would be a fight to the death.[24]

This display of Mexican bravado and the verbal exchange between Caldwell and Lara gave the Americans valuable time to prepare for the fight. The Regulars, especially Captain Thompson, assisted Doniphan by forming the volunteers into line of battle, preparing to fight on foot. This took about twenty minutes, according to one Missouri officer. Meanwhile, Doniphan calculated his options.[25]

Surveying the enemy's formidable deployment, Doniphan rejected launching a precipitate attack. Although it would call for his volunteers to show remarkable discipline under the pressure of their first engagement, the colonel decided to risk trying a *ruse de guerre* on his right wing. Most of the Mexican infantrymen carried old British Brown Bess muskets, purchased from suppliers in Europe. The Brown Bess was a single-shot, muzzle-loading, smoothbore weapon with an effective range of about fifty or sixty yards. After the Mexicans fired an ineffective volley some four hundred yards away, Doniphan responded by directing some of his men to lie down or kneel in the tall grass, emphatically imposing a strict order on everyone not to shoot back. Colonel León recounted later that "four [soldiers] in the enemy's second line were seen to fall, besides various others among the enemy, who died in the hail of fire so well sustained by the [Mexican] infantry and sections of the cavalry." After another Mexican volley, delivered at about three hundred yards, more Americans appeared to go down; actually, they responded once again to Doniphan's direction. Delivering volleys demonstrated that the Mexican units had undergone some formal training and tactical drill, but firing at such ranges made it unlikely that the Mexican Brown Bess muskets would cause any casualties among the Missourians. A third Mexican volley crashed out at a range of about two hundred yards, and other Americans seemed to be killed or wounded. Then the Mexicans cheered and surged forward, thinking that their musket shots had made casualties of many of the Americans.[26]

Doniphan wanted his men to shoot back when the Mexicans closed inside one hundred yards, a range in which their rifles would be deadly accurate. One of the Missourians, Private Marcellus Edwards, recalled how hard it was for them to withhold their fire. Continuing to show surprising discipline, the American volunteers now understood their colonel's plan and obeyed his orders, even as some agreed that they had shot game at a greater distance than the enemy line moving toward them. Drawing upon his oratorical skills, the colonel walked among his soldiers, asking them to "remember Okeechobee," the 1837 battle during the Second Seminole War in Florida in which Missouri soldiers had broken and run from the field. Doniphan wanted to remove that stain from their state's military record. "Reserve your fire" until the order, Doniphan reiterated.[27]

As the Mexicans advanced, Doniphan, conferring with Captain Thompson, determined that the attack might envelop the American line. Indeed, giving further evidence of his units' time on the drill field, León had them moving in remarkable concert in the center and on each flank. Therefore, Doniphan ordered an "elbow" to be extended in his battle line, bending or "refusing" the left wing of his formation away from the Mexicans, who, "supposing [the Americans] to be retreating, . . . increased their speed and shouted *Bueno! Bueno!*" and other huzzahs. Not knowing how much longer his men could restrain themselves, Doniphan yelled for them to stand and shoot. Perhaps two hundred riflemen responded at once to the colonel's order. The heavy American volley sent Mexican horses and riders "tumbling in all directions," as well as killing or wounding dozens of Mexican infantrymen. The attacking Mexicans suffered such serious casualties that their line of infantry visibly "faltered."[28]

Almost simultaneously, León's lancers attempted to ride around the American left flank as other infantry units moved to engage the American right flank. Receiving a deadly volley from the Americans, the Mexican infantry sheared off to their right and sought out what appeared to be the vulnerable American supply wagons. The Missourians kept up a sharp fire into the milling Mexicans, who then met "a very warm reception" from the traders' wagons. Major Gilpin had his men ready and later recalled that "our whole line delivered a sheet of fire and charged to the front." Suffering noticeable losses among their regular units, the Mexican line of battle fragmented. Almost simultaneously, two other factors undermined León's command and control of his units. León himself was wounded and rode off the field, and a Mexican "trumpet call wrongly interpreted" confused some Mexican soldiers, who began to withdraw from the fight. Indeed, León recounted his disgust that "some of the close volleys of the enemy . . . at the most critical moment of the attack, completely disorganized the [Mexican] cavalry which turned tail with incredible haste, scattering themselves . . . in all directions."[29]

At about that time, in a "charge . . . gallantly made," Captain John Reid led a sortie of fourteen mounted soldiers with the objective of capturing a Mexican cannon. The piece had fired several times, sending what seemed like "a bushel of copper ore [projectiles]" flying overhead, but remarkably those shots had not caused any casualties among the Americans. Mexican soldiers blocked Reid's path to the gun. One fired a carbine, and its bullet narrowly missed the captain,

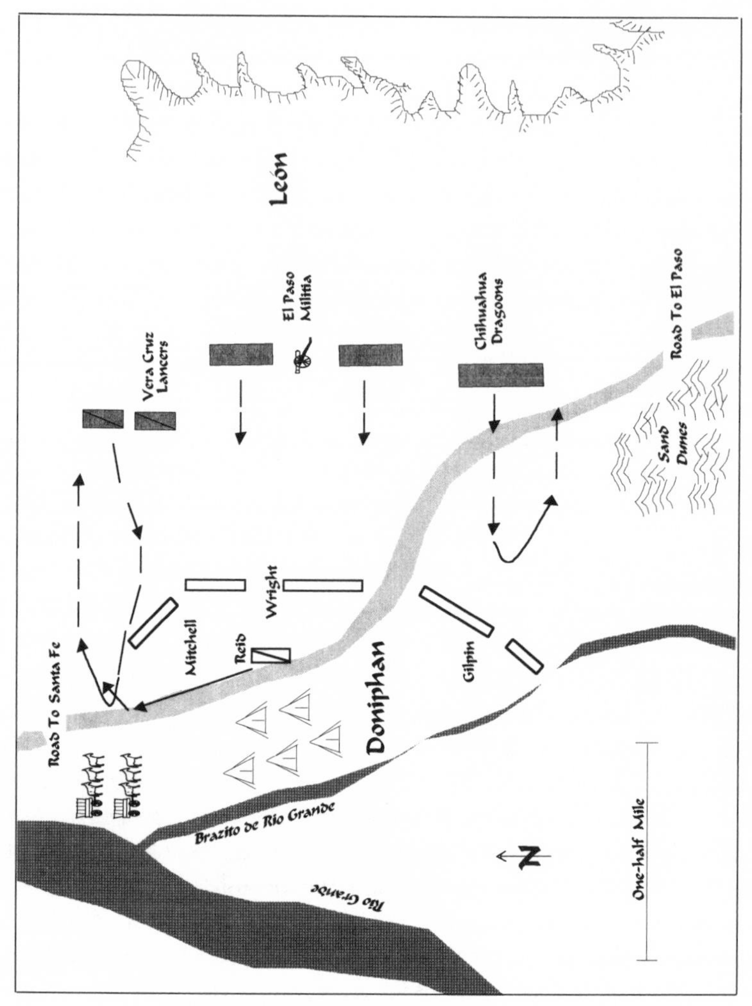

Battle of Brazito, December 25, 1846. (T. T. Smith, 1998)

who slashed at his opponent with a saber but missed; another Missourian shot the soldier dead. Reid and his men rushed the gun and drove off its crew. The losses suffered from the Missourians' gunfire, the realization that their enemy was not breaking, and Captain Reid's unexpected attack all contributed to the retreat of León's soldiers. Gathering additional riders, Reid led an ad hoc group of twenty horsemen in a pursuit for four miles. He and Major Gilpin found "the plain strewed [*sic*] far and wide with lances, arms, provisions, and dead and wounded men and horses." Behind them the "shouts & huzzas . . . echoed from one end of [the Missourians'] line to the other." The engagement had lasted less than an hour.[30]

American estimates of Mexican losses at Brazito varied from 30 to 63 killed, and between 150 and 172 wounded, and 15 or more unwounded prisoners, bringing the casualties to between 15 and 20 percent of the total force available, but higher if calculated as a percentage of the force engaged, which was around eight hundred. Colonel León, on the other hand, recorded his losses as only eleven killed, seventeen wounded, and no mention of missing. By the Americans' own count, their losses were only seven wounded, although the Mexican commander contended that his force must have inflicted casualties on the Americans "equal to ours—perhaps greater" to those his units had suffered, that is, a total of twenty-eight. The Mexicans probably suffered high casualties and also lost quantities of valuable supplies. These included a cannon, dozens of muskets with powder and shot, along with perhaps three hundred horses, providing the Americans with remounts for the next stage of their campaign. Furthermore, the Missourians promptly drank from casks of captured wine, ate quantities of bread and other foods the enemy had prepared, and smoked tobacco and cigarillos they left behind. The Americans also picked up pieces of uniforms, a few muskets, and other discarded items of equipment.[31]

For a modest engagement, Brazito received considerable attention in United States newspapers. The battle, followed by newspaper coverage of it, was a first step toward widespread national recognition for Colonel Doniphan. The New Orleans *Daily Delta* led the coverage with a full column report, complimenting the marksmanship of the Missourians and concluding that Doniphan intended to forge ahead into Chihuahua. The Cincinnati *Daily Enquirer* printed a report by one of Doniphan's officers under the banners "Battle Near El Paso!! The Americans Victorious!!" The Charleston *Mercury* allocated space for three different reports about Brazito during the month of March. The New York *Herald* set aside three-fourths of a column and called the battle a "Brilliant Affair." Numerous other newspapers around the nation offered summaries of the battle, and several described versions of the Black Flag incident.[32]

Missouri newspapers naturally gave Brazito detailed notice. The St. Louis *Republican* and the Fayette *Boon's Lick Times* both called the battle a "Glorious Victory!!" and indicated that it took place north of El Paso in New Mexico. Also using the "Glorious Victory!" headline with their reports were the Columbia *Statesman* and the Jefferson City *Inquirer*. The Springfield *Advertiser* devoted more than a column to the battle, and the St. Louis *Weekly Reveille* printed official correspondence. Naturally, the Liberty *Weekly Tribune* surpassed the state's other papers in its attention, calling the battle a "Christmas frolic" and concluding with a sectional twist that "the Western [*sic*] troops do not intend to be behind their comrades of the South."[33]

Lieutenant Roswell S. Ripley, a contemporary Regular Army officer, seldom gave volunteers or the Doniphan expedition much credit. In his book, *The War with Mexico,* Ripley took a negative view of both Doniphan's brand of leadership and the performance of the Missouri volunteers. The lieutenant demonstrated that they had been taken by surprise at Brazito. Not acknowledging the assistance rendered by Captain Thompson and the other Regulars, Ripley contended that Doniphan's companies had assembled in "uncouth formations" and only overcame with bravery what "want of method," that is, Regular leadership and tactical drill, should have provided. Ripley concluded his evaluation by asserting, "Of skill there was little demonstrated on either side," a view dismissing the commendable tactical maneuvers conducted by Colonel León's units and the Missourians' remarkable effort to hold their fire until Doniphan's order to shoot.[34]

Beyond Ripley's carping, and important for the broader picture of the war, it is useful to speculate how a Mexican victory at the Battle of Brazito had the potential to produce some significant consequences. First, in a conflict with so few bright spots for Mexican arms, a victory for the Mexicans at Brazito would have provided a needed boost in morale in northern Mexico and also potentially for Mexicans nationally. Second, if the Mexicans had won at Brazito they would have deflected the American invaders, possibly taking some of them prisoner or persuading the rest to retreat to Santa Fe. Depending on American losses of men, supplies, and wagons, a Mexican pursuit held out the prospect for defeat in detail for Doniphan's regiment. Indeed, Private John Hughes concluded that for the Missourians "defeat would have been ruinous." Furthermore, news of Doniphan's defeat might have inspired greater support for the Taos Revolt, which began on January 19, 1847, when the American governor, Charles Bent, was killed. A victorious Mexican army marching on Santa Fe could have had a galvanizing effect on Mexicans and perhaps a demoralizing effect on the Americans.[35]

As it was, Doniphan's victory contributed to the American war effort. It drove back a Mexican force numbering more than one thousand soldiers and defeated it so badly that it made no effort to defend El Paso del Norte. Scattered and disorganized, the remnants of the Mexican army retreated south to Chihuahua City, opening the way for Doniphan to continue his campaign, threatening another crossing of the Rio Grande, and posing a threat to Chihuahua City. Moreover, the American victory helped to affirm the United States' hold on New Mexico, despite a revolt by Mexicans in Taos. A force of uniformed Mexican regulars moving north would have been a serious threat to Colonel Sterling Price's 2nd Missouri Regiment. Finally, Brazito did not bring immediate glory to Doniphan and his men, but it lent momentum to their invasion. Winning the battle also gave the colonel important practical experience as a combat commander and strengthened the confidence of his volunteers.

Doniphan saw to it that all useful captured equipment and supplies taken from the Brazito battlefield were distributed among the expedition's wagons. Packing away their souvenirs and booty, the Missouri volunteers looked ahead to the next important landmark. Only a few miles ahead was El Paso del Norte, a natural gateway into the interior of Mexico.

CHAPTER SIX

"In the Midst of the Enemy's Country"

Doniphan woke up his regiment at first light on December 27 and ordered it to continue the invasion, moving against El Paso del Norte. Lieutenant Colonel Mitchell rode out ahead with some scouts. The excitement of the Brazito was still fresh in the Missourians' minds when, about six miles outside of El Paso, the colonel ordered the regiment to deploy into line of battle, preparing to engage what appeared to be a Mexican force sent out to defend the city. Then Doniphan saw that one of the Mexicans was waving a white flag, but he viewed the banner skeptically, worried that it might be a trick to lull the Americans into letting down their guard. Instead of soldiers the Mexicans proved to be a civic "deputation" of public officials and businessmen, out from El Paso to greet the American column. Leaders of the group offered Doniphan and Mitchell some local wine and implored "that their property might remain unmolested." At the same time they assured the American invaders "of the tranquil and friendly disposition of the inhabitants" of El Paso. Doniphan responded that he offered the residents of the city "liberty and protection" of U.S. military forces. Private John Hughes reported that the deputies "escorted us into the city." This cordial welcome somewhat eased the concerns of the regiment about the kind of reception it would receive in El Paso, but the Americans never forgot their status as invaders and an occupying force.[1]

The Missourians must have smiled as "the people came from their houses giving [them] apples, pears, [and] grapes." Soon the soldiers had their hands and pockets full of fruit. Other Mexicans followed the invaders to their camps, offering various edibles for sale or barter; apples went ten for three cents. In the town's markets the Americans saw plenty of corn, one of the most important staples for men and beasts, and more fruits, including melons, quinces, and dried peaches, were available. The bounty of foods, especially in December, was a welcome sight to the Americans. One observer called El Paso "an oasis in the desert," and a soldier believed that it must be "the garden spot of Mexico." Promptly confirming the arrival of a new, if temporary, regime, Doniphan ordered a soldier to run up the U.S. flag from a spire of a church near El Paso's central plaza.[2]

It was not clear how long the regiment would be in El Paso, a city with a population of around ten thousand, but the American soldiers immediately were on the lookout for diversions and any comforts they could find. One of the infantry officers who had remained with the regiment, Lieutenant George Gibson, may have overstated, but in his view Doniphan's "army was composed of men of a restless and roving disposition and the little discipline which prevailed was totally insufficient to prevent rioting and dissipation." Doniphan had to adjudicate complaints and hear accusations from the local populace, including cases of theft and assault. Knowing the potential for his volunteers' unruly behavior, Doniphan ordered the Mexicans not to sell alcoholic beverages to his soldiers and decided that most of his companies would camp away from the populace, some on the western edge of the town, others below the plaza. On the west, Private Jacob Robinson pitched his tent in "an old corn field amidst plenty of burrs and sand." Other camping spots had more sand than vegetation, and the sand, swirling constantly, aggravated the soldiers. Wolves prowled near the camps and maintained a nightly "dolorous serenade."[3]

Of course, in a city the size of El Paso all sorts of opportunities opened for the rowdy Missouri volunteers to engage in games of chance and look for alcoholic beverages. They seemed to find gamblers on every street corner, tossing dice, dealing cards, and offering other forms of betting, accepting money or items of value for the wagers. According to Lieutenant Gibson, eventually "Colonel Doniphan issued an order to prohibit it [gambling] on the street." Many of the soldiers wanted wine and liquor and were not interested in having just a drink or two but wanted to "find [any] means of getting drunk." One soldier noticed with joy that "El Paso is in fact an extensive vineyard," and the harvest of grapes in the area produced local wines that two other volunteers rated as "excellent." In this case, excellence may have involved both the wide availability and the price, for wine was only one dollar a gallon. Alcoholic beverages, including beer, were cheap and ubiquitous.[4]

Of course, the volunteers also scrutinized the townspeople and caught glimpses of young women as they rode through El Paso or went into town on errands. Lieutenant Gibson concluded that "both the men and women present a neater appearance and have more refinement [than the residents of Santa Fe]." Many of the women kept their faces hidden behind veils, arousing at least the curiosity of the Missourians. Of course, they sought public or private meetings with women. Gibson paid court to one of the young ladies, "a pretty girl with dark eyes, black hair, and a brunette complexion, and, like all women in the country, has a fine form and pretty hands and feet." Gibson was rewarded by receiving an invitation to her home, and he brought gifts of tobacco for his host, the girl's brother, and some beads for the young lady. Another soldier found the interior of the home he visited to be a comfortable domicile with a charming patio and garden, quite unlike what the exterior's "dismal doors" might have promised.[5]

A lady's charms were tempting, but practical soldiers wanted to eat three times a day, and beef turned out to be a rare commodity in El Paso. Food on a typical day for the soldiers consisted of local stringy mutton and flour tortillas, supplemented by some plentiful local fruit, served with weak coffee. Receiving any food or fodder from army sources in Santa Fe was unlikely. Doniphan's officers cataloged the available food in El Paso, finding a considerable quantity of stored corn, some of it supplied to the expedition by an El Paso wine merchant. The colonel planned for other necessities, such as wheat, to be purchased on consignment. Doniphan arranged to have some of his men repair and reopen a local mill to grind flour from local wheat, though all the soldiers expressed their dissatisfaction with the low quality of those products. The invaders relied on the local economy for other necessities, including firewood. For example, Private Frank Edwards explained that he and the members of his mess arranged for a Mexican woodcutter to bring them wagon loads of wood each week. Following negotiations with ranchers, the Missourians improved their rations by buying local cattle. The cooperation of the El Pasoans was crucial to the sustenance of the Doniphan Expedition.[6]

The colonel also looked for help from the dozens of merchants who traveled with the expedition. Around three hundred civilians were transporting goods valued by Lieutenant Gibson at one million dollars, and few of them expressed any interest in going on alone. Most were willing to continue their symbiotic relationship with the regiment: it protected them, and they sold goods and lent money to the soldiers. Doniphan also saw the merchants' assorted supplies as additional resources for the regiment. The specie was instrumental to Doniphan's ability to purchase food and fodder on the local economy. Immediately upon reaching El Paso, the traders had set up displays of their wares in the main plaza. The local populace browsed and bought from the Americans, despite the tensions of war. After all, some of these same merchants had visited El Paso in the past, and would likely do so again in the future. Doniphan also saw the goods owned by the traders as a prize that could greatly benefit the enemy, if the wagon trains were captured intact.[7]

The Americans never rejected the possibility during the time they were in El Paso that a Mexican force from Chihuahua might charge out of the desert, launching a counterattack. Therefore, Doniphan ordered his companies to carry out daily tactical drill practice. The drills kept the soldiers occupied and reminded them of the prospect of more combat, but when called upon to "parade [they presented] a ludicrous sight." There had been no resupply from the United States, and many of the men had not had uniforms even at the beginning of the campaign. By the time they reached El Paso, it was an understatement for Private Frank Edwards to say that their clothes "had seen pretty severe service." He continued: "In a whole company, no two pair of pantaloons were of the same hue; . . . red flannel or checked shirt[s] made up the 'uniform.'" Lieutenant Gibson noticed that several soldiers sported bits and pieces of Mexican uniforms picked up at Brazito, making souvenirs do a practical turn. Edwards concluded, "If General Taylor could boast of two R's, 'Rough and Ready,' we felt that we were fully entitled to three, Rough, Ready and Ragged."[8]

Colonel Doniphan also initiated a search for any Mexican military supplies and reconsidered camp assignments for his soldiers. The searches uncovered quite a cache, including twenty thousand pounds of gunpowder, four cannons, cannon cartridges, five hundred muskets, musket balls, and four hundred lances. The colonel intended to prevent any chance that El Paso's residents would be able to use hidden weapons to assault his regiment, or to cooperate with any Mexican military force from Chihuahua that might attempt to retake the city. After being in El Paso only a few days, on January 1, 1847, a sentry called out that a cloud of dust might indicate an advancing Mexican force. Responding to his call, buglers sounded assembly and the regiment formed battle lines. Hearing the bugles in his quarters near the plaza, Doniphan "came running on foot with his holster-pistols swung across his left arm, having his sword drawn in his right hand." It was a "*false alarm*." Cautious, the colonel kept the regiment under arms for most of the morning. The volunteers were glad to get the call to stand down; even better news, most of the companies could leave the sandy fields and move into the city to receive assignments for quarters. The colonel arranged for two commodious structures just off the main plaza to serve as barracks, housing several companies, as well as a smaller building, actually a wing of the city jail, for another contingent. On January 2 the commander of Company E, Captain John Stevenson, leading one hundred men who for various reasons had been left behind at Albuquerque, rode into El Paso. A pleasant surprise: several commissary wagons accompanied Stevenson, improving Doniphan's supplies.[9]

Although some of the Missouri volunteers found El Paso "picturesque" and the "scenery . . . grand," during each passing week in the city illnesses became more widespread among the troops. They dreaded the diseases but also expressed little faith in their physicians. Private Marcellus Edwards charged that "hospital affairs are conducted scandalously. There is not a surgeon or steward who can much more than determine calomel from quinine, and not one who would leave the card table to attend the deathbed of his patient." Typhoid became a serious problem and a real threat to the health of the expedition. After Private John Leland of Howard County died of typhoid on January 16, his fellows gave him an elaborate funeral "with martial honors." Among Leland's belongings, soldiers found some letters from his mother. Private Edwards summarized their content, noting Mrs. Leland had written that "she would willingly sacrifice him [her son] at the cannon's mouth" rather than have him slink home as a deserter. Now her son had been taken not by Mexican gunfire but by a kind of enemy the soldiers were powerless to fight. In the next few days Private James Madison and Private Jordan Hackley of Howard County fell to the same disease, and pleurisy killed Private John Dyer of Lafayette County. Such losses heightened the attention of some soldiers to their faith, while others sought out more worldly pleasures knowing that they, too, might be felled by such unpredictable enemies.[10]

Although newspapers such as the New York *Herald* and Hartford *Weekly Times* gladly announced "COL. DONIPHAN IN POSSESSION OF EL PASO," other Americans expressed concern about the Missouri volunteers being trapped inside Mexico. A Detroit paper made the fullest presentation of this opinion. Even after it explained that the Missourians had reached El Paso safely, the Detroit *Free Press* postulated that "the representations made to Col. Doniphan that Chihuahua would be an easy conquest were evidently intended as delusions to entrap him, and beget a spirit of security and lead him far off into the interior where he might be entirely cut off." Adding to this theme, the Cincinnati *Daily Commercial* seemed worried that a "weak and imbecile [Polk] administration" may have sent Doniphan and his regiment to disaster. Meanwhile, while Doniphan's volunteers continued to have a high level of confidence, back on the home front in Missouri some civilians expressed doubts and concerns. For example, in St. Louis James Glasgow, a merchant familiar with the Santa Fe Trail, worried about his fellow Missourians. Glasgow opined that he "would not be at all surprised to hear of Doniphan's capture as they [the volunteers] seem to be entirely ignorant of passing events in the other parts of Mexico." Along a similar line, a writer in Independence postulated that Mexicans could cut off and surround Doniphan and his regiment. Another Missourian had "foreboding that when he [Doniphan] meets with an opportunity to have one [a battle], he will be out numbered and whiped [*sic*]."[11]

To reinforce his column, on the day after the battle at Brazito, Doniphan added a controversial figure to his expedition. James Kirker, about fifty years of age when he met Colonel Doniphan, had a checkered reputation as scout, hunter, and mule skinner. An Irishman sunburned a deep, leathery brown after twenty years in the Trans-Mississippi, Kirker spoke fluent Spanish and had occupied himself in American territory and in Mexico using legitimate and questionable employments since the 1820s. A cloud of evil seemed to cling to Kirker and anyone who rode with him; several Shawnee and Delaware Indians accompanied Kirker, and they were a tough-looking lot. It was common knowledge among Mexicans and Americans that Kirker was a scalp hunter, killing Apaches—men, women, and children—and selling their scalps for bounty money awarded by Mexican governors of Chihuahua and New Mexico. In December 1846 Doniphan and Kirker became allies of convenience; the colonel never seemed to quite trust the scout, even if he was an Irishman. For reasons of his own, possibly dissatisfied about not being paid bounties owed to him by Mexican governors or seeking better opportunities to strike at the Apaches, Kirker attached himself to the Doniphan Expedition. In the weeks to come, Doniphan appreciated the valuable information Kirker provided about the terrain between El Paso and Chihuahua City as well as his opinions about the Mexican forces that the regiment would likely encounter.[12]

Doniphan would have been pleased if Kirker could have provided him with any reliable information concerning the whereabouts of General Wool, along with descriptions of the Mexican forces to the south. After questioning business and civic leaders, the colonel told his officers that he "was now pretty well convinced that Gen. Wool has not been near Chihuahua, nor will not be there" if or when the Missourians continued their campaign south. Doniphan expected to remain on his own for the near future and might not come under the command of a senior Regular army officer for several weeks. Reaching these conclusions carried multiple meanings for Doniphan. Certainly, he needed any news he could get about Mexican forces in Chihuahua. The colonel was struck by the repetition of one rumor concerning the Mexican defense of Carrizal, described as "a fortified place some distance on this side of Chihuahua." It turned out to be about ninety miles south of El Paso.[13]

Of course, the Mexican authorities wanted details about the American invaders, and they received them from one of the leading public figures in El Paso. A Catholic priest, Father Ramón Ortiz, arranged for messengers to take information about the Americans to Chihuahua. Suspicious of his actions, Doniphan had the priest watched. If they accepted Ortiz's messages at face value, Mexican military leaders probably gained an accurate estimate of the invading force. In order to stop such transfer of intelligence, Doniphan had Ortiz arrested and planned to take him as a hostage along with the column to Chihuahua.[14]

In the middle of January Doniphan again had to make command decisions. He had several options. First, and easiest, was to remain camped in El Paso. A Missouri merchant, M. L. Kritter, expressed his hope that Doniphan would elect to do that.[15] Holding El Paso for three or four months would consume most of the time remaining on the one-year enlistments for the colonel and his regiment. Second, Doniphan could return to Santa Fe, an option that had little to make it attractive. Although consolidating American control over New Mexico was one of President Polk's main strategic objectives of the war, returning to Santa Fe appeared to offer only routine duties, reinforcing the American garrison, and patrolling the Navajo country. Nothing indicated to Doniphan that embers of enemy resistance still flickered in New Mexico. A third, more appealing, option beckoned. The colonel could proceed southward toward Chihuahua, along the lines he already indicated by requesting artillery support even before the battle at Brazito.

As an independent commander, Doniphan interpreted his orders to mean that advancing into the province of Chihuahua was his ultimate goal, though, as Private Hughes remarked, the orders called for the colonel "merely to *report* to Gen. Wool at that place, not to *invade* the State." It was impossible now not to do one without the other. As far as Doniphan knew, Wool had not captured the city, which had been the general's objective in America's offensive plans. Therefore, taking the third option meant maintaining the initiative and continuing the American offensive. It also opened possibilities for keeping the enemy off balance and placing additional Mexican territory under American control. Marching into the province of Chihuahua, however, was also Doniphan's most risky choice. He could not be sure of Mexican military strength there or of enemy defenses at the state's capital city. Moreover, other factors presented potential problems for the regiment: difficult terrain, bad weather, unreliable availability of water, and the possibility of Indian attacks all had to be considered. Doniphan's regiment had already crossed La Jornada del Muerto, some of the driest terrain in North America. Between El Paso and Chihuahua City lay 250 more miles of desert. Although Doniphan may not have known it, another of Napoleon Bonaparte's maxims could be applied to the Missourian's situation: "The frontiers of nations are either large rivers, or chains of mountains, or deserts. Of all these obstacles to the march of an army, deserts are the most difficult to surmount."[16]

Doniphan reached his decision, ordering his men to prepare to march to Chihuahua. The colonel chose the most aggressive of the three options open to him, though he still did not know the whereabouts of General Wool or the outcome of the Taos Revolt. Before he moved, he would have some of Clark's artillery. According to letters from the major and a personal report from Mr. Ross, one of the army sutlers from Santa Fe, Doniphan knew it would be from ten days to three weeks before he could expect the guns to arrive in El Paso. The colonel called in Private Tom Forsyth, dispatching him back to Santa Fe, and urging that the cannons be hurried along. By taking the option that appeared to have the most opportunity for him, Doniphan also chose the way to inflict the greatest damage on the enemy.[17]

American newspapers carried numerous reports of Doniphan waiting in El Paso for the artillery, so his situation was not secret information to either Americans or Mexicans. Given the many opportunities for conversations between the Missouri volunteers and the residents of El Paso, it was likely that the Mexicans also knew Doniphan had made his decision to march south and was only waiting for reinforcements. Meanwhile, the colonel sought more information about potential enemy forces, and on January 26 he sent Captain Hudson and a detachment of "Chihuahua Rangers" on a patrol, riding twenty miles below El Paso. The patrol returned the next evening, reporting that it had seen no enemy in the area but had uncovered a cache of musket ammunition near Presidio del Eclezario. Hudson also passed on the rumor claiming that a Mexican force was or would be marching toward El Paso. More than ever Doniphan wanted Clark's artillery.[18]

Major Meriwether Clark commanded more than one hundred men and Captain Richard Weightman's battery of guns, including four 6-pounders and two 12-pounders. They rumbled out of Santa Fe on January 16 bound for El Paso. Making their way south, the Missourians were greeted by frost on their blankets each morning, although the temperature warmed during the day. The officers of the battery, wanting to make the trip as rapidly as possible, averaged about fifteen miles per day.[19]

Like their fellow volunteers who had preceded them, the artillerists ventured into the dreaded Jornada del Muerto. Sergeant William Kennerly looked around him to see "just sand, sand, everywhere." As at other times on the expedition, soldiers of the artillery unit had arranged to bring alcohol with them. According to Private Daniel Hastings's description, "Some of the officers, owing to fatigue and partial intoxication, are exceedingly petulant and arbitrary." There was a noticeable straightening in the saddles when Private Hastings recorded that "an express from Colonel Doniphan arrived urging us on to his relief as quickly as possible, for he was hourly in expectation of an attack from the enemy who were supposed to be five thousand strong." Accompanying the colonel's riders were forty-five "fresh mules in very good condition"; they helped relieve some of the tired animals that had been worked hardest pulling the battery's guns. Drawing closer to El Paso, Clark and a few others decided to ride ahead of the battery. They reached Colonel Doniphan on January 28.[20]

On the evening of January 31, Americans who had ventured north of El Paso galloped back into the city to report that Captain Weightman and the artillery were several miles away. They desperately needed food. The colonel sent out a wagon, supplying the appreciative artillerists with "cooked bread, meat . . . with some hard biscuit," plus a bonus: "a keg of very superior wine, the pure juice of the grape." The next day around noon Doniphan heard the kind of commotion that might have signaled "a day of jubilee"—Weightman's artillery was rolling into El Paso. The artillerists received a warm greeting. According to the description of one of the volunteers, "Groups of men standing on the tops of houses, waving flags and standards, [greeted the cannoneers] as the artillery marched toward the [city] plaza. . . . Shouts and exulting cries [rose from the soldiers] as one piece of cannon after another turned the corner and came into sight. . . . [The Missourians] were drunk with joy and revelry." A handful of musicians played "Yankee Doodle," while other soldiers fired off some of the four captured cannons that the regiment had found in El Paso.[21]

The arrival of additional Missouri volunteers seemed to be disturbing to the disbelieving residents of El Paso. According to Private Hastings, "The terrified Spaniards . . . gazed at us with as much wonder and astonishment as though we had been a company of fiends." After seventeen days on the march, the artillerymen were pleased and "surprised to find so large and pleasant a city." "The extreme neatness and regularity of the streets which are daily swept by females, the walks beautifully ornamented by long rows of shaped trees just resuming their green foliage" made a favorable impression on the cannoneers. The plentiful supply of fruit helped to quench their thirst. Naturally, that night the volunteers held a rowdy fandango to celebrate the arrival of the artillery. Many of the Americans got intoxicated.[22]

The day after Clark's artillery arrived at El Paso, it conducted target practice under the watchful eyes of the Regular officers assigned to the Doniphan Expedition. Sergeant Kennerly, from Battery A, recalled that one of the Regulars "remarked in rather a sneering manner, 'Pretty good shooting for civilians!'" The Regular may have been joking, or prodding the artillerymen to a better drill, or displaying a lack of respect for the volunteers. Perhaps this remark came from Lieutenant Charles Wooster, who had joined the regiment in Santa Fe, after General Kearny had paid encouraging compliments to the cannoneers during their brief training at Fort Leavenworth. Or it might have been that the artillerists had grown lazy during their sojourn in Santa Fe and had not kept up with their drills. In any event, the barbed remark stung, and the St. Louis volunteers may have vowed to show the Regular officer how well they could shoot when they met the enemy.[23]

As the colonel looked to the final details of the march south, a messenger arrived from Santa Fe on February 7 bearing the news of the Taos Revolt. Although the messenger's information was incomplete, the colonel learned that on January 19 dozens of Mexicans and Pueblo Indians had killed Governor Charles Bent and five other Americans at Taos, north of Santa Fe. In the next few days, another fourteen Americans died at the hands of the rebels and shredded all of Kearny's and Doniphan's sanguine messages about a tranquil New Mexico that had accepted American annexation. Hundreds of poorly armed Mexicans had risen up, avenging Governor Armijo's failure to defend New Mexico and challenging the American occupation of the state. Colonel Sterling Price acted swiftly to suppress the rebellion. Deploying about half of his regiment and supported by several cannon, Price fought two engagements with the Mexicans. Unknown to Doniphan, the climax of the rebellion came in a battle on February 3 at Taos Pueblo, where more than forty Americans and over one hundred Mexicans were killed. Fighting in other skirmishes, Price, leading the 2nd Missouri Regiment, and detachments of Captain Angney's infantry and Captain Fischer's artillery had quashed the uprising.[24]

Upon hearing about the Mexican rebellion, Private Marcellus Edwards, for one, grew angry. He believed that the revolt was the consequence of what he considered the Americans' "kind treatment" of New Mexico's residents. The news of the Taos Revolt put a new light on Doniphan's decision to go to Chihuahua. In Edwards's opinion, the Missourians' "situation is rather critical—leaving an enemy in our rear, marching in the heart of their country, expecting to meet a powerful one [enemy army] in front, depending upon them [Mexican civilians] for subsistence, and our strength not exceeding one thousand." Obviously, advancing through enemy country entailed numerous dangers, but at that stage it was difficult for Doniphan to assess the accuracy of reports on the strength of Mexican forces in the state of Chihuahua.[25]

After commanding the 1st Missouri for seven months, Doniphan knew his men well, but he wondered if the news of the Taos Revolt might have influenced some of the volunteers to return to Santa Fe, where they would help Colonel Price suppress the Mexican attempt to regain control of New Mexico. On the contrary, many of the soldiers expressed themselves in favor of going on into the province of Chihuahua. Private Hughes recounted that if the colonel had taken a vote, the men's response would have been a hearty "Lead Us On." Few favored a return to Santa Fe. For his part, though ill at the time with indigestion, fevers, and headaches, Private William Richardson indicated that most of the men in his outfit were "weary of our detention here" in El Paso and were ready to go south. Nerves had been wearing thin; Lieutenant Richard Wells of Company F had cut Lieutenant Robert Barnett of Company B in a knife fight, inflicting a serious wound. Lieutenant Gibson also recorded no vote being taken, but he was emphatic that the volunteers had grown tired of El Paso and "were urgent to be led against the enemy or any other place, so that they were in camp or on the march." Private Jacob Robinson, however, described the situation in just the opposite way, saying, "If a vote of the regiment was taken, we would go no farther"; because the colonel and other respected officers ordered it, however, "onward we must go." Several days before, Private Marcellus Edwards recalled widespread distaste about the monotonous food and dissatisfaction with the prospect of yet another long march through another desert. Edwards even alluded to indications of "mutiny" but did not elaborate. A new phase of the march was near at hand, and Edwards spoke for most of the regiment: "It appears as though we were just getting into the merits" of combat service against the Mexicans, and many of the volunteers relished the prospect of another battle. They would march south.[26]

Expressing their frustration at remaining idle for so long in El Paso, the volunteers committed deplorable acts. Three men from Captain Hudson's command were court-martialed for rape. Captain John Reid, commanding Company D, and James Collins, one of the regiment's interpreters, accosted two Mexicans who had recently ridden in from Chihuahua. Reid and Collins demanded to know what the men knew about the dispositions of Mexican forces around Chihuahua City. When they refused to answer, the two Americans, assisted by some others, grabbed ropes, made nooses around the Mexicans' necks, and tossed the ropes over a ceiling beam in a tavern, pulling the protesting civilians off of the floor. They hung there for some minutes, "till almost dead." According to Private Marcellus Edwards, "they were . . . cut down and when brought to their proper senses again, were quite willing to reveal what they knew about" the Mexican forces. Their report placed eighteen hundred Mexican soldiers on the march from Chihuahua toward El Paso, and Reid seemed inclined to believe them. Such brutality on the part of the Missourians appeared to have been rare, but it indicated that the role of conqueror brought out the worst in some of them, even if others, such as Private Hughes, contended that the regiment made every effort to treat the El Pasoans fairly and kindly.[27]

Prior to marching south, Doniphan ordered out Lieutenant Colonel Mitchell with Captain Hudson and the Chihuahua Rangers as a scouting detachment. Before Mitchell and Hudson saddled up, two traders named Kerford and Gentry, with their group of forty-five heavily laden wagons, struck out on their own, headed for Chihuahua City. Learning that Kerford and Gentry had gotten a jump on everyone, Doniphan sent a rider down to Hudson, directing him to overtake and detain those traders until the rest of the column reached them, but he was disappointed to find out that the two had escaped. Many days later the colonel learned that the two had sold goods to the Mexican military in Chihuahua City. Riding to catch up to the merchants, the Rangers encountered several Mexican civilians on the road, one of whom was well armed; having no specific reason to hold him, the Rangers allowed him to go on his way. Soon, Doniphan addressed the other merchants and clearly stated that all of them must follow his orders. If any failed to do so, he would be forced "to confiscate [their wagons] and the goods in them" to prevent them from falling into the hands of the enemy.[28]

On February 8, 1847, Doniphan gave the order for selected units of the regiment to start for Chihuahua. Every soldier in the regiment had become an old hand at crossing deserts and knew that their colonel wanted them to travel fifteen or twenty miles per day. On the first day out, the lead elements of the expedition marched about twenty miles, but they left other units strung out behind them. Recalling that Kearny had freed Mexican captives at Bent's Fort, Doniphan decided to release two Mexicans taken prisoner at Brazito, perhaps in hopes that their description of the regiment would undermine the morale of Mexican forces that might be assembling to resist them.[29]

The Mexicans knew that the Doniphan Expedition was marching south. Looking back upon the 1st Missouri Regiment's invasion of Chihuahua, a senior Mexican officer, General José A. Heredia, saw what appeared to be an American cordon offensive—part of cohesive American actions involving forces under the command of General Zachary Taylor near Buena Vista Ranch and General Winfield Scott's invasion force off the Gulf Coast. General Heredia recounted: "In the last days of February and the beginning of March, the enemy's cannon sounded at once on the Sacramento [River], in the Angostura [Pass], and at Vera Cruz." From the Mexican point of view, Colonel Doniphan and his regiment were contributing to American strategic plans.[30]

In order to support Taylor and Wool, Doniphan still had a long way to go. He reached the advance camp of Hudson's Rangers on February 9. The entire regiment and supporting units were consolidated and ready for the next stage of the march. The colonel reckoned their numbers to be "924 effective men: 117 officers and privates of the artillery; 93 of Lieut. Col. Mitchell's escort [some of

Wagon train. (From Gregg, *Commerce of the Prairies* [1844]; courtesy of the Museum of New Mexico, negative no. 171104)

the 2nd Missouri Regiment]; and the remainder, the 1st regiment of Missouri mounted volunteers." However, one of the artillerymen, Private Hastings, estimated their strength at 1,300 men, "four hundred wagons and seven thousand animals, including horses, mules and oxen," with the balance of 376 probably including the traders, merchants, mule skinners, and drivers who were not volunteer soldiers.[31]

At this camp, and looking ahead to the likelihood of combat, the colonel ordered the traders to organize two companies to supplement the regiment, asking the civilians to elect their leaders. Doniphan had considered such an organization as far back as December 26, the day after the Brazito fight, when he asked James Oldham, a former soldier who had to be released from active duty for health reasons, "to raise a company . . . among the traders' hands." Edward Glasgow and Henry Skillman took the most votes for captains and Samuel Owens was chosen "major" of the merchants' battalion. The soldiers got little rest that night, however. The passage of the merchants' wagons kept up a constant "rumbling [that,] together with the shouts of the drivers and the crack of their lashes, greatly disturbed our sleep." The next day brought a gray dawn that was so cold and foreboding that the colonel directed the soldiers to stay in camp one more day. The next leg of the march included what Lieutenant Gibson called La Jornada Cantarecio—a sixty-five-mile passage, similar to La Jornada del Muerto.[32]

To fortify their customers for the *jornada,* the sutlers passed among the companies and found a few men who still possessed a little cash to buy whiskey at seventy-five cents per pint; others put their purchases on credit. A rumor ran from campfire to campfire that an army of four thousand Mexican soldiers was marching north to intercept the column. With some justification, most of the Missourians could have discounted the latest rumor.[33]

Of great concern to Doniphan was the possibility that a strong Mexican army would finally materialize at some point to oppose the passage of the regiment. Therefore, he sent out scouts each day as the expedition moved deeper and deeper into enemy country. Jim Kirker had become de facto chief of scouts. He and his group of Shawnee and Delaware Indians ranged well ahead of the column, setting out the same day as the regiment but, being only a dozen riders, able to move much faster. As Sergeant Kennerly remembered, "Reconnoitering parties . . . were on constant duty."[34]

The expedition's movement again depended on the availability of grass and water. During the first two days out of El Paso the grass seemed abundant for wintertime, but, as Sergeant Kennerly recalled, the scene changed and everything seemed "very dry at this season." After only a few days Private Frank Edwards asserted that most soldiers could have "fought Old Nick himself, if he had stood between us and a full canteen." On the tenth the column passed a small farm whose owner refused to sell them any corn. In reply, "Colonel Doniphan directed some of the men to go and help themselves to the required amount." While they were at it, the soldiers also confiscated all the farmer's horses. On February 11 most of the regiment marched about twelve miles. However, many of the merchants did not move, remaining at the campground of the night before. A raid by Apache Indians, who drove off 250 mules and some sixty oxen, prevented several of the traders from moving. Successive strikes of that kind might have crippled the progress of the expedition. As they invaded Chihuahua, it seemed to the soldiers that "the Apache are constantly prowling about," and were especially seeking to steal livestock. A small patrol retrieved most of the oxen and claimed to have killed one of the Apaches. In the process, however, the soldiers wore out their horses and abandoned them.[35]

Leaving El Paso behind, the soldiers found the days quite "warm, and the night[s] very cold." On February 13, at the edge of La Jornada Cantarecio, Doniphan ordered an all-day halt so that the soldiers could attend to animals, equipment, weapons, and ammunition. Private Marcellus Edwards recalled that

"A CAMP WASHING DAY." (From Richardson's *Journal of William H. Richardson* [1848]; courtesy of the Museum of New Mexico, negative no. 171110)

several of the volunteers molded extra bullets and made them up into cartridges. He also remembered that during the day two men deserted the regiment. According to their friends, the two returned to El Paso to marry Mexican women. In addition, two other soldiers, Maxwell and Willis, died of unnamed causes. The regiment spent time preparing extra cooked food and filling water casks and canteens. Soldiers reexamined powder captured at Brazito to determine if it was worth keeping, and they discarded two small Mexican cannon and some ammunition as more nuisance than ordnance. Captain Weightman drew some of the fresher horses and had them assigned to the artillery batteries. Several soldiers went hunting and brought in some game, including "deer, antelope, hares, ducks, and geese."[36]

At this camp near San Elisario, a merchant from Independence, Missouri, Manuel X. Harmony, approached the colonel and announced that he no longer wished to travel with the invaders. Harmony had been born in Spain but had become a naturalized U.S. citizen and had operated a trading company in Independence. Deciding to remain in the vicinity of El Paso, Harmony said he would rely on his contacts with friends to sell his goods there. Not content to merely make his request, the merchant tried a trick, claiming that most of his mules had been stolen by Apaches, forcing him to stay in El Paso until he arranged to purchase others. But soldiers found Harmony's mules hidden nearby, and from that time on Doniphan was suspicious of the merchant's intentions and loyalties. By this point in the campaign Doniphan saw the privately owned trade goods of the merchants as a potential source of resupply for his regiment and their wagons as a possible means of protection. If Mexicans attacked the expedition, he could arrange the wagons into a "corral" or hasty redoubt. The Missourians were deep in hostile country, and if the Mexicans regained control of Santa Fe, Doniphan's column had no base of operations if retreat became necessary. Private Marcellus Edwards contended that Harmony anticipated a forthcoming fight between the Americans and the Mexicans and "wanted to remain behind until our battle at Chihuahua and then come in a great friend to the victors." Doniphan knew that a few merchants had already left the column and that others, following Harmony's example, might try to venture out on their own. The colonel was determined to stop such independent action; moreover, Harmony's actions raised Doniphan's suspicions that he "was anxious for the success of the Mexicans."[37]

Therefore, concluding that the circumstances qualified as a "military emergency," Doniphan ordered one of his subordinates, Lieutenant Colonel David Mitchell, to inform Harmony that he would be required to accompany the Doniphan Expedition. Acting on Doniphan's order, Mitchell told Harmony that his trade goods and wagons were being appropriated for use by the volunteers and his drivers enlisted to serve "in time of action." Doniphan indicated that if Harmony were allowed to sell his wares they might be used by Mexicans against the Americans. Furthermore, as Captain Reid recalled, the colonel related the additional "purpose of having the loaded wagons to use, if necessary, as a kind of field work" for defense against Mexican attack. Reluctantly, Harmony acquiesced to Doniphan's orders and moved south with the column. In the weeks to come, Doniphan, Mitchell, and Harmony would renew their disagreement over the merchants' rights to venture off on their own.[38]

On February 14, after burying the two men who had died overnight, the expedition resumed its southward movement at 8:00 A.M. Ahead the soldiers could see for miles, and "the countryside . . . present[ed] a barren appearance, the soil sterile; the surface rocky and mountainous." Simply put, Hughes pictured it as a "dreadful desert." Some of the wagons bogged down in deep sandy patches, requiring the soldiers to dismount and put their shoulders to the wheels of wagons and cannons. Grudgingly, the wheels turned. Looking up from such backbreaking work, Lieutenant Gibson observed that the Chihuahua Trail led through two parallel rough ridges, creating "a valley entirely surrounded by mountains, some of which are high, of all possible forms and shapes which can be imagined. It looks like an amphitheater on a large scale." The soldiers slogged ahead for twelve hours, and then the column stopped. The volunteers posted sentries and cooked dinner.[39]

As usual, the men were up early on February 15, and the lead element of the column had moved twelve miles before Doniphan called a halt for breakfast. After eating, the Missourians resumed the march, adding another twenty miles to the day's tally. They encountered more deep sand; some wagons sank nearly up to the wheel hubs. The teamsters brought around more mules, put them in the traces, and lashed them forward. Of course, men and animals worked up a desperate thirst; they had found no fresh water source for forty-eight hours. When the soldiers came across water, they welcomed having some even if it was not appealing. Private Robinson recalled that one pond was "extremely brackish and offensive to the smell," but both men and animals drank "eagerly," only to look around and see several "carcases [*sic*] of mules and horses" nearby. That evening a dispatch rider reached the camp with newspapers and letters from Santa Fe. According to those reports, admittedly unofficial and weighted with hearsay, General Wool was probably not at Chihuahua City. Having been moving southward for eight days, Doniphan discussed the matter of a return to El Paso but decided to press on. In the mail delivery were several letters to the soldiers from friends and family in Missouri. Hughes said that receiving the mail worked like a tonic on the men, boosting their morale. For days to come soldiers exchanged family news, jokes, and information from the home front.[40]

That night a thunderstorm drenched the regiment. Marcellus Edwards watched as "the rain descended in . . . torrents [running] in streams across the road." Men bent over rivulets and filled up buckets and canteens. The rain was most welcome to the oxen, and the downpour seemed to have "imparted new life" to many of the beasts, but several of them were so broken down that they had to be abandoned. Overnight another soldier died. After a comrade said a few words of solace, a squad fired a volley in his honor.[41]

On February 16 Kirker and his scouts came upon the village of about three hundred people at Carrizal, where Hughes was pleased to see "much cool and delightful water." The Mexicans had built a fortified camp at Carrizal, but they had evacuated, and all the signs showed that the garrison had left recently. The place looked as though it could have been defended. Lieutenant Gibson described the fort as "large and commodious . . . but . . . much dilapidated," including barracks and a chapel. Doniphan would not have wanted to leave a

Mexican garrison in his rear, and it was another time that the Mexicans rejected manning a defensive position, where they might have inflicted losses on the invaders and weakened their column. A farmer gave over several pigs to the Americans, although Lieutenant Gibson did not say how they were paid for.[42]

The invading force encountered a bubbling hot spring on February 17. Private Richardson was disgusted, finding that the "water is scarcely fit to drink, having a very disagreeable taste." Nevertheless, many soldiers dipped their canteens into the pool, hoping the taste would improve when the water cooled off. After "neighing and crying piteously for water," horses and mules drank their fill. The regiment proceeded to complete a fourteen-mile march. By the end of the day a number of wagons had either broken down or had to be left behind because there were too few mules to pull them. Soldiers or sutlers tossed out more than five thousand pounds of flour and barrels of salt.[43]

Doniphan's column halted and made camp again on February 19. Men and animals were exhausted. The Missourians encountered a rare delight—"good water" in abundance at a place they called "the Lagoon of the Ducks" ("Laguna de los Patos"), fed by "a large, bold stream, [flowing] clear." Private W. Tolley died there. One of the volunteers said Tolley was overheated and then drank too much cool water. The regiment rested there for nearly a full day, but part of the rest was ruined by a freak windstorm that hit in midafternoon, blowing over most of the tents and depositing gritty sand in everyone's cooking pots and on their plates at dinnertime. Rather than abating that night, the wind blew more fiercely, ripping the covers off of several wagons. That evening scouts caught four Mexicans, who proudly proclaimed that an army of some three thousand men was preparing defensive works some six days' travel away.[44]

On February 20 advance riders brought information that during the day ahead they could expect to see "the same scene of desolation" as they had seen on all of the days of the previous week. "No cultivation [was] to be seen any where, nor scarcely any natural vegetable production except the thorn and muskeet [mesquite] brush." A bit of good news: Lieutenant Gibson judged that the route coincided with "an even, smooth road, better than any turnpike" back in Missouri; taking advantage of this remarkable path, they pushed on until 11:00 P.M.[45]

The next day, after a march of ten miles, the army camped near a ranch at a place called Ojo Caliente (Hot Springs). Following their colonel's example, dozens of soldiers took baths; some found the clear waters "too warm," but others reported that the respite was "very comfortable." Not only did some find the waters delightful, but they caught trout and also had a delicious meal. An officer strode through the camp and picked Private Richardson and eighteen others to replace the advance scouting group. Gulping down a hasty supper, the patrol "mounted and rode out a long distance." When the returning scouts neared the column, they raised such a dust cloud that their fellows believed the enemy was upon them. Hastily, troops fell in line of battle and cannon were unlimbered, only to see the scouts come tearing over the rise and into view. Meanwhile, rejecting the notion that they might be set upon by Indians or Mexicans, Richardson's scouts "made a small fire of brush weed," picketed their horses and mules, posted a few guards, and turned in for the night. Private Marcellus Edwards, reflecting on the warm days and freezing nights, the wind and sand, the lack of water and wood for fires, the boring, redundant food, recalled "the warm houses, the soft feather beds, and the cool springs at home [in Missouri]." Hearing Edwards's lament, another soldier sighed and wished to sit at his table at home "and eat good bacon and collards." Although Doniphan and his officers worked to stem straggling or independent scouting, the men left the column on their own, seeking out fresh water and hunting for some game to supplement their cook fires. Others were distracted and ceased to be watchful. The expedition was vulnerable to attack.[46]

A grueling march of thirty miles sent the Missourians into camp on February 22 "at a place where the men had enough water; but none could be spared to the poor horses and mules." The pace of the march was beginning to tell: it was increasingly difficult for sergeants to roust men out of their blankets in the cold mornings. March discipline was becoming harder to enforce, especially where water was concerned. The first company to find a water hole trampled the ground all around, muddying the water and ruining it for the next unit. That night Hughes and his cohorts "tethered their animals, and wrapping themselves up in their blankets, lay down on the earth without taking their suppers."[47]

February 23 was one of the regiment's best days in Chihuahua. A bright sun warmed the soldiers, and a march of eight miles brought the Missourians to a pleasant pond for the animals. Proceeding a few more miles, they drew near a creek. The advance group approached the stream cautiously, finding dozens of antelope grazing along the banks. Some fled from the regiment; others, disoriented by the number of wagons and men, darted toward the column. Rifles went to shoulders and dozens of aimed shots brought down several of the sleek animals. The hunters distributed fresh meat to the cook fires that night. On a sad note, word spread that night that Private Robards had died.[48]

Again acting in his role as scout, Private Richardson rode ahead on February 24 and, reaching the summit of a crag after climbing for several minutes, posted himself on a promontory. "To the left a continuous range of mountains loom up, whose bare and rugged tops present . . . coldness and desolation. The whole face

"A Camp Kitchen." (From Frost, *History of Mexico and Its Wars* [1882]; courtesy of the Museum of New Mexico, negative no. 171108)

of the country is destitute of wood . . . except a species of brush or thorn bushes." Glancing down, Richardson "beheld a long line of wagons stretching along the road as far as the sight could reach." It was ragged up close, but from a distance the Doniphan Expedition made an impressive array on the march. Showing the regiment's high morale, some of the men thought up names for their companies. Captain Reid's Company D called themselves the "Missouri Horse Guards," and Captain Parsons's Company F went by the "Missouri Dragoons."[49]

Reveille on the twenty-fifth sounded an hour before first light. By sunrise Doniphan had the regiment fed, lined up, and moving ahead. Eight miles along, the men spotted a lake, which provided water for men and animals. The water tasted better and the grass was more abundant than at most of the other spots along the trail. It was too good a place not to camp, and the men scrounged enough mesquite to make several cook fires for a midday meal. Suddenly a strong wind picked up, scattering sparks from the fires and setting alight the prairie grasses and weeds near the camp. With alarming rapidity a "wall of flame," rising "twenty feet high, and threatening to devour the whole train," consumed much of the available grass. The soldiers scrambled to put out the blaze, beating at the flames with their blankets, but the wind spread the fire despite their efforts. All around "mules [were] braying, and horses neighing, conscious that some danger was at hand." Snapping their whips, drivers yelled to their teams, "urging their animals to the utmost speed." It became obvious to the soldiers that the expedition's supply of gunpowder was in danger. Captain John Reid and others jumped forward, wielding their sabers to cut at the tufts of grass and dig a shallow ditch in an attempt to stem the raging fire and discourage its spread. Some teamsters drove their wagons into the small lake to protect them from the fire. Possessing a life of their own, with a "fearful roaring and crackling," the flames danced up the slopes of the ridges and skipped across the valley. Soon it seemed that "the whole prairie, as far as the eye could reach, [was] in flames. A strange glare tinged the clouds, and all surrounding objects and presented a scene which was fearfully grand." Seeing this wildfire and how fast this "sea of flames" spread, and knowing how little water they found, the soldiers could understand why so few trees survived in the valley. One of the soldiers, William Kennerly, also concluded that the "Mexicans might have cut us off many times in this way [setting fires deliberately] had the thought occurred to them." The soldiers spent the balance of the afternoon fighting the fire or trying to escape from it.[50]

A Missouri bugler blew a sharp call to open the day on February 26, not caring if he announced the Americans' presence to any nearby Mexicans. Up ahead the scouts contacted a Mexican rancher, who contended that a Mexican army numbering between three and four thousand had dug in at Sacramento Ranch, some twenty miles away. Suddenly, a fierce sandstorm reduced visibility to only about one hundred yards, discouraging the expedition's progress.[51]

It was probably at this ranch that Private Marcellus Edwards described a story about some volunteers stealing and killing chickens. Colonel Doniphan himself drew his saber and waved it at the offenders, ordering the thievery to stop. One of the men, who had just stuffed a bird under his blanket, supported the colonel, saying that it was "very wrong for these men to kill all the Mexican poultry." Unfortunately for the scamp, at that moment the chicken, "feeling uncomfortable under his blanket, squalled out and exposed his captor." Doniphan could save only a few of the rancher's birds. Other volunteers sought out any living creature that was fit to eat. At a small corral were several other animals, and outriders brought in others; eventually the scouts had found fifty sheep and more than a dozen cattle and some hogs, some reputedly from the ranch of Governor Ángel Trías Álvaraz.[52]

On February 27 scouts, including Lieutenant Colonel Mitchell, brought Colonel Doniphan the words he had been waiting to hear since leaving El Paso. Meeting the colonel in his camp at El Sauz, a small settlement, they "reported the enemy in strength behind redoubts" only a few miles ahead, confirming the rumors they had heard for several days. As Captain John Stevenson recounted, the Mexican "force had not been exaggerated." Mexican soldiers occupied an imposing system of defensive works, strengthened by a number of cannons. Furthermore, contingents of uniformed Mexican horse soldiers—cavalry or dragoons—were mounted and apparently ready for action; their uniforms, arms, and equipment showed that they were not local militia. Seeking their own information about the invaders, a number of Mexican scouts drew close to the American camps. The Missourians chased one and captured his horse, complete with fancy saddle, although somehow the Mexican escaped on foot. In sharp contrast to all of the rumors during the expedition's approach to Santa Fe, these Mexican defenders appeared capable, well organized, and willing to give battle.[53]

CHAPTER SEVEN

The Battle of Sacramento

Rising dramatically out of the valley floor, the sixty-foot scarp above the shallow Arroyo Seco dominated Doniphan's view of the southern horizon. The colonel needed to know everything he could about the Mexican forces defending the plateau and guarding the ford of the Río Sacramento, a spot about eighteen miles north of Ciudad Chihuahua. One thing the colonel did know: water flowed intermittently through the riverbed, and the Sacramento presented no obstacle to the passage of the Missouri regiment.

On the Mexican side, Ángel Trías Álvarez, provincial governor of Chihuahua, held the rank of brigadier general and served as second in command for Major General José A. Heredia, leader of the Mexican forces in Chihuahua. Governor Trías owned a ranch situated near the Sacramento ford. Trías helped raise volunteers and scoured the countryside for any weapons to arm the militia. General Heredia had entered military service with the Spanish army in 1815 and had held several responsible commands over the years. Heredia's senior subordinates included Brigadier General Pedro García Conde, chief engineer and cavalry leader; Brigadier General Cayetano Justiniani, senior division commander; and Brigadier General Mauricia Ugarté, infantry commander.[1]

To gain a personal impression, Doniphan rode forward to reconnoiter the Mexican positions. At his request several others conducted a reconnaissance of the enemy emplacements, including Lieutenant Colonel Mitchell, Major Clark, and scout James Kirker, each of whom took selected soldiers with them. On February 27, 1847, as the evening approached, Mitchell observed the Mexicans and turned in one of the most complete reports evaluating the layout and strength of their forces. He saw Mexican infantry marching to and fro, cavalry and lancers riding in formations, soldiers improving their redoubts, artillerists preparing their cannon for battle, and messengers galloping from one place to another. The Mexican forces were well supplied with stock: an observer noted that "the vale [valley] stretching to Chihuahua was literally alive with cattle, sheep, horses, and mules." Bringing back their intelligence and combining it with Doniphan's personal observations, the Missouri officers met in council to discuss what they had seen. The enemy's strength was in the eye of the beholder, and American estimates of the Mexican force varied. Colonel Doniphan reckoned that his enemy fielded upward of four thousand men, a total he claimed was confirmed later by finding the report of the Mexican adjutant. According to Doniphan, Heredia's forces included twelve hundred infantry, including National Guardsmen, twelve hundred cavalry and lancers, three hundred artillerymen, and fourteen hundred provincial riders without uniforms and armed with a hodgepodge of weapons. Other scouts estimated that three thousand Mexicans occupied the defenses. Despite their differing opinions on the strength of their opponents, the Americans agreed that the Missouri regiment was outnumbered at least two to one and that the Mexican positions looked formidable.[2]

On the plateau Heredia was the commanding general, but Brigadier General Pedro García Conde, former minister of war for the Republic of Mexico, had designed and supervised construction of the defensive lines. Based on his experience and twenty-four years of service, mostly in engineering billets, García Conde was one of the most knowledgeable officers in the Mexican army in 1847. On the south side of the river, General García Conde set up a cannon and an observation post on the end of a prominent ridge, Sacramento Mountain, some two hundred feet high, that allowed an overview of the plateau, the road, the ford, and the valley. On his right flank García Conde's soldiers constructed some emplacements on top of another ridge, the Sierra de Nombre de Dios, overlooking the gap between that ridge and the plateau above the Arroyo Seco. In addition, they placed an *abatis* to discourage any movement through the inhospitable defile of a dry, rocky creek bed. The engineer then turned his attention to the plateau north of the river and arranged his main defenses in the shape of an inverted capital letter "U," with its open mouth facing away from the valley. García Conde then directed his men to dig some twenty redoubts, most measuring about twelve by fourteen feet, but the three facing the valley were larger. Soldiers dug entrenchments to support and connect some of the redoubts. García Conde individually emplaced ten cannon, including two 9-pounders, two 8-pounders, and six 6-pounders, at various points along the front of the curve and western axis of the inverted "U." The largest redoubts and the strength of the defense faced the plain. However, García Conde's layout of the other emplacements also gave the defenders good fields of fire if the Americans brought an assault on the Mexicans' western flank, which was guarded by a deep, rocky gully. García Conde located his gun positions to provide mutual supporting fires, but it was a single-line defense; if part of his line gave way, it would endanger the integrity of the whole position. García Conde's efforts certainly impressed one of the Missourians, who said that "the place seemed impregnable," but García Conde's defensive layout may have been too ambitious for the number of soldiers in Heredia's army.[3]

The variety of the uniforms worn by the Mexicans indicated that soldiers representing several units occupied places in the defenses. According to General Heredia, his line held 70 soldiers from the 7th Infantry Regiment, 250 from Chihuahua Battalion, and 50 dismounted troopers from the 2nd Durango Cavalry Squadron; 119 regular artillerists served the cannon. Some 180 National Guardsmen filled in the redoubts. In addition, some 1,200 horse soldiers, including units of lancers and the 1st Durango Cavalry Squadron, rounded out the regular troops assembled to turn aside the American invasion of Chihuahua—a total of nearly 2,000 officers and enlisted men. Heredia noted that his regulars were well equipped and well supplied, but most of them were recent enlistees who had been serving in uniform for around three months, only long enough to begin to be acquainted with their duties and officers, and less than half the time the 1st Missouri Regiment had been on active duty. Therefore, although Heredia recognized that his men were well armed, he did not consider them qualified to be rated as "regular troops" despite their regular unit designations. Indeed, the general characterized his field force as "perfectly raw" but enthusiastic. Heredia supplemented his units of uniformed soldiers by raising approximately 1,000 rancheros, provincial civilians variously armed. Similar outfits often carried lassos, slings, machetes, and knives but few firearms; if the Americans broke and ran, the rancheros could join in the pursuit. Including the rancheros brought the total complement of the Mexican force to around 3,000.[4]

Prior to engaging the American invaders, Heredia and García Conde discussed their prospects. Their first priority was to protect Chihuahua City, but they expected more than defense out of the upcoming battle. Winning it would provide a springboard to strike north. A Mexican victory on the Río Sacramento could lead to a counteroffensive designed to recapture Santa Fe, regain control of New Mexico, and change the strategic direction of the war in central Mexico. The Mexican commanders outlined ambitious goals and were not intimidated by their enemy: soldiers had cut hundreds of ropes and gathered handcuffs to restrain American prisoners they expected to take after the battle, and dozens of Chihuahua residents planned to sit on the hillsides to watch the encounter. Mexican officers displayed their bravado in conversations with incarcerated

American merchants, describing how they were going to "flog 'the Yankees.'" On the evening of February 27, Mexican soldiers attested to their patriotism and willingness to defend their homeland. Going into the battle, the Mexicans did not appear to be overawed by the invaders.[5]

The invading American force totaled 1,014 soldiers: 800 in the 1st Missouri Regiment, 97 Rangers with Lieutenant Colonel Mitchell and Captain Hudson, and 117 with Clark's battery (four 6-pounders and two 12-pounders). In addition, numerous merchants and their employees accompanied the expedition, somewhere between 150 and 300 all told, but no member of the expedition gave specific numbers for the civilians, although their wagons might be instrumental in providing a defense if Mexican troops attacked. The American force probably totaled around 1,200 men ready to fight. Before the battle, displaying his self-confidence and making an effort to inspire his men, Doniphan once again drew upon rhetoric. A private remembered that the colonel talked in an "off-hand manner" and "with a kind of half laugh, his eyes twinkling." Doniphan said, "'Well, boys, I have issued an order this morning that we are to camp in the enemies [*sic*] intrenchments tonight.'" As he had done before, outside of Las Vegas and at Brazito, Doniphan found a way to draw upon his oratorical skills to prepare his men for battle: they expected him to say something inspirational, and he did not disappoint them. They responded enthusiastically, yelling back: "'Yes, yes we will colonel,' in thundering tones, reiterated over and over again with loud huzzas.'" The Missourians "appeared to have the fullest confidence of success."[6]

At dawn on February 28 the chaplain of the Mexican army celebrated mass for his soldiers, and the day turned clear and sunny, giving Doniphan and his officers an unobstructed view of the Mexican positions. The colonel brought his officers together around 1:00 P.M., and they rode to a spot little more than one mile from the enemy lines. From that vantage, the volunteer and Regular officers reexamined the Mexican defenses and made observations about their redoubts and troop dispositions. The officers passed around a telescope, commenting about one and then another of the Mexicans' emplacements, cannon, and units. Heredia and García Conde had disposed several of the Mexican horse squadrons in battle alignment in front of the plateau, just beyond the Arroyo Seco itself. Some of the Mexican infantry companies, in line of battle, were also below the scarp.

One of Doniphan's officers drew a sketch of the present enemy arrangements on the ground, and it occupied their attention as they considered their options of approach and how to attack. No advantage would be gained by trying to move the American column through the defile to the Americans' left, the right flank

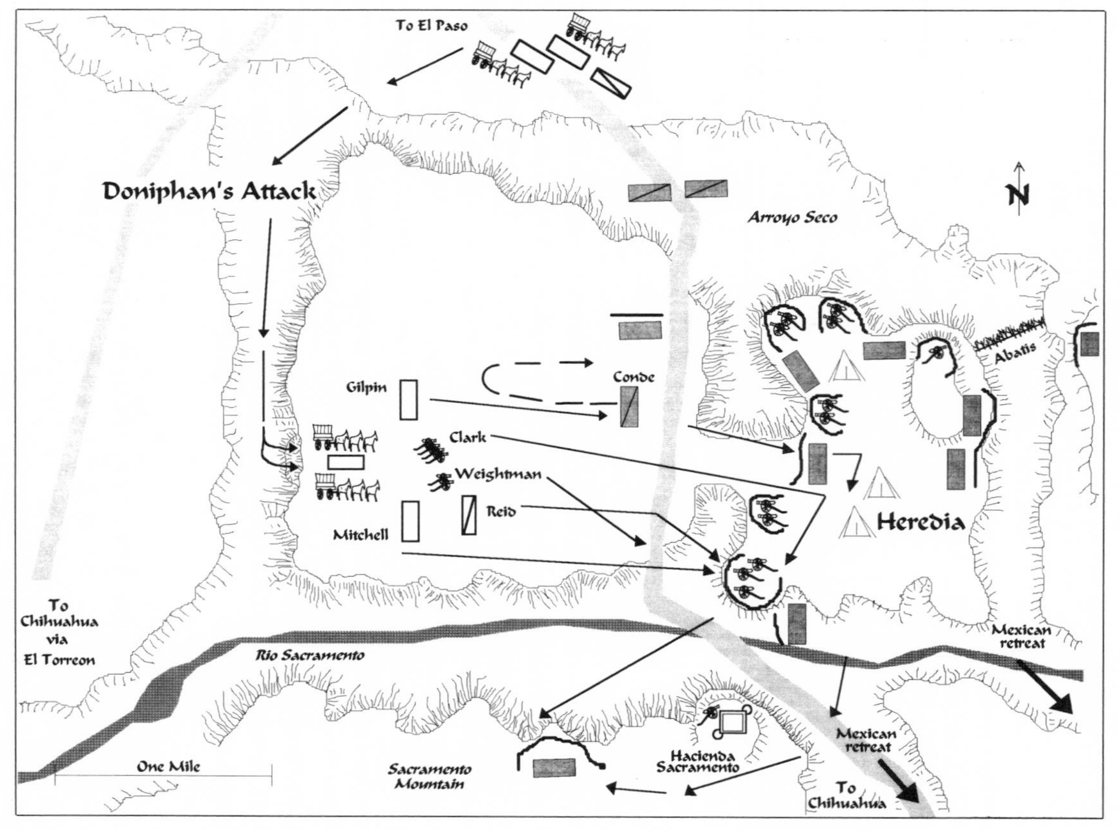

Battle of Sacramento, February 28, 1847. (T. T. Smith, 1998)

of the Mexican positions. The column would come under fire from Mexican artillery and infantry, risking the possibility of Mexican cavalry attacking their right flank and rear. Furthermore, the Missourians and their Regular Army advisers agreed that they wanted no part of an attack straight on against the plateau, requiring them to engage the deployed Mexican units and then scale the sheer face of the scarp above the Arroyo Seco. If they tried such an approach, they would be under artillery fire until the scarp prevented the Mexican cannon from firing down on them; trying to make a vertical climb, however, while being taken under fire by Mexican infantry would be foolhardy and would probably cause the regiment to suffer many casualties. Moreover, Mexican cavalry could attack the wagon train while the balance of the Missourians were trying to climb the scarp. Yet the disposition of the deployed Mexican units and defensive arrangement seemed to have been designed as if Heredia and García Conde expected the U.S. force to push headlong into the teeth of the carefully sited Mexican guns.

Sometimes success in a battle or a campaign is accomplished by someone making or approving the right decision at a crucial time. That decision may mean taking a chance, risking one's own life as well as the lives of others to bring on the action that could mean victory, and accomplishing the tactical or strategic goal for which the operation is conducted. The American officers reached a conclusion, apparently a group decision: Doniphan's regiment would outflank the strength of the enemy by swinging to their own right—thus threatening the Mexican left and avoiding the most forbidding Mexican positions.[7]

Prior to 3:00 P.M. the Americans began moving forward, directly toward the plateau. Their line of advance displayed much thought regarding how to make their approach. Several of the men carried "banners and streamets [*sic*] of different devices to make the scene as imposingly dreadful as possible" to the Mexicans. The total American force was arrayed three miles in length and about 150 feet wide, with the companies of soldiers positioned inside the "corral" of about 330 wagons—a moving rectangular box of four parallel rows about 20 feet apart—that could be halted at any time and turned into a wooden fortification, if the Mexicans presented an offensive threat. According to Captain Weightman, at about one mile from the scarp, "the whole command was unmasked by trotting out from the cover of the wagons and deploying into line." On Doniphan's order, the regiment sharply veered to its right, swinging all of its mounted men and horse artillery, followed by the supply wagons, in a great right hook. The heavy column began struggling up the slope, its movement creating a tremendous umbrella of dust, as horses, mules, oxen, and men all strained against the climb, drivers shouting at their teams, soldiers whooping until the dust clogged their throats.[8]

They had arrived at "a deep gully"—a natural moat some thirty feet deep and fifty feet wide, a natural defensive feature to the Mexican positions, one that General Heredia and his subordinates expected to help guard their left flank. To the astonishment of the Mexican officers, hundreds of the Missourians dismounted, handed their reins to horse-holders, and rushed forward carrying shovels, picks, and other tools. They worked frantically but with purpose, calling out to friends, singing songs, boasting of the speed of their work. In a short time they had partially filled in the gully, building a ramp of earth and rocks that permitted the entire regiment and its wagons to begin traversing what had appeared only minutes before as an impassable obstruction. Already showing high morale, the regiment's success in filling in the gully took its "spirits still higher." Eight hundred horsemen put spurs to their mounts. Whips snapped and cracked, artillerists and wagon masters shouted and cursed, and hundreds of wheels rolled against the rocky soil. The mules resisted, of course, but the Missourians "punched and . . . lashed" the stubborn animals, and the wagons, some weighing as much as twelve tons, rumbled forward, first going down the slope into the gully, moving across the dirt ramp, and then climbing the opposite bank. From their perch on the ridge above the Sacramento River, dozens of Mexican civilians, out from Chihuahua to watch the battle, looked perplexed as the enemy column surged through the gully.[9]

Diverse emotions must have played across General Heredia's face—amazement, anger, disappointment—indicating that the invaders had surprised him when they declined to test his main defenses. Recognizing immediately that the Americans intended "to turn [his] position," the general suddenly had "to change [his] whole plan" of battle. Heredia ordered his mounted troops and a battery of four cannon to counter this threatening movement by the Missourians. Responding to his commander's order, García Conde hastily brought up from the Arroyo Seco squadrons of Mexican lancers, numbering around five hundred men, and arranged them in battle formation outside the western shank of the inverted "U." Soon they were supported by the rest of the Mexican mounted units. A well-delivered Mexican attack could disrupt the formation of the invading Norte Americanos. In their colorful uniforms, the Mexican lancers made an impressive sight. Bright sun reflected off hundreds of lance tips and crossed belts. Unit guidons whipped in the breeze. All the martial display hid the fact that this was the first battle for most of these soldiers. Also prominent was the bellicose Black Flag with skulls and crossbones on one side and the legend "Liberty or Death" on the other, the same flag that Mexican troopers had carried at Brazito. Receiving their orders, led by their macabre pennant symbolic of no quarter, the "splendid" line of Mexican lancers rode forward to challenge the Americans' approach.[10]

On Doniphan's command, Captain Weightman and his gunners took two 12-pound howitzers and dashed out ahead of the Missouri column. Also on the colonel's order, Captains Reid and Hudson led their mounted companies to support the battery. At about nine hundred yards from the Mexican lancers, Weightman signaled to halt and his crews unlimbered the howitzers. Weightman yelled his orders: "Form battery, action front, load and fire at will!" Responding with motions practiced hundreds of times, the artillerists took their posts, sponged out their guns, stepped forward with ammunition, and rammed home the cartridges. The gunners lifted their right hands vertically in the air, signaling that their piece was ready. Lieutenant Edmond F. Choteau gave the order to fire. Well-placed shots fell among the charging Mexican lancers. Several riders and horses were killed and wounded. In almost no time, Weightman's gunners sponged out, reloaded, and fired, delivering more deadly shots among the charging horsemen, "mowing lane after lane through the solid columns of the Mexicans." Sponging out and reloading their cannon again, Weightman's gunners shouted encouragement and challenges to each other. The Missouri howitzers blasted more shots into the mounted Mexicans, bringing down several and sending the rest retreating to their lines. The American artillery had foiled the first Mexican attempt to disrupt the flanking assault.[11]

According to Private Daniel Hastings, serving with Weightman's battery, the retreating lancers moved aside, "unmasking the body of twelve hundred cavalry and the [Mexican] battery which opened upon us a continuous blaze of iron missiles." To Hastings, "the earth seemed to tremble and quiver" as the Mexican cannon fire combined with the shots from the Missourians' guns. Working with speed and efficiency, the American gunners let loose several shots, tearing "through the enemy's ranks emptying saddles and bowling them over like so many tenpins." General Heredia sat on his horse in "mortification to see [his cavalry] completely dispersed." Terrified lancers and wounded cavalrymen bolted through the gaps between the redoubts or jumped their horses over the entrenchments. Their disorderly passage was disheartening to the cannon crews and National Guardsmen, a number of whom deserted their positions. Establishing a rally point fifty yards behind the entrenchments, General García Conde endeavored to reassemble his troopers. The battle had been under way for about fifty minutes.[12]

Capitalizing on his enemy's confusion and retreat, Weightman directed his gunners to limber up their pieces and advance. Hours of drill paid off. Within minutes the mules and horses pulled the battery forward, stopping only fifty yards from the enemy redoubts. At that distance, Weightman and his crews were now vulnerable, standing within comfortable range of the Mexican infantry's Brown Bess muskets. Several musket balls whistled by their heads or sprayed dirt on their boots. A Mexican cannonball flew toward the gunners, taking off the head of Lieutenant Andrew Dorn's horse. Remarkably, Dorn was unhurt, but the horse's blood splattered the gun crew.[13]

Meanwhile, Doniphan needed to deploy his regiment for the attack. He and his subordinates probably had discussed the manner of deployment at their officers' conferences. Receiving advice from Captain Thompson of the 1st Dragoons, Doniphan gave orders dividing his regiment into three parts and directing most of his soldiers to dismount at more than two hundred yards away from the redoubts, well out of range of the Mexican muskets. One hundred men had been designated as horse-holders, well below the routine practice of one of every four soldiers acting as horse-holders in Regular U.S. Army units, but the colonel wanted as many men making the attack as possible. At this stage Doniphan knew he was relying on the effort and bravery of his soldiers and the energy of his subordinate officers to make his plan successful. On Doniphan's left, Major Gilpin and his battalion dismounted and drew up in loose line of battle, ready to step off at the colonel's call; Doniphan and Gilpin held a brief conversation, both gesturing at the Mexican redoubts to their left. To the right of Gilpin's battalion stood three selected companies, led by Captains Reid, Parsons, and Hudson, all still mounted. To the horsemen's right, Clark's artillerists busied themselves, as the battery prepared to send more shots flying at the enemy. On Doniphan's far right clustered the 1st Battalion under Lieutenant Colonel Jackson, supported by Lieutenant Colonel Mitchell's detachment from the 2nd Missouri Regiment. Jackson's battalion would assault the Mexican gun emplacements to their right. Behind the deploying Missourians waited the wagon train, still in the rectangular box formation, carrying the regiment's supplies. Should the impending attack fail, the regiment would rally at the wagons. Remaining mounted on his chestnut horse, Doniphan watched approvingly as, in response to his orders, the regiment's companies, with the exception of those of Hudson, Parsons, and Reid, dismounted and finished moving into line of battle. As the Missourians formed their lines, the Mexican cannon fire increased in volume, and one "heavy volley of musket fire" roared out ineffectively from the Mexican entrenchments. "Well, they're giving us [hell] now boys!" the colonel shouted.[14]

At the same time that Americans deployed into line of battle, showing unmistakable signs that they were about to deliver their main attack, the Mexican ranks began to unravel. Hoping to strike terror into his enemy, Heredia ordered several companies of lancers to attack the Americans' rear, falling on the wagon train. A dozen slaves, led by Lieutenant Duncan's slave, Joe, had been armed to assist the teamsters in the wagons' defense. The teamsters and slaves were ready. They opened a blistering fire and turned back the lancers. In the meantime, García Conde's retreating cavalry riding over and around the Mexican entrenchments dismayed and demoralized some of the inexperienced Mexican recruits. Despite the efforts of their officers to hold them in their positions, several of the recruits broke and fled to the rear. General Heredia himself, assisted by his subordinates, rallied some of their men in a hasty line behind the redoubts. By contrast, Captain Rafael Gonzales and his company of the 7th Infantry Regiment served as an example to the rest of the defenders: they held fast in their redoubt. Aware that he no longer needed all of the men and guns left in the emplacements facing the plain, Heredia ordered one of his artillery officers, Colonel Matías Conde, to take two cannon and set up a new gun position that would give a better field of fire against the attack that was taking shape. Disconcerted by Matías Conde's preparations to relocate his guns, some other officers and soldiers mistook this movement as a sign of retreat. Individually and in small groups, Mexican soldiers began to scatter, causing confusion and further disrupting Heredia's defense. At about that time the American artillery opened fire and the Missouri mounted units began to move toward the Mexican entrenchments, where some of the defenders opened fire on the attackers.[15]

Suddenly, half a dozen horsemen burst forth from the American line, riding hell-for-leather across the open area separating the two combatant forces. In front of them all galloped "Major" Samuel Owens, elected leader of the merchants and traders, "waving his hand in an exulting manner, and shouting out, 'Give it to them boys! They can't withstand us.' " Following behind Owens came some others, including Captain John Reid, scout James Kirker, and Private James Collins. Kirker may have made a bet with Collins about who could reach the Mexican gun emplacements first, but no one ever gave a substantiated explanation of why Owens dashed into the open. Presenting an inviting target, Owens charged one of the strongest of the enemy redoubts, on the far left of the Mexican line. As Owens approached the base of the redoubt, several Mexican soldiers opened fire. Owens was hit and reeled from his saddle; his horse, also shot, rolled back on top of him. Seeing Owens fall, Kirker and the others then abruptly changed directions, dashing northward along the front of the Mexican line, drawing fire from each emplacement as they rode past. None of the other riders were hit. Meanwhile, twenty men from Reid's company raced out behind their captain, reaching him as his horse was shot and went down. The group drew

Charge of Captain Reid at Sacramento. (From Hughes, *Doniphan's Expedition* [1847]; courtesy of the Museum of New Mexico, negative no. 171564)

rein, and a private leaped from his saddle and, in a gallant gesture, offered his horse to the captain so that he might continue the attack.[16]

The wild ride of Owens and the others caused distress among the Missourians, many of whom watched these acts of bravado as if transfixed. Shouting for revenge, other officers and small groups of men left the American line to instigate the attack. Several of Captain Reid's company reached the center Mexican redoubt, dismounted, and dashed over its parapet, but Mexican defenders drove them out. Coming to their support, Major Clark moved his guns to gain a better angle on the Mexican positions. Then another bizarre action occurred. Doniphan's adjutant, Captain James DeCourcy, broke from the circle of staff around the colonel and proceeded to gallop to his right down the American line. Apparently DeCourcy had been fortifying himself with some liquor prior to the battle, and he began shouting almost incoherently. Different soldiers reported hearing different words from DeCourcy. One said that the captain shouted several times, "Prepare for a charge!" Another contended instead that DeCourcy called repeatedly, "Halt, Captain Parsons! Halt, Captain Parsons!" In response,

Captain Parsons signaled "halt" to his mounted company and then called out, asking Doniphan for permission to join the attack. The colonel followed after his deranged adjutant, trying to confirm the order to charge. Confused by DeCourcy's tirade, some units held fast; others began the assault. Soon the colonel got the attention of his officers, who urged their units forward. The attack went ahead, but Doniphan was fortunate that DeCourcy's intemperate escapade had not caused worse confusion among the Missourians.[17]

The American line rippled forward, and Clark's guns delivered devastating fire upon the Mexican positions, causing casualties to enemy soldiers manning the redoubts in front of Major Gilpin. Clark "opened upon them [the Mexicans] a very destructive fire of grape and spherical case shot, which soon cleared [Mexican soldiers from positions facing] the left of our line." Moreover, Clark's cannon shots also inflicted several casualties among General García Conde's units of Mexican mounted troops, who had rallied and appeared ready to attempt another charge. At the other end of the line, Private Frank Edwards finally heard someone give the order to attack. Making a perfect target by remaining on his white horse, Lieutenant Colonel Mitchell led the way. By then, it appeared to Private Daniel Hastings as if the "whole army at one rush made a dash" across the open space and up to the sides of the redoubts. "With a whoop and a yell and a plunge, we were over into their fort, man to man, grappling in a merciless fray of blood curdling scenes, neither giving nor receiving quarter, unsparing and blind to all traces of humanity." Shouting and shooting, the Missourians pressed home the assault.[18]

Although delayed by DeCourcy's bizarre behavior, the Missourians' advance now included everyone but the horse-holders, merchants, and teamsters, and the regimental commander rode to join the melee. According to Frank Edwards, as the charge developed unevenly, "Colonel Doniphan [first] covered his face with his hands, and almost groaned out, 'My God! they're gone! The boys will all be killed!' Then instantly raising his head, he stuck his spurs to his horse's sides, and came dashing after [his soldiers]." Mexicans in the center redoubt kept up steady but ineffective cannon fire on the attacking Americans. The cannon shots decapitated two more American horses, but most of the Mexican rounds flew high, in part because the Mexican guns had to fire downhill. Therefore most of the shots missed the attacking soldiers, falling toward the rear near their wagons, where several other horses and mules were killed or injured. By that time, however, the Missourians' attack was becoming "an irresistible torrent."[19]

The attacking Americans scurried forward, but to some of them what first appeared to be a gentle slope leading up to the redoubts seemed to grow steeper and the line of forts seemed more imposing as they got closer to them. "On

"THE BATTLE OF SACRAMENTO." Note: inaccurate portrayal of Americans in uniforms. (Currier & Ives print, courtesy of the Library of Congress)

arriving on the summit, [the Missourians] gave one shout, one hurrah," and some proceeded to open fire on the defenders with pistols or rifles; others, swinging clubbed rifles or wielding knives, jumped in among the Mexicans. Clark, who scrambled up the face of the redoubt to his front, found dead and wounded Mexican soldiers lying around their guns. Not hesitating a moment, Clark called over his gunners, who began shifting one of the Mexican cannon and training it on the center redoubt. Suddenly, from the well-sited Mexican cannon atop Sacramento Mountain, "shot after shot" fell around the Americans. Disregarding these salvos for the moment, Clark's men managed to train their captured cannon, firing first on some of the fleeing Mexicans, "mow[ing] them down [and leaving the area] strewn with corpses and the mangled bodies of their wounded."[20]

Doniphan saw that "the main [Mexican] battery to our right still continued to pour in a constant and heavy fire." Shouting encouragement, Mitchell and Jackson led their men forward on the right. They paused to deliver a volley at seventy yards out, and at that range fire from their well-aimed rifles produced several Mexican casualties. In reply, a scattering of shots came from Mexican soldiers, several of whom hurriedly discharged their muskets. Recognizing the

"Battle of Sacramento, Feb. 28th, 1847." (Currier & Ives print, courtesy of the Library of Congress)

strength of the defensive lines, some of the Missourians understood then that if the Mexicans had "only fought cooly and directed their musketry well we must have suffered a heavy loss." Instead, some of the Mexicans kept down in the redoubts and "behind the breastworks and in the ditches," sometimes firing their muskets by placing them on the parapet and pulling the trigger without taking aim, which indicated both deficient training and inadequate leadership from company-level officers—the captains and lieutenants. The Missouri volunteers reached the main redoubt: they scrambled up and over the sides, confronting the Mexican defenders, several of whom staunchly held their positions, fighting back with whatever weapons came to hand. Mitchell discharged a double-barreled shotgun at the Mexican artillerymen, and other Missourians drew pistols and fired point-blank, killing the gallant defenders where they stood. Mitchell saw that a determined Mexican officer had rallied about two hundred of his soldiers outside the south corner of the redoubt. Mitchell reacted instantly, yelling for his men to form into a hasty line. Some of the mounted Missourians from Reid's and Parsons's companies had ridden across the rear of the Mexican defenses and, seeing Mitchell's line deploying, cantered over to assist him. Giving his men a glance, Mitchell called for a charge, and they ran headlong down the

"Colonel Mitchell bearing off the Mexican Standard." (From Frost, *Pictorial History of Mexico and the Mexican War* [1848]; courtesy of the Museum of New Mexico, negative no. 171109)

slope toward the enemy, dispersing them. Following behind the attacking battalion, the American horse-holders pulled the reins of the mounts and brought the excited animals toward the soldiers. Swinging into their saddles, Mitchell's men took up the pursuit of the retreating Mexicans. They galloped down the slope to the Sacramento River and reached the road to Chihuahua. In several places the pursuit turned into dozens of individual fights. Soldiers shot, stabbed, and jabbed at their enemies. Symbolic of the victory, Mitchell picked up a Mexican flag and rode to find Colonel Doniphan.[21]

The battle was ending, and from across the Río Sacramento the Mexican cannon sent shots at the Americans to provide some cover for Heredia's retreating army. Not content to let the Mexican shots go unanswered, Clark turned his attention to the Mexican gun position some twelve hundred yards away. Clark reported that "the first fire of our guns dismounted one of his largest pieces, and the [American] fire was kept up with such briskness and precision of aim, that the battery was soon silenced and the enemy seen precipitately retreating." Noticing other likely targets, the artillery major then directed his crews to shift their fire to Rancho Trías and the Mexican supply wagons parked nearby. By then, clusters of Americans were running or riding across the plateau, which was "strewn with lances, arms, provisions, dead men, etc." The battle had shattered Heredia's army, "leaving the American forces master of the field."[22]

As nightfall approached, Doniphan ranged across the scene of his victory and happened upon a wounded Mexican artillery lieutenant in one of the redoubts. Having the advantage of seeing the outcome of the battle, the colonel conversed with the man, asking him "if he did not know, before the action came on, that the Mexicans would be defeated." Facing the commander of the invading enemy force, the young lieutenant responded, "'I did not; and if they [the Mexican soldiers] had stood to their posts, as I encouraged them to do, you never could have driven us from our strong position. I am now your prisoner but I do not regret fighting for the liberty and honor of my country. I will still encourage my people to resist foreign invasion.'" This patriotic reply impressed Doniphan, who magnanimously paroled the lieutenant rather than keeping him with the other prisoners.[23]

Doniphan requested reports on Mexican casualties as well as lists of killed and wounded from his own battalions. On the American side, Samuel Owens, the foolhardy merchant, was the only fatality; however, three soldiers were mortally wounded and died the next day. These included Sergeant A. A. Kirkpatrick and J. L. MacGruder, rank not specified, both of Captain Reid's Company D, and Private William Henkle, of Captain Parsons's Company F. Eight other Missourians were wounded in the battle. A couple of these suffered serious wounds, including Sergeant A. Hughes of Parsons's company, who had both legs broken by a Mexican cannonball. Doniphan noticed that all of those who died of wounds came in the units that remained mounted during the assault.[24]

The Americans gave various tallies of Mexican casualties, but all agreed that the Mexican losses were high. The estimates ranged from three hundred to five hundred Mexicans killed in action, and another three hundred to five hundred wounded. The count of prisoners should have been more accurately rendered, but even that number shifted between forty and seventy-nine. Taking an approximation of nearly eight hundred Mexicans soldiers killed, wounded, and made prisoner meant that Heredia's army suffered around 25 percent casualties. If the Mexicans losses totaled over one thousand, then casualties would have been about 30 percent. Whatever the total, Sergeant William Kennerly recalled that it took the Missourians most of the next day, March 1, to bury the dead.[25]

The Missourians described a variety of Mexican equipment and supplies captured after the battle. They claimed to have taken several Mexican regimental flags and national banners, and Major Clark took a special trophy, Brazito's infamous Black Flag. Although once again the American accounts varied in the totals they rendered for supplies and so on, included in the booty were several cannon, hundreds of pounds of powder and ammunition, thirteen thousand pounds of bread, sixteen thousand pounds of meat, one hundred mules, thousands of cattle and sheep, twenty heavy wagons plus several other horse-drawn vehicles, numerous boxes of cigars, and some three thousand dollars in gold and silver coins. This booty not only provided trophies and souvenirs for the victors but also resupplied the Missouri column for weeks to come, and the money revitalized the expedition's buying power. Furthermore, that so much was abandoned on the field indicated the extent of the Mexican defeat.[26]

In his after-action report, General Heredia tried to put the best face on the defeat. Summarizing his army's "desperate effort" to prevent the loss of the province of Chihuahua and its capital, Heredia's gloomy words revealed his disappointment and supported the decisiveness of the American victory. For his part, the general calculated his losses at a remarkable total of only one hundred killed, wounded, and missing—only about 3 percent of his army. Many of these came from the redoubtable company of the 7th Infantry, which was nearly annihilated. In his conclusion Heredia revealed that "having lost all hope of regaining the day," his "terrified" soldiers "fled to the mountains," displaying more "confusion" than cohesion. His "camp remained in possession of the enemy, [and] nothing was saved" but a few rounds of ammunition. Although his officers tried, their "efforts were useless" to gather stragglers, and the army had disintegrated, thus indicating that under the category of "missing" the total certainly must have been higher than one hundred. In light of Heredia's own admission of suffering such a resounding defeat, and the fact that his army no longer existed as a fighting force, Mexican losses were probably closer to the American estimates than the incredibly low number Heredia recorded.[27]

While Heredia wanted to downplay his losses, the victors displayed some disagreement over assigning credit for the Battle of Sacramento, which one member of the regiment contended immodestly would "safely be regarded as one of the most signal and brilliant victories ever achieved by American arms." To another veteran, Private William Richardson, the American "success is to be attributed entirely to the superior skill of our commander [Doniphan]." Likewise, John Hughes showered the lion's share of the credit on Doniphan, writing that "he was all the while at the proper place, whether to dispense his orders, encourage his men, or to use his sabre in thinning the enemy's ranks. His courage and gallant conduct were only equalled by his clear foresight, and great judgment." A sharply contrasting view came from Lieutenant Charles Wooster, one of the

Regular dragoon officers assigned to the regiment as an adviser. Wooster contended that "Col. Doniphan . . . was rather at a loss what to do during the action, and readily assented to any advice given by myself [Wooster] or by Capt. Thompson of the Dragoons who was present. In fact, . . . without assuming too much to myself, that the movements generally during the engagement were made at my suggestion." None of the other veterans, whatever their rank, accorded Lieutenant Wooster such influence during the battle. Other Missourians wanted to give the greatest glory to another one of their own officers—Lieutenant Colonel Mitchell. For example, Lieutenant Robert B. Todd believed that Mitchell "seemed to be every where," providing inspiring leadership on the battlefield, and that Doniphan had slighted Mitchell in the official report of the battle. Indeed, Mitchell inspired the Missourians on the right side of the line and during the pursuit after the Mexican redoubts were taken, but he did not give central direction to the assault. Even Todd admitted that there was "glory enough for one campaign—Glory enough for our gallant State" and its soldiers who had fought so well.[28]

Many newspapers from around the United States considered Sacramento a notable victory and devoted varying amounts of attention to the battle. While news of Doniphan's victory competed for space with coverage of Zachary Taylor's victory at Buena Vista (La Angostura, February 22–23) and Winfield Scott's landing at Veracruz (March 9), journalists' reports about Sacramento built recognition for the colonel and boosted him to the level of a national hero. Several of the accounts bestowed compliments on the Missouri volunteers for their victory, glowed with nationalistic pride, and implied that the regiment represented an expanding America. For example, giving the flavor of the positive coverage, the Natchez *Mississippi Free Trader* intoned, "This battle, considering the disparity of forces engaged, is one of the most brilliant achievements of American arms during the existing war, and reflects imperishable honor upon the Missouri volunteers, whose gallantry and bravery won it." The New Orleans *Picayune* ran one of the few wartime maps of the battlefield and proclaimed that "the battle of Sacramento and the capture of Chihuahua are among the most glorious events of the whole war." The Indianapolis *Indiana State Sentinel* and the Cincinnati *Enquirer* used the same headline heralding the "Glorious News!! Fall of Chihuahua!" In a later issue the *State Sentinel* complimented the "Missouri sharp shooters" on their victory over a "strongly entrenched" Mexican force. Vying to place the battle on a pinnacle, the Savannah *Daily Republican* termed it "a very brilliant achievement," the Baltimore *Daily Republican and Argus* called it "a most brilliant victory," the Columbia *Missouri Statesman* hailed it as a "splendid victory," and both the Charleston *Courier* and the Tallahassee *Floridian* echoed a story from the Washington *Union*, calling the battle a "brilliant action" in which Americans achieved victory although outnumbered four to one. Referring to Sacramento, the Little Rock *Arkansas State Gazette* concluded that "it must be a matter of national pride to know that wherever our arms appear they prove invincible." Taking a similar stance, the Newark, New Jersey, *Advertiser* expounded: "Wherever the American Arms encounter the Mexicans they triumph, whatever may be the odds." The Fayette, Missouri, *Boon's Lick Times* stressed the "Victory of the Missourians!" and heralded "Huzza for the Missouri boys!" The St. Louis *Republican* congratulated the state of Missouri for producing such fine soldiers, and the St. Louis *Reveille* contended that Sacramento was sure to bring the "admiration and the applause which a whole country will shower upon the victors."[29]

Other newspapers limited their coverage to recapitulating one or two official postbattle reports without offering editorial comments. They especially favored quoting Doniphan's lengthy and positive letter reporting the battle's results to the adjutant general of the U.S. Army in Washington. Regarding Doniphan's letter, the *Niles National Register* noted the brief compliment: "Our officers write as well as fight." In an odd departure from the other papers printing accounts of victory at Sacramento, the Baltimore *Sun* offered the rumor that instead of winning Doniphan may have been severely defeated.[30]

In contrast to the positive tone of most journalistic reports, and notwithstanding Doniphan's membership in the Whig party, some Whig papers called for Americans to reevaluate the war effort. The New York *Tribune* duly noted the victory at Sacramento and the fall of Chihuahua, but it contended, "Against any country except Mexico . . . it would seem the height of madness and folly thus to make war by marching handfuls of men into the populous districts and States, and taking possession of large towns. [The United States] may receive a check to our overweening confidence ere long; though God forbid it should be Col. Doniphan" who would suffer a reverse. The Richmond *Whig and Public Advertiser* deftly complimented Doniphan's exploits while criticizing the leaders of the Polk administration. The *Whig*'s approach contended that the march of the Missourians and the victory at Sacramento "deserves to be ranked among the most adventurous and brilliant exploits of the Mexican War." On the other hand, the Richmond writer asserted that Doniphan's "movement to Chihuahua formed no part of a well digested plan of operations" and that, placed in danger "beyond the reach of aid from any quarter," Doniphan might well have fallen to "defeat and massacre from the superior force" that the colonel engaged. The *Whig* concluded: "That he [Doniphan] was not cut off is ascribable not to the 'eminent ability' of those by whose orders he undertook this fruitless expedition, but to the skill and courage of himself and of the men he commanded." America's senior political and military leaders deserved censure because "the expedition seems to have been undertaken without any object—as the conquered territory will be necessarily abandoned [following peace negotiations]. Whether the 'glory' won by Col. Doniphan and his men is deemed sufficient recompense for the hardships and perils they have successfully encountered, must be left for wiser heads . . . to determine." Along similar lines, the Washington *National Era* wondered what another victory "by flogging poor Mexico" would really mean. In the view of the *Era*, "The warfare upon the Mexicans [was] becoming a continued science of slaughter."[31]

Reading the report of Doniphan's victory in the Washington press, President Polk allowed his hyperbole free rein when he wrote emphatically in his diary, "The battle of Sacramento I consider to be one of the most decisive and brilliant achievements of the War." Overjoyed at yet another American triumph, the commander in chief paid the volunteer colonel a high compliment, especially considering that Polk was a Democrat and Doniphan a Whig, but the president recognized that the Missourian's victory supported the administration's overall strategy for the war.[32]

For an engagement involving modest-sized forces,[33] the battle at Sacramento had several significant consequences. First, fought only a few days after Zachary Taylor's triumph near Saltillo at Buena Vista,[34] Doniphan's victory at Sacramento protected Taylor's flank. Second, Sacramento put to rest any hopes of Mexico's retaking Santa Fe, and contemporaries expressed the opinion that it helped pacify New Mexico and protect America's hold on that province.[35] Moreover, the fall of the provincial capital of Chihuahua City on March 2, 1847, lowered Mexican national morale. Furthermore, there was a possible economic consequence: the state of Chihuahua produced large quantities of silver from its mines, bullion turned into specie for the government. American occupation of the province, rated by one American observer as "third in wealth and resources" among Mexican states,[36] disrupted a major source of silver to the Mexican government.

Yet another Mexican defeat highlighted the deficiencies of Mexico's army, which had been unable to mount sturdy defenses or repulse any of the United States invasions into Mexico's northern states. In addition, one of Doniphan's soldiers contended that the American victory "prevented a large amount of property [guns, ammunition, trade goods] in the hands of the traders from falling into [the Mexicans'] hands—property which was sufficient to have supported the whole Mexican army [of Heredia] for several months."[37] Furthermore, Doniphan's win over an entrenched army also deprived the Mexicans of the intangible yet potentially significant uplift that a victory over any American force would have given Mexican arms. Thus Sacramento's outcome reinforced both the image and the reality of U.S. military prowess and Mexican ineptitude.[38]

The El Paso–Chihuahua campaign added strength to the tradition of the American volunteer army officer. Essentially a novice in military matters in 1846, Doniphan appeared to many of his contemporaries to personify the widely held American faith that natural military leaders would step forward when the nation needed them. The New Orleans *Delta* accurately characterized Doniphan as a "citizen commander of citizen soldiers," but the Washington *Daily Union* went so far as to rank Doniphan among Taylor, Scott, Kearny, Sterling Price, and John C. Frémont as the top officers of the war, concluding, "What can the Mexicans expect from any contest with such soldiers?" Certainly Doniphan's regiment accomplished remarkable things, and the battle at Sacramento demonstrated that he was one of the best volunteer commanders of the war.[39]

By March 1847 Doniphan had been on campaign for nearly nine months. He had fought and won two engagements with the Mexicans. Now located deep inside the enemy's country, Doniphan began thinking about how he and his soldiers would conclude their service and how they would arrange to get back to Missouri.

CHAPTER EIGHT

From Chihuahua to the Coast

On March 2, 1847, Doniphan saw the late afternoon sun reflecting off of the impressive spires of a cathedral and the sandy adobe of hundreds of flat-roofed houses of Ciudad Chihuahua, a metropolis with a population of about fifteen thousand. Around 4:00 P.M., with the "grand" tones of the cathedral's bells ringing in their ears, Doniphan and his Missouri regiment entered a civilized haven in the desert and prepared to occupy the second capital of a Mexican state. The colonel arranged for Major Clark's artillery bandsmen to play "Yankee Doodle" and "Hail Columbia," and his soldiers fired twenty-eight cannon shots to salute the American flag as it ran up the pole in the city's central plaza. Many of the city's residents were not there to see the flag raising; perhaps half of the population had fled in fear of the conquerors. A number of foreign nationals turned out to welcome the victors of Sacramento, showing Lieutenant George Gibson that they were "greatly relieved" by the triumph of American arms.[1]

The city made a favorable first impression on the Americans, who, gratified by their victory, gladly ensconced themselves at a place with plentiful water and food. In the opinion of Private Frank Edwards, Chihuahua was "a city far superior to any place we had before entered," and Lieutenant Gibson believed that Chihuahua was "really pretty." The city was well laid out, with clean, wide streets lined with cottonwood trees. An impressive stone aqueduct, more than five miles long, supplied some of the city's water needs. Several public squares, graced with fountains, provided places to socialize and relax. Doniphan and his soldiers toured what the Americans called the "Congress Hall," the Chihuahua state assembly building, containing the archives, meeting rooms, and officials' chambers, ornately decorated with gilt and paintings. Incongruously, the Mexicans displayed several Indian scalps on a railing in front of the hall. The Yankees

"Chihuahua About 1850." (From Webb, *Adventures in the Santa Fe Trade, 1844–1847* [1931]; courtesy of Arthur Clark Co. and the Museum of New Mexico, negative no. 171105)

also walked through the handsome treasury building, and Colonel Doniphan decided that, since it contained so many vacant rooms, it would make good quarters for some of Major Gilpin's troops. Posted to the city's bullring, Lieutenant Colonel Congreve Jackson's battalion fit comfortably onto the grounds of the large structure. A lovely *alameda*, or public walkway, extended through and around the city. More cottonwood trees shaded the *alameda*, and stone benches, placed intermittently, allowed pedestrians to pause and rest. Doniphan himself concluded that it was a "beautiful city."[2]

The Missouri volunteers soon understood why the pride of the city was its magnificent Roman Catholic cathedral. Dominating the main plaza, the shrine made a deep impression on all visitors to the city. It was built in the Gothic style and measured "180 feet long and 80 wide with two steeples 100 feet high"; the twin towers each contained a matching set of a dozen bells. A variety of carvings and sculptures, including life-sized statues of Jesus Christ and the Twelve Apostles, decorated the cathedral's front elevation. Beautiful Corinthian columns flanked an arched entryway holding two heavy wooden doors. Suitably awed, Private Jacob Robinson, originally from Portsmouth, New Hampshire, called it "one of the most splendid buildings in America." Under construction for half a century and completed in 1789, the cathedral contained a ornate interior that Lieutenant Gibson concluded was too "gaudy" for his taste, with "every corner being occupied by paintings or some scriptural representation."[3]

On March 3 the cathedral served as the ceremonial departure point for "Major" Samuel Owens, late leader of the merchants' battalion. Many of the soldiers assumed that Owens was a Catholic (though he was not), but his friends planned an elaborate funeral regardless of his religious conviction. Owens's friends paid six Mexican priests to officiate at a mass, and one American cogently observed, "Perhaps nothing could have been better calculated to allay the terror and dislike of the citizens [of Chihuahua], than to see their priests thus performing funeral service over one of our officers." As the cathedral bells tolled, the funeral cortege wound across the "white polished stone" pavement of the plaza. Removing their hats, members of the regiment lined the street or stood on the stone benches to watch the procession.[4]

Within a few days, many of Chihuahua's residents returned from the countryside to the city, and shops and markets resumed their business. Calling to potential customers, street vendors peddled "sugar candies, cakes, pies, oranges and other refreshments." Soldiers with money to spend or items to trade bargained with local merchants selling "bread, red peppers, beans, dried pumpkins, and parched corn." By the end of March the city was lush with "peach and pear trees . . . in full bloom, and fig trees . . . putting forth their leaves"; quantities of plums, apricots, and quinces soon became available.[5]

While the fruit trees promised an abundant harvest, Doniphan and his soldiers hoped they could confiscate some of the bounty of Chihuahua's renowned silver mines. Several mines operated within a few miles of the city, providing some of the specie that helped Mexico finance the war. Workers transported the ore from the mountains to the Mexican government mint in Chihuahua City. Hoping that it might contain coins with which he could pay his soldiers, Doniphan demanded entry to the mint on March 3. The director of the mint, an Englishman named John Potts, at first refused Doniphan's demand, asserting, in the words of Private John Hughes, "that he had a private claim upon the mint, and did not intend to permit the Americans to go into it." Potts's refusal brought this response from the colonel: "Sir, I neither fear you nor your government [did he mean the Mexican or the British?], and shall enter by force if necessary." After many months on campaign, the Missouri volunteers had developed what Dr. Frederick Wislizenus called a "ragged" and "savage" appearance. "There was not one among them in complete uniform, and not two in the whole regiment dressed alike." Unsurprisingly, Mr. Potts considered that the Missourians looked more like bandits than soldiers. Undeterred by Potts's refusal, Doniphan deployed five companies of his men and directed Captain Weightman to bring around two of his cannon. Seeing these scruffy but efficient troops arrayed in only a few minutes, Potts responded, "Gentlemen, the doors shall be opened if you will wait a moment til the keys can be obtained." Enjoying the chance to put a humorous touch to Potts's statement, Doniphan exclaimed, "We have keys [the cannon] which will fit any lock and can as well enter the building without your aid as not." When the doors swung open, the building was found to contain no money, and the disappointed troops received no pay from Mexican coffers. To keep his disappointed troops occupied, the colonel rotated required tactical drills through the regiment's companies on a daily basis.[6]

After the incident at the mint, and following Kearny's example from earlier in the campaign, on March 6 Doniphan read a proclamation to the people of Chihuahua. In the words of the "commander-in-chief of North American forces," they would be occupying the city indefinitely, and, as in New Mexico, Doniphan claimed that capturing the state capital had put the whole state under American control. He urged everyone to go about their "ordinary occupations," including coming into the city to conduct business with the American merchants who had accompanied the expedition. The colonel pledged to protect the city's residents in their persons, property, and religion. Doniphan also promised that any crimes against his soldiers would be punished, but he stressed that wars were between armies and that violence would not be visited "against individual citizens who are unarmed." Putting a hard edge on the American occupation, and as he promised in his proclamation, during the coming days Doniphan dealt harshly with Mexican thieves, ordering several public floggings to punish those considered guilty even of petty crimes.[7]

After residing only a few days in Chihuahua, some of the volunteers decided to create a record of their sojourn by establishing a newspaper. In mid-March Lieutenant Christian Kribben, one of the artillery officers, became editor of an occupation newspaper, the *Anglo Saxon*. Boasting of some experience in journalism, Kribben also practiced law in St. Charles, Missouri, and had enlisted in Company B of the St. Louis artillery. The paper was a diversion for Kribben and probably entertained the Missouri volunteers, who enjoyed seeing their exploits in print. Kribben complained, however, that due to shortages of newsprint it had been easier to overcome "big obstacles" on the campaign than it was to publish the newspaper.[8]

Cut off from routine contact with other Americans, the expedition never received enough news about what was happening in Missouri and the United

States or how their own adventures might be covered back home or understood by military superiors. Scattered reports in American newspapers expressed some skepticism that Doniphan's small force could survive so deep inside the enemy nation. Receiving no official reports from the U.S. War Department, editors printed speculations on the possibility that the Doniphan Expedition had been defeated. In contrast, General Taylor at Monterrey had been handed a report that *Kearny* had reached Chihuahua, but Old Rough and Ready did "not attach much credit to the rumor." Now that he had succeeded in capturing Chihuahua, Doniphan doubtless would have been disappointed to learn that Secretary of War William Marcy "much regretted that Colonel Doniphan was sent down the Rio Grande towards Chihuahua. As General [John] Wool did not proceed with his expedition to [Chihuahua City], the Colonel and his command may find themselves in an exposed position." Indeed, Doniphan's regiment was in an "exposed position," but, as Private Hughes described so well, the men of the 1st Missouri held a low regard for most Mexicans and believed they were capable of defeating any Mexican military force brought against them.[9]

Doniphan wanted to relay both official reports and unofficial information on the status of the expedition to the United States. Around March 6 he dispatched a messenger to Santa Fe through El Paso, with a description of the regiment's victory at Sacramento and position in Chihuahua. Next, on March 14 the colonel sent "Major" John P. Campbell, one of the Missouri merchants, and an escort of thirty-eight men back to the States carrying letters to the authorities. Campbell's party traveled north to El Paso, then across Texas and Louisiana, eventually reaching New Orleans on May 10. A week later he stepped off a steamboat in St. Louis, giving the city and the state substantive descriptions of the circumstances and adventures of the Doniphan Expedition. Writing to U.S. Army Adjutant General Roger Jones, Doniphan revealed his fear that General Santa Anna had surrounded General Wool at Saltillo. If Wool suffered a defeat, Doniphan concluded that "an immediate retreat [by the Missouri regiment] will become necessary." In a similar letter intended for publication back home, Doniphan elaborated to E. M. Ryland, editor of the St. Louis *Republican:* "Our position will be ticklish, if Santa Anna should compel Taylor and Wool . . . to fall back. All Durango, Zacatecas, and Chihuahua will be down upon my little army." The colonel gave a stark analysis of his situation: "We are out of the reach of help, and it is as unsafe to go backward as forward. High spirits and a bold front, is perhaps the best and safest policy." The colonel could not resist adding a flash of humor. "My men are rough, ragged, and ready, having one more of the R's than General Taylor himself." Unpaid for nine months and veterans of hundreds of miles of marching, the Missouri soldiers existed on "half rations, hard marches, and no clothes!—but they are still game to the last, and curse and praise their country by turns, but fight for her all the time."[10]

The numerous attractions of Chihuahua City diverted the Missouri volunteers away from warlike pursuits. Many of the Americans sought familiar entertainments such as cockfights and fandangos. Although they had heard much about bullfights, few of the Missourians actually had seen one. Chihuahua held its bloody events in a remarkable large public arena, which appeared to Lieutenant Gibson to reflect the style of a "Roman amphitheater." The bullring was "one hundred yards in diameter," with stands that seated five thousand people. During the American occupation, however, there was a shortage of bulls, and the matadors either refused to perform or had left the city. Tired oxen replaced spirited bulls, and neophytes substituted for experienced matadors, detracting from the spectacle the Missourians expected to see.[11]

On the way to the bullring or returning to their quarters, the soldiers were pleased by the availability of all sorts of foods in the city. After the tiresome, limited fare on the march from El Paso, the soldiers could feast from a cornucopia, including "eggs, chickens, lettuce, asparagus, and beans and peas." According to Lieutenant Gibson, "mutton and pork [were] plentiful but generally not good," though it was refreshing to have some variety in their menus again. Among the most notable commercial repasts, the turkey dinners spread in the dining room of one of the large hotels soon gained a reputation for being like ones in restaurants in the States, "remind[ing] us of home."[12]

On another, more lovely, subject altogether, one of the volunteers decided that the women of Chihuahua City were very "attractive." Dr. Wislizenus commented that "the señoritas are celebrated for their beauty and natural grace." Lieutenant Gibson agreed, observing that "the women are of good size, well made, and some very beautiful and fascinating." One of the astounding attractions of the city was a sequence of "bath houses and refreshing pools of pure water arranged for public accomodation [*sic*]." Private Daniel Hastings recorded that "groups of both sexes may at any time be seen swimming diving and splashing in great glee, without one thought of modesty or impropriety, considering it a great luxury." Obviously drawn to the ladies' charms, Private Hughes offered more than just detached observations: "Modest, chaste, virtuous, intelligent females are rarely to be met with [in Chihuahua], yet, notwithstanding they are few, there are some such. Many of the females of that country, are gifted with sprightly minds, possess rare personal beauty, and most gentle and winning grace of manners. Their lustrous, dark, sparkling eyes, and tresses of glossy, black hair, constitute a fair share of their charms." During their days in Chihuahua, many of the Missouri volunteers sought liaisons with the city's women.[13]

After nearly nine months on campaign, many of the undisciplined Missouri volunteers demanded more than good food and innocent pastimes. Private Hastings noticed that among the volunteers "debauchery [was] becoming more and more prevalent." Private Robinson agreed, writing that "drunkenness [was] much less common among the Mexicans than with us." It became routine for the Missouri soldiers to seek out "improper indulgences" and other "transactions of so heinous and obscene a character" that Hastings refused to detail them in his diary. The soldiers had an increasing tendency to squabble and fight among themselves or be lured into gaming dens and cockfights, where they had altercations with Mexicans, though incidents of significant violence were few.[14]

Susan Magoffin, wife of James Magoffin, one of the Missouri merchants, gave a graphic and sarcastic description of her opinion of the Missourians' residence in the city after they had been there about one month:

> We found Col. Doniphan's command occupying the city, and a beautiful sight they have made of it in some respects. Instead of seeing it in its original beauty as I thought to have done twelve months since, I saw it filled with Missouri volunteers who though good to fight are not careful at all how much they soil the property of a friend much less an enemy. The good citizens of [Chihuahua] had never dreamed I dare say that their loved homes would be turned into quarters for common soldiers, their fine houses many of them turned into stables, the rooves [*sic*] made kitchens of, their public *pila* [drinking fountain] used as a bathing trough, the fine trees of their beautiful alamador [*alameda*—public walk] barked and forever spoiled, and a hundred other deprivations equal to any of these.[15]

Although some of the volunteers later wanted to deny any serious problems, the matter of indiscipline in Doniphan's regiment was beginning to take on paramount importance, and, exotic though it was, Mexico had lost its appeal for him and many of his soldiers. To the colonel, Mexico was a "sterile and miserable country," and he heaped "hearty curses [on] everything Mexican." The state of Chihuahua was desolate, according to Lieutenant Gibson, and the provincial capital had "an immense number of beggars . . . at every corner. . . . They are a great nuisance, and consist of men, women, and children in filth and rags." Doniphan's soldiers were losing their patience, tired of field campaigning, and ready to end their enlistments. This combination of factors led Doniphan to conclude, in a letter to General John Wool, that by this point in their service, the men of the 1st Missouri were "wholly unfit to garrison a town or city." The colonel recognized that his men would "soon be wholly ruined by improper indulgences." The soldiers began to take out their frustrations on the local population, and some of the city's women and children again sought refuge in the countryside. According to Private Hastings, "horseracing [*sic*], gambling, and street fighting have become the chief business of the day, while drunkenness, licentiousness, profanity, the needless destruction of property, and uncalled for abuse practiced upon innocent natives are engaged in with impunity." Receiving the news of General Scott's victory at Veracruz prompted the Missourians to hold a round of boisterous fandangos.[16]

Not knowing how long he would remain in Chihuahua, Doniphan set a meeting with local authorities to discuss the release of Americans held prisoner in the city and elsewhere and to resolve the status of American merchants who had traveled with the expedition. Foreign residents of Chihuahua had told the Americans, "So confident were they [i.e., the Mexicans] of success [at Sacramento] that they had made arrangements to dispose of all goods of the [American] traders." Therefore, Doniphan was protective of the merchants. The colonel invited Governor Trías to return to Chihuahua to participate in the meeting, but the governor declined. Held in Doniphan's commodious rooms in the governor's palace, the conference resulted in a "treaty" by which the Mexicans agreed to allow the traders to sell their goods without reprisal. The colonel also demanded that the Mexican authorities release six Americans held hostage in Durango, including merchant James Magoffin, threatening to execute six Mexican army officers captured after the battle at Sacramento if the Americans were not set free.[17]

By this point in his adventure, Doniphan knew the merchants all too well, and he was not going to let them issue orders to him. Some of the merchants were strongly opposed to Doniphan's leaving Chihuahua until they could sell their goods, which might take months. The merchants wanted to both complete their transactions and enjoy the protection of American arms before returning to Santa Fe. Doniphan told General Wool that the entrepreneurs had "several hundred thousand dollars at stake." Several implored Doniphan to remain in Chihuahua until the enlistment of the regiment expired—about three more months—but even they admitted to the colonel "that their [quantity of] goods could not be sold here in five years." Clearly, Doniphan was growing impatient with the merchants, after making efforts to accommodate them during the previous eight months. He opposed "remaining here as a mere wagon-guard" for the businessmen. Doniphan made it clear, instead, that he favored taking a prompt path to Missouri—through El Paso to Santa Fe and then eastward, or across to the Gulf Coast and then by boat to New Orleans. Only the route was yet to be decided.[18]

On March 18 Doniphan learned that Zachary Taylor had fought a battle at Buena Vista (La Angostura) on February 22 to 23. Although Mexican rumors held that Santa Anna and his troops had defeated Taylor's army, the Missourians dismissed that assertion. Confident that there had been another American victory, Colonel Doniphan ordered the Missourians to celebrate by firing off twenty-eight cannon.[19]

Interpreting the news of Buena Vista to their own satisfaction, the volunteers speculated on how much longer they would be in Chihuahua and where they would be going next. The Missourians bandied about the names of their next likely destination. Some guessed Durango or Saltillo or Parras or, outrageously, Mexico City. Others favored returning to the United States, aiming for San Antonio, Texas, or Fort Towson, Indian Territory. At an officers' council of war held on March 19, Private Frank Edwards recalled hearing that "a few of the officers proposed staying in Chihuahua, others were for trying to join General Taylor, and some suggested a retrograde march to Santa Fé; most, however, were in favor of pressing home by way of Monterey [*sic*]." Colonel Doniphan and the group made no decision but met again a few days later, when the vote of the majority favored staying in Chihuahua. Doniphan, in the meantime, made plain his own decision: he wanted to return to Missouri. Learning of Doniphan's opinion, several of the merchants realized that they should start selling off their goods, even if that meant disposing of them to Chihuahua's businessmen at reduced prices.[20]

Determined to leave Chihuahua, the colonel decided on March 20 to send messages to Wool and Taylor. Doniphan picked one of the merchants, "Major" James L. Collins of Boonville, Missouri, to lead an "express party" of twelve men, including Private John T. Hughes, to Saltillo, more than six hundred miles away. The colonel wrote a lengthy letter to General Wool, explaining circumstances in Chihuahua. Based on a pace of twenty-five miles per day and hoping there would be no delays, Doniphan expected Collins to take several weeks to reach Saltillo, meet with Wool, and then return to Chihuahua. Traveling mostly at night to avoid encountering Mexican soldiers, Collins set out at breakneck speed, setting an exceptional pace of nearly fifty miles per day.[21]

Before Collins could return, Doniphan learned that the Mexicans might have stored a quantity of military supplies at the town of San Geronimo, near Parral, more than 150 miles to the southwest. Although some doubted the rumor, Doniphan ordered Gilpin's battalion, plus Clark's artillery and Hudson's

Rangers, more than half of the regiment, to sortie and destroy the cache. The colonel's orders resulted in two feverish days of gathering supplies, "shoeing horses, . . . repairing wagons," and packing them. Accompanied by Dr. Wislizenus, newly appointed as one of the regimental surgeons, the contingent left Chihuahua on April 5. In sharp contrast to the march south from El Paso, the Missourians had food on the hoof; many head of cattle and sheep grazed in the countryside, available for the regiment's cook fires. About 50 miles from Chihuahua, an American dispatch rider brought the column to a halt, claiming that five thousand Mexicans were marching to retake the city. If the report of this large Mexican force was valid, Doniphan had to reunite his contingent with the rest of the regiment. Believing he had no choice, the colonel ordered the men to return to Chihuahua without confirming if military supplies were in San Geronimo and without sending scouts south to check on the truth about the advancing Mexicans. No substantive information was ever received about Mexican forces operating near Chihuahua City, but a number of its residents, some of whom had only recently come back to their homes, left the city, fearing a battle in the streets. It was the regiment's only retrograde movement of the entire expedition, and two days later the battalion and supporting units were encamped again at Chihuahua.[22]

"Major" James Collins and his dozen Missouri volunteer riders, accompanied by twenty-six Arkansas cavalrymen from General Wool's command, arrived in Chihuahua on April 23. The cathedral bells rang, and Weightman's cannon boomed their welcome. The Collins express brought word from General Taylor that the Doniphan Expedition was to report to him near Saltillo as soon as possible. Doniphan announced Taylor's order to the regiment, and everyone began making arrangements to depart within two days. Of course, receiving the orders to leave Chihuahua created another reason for a fandango at the biggest hotel. To no one's surprise, the party became an "evening with merry drunkenness."[23]

As before with major marches, Doniphan divided the regiment into segments that departed at staggered times. The morning of the first departure on April 25 presented an unusual scene. Despite the fact that several unpleasant incidents and episodes had taken place in and around Chihuahua between Missourians and Mexicans, Private Hastings marveled to see a "great number of young ladies assembled on the side of the street to bid [the soldiers] adieu, and in many instances their tearful eyes and quivering lips betrayed their deep sorrow at parting with the Americans." Some of the women asked the colonel if they could travel with the regiment; assuming his strictest tone, Doniphan forbade it. Later, however, other women hid themselves in wagons; some, dressed in pants and shirts, rode out of the city on horseback. One by one, Doniphan discovered them and sent them home.[24]

Accompanying Doniphan once again were several American merchants, including Manuel X. Harmony. The colonel brought along the merchants for the reasons he had established earlier: some carried supplies that might benefit the expedition, and their heavy wagons could serve as a kind of moving redoubt to provide protection should the column be attacked. Engaging Mexican regular soldiers was still a possibility. The numbers of merchants traveling with the column by this time was not certain, but there were many fewer than before. Some had left Chihuahua during the occupation; others took their chances on their own when it was clear that the regiment would be moving east rather than north to El Paso. Because he had been attached to the expedition, Harmony had been treated as persona non grata by the Mexicans, who had boycotted his goods. Now he had to travel with the Americans to escape persecution by the Mexicans. Weeks earlier, Doniphan had suspected Harmony of collusion with Mexican authorities, but now the colonel allowed ten other merchants to stay in Chihuahua.[25]

The traders and the regiment faced yet another arduous march. They knew the prospects: not enough water, lack of wood for cooking, blazing hot sun in the daytime, and evening chills requiring blankets pulled to their chins at night. But with the fresh information brought in by Collins and Hughes, Doniphan knew enemy dispositions and the lay of the land between Chihuahua and Saltillo. As in New Mexico, the threat of Indian attacks had to be considered. The Collins-Hughes express encountered no Mexican army units, and would have avoided them if they had crossed them. The American volunteer soldiers proposed to travel over hundreds of miles through the interior of Mexico, but it was unlikely that they would go into battle with either regular units of the Mexican army or organized militia. Once again the deficiencies of the Mexican defenses were evident. But the land opposed the Missourians. They faced one bad seventy-five-mile *jornada* and other stretches where water would be scarce, but the Missourians had been through worse. In some places they could expect water to be available rather than nonexistent. The campsite of the first night out was comfortable, with water and plenty of grass for the horses and mules.[26]

Of course, the full regiment could not make the same speed logged by the Collins-Hughes express; the expedition was burdened with its own wagons, the merchants, and all of the artillery. But after fighting to take Mexican cannon, the volunteers were determined to bring home those heavy trophies, even if it took considerable extra effort. "Traversing ravines demanded letting them [the cannon] down the steep places with ropes and taking twenty mules to raise them to the [next] levels," Sergeant Kennerly recalled. Twenty miles out of Chihuahua a narrow, deep canyon looked like it might have been a perfect place for an ambush, if there had been Mexican troops there, but the column passed uncontested.[27]

On rough roads and across the countryside filled with thorny mesquite plants, the 1st Missouri moved at a steady pace. Even soldiers who had wanted to stay in Chihuahua or others who had wanted to take a more adventurous route to the south must have sensed the feeling of momentum toward the coast. On April 27 they passed through Santa Cruz, "a fine town" in Private Frank Edwards's opinion, having a population of about five thousand. They camped near a handsome hacienda supported by cotton fields watered by irrigation, and they heard reports of Apache raiders active up ahead. The regiment reached Santa Rosalía, which Private Robinson described as "a considerable town." Private Richardson and two hundred others bathed in the river, later tearing down a private corral and distributing the wood for cook fires. On May 1 Doniphan held an inspection of the regiment at Santa Rosalía: they had traveled 120 miles in four days.[28]

The days and the miles ticked by. A place called Rancho Remanda provided plenty of good water. From that spot, on May 2 Doniphan assembled an outfit of 116 men to push forward, conduct a reconnaissance, and arrange for provisions at the town of Parras. This advance guard consisted of Captain John Reid's Company D, the Arkansas cavalry detachment that had escorted the Collins-Hughes express, and Lieutenant Colonel Mitchell with twenty men. In the town of Guajuquilla, where irrigation canals from the Río Florida watered prosperous cotton fields, Doniphan was informed that the *jornada* of seventy-five miles lay ahead. To prepare for the crossing, on May 3 the Missourians purchased forage for their animals and a large quantity of fresh food for themselves.[29]

As before in such circumstances, the soldiers planned to traverse the *jornada* as rapidly as possible. On May 4, after several hours of travel, they came to "a pond of brackish water" and were glad to have something to drink, "notwithstanding it was a disagreeable mixture of salt and sulphur." Ahead of the column, heavy clouds rolled across the sky, and after dark heat lightning crackled, showing the outline of the roadway. Private Hughes recalled that "the artillery rumbled over the rocks, and [flickers of] fire sparkled beneath the wheels" as cannon passed over the road. Half asleep, soldiers swayed in their saddles; some sang songs to stay awake. The march continued until midnight, when Doniphan finally called a halt. The men were up early on May 5, shaking lizards and scorpions out of their blankets. They saddled up and rode through a dusty, waterless day. Hughes saw that "the dust filled the mouths, and nostrils, and eyes, and covered them completely." Swollen tongues added to the soldiers' discomfort. Reaching a grassy plateau, Dr. Wislizenus used his barometer and measured the spot at forty-seven hundred feet above sea level. The men chanced upon some Mexicans driving a string of mules transporting sugar and loaves of bread, buying some of the bread for only a few cents per loaf. That night they found trickling muddy water so bad that the horses refused to drink. Pressing on another three miles in hopes of finding better water brought them to another stream, containing the same muddy sludge but with sulphur added. Eventually, after a forty-mile day, they were gratified to come to a good spring, a spot that Hughes considered a true "oasis, a smiling, inviting retreat in a desert." "The long distance, as well as the want of water, the excessive heat, and especially the tremendous dust in the narrow road between the chaparráls, made to-day's march one of the most fatiguing," Dr. Wislizenus reported.[30]

On May 7, ranging beyond the regiment, Mitchell and the advance party encountered a group of thirty armed Mexican civilians. Avoiding a fight, Mitchell's force overawed and disarmed the Mexicans. Following an extended discussion, Mitchell found that the rancheros had not gathered to oppose the Americans but to watch out for Indian raiders. After receiving a pledge that they would not use their arms against the Doniphan Expedition, Mitchell returned their weapons. Meanwhile, with the regiment, Hughes reported that the hungry soldiers had helped themselves to cows, pigs, and chickens they found at Rancho Pailayo, not bothering to offer any payment for them.[31]

As the Americans entered the state of Durango, the land itself again became their enemy. Private Robinson remembered the regiment "marching through sand and dust, sometimes so thick that we could not see the steps before us." Patches of the road contained ruts six or eight inches deep and filled with a light, powdery silt. On May 9 Mexicans related news of an American victory: General Winfield Scott had defeated Santa Anna at the Battle of Cerro Gordo. Doniphan arranged for a salute to honor Scott, having twenty-nine cannon shots fired. The next day provided an enjoyable interlude: the regiment crossed a brisk-flowing stream, wonderful for swimming. Some miles farther on, Collins informed Doniphan that the residents of the village of San Sebastian "had been hostile" to his express party. Consequently, the troops took all the corn they wanted without paying. Coming to a ranch with little water on May 11, Private Robinson disparaged the countryside as having "not a blade of grass . . . and where there was any, it was dry as a nearly vertical sun could make it." Soldiers looked in the water of a murky pool and saw leeches stirring. Three soldiers, including Lieutenant Stephen Jackson, who had been ill with typhoid, died and were given military burials, assisted by a local priest.[32]

Since leaving Chihuahua, Doniphan and his men were aware of the dangers of Indians in the region. According to Private Frank Edwards, "The word *Apache* is enough to make a Mexican herdsman tremble." The constant threat from Indian raids prompted Mexican ranchers, farmers, and travelers to go everywhere armed, carrying one or more weapons, such as "a sabre, carbine and lance." Edwards went on to ascribe notable raiding prowess to the Apaches, claiming that they had been known to run off "several thousand head [of cattle] at a time." Recalling Jim Kirker's reputation as a bounty hunter, Edwards knew that "the government of Chihuahua at one time set a price on every Apache scalp."[33]

On May 12 Apache raiders drove off several dozen of the regiment's horses. Doniphan and Captain John Reid determined to get them back, though the colonel knew it was risky to send a small patrol away from the main column. Nevertheless, on May 13 Reid volunteered to lead a patrol, though only eight men stepped forward to join him. Among the riders were Sergeant Kennerly from the artillery. A few hours later Mitchell and another twenty men of the advance guard joined Reid, creating a more substantial force to operate independently of the regiment.[34]

Needing food and resupply, on May 13 Reid approached the hacienda of Don Manuel Ibarra, who already had established good relations with the regiment. Ibarra spoke English fluently, having received schooling at a frontier academy in Bardstown, Kentucky. Moreover, the month before, Ibarra had assisted James Collins's express riders, giving them food and exchanging fresh mounts for tired American horses. When Reid requested assistance, Don Manuel not only gave supplies to Reid's patrol but also offered, with Reid's permission, to lead several of his own rancheros to join the Missourians. The *patrón* explained to Reid that the Indians had captured more than a dozen women and children, run off hundreds mules and horses, and stolen equipment and belongings, including religious relics. Ibarra wanted to rescue the hostages and recover the animals and property. Knowing that the war between the United States and Mexico was still being fought, Ibarra nonetheless proposed to put his men under Reid's command in order to improve the chances of effecting the rescue. Reid graciously accepted Ibarra's offer, and now some sixty riders—Americans and Mexicans—set out together to find the Apaches.[35]

Later on May 13, near a spot called "El Pozo" (the Well), Reid's Missourians and Ibarra's Mexicans encountered the Lipan Apache raiders, estimated at forty or more warriors. The engagement opened with Reid, Ibarra, and two Mexican vaqueros serving as a decoy to lure the Indians into a trap. When the Indians pursued the four riders, the Missourians and Mexicans left a place of concealment and attacked the Lipans. Each group of mounted men commenced shooting at the other, producing what Reid termed a "conflict [that] was warm and close." Some of the Indians were armed with muskets; others had bows and arrows. Unwilling to give up their captives, animals, and loot, the Apaches counterattacked. This offensive tactic appeared to succeed, for although Reid's troops fired several shots, none seemed to hit their marks, and the Missourians beat a hasty retreat for one hundred yards.[36]

Then, at Reid's signal, the combined force suddenly swung around in a counterattack while several of the Missourians dismounted, in order to take better aim. About that time, fortunately for the Mexican-Missouri contingent, another group of Missouri riders crested a nearby hill; they were the escorts for the merchant wagons of Manuel Harmony. Recognizing Captain Reid, the soldiers brandished their weapons and charged down the slope, yelling like banshees. Their whoops startled the Indians, who knew instantly that these belligerent attackers were not rancheros. The Apaches jumped to the conclusion that they might be Texas Rangers. "*Tejanos! Tejanos!*" the Indians yelled, suddenly having to deal with two groups of battle-worthy enemies. In the resulting melee, Reid's Missourians and Ibarra's Mexicans claimed several Indians killed and wounded as the mounted combatants clashed and rode through the lines and clusters of their enemies, shouting and firing. Undaunted by casualties, each side reversed direction and charged again. Facing strongly armed and aggressive forces, the Indians broke off the engagement, leaving their dead behind. One Missourian wrote that, to him, the fallen Indians "resembled bronze statues thrown upon the ground."[37]

Reid was among several Missourians wounded, but the combined forces counted fifteen Apache dead on the field and claimed that another five wounded were carried off by their fellows. One of the principal warriors, thought by the Missourians to be a chief, was among the dead. Measuring and evaluating the fallen warrior, Dr. Wislizenus concluded that he was "a fine specimen." Using a hatchet, Wislizenus proceeded to decapitate the Indian, "boiling his head, daily, until the skull was in a condition to pack away."[38]

The chief's tribesmen abandoned five hundred horses and mules, and left behind a variety of loot and booty as well as eighteen Mexican women and children. Some of the horses belonged to Captain Reid's company; others were from the hacienda of Don Manuel de Ibarra. Doniphan ordered those horses returned to the hacienda. The *patrón* hosted a fiesta in honor of the Yankee regiment, bringing out "barrels of wine" and setting "long tables, loaded with everything the ranch afforded." Don Manuel led the Mexicans in making toasts to Doniphan and his men. Ibarra also swapped some horses with Reid, allowing him to gain fresh mounts for the remainder of the journey to the coast.[39]

From Ibarra's hacienda to Parras was a thirty-six-mile route almost as bad as the *jornada*—a passage Private Hughes remembered as being "without one drop of water, and almost without . . . one sprig of green vegetation." As the column approached Parras, a prosperous town of about nine thousand people, situated at almost five thousand feet above sea level, Private Robinson noticed that the landscape took a remarkable "change of appearance for the better [a change so sharp that it] can hardly be imagined." While cottonwoods predominated, several kinds of trees dotted the landscape, including ones yielding various fruits. Private Richardson wrote that "the gardens in and around the city are beautifully arranged, and *tastefully* supplied with ripe apricots, oranges, and lemons; also a great variety of flowering shrubs and plants." Numerous roses bloomed and giant mescal plants abounded, from which the Mexicans made a fermented drink. Productive grape vines yielded good local wine—at least, it tasted quite good to the Missourians. Dr. Wislizenus wrote that "the town itself was much handsomer than I expected. It has some fine streets, with old substantial buildings, a large 'plaza,' and a general appearance of wealth and comfort." According to the doctor, the city was so pretty that Doniphan decided to place the volunteers' camp away from Parras's *alameda* so that the expedition's horses would not eat the bark off of the trees lining the walkway. Robinson gushed that the town "was one of the most beautiful places I have ever seen." Obviously, water was plentiful.[40]

Adding a personal touch to the regiment's arrival at Parras, a delegation of townspeople lauded Captain Reid and his men for their victory over the Apaches. The civic leaders handed the captain a glowing "letter of thanks" complimenting the "celerity, skill, and heroism" of the Missourians, and particularly the "gallantry" of Reid himself. The letter emphasized that the citizens were grateful for the safe return of those who had been held captive by the Indians. Filled with pride and glad to be showered with praise rather than bullets, the regiment pitched camp near Parras on May 14.[41]

A violent incident ruined the cordial relations—the kind of episode that could occur at any time in an occupied country. None of the Missouri veterans related identical stories, but on one matter they agreed: Mexicans attacked and seriously injured a member of the expedition, probably a civilian teamster. He later died of his injuries when the regiment reached Monterrey. Violating the U.S. Army's *Articles of War* and circumventing the supervision of the expedition's officers, the teamster's friends sought revenge by beating several Mexicans. This breach of military discipline soured the convivial welcome given the expedition by the city of Parras. While the regiment had no need to linger in Parras, Doniphan was concerned that indiscipline would become rampant among men of the expedition. He hastily arranged to buy food and forage, and the expedition resumed its march on May 17.[42]

Leaving Parras behind them, the Missourians were cheered by the prospect of meeting General Taylor and the elusive General Wool. Filled with anticipation, Doniphan's men spruced up their appearance, washed their clothes, and patched holes in their shirts and pants, preparing to pass in review for the senior officers. Despite such efforts, they looked more like beggars and derelicts than soldiers; without access to a quartermaster and with no opportunity to buy clothing on a government account, the 1st Missouri Regiment was unable to put itself into a more uniform appearance.[43]

During the next five days the regiment passed isolated ranchos and haciendas, crossed slender creeks and sluggish streams, and rode through modest towns and deserted villages. The expedition made a steady twenty or twenty-five miles a day. The attitude of the soldiers combined frolic with impatience and individualism. Dr. Wislizenus recognized the lack of discipline: "Usually, during the march, the men selected their paces more according to fancy than military rule, and it was not uncommon to have our line stretched out to five miles, or three-fourths of the regiment marching in the vangard [*sic*]." Obviously, if they had collided with Mexican regular soldiers, the results could have been disastrous for the Missourians, who no doubt behaved nonchalantly because they knew there was little likelihood of battle. Doniphan ordered the regiment to form up in more regular order in the prospect of seeing General Wool or other senior officers. When the generals did not appear, the line disintegrated again into individual riders, pairs, and scattered groups.[44]

On May 22 Doniphan and his men arrived near the main American military encampment at Saltillo, a substantial city having a population of fifteen thousand. The colonel reported to General Wool, who had ridden out to inspect the 1st Missouri Regiment. Some of the volunteers made a visit to the Buena Vista battlefield, picking up souvenirs such as buttons and coins while listening to General Wool offer commentary about the battle. Once they made their camp about five miles from Buena Vista, General Wool watched as the volunteers rode by on horses and mules. Resplendent in his full dress uniform, the general was appalled by the volunteers' behavior. Many were rowdy and showed no interest in maintaining formation or in taking part in an afternoon of tactical drill that the general wished to see. In his first discussions with Doniphan, Wool mentioned the possibility that the volunteers would reenlist but, after observing their behavior during the review, he may have been satisfied when they declined to do so. In the nineteenth century, Americans signing for military service talked about "going to see the elephant"—the lure of battle. Jonathan Buhoup, a visitor from the Arkansas regiment, observed that Doniphan's "men looked as though they had not only seen the elephant but the kangaroo, also." In public, however, General Wool issued the obligatory compliments and praise, emphasizing that the Missourians "in the course of [their] arduous duties [had rendered] a series of highly important services, crowned by decisive and glorious victories."[45]

Near Saltillo on May 23, the artillerists and the colonel had important duties to perform. Captain Weightman and Major Clark turned in the six cannon belonging to the federal government to an ordnance officer. There also Doniphan bade good-bye to Captain Philip Thompson, the most reliable and supportive of his Regular Army advisers, and the other Regulars who, in one way or another, had been helpful during the last months. Fittingly, Thompson became acting inspector general on General Wool's staff.[46]

On May 24 the Missouri column left Saltillo, with Dr. Wislizenus noting their elevation above sea level—they were below three thousand feet and steadily moving toward the coast. They marched sixty miles to contact General Zachary Taylor about noon on May 26 at his camp at Walnut Springs, outside Monterrey, another major town with a population of about fifteen thousand and located at an elevation of 1,626 feet. On the way two soldiers (Smith and Smart) died of unspecified causes.[47]

By the spring of 1847, Taylor knew his popularity benefited from such formalities as reviewing volunteer units on their way back to the States. The Missourians noticed that Taylor was "such a contrast to Wool." Dressed informally, wearing his trademark straw hat and a checkered shirt, Taylor walked into the expedition's camp to inspect its captured Mexican trophies of cannon and flags. Sergeant Kennerly heard him give "some kind and complimentary words" to Clark's artillerists. Taylor went around camp shaking hands with volunteers, and the general's adjutant wrote up a formal order paying his "grateful tidings" to the Missourians on their victory at Sacramento. Taylor posted official orders for Doniphan's regiment to proceed nine miles to Camargo and then on to New Orleans. The army gave the soldiers the option of selling their horses or having a small detachment drive the mounts to Missouri. The market for horses near Taylor's camps was saturated; Missourians who sold their animals got only a fraction of their value, but at least they got some cash. Among those horses taken overland to Missouri, about half were stolen, died, or lost.[48]

Now the Missourians were only a few days away from the Gulf Coast. On May 27 they left Walnut Springs, headed for Camargo. Zachary Taylor came out to bid farewell, riding "along the lines, with his hat off," enjoying their cheers.

Hudson's Rangers responded by giving the general a saber salute. Taylor rode with Doniphan's column for several miles.[49]

During the next three days the volunteers showed little interest in security, believing there was no prospect for action. Companies and small groups of riders were strung out on the road for several miles. They camped at deserted ranchos, and mirages of lakes danced ahead of them. On May 30 they stopped at the Mexican town of Mier, scene of the infamous decimation of the Texan raiders in 1842.[50]

They reached Camargo at about 2:00 P.M. on May 31, after burying another one of their fellow soldiers, who had died of some unidentified malady. Camargo had a population of about one thousand people, but it had turned into one of the most important American military depots in northern Mexico. Private Frank Edwards took note of "quite a large number of canvas houses used for the protection of provisions and other stores." Hundreds of mules and horses, used for pulling supply wagons, made their presence known. Dr. Wislizenus saw little to recommend about Camargo. "Deep sand" drifted over the streets, "a constant disagreeable wind [was blowing], and "the brackish, sulphurated [*sic*] water of the Rio-San Juan" made the town "a very unpleasant place" in the doctor's opinion.[51]

Leaving Camargo on June 1, the Missourians no longer expressed concern about the Mexicans; the war was over for them. Unexpectedly, the soldiers witnessed a violent tableau. Private Robinson recalled the incident: "One of the men, named Swain, was about sixty yards in advance of the column, which was much scattered; when suddenly a Mexican rode from the chapparral [*sic*] and shot him through the heart, dismounted, robbed him of his rifle and sabre, and rode off again into the chapparral, defying all pursuit." Captain Reid and fifty men mounted chase and returned with "seven suspicious [looking] Mexicans. No proof could be found against them, but our men were . . . much excited." That night, men of the regiment again carried out a vendetta that violated the U.S. Army's *Articles of War.* Missouri volunteers murdered three of the Mexicans and burned down a house in retaliation for Swain's death. The next day, Captain Reid took fifty men and tried to track down other Mexicans who may have been involved in Swain's murder.[52]

At Reynosa, only 184 feet above sea level (according to Dr. Wislizenus's barometer measurement), the Rio Grande was "about 200 yards wide, and six or more feet deep." Two river steamboats were docked there, and two more were anchored in the river. Remarkably, a savage rainstorm pelted the regiment for three days. Water coursed across the mudflat where the soldiers had camped, flowing through their tents and soaking their blankets and belongings. When the rains stopped, thousands of blue flies assaulted the volunteers, covering everything—blankets, pans and mess kits, weapons, and the arms and bodies of the soldiers, making everyone miserable.[53]

There was a final turn-in of heavy government equipment and animals on June 3. According to a merchant, Josiah Gregg, a disagreement erupted between the colonel and one of the quartermasters. "Capt [James] Lee was much vexed at Col. Donophan [*sic*]" over when and how "to deliver all the Government [property]." Of course, Lee insisted that the volunteers follow his procedure. The regiment turned over about fifty government wagons and four hundred mules to the army quartermaster. Government officers informed the volunteers that they would be taking only a few personal possessions on the boats—bulky items, such as saddles, would be left behind. Virtually all the men were disappointed at this news, and none wanted to leave their saddles to the Mexicans. Although a few sold their saddles for small sums, Private Frank Edwards watched the rest build "a funeral pyre" of saddles and other tack; "extra blankets, buffalo robes, and everything [else not permitted on the boats] we cast upon the [flaming] pile."[54]

Loading the regiment onto the steamers began on June 3, but due to a mix-up they did not sail. Some men spent the night on the steamers, while others went back on shore and slept in tents. Several companies reloaded again and sailed on June 4; others boarded and departed on June 5.[55]

"Point Isabel from Brazos Santiago." (From Thorpe, *Our Army on the Rio Grande* [1846]; courtesy of the Museum of New Mexico, negative no. 171111)

American soldiers' arrival and departure and the docking of army supply boats added to the hustle and bustle of the trading center of Matamoros, a city of about five thousand population. The town impressed few Americans, however. Caleb Cushing, a volunteer brigadier general from Massachusetts, called it "a sink of pollution." A reporter for the Matamoros *Flag* caught sight of the 1st Missouri, describing the men as having "unshorn beards and goat and deer skin clothes [and they] reminded us of descriptions of the [people inhabiting the] countries of the Russian empire."[56]

On June 6 several companies of the regiment disembarked at a beach near the mouth of the Rio Grande and frolicked in the Gulf of Mexico. The soldiers walked out through the surf, going some distance from shore, letting "the breakers pass over our heads." The waves were so strong that they knocked over some of the men. Dr. Wislizenus took a "refreshing sea bath," and Private Hughes recollected "the most refreshing and pleasant bathings in the River and the Gulf."[57]

For the first time the regiment was without mounts, and on June 9 the soldiers hiked down to the small island of Brazos Santiago. Dr. Wislizenus saw the island as just "one wide sheet of sand." Several types of vessels lay anchored in the harbor, and undoubtedly the soldiers speculated on which steamers would carry them back to the States. Several days earlier, back near Saltillo, General Wool had issued the order praising the men of the 1st Missouri Regiment, also saying that "the State of Missouri . . . will without doubt, receive them on their return with all the joy and satisfaction to which a due appreciation of their merits and services so justly entitle them." For Doniphan and his volunteers, it was time to go home.[58]

CHAPTER NINE

Coming Home a Hero: "American Xenophon"

On June 10, 1847, at Brazos Santiago, near Matamoros, Doniphan and most of his regiment—men of Companies A, B, C, D, F, G, H, and K—clambered aboard the steamer *Republic*. Major Gilpin, Captains Weightman and Hudson, and 250 other soldiers departed in the *Murillo*. Federal officials had contracted steamers and sailing vessels to transport soldiers to New Orleans or Mobile. While the brig *Murillo* looked "beautiful" from the dock, one of the soldiers was very disappointed by what he saw on board, finding the interior "filthy"—"worse than a hogpen." A typical meal consisted of coffee, crackers, and molasses, supplemented by anything the soldiers pulled from the Gulf of Mexico, such as dolphin, small sharks, or turtles. Until a supply boat delivered some water casks, the men complained of short rations of water, which seemed ironic as they sailed across the Gulf. Demonstrating that the hazards of active service were not yet behind them, two soldiers died of unspecified causes on the five-day trip. When they sighted the Louisiana coast, several members of the regiment cheered but others prayed, giving thanks for having survived the voyage through the Gulf, as well as having endured all the other hazards of their adventures. Coming up the Mississippi, the volunteers noticed that flags and bunting adorned the houses along the river, signs of welcome by the Louisianians to all returning veterans. From balconies and porches, ladies waved their handkerchiefs in greeting to the men on the *Republic* as it steamed by, adding a genteel touch to the homecoming.[1]

Word of the pending arrival of Doniphan and his men reached New Orleans ahead of the regiment, because Major Gilpin and Captain Weightman had left their group in order to land at the Crescent City in another steamer on June 13. Of course, it had served as the port of embarkation and return for thousands of

American soldiers during the war. The comings and goings of volunteers and Regulars had become a routine part of wartime in New Orleans. According to a story in the New Orleans *National*, the prospect of "the arrival of Col. Doniphan and his regiment in this city has created an unusual degree of interest, although it has for the last fifteen months been wrought up to the highest pitch of excitement by military novelties." The New Orleans *Picayune* urged that "some fitting form" of greeting be arranged for Doniphan's men, no doubt involving the opportunity for oratory.[2]

Over three days, on June 15, 16, and 17, the 1st Missouri Regiment stormed into the Crescent City, ready to celebrate the end of their one year of military service, while the war continued for thousands of soldiers of both nations on campaign in the Valley of the Montezumas and hundreds of other U.S. troops on garrison duty across northern Mexico. The returning Missourians set up a public display of their captured war trophies, including "lances, with gay pennons attached to them; escopetas, swords, [and] pistols."[3]

Reports in the New Orleans newspapers delineated so well the prevailing attitudes of America on the verge of victory in the summer of 1847 and set the tone of descriptions of Doniphan's return to the United States. A writer for the New Orleans *National* noted that Doniphan was "a man of giant frame, of that loose carriage peculiar to the west, that deceives the eye as to proportion and strength." Some observers could easily have been unimpressed by the Missourians' "strange uncouth appearance." The *Delta* remarked that the long hair and unkempt beards of the "bold, fearless, indomitable" men of the 1st Missouri Regiment "reminded us of the pictures of Robinson Crusoe and other shipwrecked adventurers, who having been a long time banished from civilization and compelled to live among savages and wild beasts are suddenly transferred to their homes and to the society of cultivated men." According to the *Courier*, the volunteers were clad in combinations of calico, goatskin, deerskin, linsey-woolsey, and jackets "once worn by some proud lancero." The volunteers' dress supposedly showed "in striking light the hardihood, the enterprise, the bravery and intelligence of the American backwoodsman." A Regular Army officer watched as the Missourians prowled the streets. "If you can imagine a man about six feet two to four and a half inches high, and well proportioned, with a deer skin (hair on) hunting shirt and pantaloons, the seams fringed with the same material cut into strings, and a bear skin stretched over his face with nothing but eye holes cut in it, you can see a large portion of Doniphan's Regiment." The *Delta* concluded that "altogether such a motley band were never before paraded on our soil."[4]

But the New Orleans *National* emphasized the claim (or wish) of many

The veteran colonel: Doniphan after the campaign. (Courtesy of Colonel Doniphan Carter, U.S. Army, retired, Falls Church, Va.)

Americans that "beneath those rough exteriors, are concealed minds of educated and high toned sentiments, full of lofty thoughts and love of liberty." Watching the Missouri volunteers mingle with gawking onlookers, a reporter took the occasion to recapitulate "a wonderful picture, this marching of a few hundred men though populous states, conquering their inhabitants in pitched battles, and occupying their cities and towns as garrisons." Confirming the American devotion to relying on citizen-soldiers, the journalist described in glowing terms the "men who, up to the time they enlisted under the banner of their country, were employed exclusively in the arts of peace, using the rifle only as a source of amusement, and looking to the annual return of the militia muster as a subject of ridicule—yet when a demand is made upon them, they seem easily to put on the full panoply of the ancient crusader and go forth conquering, as if they had been schooled in the camp, and been disciplined from youth amidst the clamor of war." Extrapolating from the success of one regiment, the reporter contended, "Of such [human] materials is composed this mighty race of North Americans, who seem destined to overshadow the greatness of all nations of times past."[5]

With some reluctance, the volunteers turned in their government-issue Hall's rifles to an army ordnance officer, but they relished the prospect of receiving their official discharge papers and having money in their pockets. Back pay and various allowances for clothing and forage—averaging more than three hundred dollars per soldier, for the regiment had not been paid for its entire year of service—meant that any of the delights and temptations of New Orleans would be available to them. Like the men from other regiments, the Missourians boisterously lined up at the counter of the paymaster's office, enjoying the scene as, under the eye of senior paymaster Lieutenant Colonel Benjamin F. Larned, Captain William H. Churchill counted out their coins. First things came first, and for most of the men that meant a long bath and a visit to a barber. New Orleans store owners and tailors vied with one another to sell new clothes to the shabby volunteers. Enjoying themselves immensely, the Missourians bought new hats, trousers, shirts, jackets, shoes, socks, and underwear. Their purchases totaled into the thousands of dollars. After patronizing the stores and tailor shops, the volunteers reappeared rigged "up in handsome style." The Missourians strode through the French Quarter as "the lions of the town," exciting "universal attention by their appearance." They were invited to attend parties, masquerade balls, and dances; they could not resist displaying their knives and pistols at the soirees.[6]

Naturally, the lures and haunts of the Crescent City excited the returning veterans, but they had to be careful. Police arrested confidence artists for "selling pinchback rings to volunteers, warranting them to be pure gold" and at least one volunteer was robbed of his back pay on the streets. According to the *Delta*, however, while the volunteers might have been expected to "give free rein to their passions and appetites," most of them deserved to be complimented on the "strict propriety of their deportment." Indeed, many men of the regiment "deported themselves in the most correct and manly manner . . . respectful and obedient to the laws." The *Delta* reported that only a dozen Missourians had been arrested for public intoxication before they left New Orleans.[7]

Highlights of Doniphan's sojourn in the Crescent City included having rooms at the prestigious St. Charles Hotel, a visit to the St. Charles Theater to see Junius B. Booth in Shakespeare's *Richard III*, and an afternoon at Stickney's

Circus, but among the most pleasurable were opportunities for speechmaking. On June 16 Thomas F. Marshall of New Orleans welcomed the Missouri regiment with a speech at the St. Louis Commercial Exchange. Marshall congratulated the Missourians for "capturing one of the enemy's largest cities [Chihuahua] . . . after marching a distance of 3,500 miles." Reaching his peroration, Marshall "defied an example . . . since the days of the ancient Greeks to the present, in all the pages of history . . . to be brought forward of better, braver, more patient or more indomitable soldiery having ever existed." There followed rounds of cheering—three cheers for Marshall, three for Doniphan, and three more for Zachary Taylor. Doniphan then rose to address the gathering, according to the *Delta,* "not as [a] regular soldier, not as [one] whose trade war had long been, and from whom honor and duty demanded the sacrifice, but as [a] volunteer, seeking glory, and supporting the honor and rights of our Proud Republic." The colonel thanked Marshall for his kind words and the people of New Orleans for their generous hospitality but then brought "roars of laughter" from the appreciative crowd when he said, tongue in cheek, "I am not certain whether these are my men or not. They look very differently from their yesterday's appearance; and the fact is, as I have a new coat, I am not sure that I know myself." A few days later local dignitaries and townspeople joined soldiers from other regiments in a rally at Lafayette Square to give a send-off to Missouri's heroes.[8]

On June 28 the steamer *Old Hickory,* black smoke belching from its stacks, pulled away from the dock at New Orleans. On board rode Colonel Doniphan, Major Gilpin, Captain DeCourcy, and almost 200 other volunteers, including Captain Moss and a Clay County contingent, beginning the upriver journey home to Missouri. No longer under military orders, the veterans of the regiment had booked passage into several boats for the trip. *Harry of the West* carried 100 volunteers of Jackson, Clay, and Howard and Franklin Counties; Captain Weightman and 144 soldiers and officers rode in the *Clarksville.* Soon there followed *Pride of the West,* transporting Captain Hudson and the Leclede Rangers. *Hard Times, Memphis, J. M. White,* and the *Vernon* each transported thirty or forty Missouri veterans. The citizen-soldiers enjoyed the passage, luxuriating in their new clothes, playing cards in the saloons, and, after months of eating too much "hardtack, salt pork, and beans," dining on fare unavailable to them for the past year—smoked hams with black-eyed peas and yams, roast turkeys with baked Irish potatoes, pork chops with rice and gravy, as well as "Pompano, Spanish mackerel, [and] luscious fruits."[9]

Most volunteers found the three- or four-day trip relaxing following the hectic pace and Creole foods of New Orleans. There was some minor excitement on the stop in Memphis when a local tough knifed one of the volunteers on the street. But as the lush green banks of the Mississippi River slipped easily by, the thoughts of the volunteers turned to wives, sweethearts, family, and friends unseen for more than twelve months.[10]

The men of the 1st Missouri Regiment already had some inkling that a reception awaited them in St. Louis, but exactly what its form and proportions would be was not yet clear. They had enjoyed receiving the public accolades and speeches given in their honor at New Orleans, and, in an era when extemporaneous public speaking was both a major form of popular entertainment and a mainstay in politics, the volunteers assumed that their return to Missouri would offer appropriate occasions for speakers to demonstrate their oratorical skills at parks and dinners. They were not disappointed.[11] The receptions accorded to them equaled or surpassed any given to a returning volunteer regiment after service in the Mexican-American War.[12] Displays of patriotic fervor, such as those given to returning veterans in 1847–1848, not only helped celebrate the victorious conclusion of the war with Mexico but also contributed to the expectations of victorious Americans looking for ways to mark the military service of other soldiers during the remainder of the nineteenth century and on into the twentieth century. The festivities made a symbolic point, drawing together the citizenry to honor the veterans for their sacrifices of time and health undermined or wounds sustained while on active duty. Moreover, the special occasions also honored the memories of those military personnel who were killed or missing in action, and let their relatives know that the community, state, and nation appreciated their sacrifice for the common cause.

In St. Louis organizers had been busy for more than a week before most of the state's most illustrious volunteers were expected. Of course, traveling on half a dozen steamboats meant that the volunteers would be coming to St. Louis over several days. For instance, on June 27 and 28 more than 150 volunteers, including Captain Reid, had come in on three different steamers. Members of the reception committee met with the early arrivals and urged them to stay in St. Louis for a few days until Doniphan returned. The colonel himself arrived with most of his senior officers on June 30. Understandably, the city dignitaries wanted to delay the public gala in honor of the regiment until the homecoming of Captain Hudson's Leclede Rangers and Major Clark's artillery battery—the volunteers from St. Louis who had ridden with Doniphan. Therefore, the "Marshal of the Day," Thornton Grimsley, confirmed plans for a joyous reception involving a sequence of events, to include a parade through the city, speeches, and a picnic. Thomas Hart Benton, a Democrat and Missouri's irrepressible U.S.

senator, accepted the invitation to deliver the keynote oration to the throng expected to hail the return of the stalwart soldiers of the 1st Regiment of Mounted Volunteers. Picking up on the theme of the grand campaign, the St. Louis *Republican* reminded its readers that the volunteers had "borne the name of their State triumphantly over the longest march known to modern warfare." The mayor, city council members, Regular U.S. Army soldiers, several militia units and fire brigades, as well as local clubs and civic organizations and citizens in carriages, on horseback, and on foot, were invited to participate in the parade. In order to assemble those in the parade, the reception organizers agreed to use the mass ringing of church and fire station bells to signal the arrival of the St. Louis volunteers. The city would "spare no honors" for its returning heroes.[13]

Friday, July 2, was the big day; the *Clarksville* with Major Clark, Captain Weightman, and other officers of the artillery battery arrived after dawn. The rest of the regiment was somewhere behind. The reception committee made all ready to receive the latest veterans and was about to authorize the full festivities when shortly before 11:00 A.M. a messenger galloped into St. Louis with the long-awaited news: the steamer carrying the Leclede Rangers and three hundred of Doniphan's regiment was about three hours away from the city! The dignitaries decided to delay the parade until the next boat docked.[14]

Before 2:00 P.M. a lookout sighted *Pride of the West*, and church bells pealed and signal cannon boomed the message that the St. Louis contingent was arriving at last. Within a few minutes taverns, hotel lobbies, businesses, and shops disgorged their clientele; hundreds of people rode and ran for the docks, the sounds of hundreds of horses' hooves and boots and shoes hitting the streets creating an audible rumble. Pandemonium seized St. Louis as "crowds of eager expectants rushed down to the levee in anticipation of the welcome arrival."[15]

From the deck of the *Pride of the West*, Captain Hudson could see the upper stories of buildings decked out with banners and bunting. Flags flew from the porches of houses and doors of businesses. People jammed the streets. Stretching more than four blocks in all directions flowed a "living torrent" of humanity, pushing, shoving, and shouting hurrahs. More cannon shots sounded as artillerists fired their guns to excite the throng crowding up to the steamer. Plumes of white smoke erupted as its whistle blasts added to the general din.[16]

In a remarkable show of cooperation, some of the multitude grew quiet, straining to hear the words of hospitality spoken by R. S. Blennerhassett, of the reception committee, and Bryan Mullanphy, the mayor of St. Louis. Then the dignitaries asked Captain Hudson to address the crowd. The young attorney responded promptly, noting that he was pleased to return healthy to his family after so many hardships on campaign. But he said that this welcome was "such a reward" that it "would obliterate all recollections" of the hardships. Warm clapping rippled through the huge gathering. Hudson responded to that ovation by yelling two words: "Brazito! Sacramento!!" The air became electric, and Hudson "felt as if his skin was scarcely large enough to contain himself" as waves of huzzahs and loud applause thundered from the assembly.[17]

The mass of humanity opened lanes for Doniphan, Hudson, the city dignitaries, and the other volunteers to make their way to the Planter's House Hotel, where the next phase of the reception would be held. There several speakers regaled the throng, including Judge James B. Bowlin and Lieutenant Colonel David Mitchell.[18]

Then the parade commenced. According to the arrangements, the parade's leading units included seven fire company bands, totaling more than two hundred musicians, some carrying banners identifying themselves. The Franklin Fire Company and the Washington Fire Company forged ahead. Following the musicians came the grand marshal and the dozen members of the reception committee, trailed by representatives of the U.S. Army and U.S. Navy. Behind the Regulars marched local militia units—the St. Louis Grays, the Montgomery Guards, the St. Louis Jaegers, the Missouri Dragoons, and two unnamed companies—a total of 180 men decked out in diverse colorful uniforms. Colonel Doniphan and more than 300 of his volunteers were next in line, some on foot and some mounted, waving five captured Mexican flags, including Brazito's infamous Black Flag with its skulls and crossbones. The volunteers proudly displayed the ten cannon taken from enemy forces at Brazito and Sacramento. Spectators cheered the procession as it made its way down Fourth Street, up Walnut Street to Fifth, up Fifth to Washington Avenue, and down Washington to Camp Lucas, site of the next phase of the festivities.[19]

Senator Benton gave a lengthy, stirring oration, and the crowd of seven thousand expected nothing less. Benton told the throng what they wanted to hear about their regiment: "Your march and exploits have been among the most wonderful of the age." Benton congratulated the volunteers on having successfully completed an expedition equal in distance to one-fourth of the circumference of the world. He recorded, in some detail, the activities of the volunteers over the past twelve months, including making an allusion to a famous campaign of ancient times—the march of the Ten Thousand Greeks under Xenophon. The senator concluded: "And now let boundless honor and joy salute, as it does, your return to the soil of your State . . . and to . . . your families."[20]

Called upon to offer remarks after Senator Benton spoke, Colonel Doniphan stood and responded. He first extended his own welcome home to his assembled soldiers, reiterating how the splendid civic display recognized "your patriotism, your valor, your self-sacrificing devotion to country." He continued: "We feel proud, as your countrymen, in sharing that halo of glory which your gallant deeds have thrown around the name of the 'Missouri volunteer.'" Such soldiers had demonstrated, "to the astonishment of the world, that volunteer troops can be depended upon—that private citizens can be transformed into good soldiers by a proper discipline" through training given by professional officers of the Regular Army. Complimenting Benton on his command of so many of the details of the expedition, the colonel could not resist adding facts of his own, including the march to Santa Fe and the battle at Sacramento. Doniphan stressed that "republics are not ungrateful, for all who fought in the service of the United States had received a reward more munificent than a monarch ever bestowed"—that reward was the "gratitude, and warm reception, and honor of his fellow-citizens." Doniphan extolled the conduct of his soldiers: "You have fulfilled every trust with faithfulness, . . . you have performed faithfully every duty required of you." Most important, he emphasized, "Your noble, heroic conduct on the battle-fields of Bracito and Sacramento will ever be remembered with gratitude by your countrymen." On a personal note, the colonel reminded his men that "you carry with you my gratitude, which never can be effaced." He went on to call for the vigorous prosecution of the war, including the capture of Mexico City itself. Thunderous applause followed Doniphan's speech.[21]

As the food and beverages were prepared, several other speakers gave their views on the war, the regiment's march, and the warmth of the reception in St. Louis. These orators included Lieutenant Colonel Mitchell, Major Clark, Captain Weightman, Captain Hudson, Captain Reid, and again Senator Benton. The refreshments were served; one of the revelers, James Glasgow, called it "a grand fete." Another participant recalled that the soldiers—"poor fellows"—"looked bright and happy, though sun burnt and weary." The Jefferson City *Inquirer* proclaimed, "Every one, without distinction of party, sect, or creed, joined in doing honor to this little conquering army." Then the throng removed to St. Louis Park for a grand barbecue. It was a memorable and delightful afternoon.[22]

In the weeks to come, the colonel, other officers, and the individual soldiers enjoyed heroes' welcomes all over again in towns and county seats. Speeches, picnics, and more speeches were the order of the day. For example, on July 10 celebrants held a barbecue at the state capital in Jefferson City for the Cole County veterans; a few days later the town of Bloomfield sponsored another barbecue. Doniphan's hometown of Liberty followed suit. At Liberty, following Doniphan's account of the expedition, Missouri state senator David Rice Atchison, who was also Doniphan's former law partner, gave a thoughtful speech. Atchison emphasized the factor of contingency—that Doniphan's victories could have turned out to be defeats; that no one knew the outcomes of those battles in advance, and the same persons giving compliments then instead would have been offering criticisms and condolences if defeat substituted for victory. Atchison hailed the 1st Missouri Regiment's commander as deserving of the widest respect and praise. A raft of local residents then led in toasting the heroes' "military ingenuity" and "gallantry," among other attributes, before the throng moved to the tables spread with food. In the town of Independence, a crowd of five thousand cheered as Colonel Doniphan knelt before a local dignitary, who placed a traditional laurel wreath on the hero's head. The Jefferson City *Inquirer* contended that "in every little town and village, not only in this State, but in the Union, are the achievements of this Regiment of volunteers a theme of universal applause."[23]

In August the town of Gallatin hosted its own parade and a "fantastic repast" for the 1st Missouri Regiment; hundreds of men, women, and children flocked to the town. The visitors listened to Doniphan deliver a two-hour speech on the expedition in which he compared his men's displays of fortitude, stamina, and patriotism to those of soldiers who fought in the American Revolution. Doniphan also asserted that, in his opinion, the present war was justified against Mexico because of the various offensive actions that the Mexicans had perpetrated against U.S. citizens during the 1830s and 1840s, concluding that the U.S. "government had the *right* to make war." According to one auditor, "When Doniphan took his seat, thundering shouts [and] applause broke forth from all parts of the great congregation." Various observers discussed Doniphan as a candidate for political office, including governor or U.S. senator. On a more practical note, Davis and Forbis, attorneys-at-law, ran a notice in the Liberty *Tribune* advertising their abilities to assist veterans (and their widows and heirs) in obtaining federal pensions and land warrants due them for their service in the war.[24]

Doniphan's exploits justified Missourians' accolades and celebrations, and he became nationally acclaimed. Volunteer officers of other ranks, such as Major General John Quitman of Mississippi and Captain Ben McCulloch of the Texas Rangers, received special treatment by the national press and from fellow citizens of their states. Of the sixty-three other volunteer colonels serving in the Mexican War, Doniphan achieved a remarkable level of national recognition, certainly the highest recognition of any of those with no prior service in the Regular Army.[25]

Most of the fifteen former Regulars who became volunteer colonels had served only a few years on active duty before resigning; the best known was

Jefferson Davis, commander of the 1st Mississippi Rifles. Davis earned plaudits for his leadership during the Battle of Monterrey but was especially notable at Zachary Taylor's signal victory at Buena Vista (La Angostura). There he led his regiment in a counterattack that helped turn the tide of the battle. A former member of Congress before the war began, Davis drew upon his military renown to gain an appointment and then win election to the U.S. Senate from Mississippi before the war ended. Also touted as a hero, Colonel William McKee led the 2nd Kentucky Volunteer Cavalry and was killed in action at Buena Vista. George Hughes, a topographical engineer officer with twenty years in uniform, was appointed by President Polk to command the Maryland and District of Columbia Volunteers; he fought at Cerro Gordo, where he was cited for gallantry. Likewise, Ward Burnett received praise for leading the 2nd New York Regiment at Cerro Gordo and Contreras and was wounded at Churubusco. Other former Regulars fared less well. For instance, Pierce Butler of South Carolina, Humphrey Marshall of Kentucky, and John F. Hamtramck of Virginia displayed various problems controlling their regiments on the battlefield or in camp. Of course, other former Regulars served commendably in a variety of assignments but did not achieve sustained national attention.[26]

Although some of the forty-seven volunteer colonels without experience in the Regulars earned commendable records, only a few rated highly as army officers. Besides Doniphan, the most significant was William Campbell of Tennessee. Commanding the 1st Tennessee Volunteer Infantry, Campbell devoted hours to studying Winfield Scott's manual of *Infantry Tactics* and was pleased by the gradual improvement of his regiment in tactical drill. The regiment went on to fight well in the Battle of Monterrey. Campbell, Davis, and the others distinguished themselves in conventional battles, but Doniphan's exploits stood out because his regiment not only won battles but also operated independently and marched long distances through the enemy's country.[27]

Many of the contemporary reports in American newspapers describing Doniphan's March drew analogies between the Missouri colonel and warfare in other times and places. Some favored linking Doniphan with the Spanish conquest of Mexico. For instance, the New Orleans *Bee* pointed out that Doniphan's "triumphant march resembles the progress of Cortez." Finding a similar theme, a reporter for the New Orleans *National* was overcome with the image that "some ancient Spanish grave had yielded up a follower of Cortez, to recount his adventures and personal experience as he progressed toward the capital of the Montezumas." But most of his contemporaries preferred to draw analogies between Doniphan and combat leaders from the Mediterranean in ancient times.[28]

Proposing a broad approach, the New Orleans *Commercial Bulletin* maintained that "the march, of itself, is without parallel in the annals of modern [or] ancient, warfare." Reading Latin and Greek and studying the military maneuvers and political machinations of the Greeks and Romans was part of the standard academic regimen for well-educated nineteenth-century Americans. They pointed with pride to comparisons between the United States and ancient republics of Greece and Rome, and they borrowed from the Greeks and Romans in several aspects of architecture and government. There were many notable examples of such borrowings. An introductory list included the concept of democracy from ancient Athens; variations on the theme of representative democracy from the Roman republic; the design of numerous buildings of the federal government in Washington, D.C., boasting impressive Corinthian, Ionic, and Doric columns and pediments drawing on styles of ancient Athens and Rome; using the Roman term "senate" for the upper house of the U.S. Congress; adopting the name of the Athenian lawmaker "Solon" as a generic term to refer to U.S. senators; and displaying behind the podium of the Speaker of the House replicas of Roman *fasces,* representing symbols of the power granted by citizens to their elected representatives, to name just a few. U.S. citizens also sought military parallels between themselves and the Mediterranean ancients. During and after the American Revolution, many drew the analogy between the Roman general Cincinnatus, a patriotic farmer who left his plow and took up his sword, and George Washington, the Virginia plantation owner who answered Congress's call to command colonial forces.[29]

One search for a comparison, obviously charged with hyperbole, came from the New Orleans *Courier,* which postulated, "We know of no military operation that can be compared to this [march by Doniphan]. The march of Alexander the Great to the Indus [River] was as long, in point of distance, but the time consumed in it was much greater." To be a rival of Alexander, "the commander of this famous regiment, Col. Doniphan, must be an officer of great courage, hardihood, and perseverance, of most uncommon resource, and extraordinary power over the minds of men." Echoing the nationalistic tenor of the day, the *Courier* continued: "These [citizen-soldiers] are the men who constitute a strong and unconquerable nation—men who, to uphold the rights of their country, cheerfully submit to perils and privations, which it is almost fearful to contemplate."[30]

Among all the efforts made by Americans to compare Doniphan with military commanders of other eras, in their search for elevating the stature of their own heroes, the great favorite was the venerated Greek commander Xenophon. Long marches through enemy territory have fascinated people since ancient times, and in the war with Mexico U.S. forces conducted several long marches.

Captain Philip St. George Cooke and the Mormon Battalion went overland from Santa Fe to California, but no Mexican military forces blocked their way. Brigadier General Stephen W. Kearny and the Army of the West marched from Fort Leavenworth to Santa Fe, and then Kearny took a small detachment on to California, where they fought in skirmishes near the Pacific Coast. The largest U.S. military contingent making a long march was Major General Winfield Scott's army, varying in strength from ten to fourteen thousand. Scott led his invading army more than two hundred miles along the national road from Veracruz to Mexico City, going through several towns, obtaining food from the countryside, and fighting several pitched battles before bringing the war to a close. But the most notable independent march commander of the war and the most important example of a comparison between a figure from ancient times and a U.S. hero of the war was that of Doniphan and Xenophon. No other American officer, Regular or volunteer, received such recognition.[31]

Out for adventure and the chance to make his fortune, Xenophon was an Athenian mercenary in the service of Cyrus, pretender to the Persian throne held by his brother, the Emperor Artaxerxes II. Building his rebel army of fifty thousand, Cyrus recruited about thirteen thousand Greeks, led by the Spartan commander Clearchus. Most of the Greeks were veterans of the Peloponnesian civil war. In 401 B.C. at the battle of Cunaxa, near the city of Babylon (in modern Iraq), Cyrus was killed and his own soldiers fled, but the Greek contingent counterattacked and defeated a portion of Artaxerxes' larger army. Recognizing their military prowess, Artaxerxes promised the Greeks safe passage to their homeland and invited twenty-five of their senior officers to attend a banquet in their honor. It was a trap. Following the emperor's orders, a contingent of Persian soldiers surrounded and executed the Greek commanders. Thus command fell to newly elected younger officers, including Xenophon, who led the twelve thousand surviving Greek mercenaries on a military march second in fame only to that of Alexander the Great, a fighting retreat of approximately one thousand miles from Babylon to Trapezus, a Greek colony on the Black Sea. To reach the sea, Xenophon and his soldiers (in later years, their number was rounded off, so that they were hailed as the "Ten Thousand") endured deserts and food shortages, crossed flooded rivers and rugged mountains, engaging various hostile tribes before reaching Trapezus after five months of marching. All told, Xenophon and the other Greek mercenaries traveled about thirty-five hundred miles during the entire campaign. About half of the Greeks died or were killed on the *Anabasis* (the "Upcountry March"), immortalized by Xenophon in a renowned book by that title. *The Anabasis* became a classic tome of ancient times and continues to be recognized as a major work in Greek history and military history. After seeing the weaknesses and internal problems of the Persian Empire firsthand, Xenophon offered the conclusion, snapped up by Alexander the Great, that "Persia belongs to the man who has the courage to take it."[32]

Xenophon's remarkable military venture naturally drew the attention of American writers and politicians of the 1840s, including Missourians, who compared it to Doniphan's March. Not surprisingly, some differences highlight the two expeditions. Xenophon led a force ten times the size of Doniphan's, but the Greek's losses were significant—about 50 percent—whereas Doniphan lost only about 10 percent of his men. Xenophon's soldiers were mercenaries hired to fight; Doniphan's were citizen-soldier volunteers who enlisted to expand their nation's territory but were not paid (and then only a modest sum) until after the campaign ended. Doniphan conducted an offensive operation into enemy territory, helping to confirm his nation's hold over part of those lands; although Xenophon served on the offensive in the early phase of Cyrus's campaign, he supervised a retreat through the enemy's empire, which did not come under Greek control until Alexander's invasion many years later. Xenophon's expedition went on foot; most of Doniphan's men rode horses and carried supplies in wagons. Doniphan's March totaled nearly fifty-five hundred miles by sea and land; Xenophon traveled about thirty-five hundred miles. Xenophon wrote a personal narrative of his march and went on to become a writer of some distinction. Doniphan declined to write a history of his year in Mexico, in part because of the popularity of the account written by one of his soldiers, John Hughes.

Some points in common can be discerned between the two commanders and their marches. Both men were military novices of a comparable age at the time of their expeditions: Doniphan was thirty-eight; Xenophon's age was undetermined, but he was probably also in his thirties. The two were considered well educated for their times, though Doniphan's matriculation at Augusta College, a Kentucky frontier academy, did not equal the several years that Xenophon spent studying with Socrates, the most notable tutor of ancient Greece. Both expeditions lasted about one year. Native peoples in the countryside hindered the progress of the expeditions—such as Armenian hill tribes in Xenophon's case, Navajos and Lipan Apaches in Doniphan's. Both expeditions faced inhospitable conditions while traversing rough terrain. Their soldiers supported both Doniphan and Xenophon for positions of leadership. Elected leader of his regiment, Doniphan was a subordinate officer on the first leg of the march and then became the commander after the capture of Santa Fe; Xenophon was a young officer in a position comparable to that of regimental commander; after the battle of Cunaxa he was elected to be one of the five new commanding generals, and may have been the most influential of that group. The two commanders used rhetoric to encourage and persuade their men and led by personal example. On a strategic level, the march of Xenophon's Ten Thousand demonstrated the vulnerability of the Persian Empire, and the foray of Doniphan's Thousand into northern Mexico confirmed the vulnerability of the Mexican nation.

Although the contrasting points outnumbered the ones in common, those differences did not make drawing the analogy less important for nineteenth-century Americans, who had always looked for ways to compare themselves with the ancient Greeks and Romans. In fact, not reluctant to exaggerate to their nation's advantage, some Americans and Missourians delighted in concluding that Doniphan's March was more remarkable than Xenophon's, just as American elites contended that the United States—the nation and its government—was superior to both the Greek city-states and the Roman republic. Moreover, because of the renown and respect that Xenophon achieved in the ancient world, seeing Colonel Alexander Doniphan as an "American Xenophon"[33] built a prideful national image for the United States and validated its military accomplishments. Americans delighted in hearing orators and journalists liken the Missourian to the Greek. That a small-town attorney—evidently a "natural leader"—could raise, train, and lead one thousand of his fellow citizens on an expedition covering more than five thousand miles and return home victorious in only one year allowed Americans to claim much about the strength, talent, resourcefulness, and promise of the United States.

The most important analogy between Doniphan and Xenophon came in a tribute by William Cullen Bryant, founder and editor of the New York *Evening Post*. A notable journalist and poet, Bryant praised Doniphan in an editorial that was quoted across the country. Bryant asserted: "Xenophon and Doniphan—these are the names of two military commanders who have made the most extraordinary marches known in the annals of warfare of their times. Col. Xenophon, as in modern phase he has justly a right to be called, [served on] a campaign [across] Asia Minor, Syria, and the sandy tract east of the Euphrates [River]." Bryant related that after the battle at Cunaxa, "Xenophon stepped forward, and soon became one of the most active leaders; and under his judicious guidance, the Greeks effected their retreat [to the] coast of the Black Sea." After delineating some contrasts between the two officers, Bryant asserted that "our object is not so much to draw comparisons between these two expeditions as to notice the circumstances that these two men, whose names are in sound so similar, have each performed the most wonderful march in the annals of warfare."[34]

Bryant's was the most important single piece comparing Doniphan to Xenophon, but articles published in the New Orleans *Delta* may have appeared before any others. In one lengthy article, the *Delta* contended that the Missourians' march "will certainly be regarded in history as one of the most brilliant achievements in ancient or modern times. Neither the retreat of the ten thousand Greeks, under Xenophon—the bloody march of Cortes through the swarming myriads of the Aztecs . . . nor any of the various enterprises accomplished by small bodies of men, traversing hostile territory, of which history has any record, exceeded in difficulty, in danger, or in success, the masterly march of Doniphan over vast plains and through the populous valley of New Mexico." In contrast to Xenophon, the *Delta* contended, Doniphan deserved not only the classic "crown of laurel" but also a "still more glorious civil wreath"—a "double glory" for winning military victories and wisely administering hostile territory, where Colonel Doniphan drew upon the language of Cicero in compiling laws for New Mexico. The *Delta* concluded that Doniphan was a "citizen commander of citizen soldiers" who deserved to rank alongside Xenophon, Hannibal, and George Washington, an illustrious trio indeed. The conclusions of the *Delta* might be dismissed as hyperbole coming in the euphoria of victory, except that William Cullen Bryant and other respected writers and speakers, North, South, East, and West, shared or supported the *Delta*'s point of view.[35]

Other contemporaries played upon the Xenophon theme. The St. Louis *New Era* stated that it was pleased to hear "that the American Xenophon, Col. *Doniphan*" had completed his successful campaign through Chihuahua and arrived at New Orleans. The Baltimore *Niles National Register* approvingly quoted the *New Era*'s piece on June 12. It was common practice in the nineteenth century for newspapers to print pieces from other papers, but the Baltimore *Daily Republican and Argus* featured the *Delta* article prominently on its front page. Of course, in his welcome-home speech on July 2, 1847, Senator Thomas Hart Benton could not resist referring to Xenophon's Greeks: "'The Ten Thousand' counted the voyage on the Black Sea as well as the march from Babylon, and twenty centuries admit the validity of the count. The present age and posterity will include in 'the going out and coming in' of the Missouri volunteers the water voyage as well as the land march, and then the One Thousand will exceed that of the Ten by some two thousand miles." Naturally, several Missouri newspapers quoted Senator Benton's speech, but papers in other cities quoted it at length as well. Missourian John Hughes, chronicler of the expedition, delighted in noting that the state's brave volunteers "bore with Roman fortitude and patience the fatigues of the Western Expedition"; he contended that "this most extraordinary march, conducted by Colonel Doniphan, *the Xenophon of the age*, with great good fortune, meets not with a parallel in the annals of the world." Hughes emphasized that "the retreat of the ten thousand Greeks, famous through time, conducted by Xenophon . . . , forms the only parallel to Doniphan's expedition, recorded in history." "In fifteen months . . . Xenophon conduct[ed] this expedition about 3450 English miles, with the loss of several thousand brave men, and finally return[ed] to Greece, possessing nothing save their lives and their arms." John Jenkins, in his *History of the War between the United States and Mexico* (1850), compared Doniphan favorably with Xenophon, except to note that the Missourian had marched 2,000 more miles than the Greek. By the time a New Mexico reporter for the Santa Fe *Era Southwestern* interviewed the colonel in 1880 and compared his exploits to the "familiar march in classic history of Cyrus and Xenophon," the analogy had been widely accepted.[36]

Support for Doniphan's future advancement naturally came from Missouri. Several of Doniphan's friends wrote to President Polk, urging continued prosecution of the war and calling for Doniphan to be made a division commander in the next campaign. The friends emphasized that "not only courage, but genius should lead our armies. . . . Courage, system, and experience [of Regular officers alone] will not suffice to lead the arms of the republic. Without travelling beyond our own great [Mississippi] Valley, we have but to look at the genius of a Jackson in the last war as that of a Doniphan in this. . . . Hannibal-like, [he] can overcome obstacles, which to the . . . [Regular officer] are utterly unfathomable. And in the trying hour of battle, they [volunteer officers] can seize upon and turn to advantage circumstances as they rise." Because Doniphan had already demonstrated that he could "stride through an enemys [*sic*] country with unexampled rapidity, [he] should be placed in command of some division of the army." The Missourians had no qualms about assuring President Polk that such an appointment for Doniphan would be for "the country's good."[37]

What other accolades could the nation provide to "this distinguished hero of the extraordinary march and brilliant victory in Chihuahua"? The indefatigable New Orleans *Delta* judged that "this volunteer officer, who has led our soldiers, in glory and honor, through so many perils, and surmounted such appalling difficulties," should be ranked "second only to the glory of the old chief of Buena Vista"—Zachary Taylor. Doniphan's contemporary, Isaac Smith, postulated, "When the deeds of the citizen soldiery shall be appreciated then will the deeds of Doniphan and his gallant men shine forth with a brilliancy not to be surpassed." The *Delta* asserted that Doniphan's must be seen as the "most remarkable march in modern times," a sentiment soon echoed by John Hughes, who concluded that it had been "the most extraordinary and wonderful expedition of the age."[38] For Doniphan the volunteer and citizen-soldier, the final accolade came a few months later when the War Department appointed him to serve on the Board of Visitors to the U.S. Military Academy. Not only was this assignment a fitting one based on merit; it also indicated a high compliment being paid by the Regular Army establishment to a respected and popular volunteer officer. Moreover, it was one that many Regulars could tolerate, considering how well Doniphan had gotten along with General Kearny and Captain Thompson. Doniphan was pleased to accept the appointment and began making plans for the trip east. He was expected to address the graduating cadets of the Class of 1848.[39]

Doniphan enjoyed traveling to New York, and he hobnobbed with the visiting dignitaries, members of the Board of Visitors, relatives and friends of the cadets, and journalists who crowded the grounds of the Military Academy. June 16, 1848—graduation day—was picture-perfect: "The sky was almost cloudless, [and] a fine breeze swept over the beautiful plain." Beginning at 8:00 A.M. a band played "several favorite national airs" as more than three hundred people took their seats, filling every pew in the Academy chapel. Among the graduating cadets were John Buford, later to earn fame as a Union cavalry leader at the first day of the Battle of Gettysburg; James C. Duane, later chief of engineers of the Army of the Potomac; and John C. Tidball, later a Union artillery officer. The attendees grew solemn and quiet, preparing themselves for the oratory to come. Ashbel Smith, a physician, political leader from Texas, and president of the Academy's Board of Visitors, spoke briefly, naturally reminding the gathering that among them was the American military officer to be compared to the great Xenophon. Smith then introduced Doniphan, saying that he would "not discredit your intelligence, nor do injustice to the reputation of the gallant gentleman, by an attempt to inform you who Col. Doniphan is."[40]

When the American Xenophon stood before the gathering, his first words were ones of apology, for he explained that he had not been well. But he warmed to his address, and the chapel full of people responded. Doniphan urged the cadets and his audience to consider that in the future, what he called "modern" U.S. Army officers would have to be educated broadly, to include law and literature, diplomacy and economics, science and technology. The colonel cogently warned his auditors that, unlike businessmen or townsfolk, officers serving on campaign in the field must steel themselves against danger and prepare for the numerous physical demands of leadership, such as "hunger, thirst, fatigue, scorching suns, piercing colds, drenching rains, or pestilential diseases." Speaking from experience, Doniphan stressed that "all [of these burdens] must be borne, and . . . with such cheerfulness as to dispel all gloom from [the officer's] companions and followers." Ironically, after speaking for several minutes, the colonel became faint and had to be seated.[41]

Doniphan rested briefly and resumed his presentation, saying "that it occasioned him greater embarrassment to appear before such an audience than it would to meet the enemy on the battlefield." The assembly politely applauded. Then, in a word of cautionary advice applicable to military men of any age, Doniphan demanded that the cadets "remember your country wars with nations, not with individuals—she never revenges national wrongs on private citizens." The colonel complimented the Military Academy on its thoroughness, sense of discipline, and the qualifications of its professors and officers. He reminded the audience that several of the officers in his regiment—Captain Weightman, Lieutenant Colonel Ruff, Major Clark, and Major Gilpin—had attended the Academy and that their training and military bearing had contributed significantly to the success of the expedition. Indeed, Doniphan might have added that by attending the Academy, returning to civilian life as engineers and legislators, then volunteering for active service, the West Point alumni fulfilled Thomas Jefferson's expectations of a republican military institution that benefited the nation in several ways; it was more than a school for producing professional officers. Many Americans, relying as they did on the volunteer military tradition, might not have wished to acknowledge them, but Doniphan believed that the citizen-soldiers owed much to officers educated at West Point.[42]

Continuing along those lines, Doniphan emphasized the important example that Regulars could provide to volunteers. He "always deemed it very fortunate that we had been for three months with Gen. Kearny and his regulars," indicating that it was important for Regulars and citizen-soldiers to be able to work together. His "stirring speech" complete, Doniphan took his seat, and "the most deafening bursts of applause" rolled from the people in the chapel. Doniphan was gratified at the reception given his address, but he seemed glad that it was over. Still not feeling well, Doniphan made the effort to enjoy a marvelous display of fireworks that followed the speechmaking. The visit to the Military Academy and the honors accorded him during his stay at West Point marked one of the high points of the colonel's life. Doniphan returned to Missouri, his law practice in Liberty, and his family. No longer a soldier, he was forever ranked as extraordinary by his contemporaries for his accomplishments as a military commander.[43]

CHAPTER TEN

The Hero in the Crisis of the Union

In the years to come, Colonel Doniphan proudly recalled his military service in the war against Mexico. Pleased by the recognition accorded to his long marches and victorious battles, he believed his expedition had contributed significantly to the American war effort. The colonel shared the assessment of President James Polk, who wrote in his annual message to Congress near the end of 1848: "Before the late war with Mexico European and other foreign powers entertained imperfect and erroneous views of our physical strength as a nation and of our ability to prosecute war, and especially a war waged out of our own country." Disdainfully, the president charged that Europeans relied on "large standing armies for the protection of thrones against their own subjects, as well as against foreign enemies." Europe and Mexico had underestimated America's martial potential, but Polk congratulated America's "citizen soldiers" for stepping into the breach and performing as well as "veteran troops" in conquering Mexico's northern states.[1]

The shift of half of Mexico to American sovereignty caused regret and recrimination among Mexicans. Disappointed and angry Mexicans hurled charges of negligence, corruption, malfeasance, incompetence, and even treason at their leaders of the 1840s, but the fault rested with no single leader or party. Mexico's impractical notions of regaining Texas, its immature nationalism, and its inability to organize adequate defensive measures prior to 1846 all played parts in the country's defeat. Pierced by America's cordon offensives, including Doniphan's strikes into New Mexico and Chihuahua, Mexico failed to muster the military force necessary to turn back even one of America's invasions. Based on the war's outcome, astute critics questioned the viability of Mexican nationalism. The depth of Mexico's despair was expressed in an anonymous essay, probably written by Congressman Mariano Otero: "In Mexico that which is called national spirit cannot nor has been able to exist, for there is no nation." Other Mexicans related their disillusionment over the fact that the United States, a democratic nation whose institutions they admired and respected, committed aggression against them. The loss of Alta California, Pimería Alta, and Nuevo Mexico—the national patrimony—and the decisiveness of Mexico's defeat haunted Mexicans like ghostly specters.[2]

While Mexicans wept over their losses, Americans rejoiced over their gains. New Yorker Philip Hone, a Whig businessman who had bitterly opposed the war, wryly noted, "*Annexation* is now the greatest word in the American vocabulary. 'Veni—vidi—vici!' is inscribed on the banners of every Caesar who leads a straggling band of American adventurers across the prairies, over the mountains, up the rivers, and into the chaparral of a territory which an unprovoked war has given them the right to invade." Favoring annexation and Manifest Destiny as they did, Doniphan, most Missouri veterans, and many other Americans would have disagreed with Hone's attitude and reinterpreted his words to their own satisfaction. The successful American military campaigns by Taylor, Scott, Stockton, Kearny, and Doniphan across Mexico's borders and into its heartland electrified nationalism in the United States. Confirmed by the Treaty of Guadalupe Hidalgo, those American campaigns stretched the boundaries of the United States west to the Pacific and south to the Rio Grande, giving America Santa Fe, San Francisco, and vast lands of great potential. Furthermore, only a few months of war decided that Texas and California were no longer targets of European meddling and the United States would dominate North America.[3]

Even before the war ended, however, military success brought on contentious debate in the United States over the issue of slavery expanding into the conquered lands. According to the venerable Missouri Compromise, all lands within the Louisiana Purchase belonging to the United States below 36°30′ north latitude were reserved for potential slave states. Texas had entered the Union in 1845 as a slave state, but whether slave owners would transport their slaves to New Mexico, Arizona, Utah, and California, and whether slave labor could be used profitably in such places, were open questions. In the House of Representatives, Pennsylvania Democrat David Wilmot introduced his resolution opposing slavery in any lands America had taken from Mexico. Wilmot repeatedly introduced his proviso, and although it passed the House, the Senate never approved it. By reintroducing the resolution, Wilmot kept the issue of slavery in the territories before the public. Several months after the war, Doniphan chaired a meeting in Liberty that condemned the controversial proviso. The colonel and his neighbors resolved "that we are in favor of the Union, under any, and all circumstances, yet regard the Wilmot Proviso and all kindred measures, with the most perfect abhorrence."[4]

The debate over slavery in the territories carried over into the elections of 1848. Doniphan and his fellow volunteer soldiers put behind them the last of the parades and festivities held in their honor, returned to their jobs, and anticipated the electoral contest. The Whig nominee for president was none other than General Zachary Taylor, a war hero, Southerner, and slave owner. The Whigs had picked an excellent candidate, as far as Doniphan was concerned. Some Missouri Whigs wanted Doniphan to run for governor. It was the colonel's best chance to capitalize on his fame and boost his party at the same time. Whig organizer John Wilson in St. Louis envisioned an unbeatable combination. Cheering for "Taylor [and] Buena Vista & Sacramento & Doniphan . . . shall carry this state," Wilson predicted. Doniphan begged off, citing the needs of his law practice and his wife's poor health, but the coming months showed that his own health had suffered from the Chihuahua campaign. Although he would not be a gubernatorial candidate, as a loyal Whig Doniphan took time away from his law cases to give several speeches on behalf of Old Rough and Ready. Taylor won the election over two opponents, Democrat Lewis Cass and Free Soil candidate Martin van Buren. Staunchly Democratic, Missouri cast its electoral votes for Cass.[5]

The year after Taylor's election, thousands of gold-seeking "forty-niners," mostly from the Northern states and Europe, poured into California. The rapid settlement from nonslaveholding areas guaranteed that California would come into the Union as a free state, and much sooner than anyone had predicted. In one stroke the Pacific Coast would be closed to slavery. Furthermore, after his election Taylor took an innovative approach to the debate over slavery in the territories: end the disputes by quickly making both California and New Mexico states, even if the latter did not have the requisite number of settlers. Such action would have resulted in great chunks of the West being admitted as free states, and would have reduced the influence of slave state politicians in the Union. These possibilities intensified debate over slavery's status in the Mexican Cession.

With misgivings, Doniphan watched as the disagreements escalated about slavery in the nation and in Missouri. Disputes about slavery in the territories fed into a broader national debate, and Congress consolidated several issues in the Compromise of 1850. The steps toward compromise were led by Senator Stephen A. Douglas of Illinois and given crucial support by Doniphan's idol, Senator Henry Clay. A sequence of separately passed congressional acts made up the compromise, signed by President Millard Fillmore, who had succeeded to office on Taylor's death. One act admitted California as a free state, another ended the slave trade in the District of Columbia, and a third created the federal Fugitive Slave Act, requiring Northern law officers to return runaway slaves. A fourth bill organized the new territories of Utah and New Mexico. The wording of this bill implied that slave owners could take slaves into that sliver of New Mexico *above* the old 36°30′ line established by the Missouri Compromise as slavery's northern limit. That provision of the Compromise of 1850 raised the possibility that the venerable 36°30′ line would not be continued.

Like many Americans of the 1850s, Doniphan desired a grand nation reaching to the Pacific Ocean, but, like most white Southerners, he also expected slavery to remain a part of American life. The colonel would have preferred to quash the debate over slavery in the territories. If the Congress maintained the 36°30′ line, at least some territories would be set aside for slavery's growth, and the federal government would continue to give its approval of slavery's expansion into the West. In the years to come many Southerners soured on the Compromise of 1850, and some Southern political leaders saw that it would be difficult for any future slave states to enter the Union. The nation's sectional issues and divisions intensified.[6]

Doniphan remained an attractive candidate for every vacant office, and Missouri's partisan contests of the 1850s offered him the chance to run for election at any time. One observer wrote that Doniphan was "a firm unswerving Whig," someone "against whose moral & intellectual deportment nothing prejudicial can with success be alleged & he is also well qualified to make himself acceptable to the masses." No doubt, the colonel would have been a prime nominee for Congress, either the House or the Senate, or for the governorship, but he demurred. In a letter to leading Whigs printed in the Liberty *Tribune,* he cited a terrible case of "Bronchittis" and his worry that the chronic condition would intensify and lead to his death. He had to decide: winning a congressional campaign meant traveling to Washington, D.C., living in a rooming house, and being separated from his wife for months at a time. Alternatively, if he applied himself to his law practice, went out of town only a few days per month, rode the familiar judicial circuit, and visited nearby courtrooms, he could remain close to home. He chose home. In 1852 Missouri Whigs nominated Doniphan to run for governor against Sterling Price, another volunteer officer who had served in the Mexican War as colonel of the 2nd Missouri Mounted Regiment and as one of President Polk's appointees to brigadier general of volunteers. Price was an ardent pro-slavery Democrat. Once more, Doniphan declined the nomination for reasons of health, disappointing many Whigs, who were sure that he represented the best chance of undercutting the Democrats' consistent strength in state politics. The flamboyant Price easily won the governorship, defeating another Whig.[7]

Turning away from politics temporarily, the colonel entered into various business pursuits in the 1850s to provide for his family. He invested in the Liberty Insurance Company and served as its president for several years. He considered promoting the construction of trunk line railroads in western Missouri. Receiving an endorsement from Mordecai Oliver, Whig congressman from Richmond, Missouri, Doniphan arranged to sell "first rate beef cattle" to the U.S. Army and offered to transport military supplies to forts in Nebraska, Wyoming, and Dakota Territories. Along with other veterans, he sought to recover from the federal government the cost of personal horses that had died on his marches through Mexico. All of these moneymaking ventures, plus his law practice, combined to sap Doniphan's fluctuating health. From time to time for reasons of health, he declined offers to give speeches or missed meetings of the Board of Trustees of William Jewell College, which he had helped to establish in 1849.[8]

While several of his business schemes made money during the 1850s, personal catastrophes destroyed Doniphan's family. Both of his sons died in accidents, and his wife's health became precarious. John Doniphan died on May 9, 1853, in Liberty after mistaking poison for medicine. A few days later, Jane Doniphan suffered what may have been a stroke or a severe case of depression. In any event, Mrs. Doniphan, then thirty-three years of age, never recovered her health. The parents received a second shock when Alexander Jr., a student at Bethany College in western Virginia, drowned in a flooded stream near the campus on May 11, 1858. Never particularly religious before the deaths of his sons, Doniphan soon joined the Liberty Christian Church and thereafter became a devoted member of the congregation.[9]

Along with family tragedies, Doniphan suffered political travail. Between 1852 and 1855 the national Whig party broke apart, leaving the colonel without a political home. Disagreements between Northern and Southern Whigs over slavery and its expansion into the territories contributed to the party's demise, and in Missouri factional disputes undermined the Whigs. Southern and Northern Whigs also divided over how to react to the flood of new European immigrants, many of whom were Catholics. Finally, nominating General Winfield Scott proved to be disastrous in the presidential election of 1852, in which the Democrat, former volunteer general Franklin Pierce, won an overwhelming electoral triumph. Like many Whigs, Doniphan tried to remain loyal to Whig principles while seeking a new party to join.[10]

As a hero to Missourians, it was impossible for Doniphan to remain away from politics for long. In 1854 he won election to the house of representatives in the Missouri General Assembly, taking his seat in December. His return to the legislature put him in an advantageous situation. As its session opened in January 1855, the legislature was called upon to elect one of Missouri's U.S. senators. The Democrats divided sharply between two party wheelhorses, Thomas Hart Benton and David Rice Atchison. Although the Whigs never nominated another presidential candidate, this bitter split among Missouri Democrats opened the door for the state's discouraged Whigs to propose an attractive compromise candidate for the Senate. That nominee was Doniphan, but the colonel declined to vote for himself, repeatedly casting a lone vote for a man who was not a candidate. His action raised the question whether Doniphan really wanted to win the election. The legislature struggled through the election during sixteen days and forty-one ballots. By then Benton's adherents realized that they could not elect their candidate but, by switching their votes to Doniphan, they could unseat their rival, Atchison. Stubbornly, Benton's die-hard Democrats refused to desert him. This impasse blocked Atchison's election and drained Doniphan's health without producing a senator. The legislature adjourned, leaving the Senate seat temporarily vacant. Another chance for Doniphan to hold high office had slipped away.[11]

Meanwhile, Democrats and Whigs rearranged themselves into factions over one of the most controversial federal laws of the nineteenth century, the Kansas-Nebraska Act, which was passed by Congress in May 1854. David Atchison and Stephen Douglas both staked their political futures on the popular sovereignty concept, allowing settlers to decide on slavery in each territory, regardless whether it was part of the Louisiana Purchase or the Mexican Cession. The Kansas-Nebraska Act officially nullified the Missouri Compromise line of 36°30′. The Kansas-Nebraska arrangement implied that Kansas, adjacent to Missouri, might be a slave state, while Nebraska, next to Iowa, would become a free state. Rather than maintaining a federal protection or endowment for future slave states south of the 36°30′ line that the Missouri Compromise had represented, Southern leaders like Atchison discarded the once-sacred line on the vague prospect that future slave states could be carved out of such places as Nevada, Utah, and Colorado. In the opinion of Benton and other nationalists, throwing out the Missouri Compromise line guaranteed more controversy.[12]

Stepping away from Northern Whigs, Doniphan and most Southern Whigs favored the Kansas-Nebraska Act because it opened the possibility of Kansas becoming a slave state. At a public meeting held at Liberty in December 1854, the colonel advocated that Missourians migrate to Kansas and support the formation of a new slave state. As paraphrased by his hometown newspaper, "Col. Doniphan urged upon the people to take all legal and constitutional steps to prevent Kansas from becoming an abolition den." Other pro-South spokesmen later harped on the same theme. There was no residency requirement for voting in Kansas Territory, and in the months to come hundreds of Missourians crossed into Kansas at election times, casting votes for pro-slavery candidates and for a territorial constitution that authorized slavery. These actions contributed to years of hard feelings between Kansans and Missourians and violence between pro-slave and antislave forces in Kansas Territory.[13]

Despite mounting controversy over slavery, and criticism of the institution from former Northern Whigs and some residents of Missouri, Doniphan maintained his status as a slave owner. Clay County, with a population nearly one-third slaves in 1860, formed part of the belt of counties having high slave populations that followed the Missouri River running through the central part of the state. Missouri's population grew and shifted remarkably during the 1850s. Many of the new settlers, especially those moving to St. Louis, were Europeans and other nonslaveholders. Meanwhile, the percentage of slaves in the state's population fell from almost 22 percent in 1830 to less than 11 percent in 1860. Slave owners still exercised exceptional influence in Missouri's politics and economy, but the shift in the state's population indicated that their influence would be reduced in the future. The colonel owned five slaves in 1860, with an estimated value of more than four thousand dollars, a substantial investment by standards of the day. Owning these few slaves did not make Doniphan economically dependent on slavery, but it did give him status in a slaveholding society. Nothing he heard or saw persuaded him to reject slavery or free his slaves.[14] On July 12–14, 1855, more than two hundred pro-slavery advocates, including Doniphan, Atchison, Governor Sterling Price, former governor Austin A. King, and Congressman Mordecai Oliver, gathered at a state Proslavery Convention held in Lexington, Missouri. Three years later Doniphan was president of the Clay County Pro-Slavery Aid Association, one of several county organizations encouraging pro-slavery settlement of Kansas to counteract similar Northern groups bringing free-state settlers there. He wanted no part of Kansas becoming a free state and a possible magnet for runaway slaves. Therefore, through the 1850s Doniphan's support for slavery never wavered.[15]

During the presidential election year of 1856, acts of violence increased in Kansas. After a pro-slavery sheriff was murdered in April 1856, an intimidating force of pro-slavery men gathered, numbering perhaps in the hundreds. Targeting the town of Lawrence, where most settlers were from the North, on May 21 the pro-slavery raiders burned a house and ransacked two antislavery newspaper offices. In an effort at bipartisanship, Doniphan and Atchison denounced the violence, but critics of both men asserted that they had, in one way or another, sustained the pro-slavery raiders. Atchison had admonished Missourians to cross the border well armed and had been in Lawrence just before the raid; Doniphan may have lent his name to the "Doniphan Tigers," a company of toughs who may have been involved in the attack. Greatly intensifying the violence, a few days later, Ohio abolitionist John Brown murdered five Southerners who had settled along the Pottawatomie Creek, creating the image of "Bleeding Kansas" in the minds of Americans.[16]

The disturbances in Kansas formed the backdrop to the presidential campaign, and Doniphan searched for a candidate. As a border state slave owner he disdained the new Republican party, even though it nominated another popular hero of the Mexican War, John C. Frémont, who was a remarkably strong candidate. Formed in part as a response to the Kansas-Nebraska Act, the Republican party clearly announced the primary reason for its existence: to stop the expansion of slavery into the western territories. For twenty years the Democrats had opposed Henry Clay's "American System" (a national bank, internal improvements, and a high tariff), and the strong states' rights stand taken by many Democrats had never appealed to Doniphan, though their candidate, James Buchanan, was known to be friendly to Southern interests. In other words, Buchanan would not criticize or take action against slavery. Presented with such unpalatable options, Doniphan and other former Whigs in Missouri adopted the nativist American (Know-Nothing) party and its nominee, former president Millard Fillmore. Naturally, Doniphan backed his choice by delivering several speeches on Fillmore's behalf. Nevertheless, Buchanan carried Missouri and won the presidency.[17]

Making poor policy choices and controversial appointments to territorial offices, Buchanan had more difficulties with Kansas politics than did President Pierce. Threats, diatribes over drafts of territorial constitutions, and more bloodshed branded "Bleeding Kansas" during the rest of the decade. Few admitted that the first flickers of a civil war were smoldering next door to Doniphan's home state.

During 1860 the national Democratic party fell apart, while the Republicans united behind Abraham Lincoln. Northern Democrats nominated Stephen Douglas, and Southern Democrats endorsed Buchanan's vice president, John C. Breckinridge, a states' rights Kentuckian strong for slavery in the territories. Blocking slavery's expansion remained the Republicans' cardinal principle, but in 1860 they added new planks to their platform, including Whiggish propositions such as a high tariff along with federal assistance programs—land grants to state colleges and to a transcontinental railroad.

Rejecting the Know-Nothings, discarding both of the Democrats, and scorning the Republicans, Doniphan supported John Bell, the nominee of the Constitutional Union party and a former Whig from Tennessee. In order to attract a wide following and appear to be the best compromise among the sectional candidates, Bell and his party vaguely proclaimed "the Constitution of the country, the Union of the States, and the enforcement of the laws." In full agreement with each of these high-minded concepts, Doniphan spoke on Bell's behalf to several rallies across Missouri.[18]

In a speech on November 5 at Liberty, Doniphan asked voters to recall the "unity, and indivisibility . . . of our admirable form of government." Directing his listeners' attention to the Republican candidate, Doniphan was "apprehensive of Mr. Lincoln's election," fearing that it would lead to "inevitable strife, the sanguinary feuds, and border warfare which must follow in a greater or lesser degree, the inauguration of Black Republicanism, with its sectional hate and oppressive policy." To Doniphan, a vote for Bell would be the best way to unify the nation, and he called for other Unionists to rally to Bell's banner. Bell's makeshift party represented in its name what Doniphan favored: the Constitution and the Union. As an experienced and talented orator, Doniphan often ended his speeches on a positive or uplifting note, but this time he forecast "four years of incessant broils, and jealousies and bloody contests" if the Republicans won the White House. Although he sounded grim, Doniphan stopped short of predicting a civil war. Over the years, the Constitution and the Union had survived imbroglios over Missouri statehood, South Carolina's nullification of the tariff, the Wilmot Proviso, the national Fugitive Slave Act of 1850, and the Kansas-Nebraska Act. Doniphan expected that the Union would survive the presidential election of 1860.[19]

John Bell carried Clay County, but Stephen Douglas carried Missouri for the national Democrats by a narrow margin—less than five hundred votes—the only state Douglas won outright in the election. Breckinridge finished third and Lincoln fourth in Missouri. The state's new governor, Claiborne F. Jackson, though nominally a Douglas Democrat, ardently supported states' rights and slavery. Lincoln's electoral victory prompted South Carolina to secede on December 20, just a few weeks after the November ballots were counted. Contending that the Union was only a compact of the states, leaders in other Deep South states favored secession and promised to follow South Carolina's example.[20]

Unlike Governor Jackson and Southern "fire-eaters" who considered themselves adherents of secessionist theories proposed by John C. Calhoun, Doniphan refused to condone secession and the destruction of the Union in order to protect the permanence of slavery. At heart, Doniphan's attitude toward the sacred Union was close to that of one of the greatest Whig stalwarts, Daniel

Webster, U.S. senator from Massachusetts. Reaching the height of his powers in the 1830s, Webster had regaled audiences with speeches stressing devotion to the Union. For example, in 1830 Webster replied to combative words from South Carolina congressman Robert Y. Hayne, thundering out one of the best expositions of an indissoluble United States. "Liberty *and* Union, now and for ever, one and inseparable!" Webster had exclaimed. Doniphan knew well Webster's foreboding words from that same speech: "While the Union lasts we [Americans] have high, exciting, gratifying prospects spread out before us." But those aiming to disrupt the Union for personal or political reasons were creating nightmares for Webster and all patriotic Americans: "States dissevered, discordant, belligerent; or a land rent with civil feuds, or drenched, it may be in fraternal blood!" In another address to the Senate in 1833 ("The Constitution—Not a Compact"), Webster held that "that no State authority has power to dissolve these [binding constitutional] relations; that nothing can dissolve them but revolution; and that, consequently, there can be no such thing as secession without revolution."[21]

The revolution came during January 1861, and Doniphan could have recognized a bitter irony: the United States was experiencing a secession crisis like Mexico's. Mexican federalism was not strong enough in the 1830s to prevent Texas from winning a revolution and seceding from Mexico, and Texas's claims of state sovereignty boosted states' rights proponents in Yucatán and Tabasco to announce for secession in the 1840s, though they were unsuccessful. But South Carolina's effective announcement of secession in 1860 presented a dire threat to American federalism in early 1861. During January, five Southern states—Mississippi, Florida, Alabama, Georgia, and Louisiana—carried out ad hoc procedures for secession. Texas followed suit on February 1. On the horizon civil war loomed, a war that endangered federal control of the Mexican Cession, lands that Doniphan and many other soldiers had fought to gain for the United States. Other states teetered on the verge of disunion—Virginia, Arkansas, Tennessee, and perhaps Kentucky and Missouri as well. For Doniphan, it was horrible to contemplate such degradation. America had fallen into a secession crisis worse than that of Mexico.[22]

On January 28 two thousand people gathered outdoors in Liberty to hear the colonel's views on the crisis. Standing in the snow, Doniphan's friends and neighbors listened to him for more than an hour. He stressed the theme of preserving the Union and criticized South Carolina's claim of secession. This informal meeting endorsed the notion that Missouri should send delegates to a so-called Peace Convention at Washington, summoned by Virginia's legislature to solve the sectional crisis. At first Doniphan disclaimed his interest in such a venture, but, encouraged by this hometown show of loyalty and backed by a resolution in the state legislature on February 4, he agreed to serve as one of five Missouri delegates. A veteran of Doniphan's expedition to Santa Fe, Waldo P. Johnson, was one of the others. After learning that the legislature had announced an election for a state convention to consider secession, the colonel packed his bags for the trip to Washington.[23]

By early February, twenty-one states had acted to select and send more than 130 delegates to the Peace Convention, which opened on February 4, 1861, at Willard's Hotel in Washington, D.C. Those delegates represented fourteen non-slave states (Wisconsin, Minnesota, and Michigan declined to send delegates; California and Oregon were too far away), four border slave states (Missouri, Maryland, Kentucky, and Delaware), and three Southern slave states (Virginia, Tennessee, and North Carolina). At the same time, representatives from seven Deep South states assembled in Montgomery, Alabama, to build the framework for a new Southern confederacy.[24]

On the way to the East Coast, on February 4 Doniphan's train stopped in Springfield, Illinois. Boarding the train was Orville H. Browning, like Doniphan an alumnus of Augusta College and fellow admirer of Henry Clay. Thirty years before, when Doniphan had moved to Missouri, Browning went to Illinois, where he began a law practice, served as a Whig in the Illinois legislature, and developed a friendship with Abraham Lincoln. Like Lincoln, Browning was a founding member of the Illinois Republican party and a devout Union man.[25]

Pleased to see Doniphan, Browning was disappointed that he seemed ambivalent toward secession. The colonel supported neither disunion nor coercion. Browning told his fellow Augusta alumnus that he opposed any notion of secession. Doniphan appeared to concur, but he stipulated that "there were some grave difficulties to overcome in the settlement of our [states' rights] troubles." To deploy the U.S. Army against the secessionists, Doniphan warned, would "drive all the slave states into combination with the *traitors of South Carolina*." Browning curtly replied that the federal government must enforce national laws. Doniphan wondered how that could be done without further disrupting the Union. "If you use forces like the army you would be recognizing their right to secede and you'd have to bring them back as territories," the Missourian concluded, ironically striking the exact note soon put forward by Radical Republicans during debates over Reconstruction. Browning hoped that the crisis would never come to such a drastic conclusion, but, after listening to Doniphan's opinions, he had "no hopes of anything being accomplished by the border State [Peace] Convention."[26]

Doniphan found himself in good company when he got to Washington. Of course, he knew many of the delegates either personally or by reputation. Former president John Tyler chaired the Peace Convention. General John Wool was one of eleven New Yorkers present; Pennsylvania's delegation included Congressman David Wilmot, author of the controversial proviso; and from Kentucky came the younger son of the Great Compromiser, former congressman James B. Clay, who had resided in Missouri for two years. Among the other distinguished members of the convention were current or former U.S. senators or congressmen such as Republicans William P. Fessenden and Lot M. Morrill of Maine, Republican Samuel R. Curtis of Iowa, Reverdy Johnson from Maryland (a Whig who also served as attorney general under President Taylor), Democrat and pro-secessionist James A. Seddon of Virginia, Democrat-turned-Republican Salmon P. Chase of Ohio (who had also been his state's governor), Felix Zollicoffer, a Whig from Tennessee, and Whig Caleb B. Smith of Indiana. Also attending were former Democratic governor of Massachusetts George S. Boutwell and former navy commodore Robert F. Stockton of New Jersey.[27]

The gathering became known as the "Old Gentlemen's Convention" due to the advanced age of many of the delegates. Only seven of them were under forty years of age. Seventy-four others had reached their fifties (with Doniphan among them at age fifty-three), thirty-four were over sixty, and twelve tallied seventy years or more, including Tyler, who was seventy-one. A master of invective, Horace Greeley, editor of the New York *Tribune*, called the delegates "political fossils," but his aspersion did not dissuade them from their efforts to achieve some sort of national compromise that might stop secession and avert civil war. The "Old Gentlemen" looked for enough common ground for Unionists and secessionists to gather together.[28]

After being in Washington for several days, Doniphan was displeased with the convention. Listening to numerous self-serving speeches, the colonel decided it would be difficult for the delegates to reach a compromise that would be acceptable to the country and the Congress. Although numerous possibilities for compromise were discussed, the most important revolved around the ideas of Kentucky senator John C. Crittenden. Casting himself in the mold of Henry Clay, Crittenden wanted an agreement to resuscitate the old 36°30′ line of the Missouri Compromise and frame a permanent amendment to the U.S. Constitution. Had Crittenden limited his proposal simply to reviving 36°30′, he might have gained the support he needed in Congress. But the senator embellished his central theme with extra trappings, reducing the likelihood that his compromise would gain approval from moderate Republicans, including President-elect Lincoln. These trappings included preventing Congress from abolishing slavery in the District of Columbia, unless Maryland and Virginia agreed; insisting that the Fugitive Slave Act of 1850 be rigorously enforced; reconfirming that Congress could not abolish slavery in any state; blocking Congress from regulating the interstate slave trade; prohibiting slavery north of 36°30′ but indicating that below the line new territories suitable for slavery could be acquired. When the Peace Convention gathered, Congress already had voted down Crittenden's Compromise package.[29]

The delegates resolved that their proceedings must be held behind closed doors without admitting reporters to their convention. The majority agreed that they would be more likely to treat issues and proposals seriously if their speeches were not quoted or paraphrased the next day in the newspapers of Washington, New York, Boston, and Richmond. According to the confidential minutes of the convention, Doniphan spoke on only a few matters. Several delegates, including Doniphan, liked the notion of calling a new general "convention of the people" of all the states. At such a nationalistic gathering, amendments to the Constitution and other potential solutions could be discussed that might quiet the sectional discord. Another issue prompted Doniphan to speak. Some delegates favored reopening the African slave trade, but Doniphan adamantly opposed such a step. His views reflected a majority of the convention.[30]

Over many days of debate, the Peace Convention delegates took the components of Crittenden's proposed amendment, modified their wording slightly, and sent them over to Congress, which was just about to adjourn. The Peace Convention's solution embodied the old 36°30′ line, and included several supplements. For instance, new territories below 36°30′ could not be added without the approval of four-fifths of the Senate; "the foreign slave trade" was "forever prohibited"; and the price of fugitive slaves who could not be recaptured would be paid to the owner from the federal Treasury.[31]

At one point during his stay in Washington, Doniphan appeared to edge toward the secessionists, concluding in a letter to his nephew that "the border slave states must stand or fall together as a unit and by one act, and form a new government or *go with the South*, and this last is best. As one respectable republic in numbers and power is better than twenty little rickety concerns." Although Doniphan firmly believed that adopting Crittenden's ideas would be beneficial to the nation, he was creeping closer to the fact that Congress would not approve a workable compromise.[32]

Toward the end of the convention Doniphan met Lincoln. The president-elect walked into Willard's Hotel and shook hands with several delegates, complimenting Doniphan on his prowess in the Mexican War. Quite likely, the colonel bitterly recalled how attitudes toward that war had separated them. Going against a majority of Whigs, Doniphan had advocated the war and reveled in its prospects for adding new lands to the United States. Representing Illinois in the U.S. House of Representatives, Lincoln, like many Whigs, had criticized Polk's policies and the way he handled the war. In an address to the House late in the war, on December 22, 1847, Lincoln had expressed his doubt that the Mexican War started on American soil by introducing the "Spot Resolutions," demanding to know the exact spot where the first skirmish had occurred between Mexican and American soldiers. In Lincoln's view, that war was unjust and without purpose—a siren calling men to their deaths for nothing but glory. "Military glory," Lincoln had said during a later speech in the House on January 12, 1848, was "that attractive rainbow, that rises in the showers of blood—that serpent's eye, that charms to destroy." Lincoln also clinically noted that the war was something President Polk found difficult to control. Along with almost every other congressional Whig, Lincoln had voted for a resolution with a rider attached that condemned Polk's war and, by association, Doniphan's. Now one of the consequences of Doniphan's war—the long-term debates over slavery in the territories—was being placed on Lincoln's desk during the nation's worst crisis. It remained to be seen if Lincoln would find war—applying military force to achieve national policy objectives—more appropriate and useful in 1861 than he had in 1847.[33]

From Doniphan's point of view, Lincoln made a distinctly unfavorable impression in 1861. Of course, another reason for the Missourian's attitude toward the president-elect came on the basis of Lincoln's public statements opposing slavery's expansion into the national territories, the primary aim of the Republican party. Those statements demonstrated to Doniphan's satisfaction that Lincoln opposed the institution of slavery itself. Writing to his nephew, Doniphan held back nothing in his view of the Republicans' leader: "It is very humiliating for an American to know that the present & future destiny of his Country is wholly in the hands of one man & that such a man as Lincoln—a man of no intelligence, no enlargement of views [—someone] as ridiculously vain and fantastic as a country boy with his first red morocco hat." Furthermore, Doniphan asserted that, according to his reading of the newspapers, most of the speeches Lincoln gave on the trip from Springfield to Washington were "ridiculously childish displays of eloquence" rather than measured pronouncements that would mend the bonds of the Union shredded by the secession of several Deep South states. Doniphan concluded emphatically: "Jesting aside old Abe is simply an ignorant, country buffoon who [was not] fitted intellectually for [the office of] President. . . . " Doniphan was not alone in his low opinion of Lincoln in 1861. In the coming months, however, many Republicans and even some Democrats decided that the president was a better leader than they first thought.[34]

But in 1861 Doniphan's and Lincoln's mutual love for the Union superseded their past differences concerning the Mexican War and their current contrasting views on slavery. A crafty natural politician always looking for political allies and evaluating potential foes or patronage appointments, Lincoln knew the Missourian's politics and probably complimented Doniphan and his famous march in order to court his support in the future. Missouri still hung in the balance, and during the crisis of the Union, men changed sides every week. Although Doniphan refused to move an inch toward Lincoln's antislavery precepts, at least the president was grateful that, so far, Doniphan had declined to lend his military reputation to the service of the Confederacy. Shortly after the two men met, congressional Republicans spurned the Peace Convention's proposals based on the Crittenden formula, and Doniphan learned that he had been elected to the special state convention designed to consider Missouri's status in the Union.

Doniphan returned to Missouri around March 1 and made his way to St. Louis. The legislature, which had called the election for the special convention, also stipulated that if the convention endorsed secession, Missouri's voters must go to the polls in a referendum on the matter. Opening on February 28 in Jefferson City, the convention elected Sterling Price as president. Price had supported Douglas in the presidential election and was considered by some to be a "Conditional Unionist" and by others to favor the Southern Confederacy. Encouraged by pro-Union members, led by Frank Blair Jr., the convention agreed to move to St. Louis to meet in a larger building. On March 4, the day that Lincoln took the presidential oath in Washington, the delegates reconvened in St. Louis, with Doniphan in attendance. Like the nation, the delegates split into factions. Some overtly favored the Confederacy and secession. Others stood unconditionally for the Union, including Blair, Edward Bates (Lincoln's choice for U.S. attorney general), and B. Gratz Brown, editor of the *Missouri Democrat*. Doniphan, with the majority, including former governor Robert M. Stewart, ex-Whig leader James S. Rollins, and Judge Hamilton R. Gamble, collected in the middle, in the "Conditional Union" group. He and like-minded fellows wished to hold the country together but still opposed employing the army to force a seceded state to return to the Union.[35]

During his trip from Washington to Missouri, Doniphan must have been tormented by both the ongoing national crisis and his need to make a personal decision. If his sentiments to his nephew accurately reflected his state of mind, Doniphan briefly entertained thoughts of condoning secession. Soon he would have to decide if he would support the Confederacy. In St. Louis a number of the state convention's delegates proposed what seemed like a compromise: Lincoln and the Republicans must adopt the Crittenden Compromise or an amendment to the Constitution protecting slavery, or else Missouri would secede. Doniphan, of course, had been disappointed that the Congress had not passed some version of Crittenden's Compromise, and he knew that many of his fellow Mexican War veterans were ready to support secession and slavery. These conflicting emotions and opinions shrouded him as he prepared to serve on the convention's crucial Committee on Federal Relations, along with Willard P. Hall, a fellow veteran of the Santa Fe expedition, and Hamilton R. Gamble, a notable former Whig and chair of the committee. Ten other delegates also sat on the committee. These men were to issue a recommendation about Missouri and secession.[36]

Before the committee issued a report, the convention called upon Doniphan to address it concerning his trip to the Peace Conference. On March 5 Doniphan complied. In the second sentence of his address, the colonel specified the "cause for the difficulties that now agitate and disturb the country," namely, "the question of negro slavery." In a prosperous nation having much to unite its citizens in common cause, slavery had surfaced to create "sectionalism," and sectionalism had "assumed a gigantic shape." In Doniphan's view the question of slavery "must be removed from the arena of politics." If this thorn was removed from the body politic, sectionalism would cease to exist. Briefly viewing forty years of America's history through the lens of the slavery question, Doniphan pointed out that there were those to blame in both sections: "Many imprudent men have done many imprudent things at the South, calculated to inflame the minds of men at the North." But now the nation was governed by a Northern political party and by a new president from the North whose stance was "antagonistic to the South." The crisis of the Union had "weakened the cords that bind us [Americans] together, and disintegration is the natural consequence." A "revolution has grown out of the triumph of sectionalism," but it was a sectional upheaval "inaugurated" not in the South but in the North, climaxing in the presidential election of 1860. The results of that election were like a "bolt [of lightning] from heaven that shattered and destroyed" the branches of the oak of the American nation. Consequently, at the Peace Convention Doniphan had voted for a modified version of Crittenden's Compromise, stressing the venerable concept of the 36°30′ line that would maintain "the right in slave property and its ample protection" below that line in the future, thus protecting indefinitely the nation's minority—slave owners. Much to Doniphan's disappointment, Congress had rejected such a constitutional amendment, and he was worried that anyone could find any "such guarantees to slave-holding states that are now in [the Union] to remain, and induce the States that are now out eventually to come back." The colonel was not sure if any amendments, no matter how they were worded, would lure the seceded states back into the Union. Some Missouri secessionists took heart: Doniphan's speech appeared to have a pro-Confederate tone.[37]

On March 9, 1861, however, Gamble's committee reported foursquare against secession, and Doniphan signed the report. The committee decided that there were no reasons for Missouri to sever its ties with the Union, and it maintained that Missourians remained devoted to American institutions. The committee favored reconciliation between the sections. Like Doniphan and the majority of delegates at the Peace Convention, Gamble's committee recommended passage of the Crittenden Compromise as the best solution to end the crisis of the Union.[38]

Many of the pro-Confederate delegates to the state convention could admit to the truth of all that Gamble's committee reported, but a secessionist offered an amendment to the report. It called for Missouri to secede if the federal government rejected some accommodation on slavery. Although the amendment failed to pass, Doniphan stood to speak in response to the secessionists. The colonel said that it was not Missouri's place, as an individual state, to issue demands to the national government. Emphatically, Doniphan proclaimed that he was "a Union man. I go for the whole Union, the entire Union. I go for it North, South, East, and West. I do not intend to bring about a calamity that will destroy the Border Slave States and the whole Union." He would never vote for secession. The colonel stressed that it had taken seven years of the American Revolution against England and more years of testing the new nation to bring about the Constitution. He could not abide the secessionists' demand for a vote on that day to break up the Union after it had taken so many years to forge the United States.

Continuing his address, Doniphan let his listeners know that he "was willing to serve here seven years, and take every means for the preservation of this Union. I am willing to serve as long as Jacob served, before this Union shall be dissolved. I am not going to say when I shall stop; I am not going to say when Missouri shall stop. Never! Never, while hope is left, I live by hope, and as a Union man I shall only die when hope dies." Strong applause from fellow Unionists greeted the colonel's impassioned speech. Quite likely, looks of disappointment or even shock must have crossed the faces of secessionists. They had lost the endorsement of one of the state's most popular figures, a revered man whose passion directed in favor of secession might have helped swing the convention to disunion. No doubt this speech impressed Thomas L. Snead, an aide to Governor Jackson, who recalled that Doniphan was one of the "formidable opponents of the Secessionists." Voting to approve Gamble's committee report, the state convention adjourned on March 22, subject to recall. Missouri remained in the Union.[39]

Meanwhile, on March 13, 1861, the legislature took up the election to fill one of the state's seats in the U.S. Senate. Once again, as in 1855, Doniphan was offered as a compromise candidate, championed mostly by those who had voted for John Bell. Although Doniphan received more than thirty votes during the balloting, Waldo P. Johnson, a former volunteer soldier from the colonel's regiment, was elected instead. Johnson was a Breckinridge Democrat who leaned too close to secession for Doniphan's taste.[40]

The political cracks between Unionists and secessionists grew so wide that Missouri's state government began a slide into chaos. On April 12 Confederate forces opened fire on the Federal garrison in Fort Sumter, South Carolina. President Lincoln reacted by calling for seventy-five thousand militia to serve for ninety days to put down an insurrection. Several Northern governors mobilized units, but Governor Jackson, sending a scornful message, declined to comply with the president's call. Missouri Unionists, led by Frank Blair, organized their own Home Guard, which drew weapons from racks of hundreds of muskets at the Federal arsenal in St. Louis. The arrival of a company of Regular Army infantry under Captain Nathaniel Lyon, a no-nonsense pro-Union officer, was a crucial development. Lyon displaced a moderate Unionist, Brigadier General William S. Harney. Although Harney was temporarily reinstated, Lyon soon was promoted to brigadier general of volunteers and became commander of Federal forces at St. Louis.[41]

By early May, Sterling Price and David Atchison balanced precariously on the edge of becoming Confederates, and Governor Jackson intended to push them and the state into the Confederate column. Led by John Reid, a former captain in Doniphan's regiment, secessionists on April 20 had seized more than one thousand rifles from the Federal arsenal near Liberty; then Governor Jackson set up a training depot outside St. Louis, dubbed "Camp Jackson," for the pro-Confederate Missouri militia. Determining that Camp Jackson harbored potential traitors, on May 10 General Lyon and his troops surrounded the governor's militia and made them his prisoners. An altercation erupted, leading to a riot in the streets. Twenty men were killed or wounded. Many legislators shifted to the governor's side, and Jackson commissioned Price to lead the state militia, firmly placing him on the side of the Confederacy. The Civil War had come to Missouri.[42]

The sectional lines crystallized in the spring of 1861, and men across Missouri had to decide for the Union or the Confederacy. Doniphan's old friend

John T. Hughes, author of the memoir *Doniphan's Expedition*, had supported the Union but switched to the Confederates, as did the colonel's former artillery captain, Richard Weightman. Both sides wanted Colonel Doniphan. Jackson hoped to tempt him with the rank of brigadier general and command of one of the state's nine militia districts. Sterling Price, David Atchison, John Reid, and ex-artillerist Meriwether Lewis Clark were among several others mentioned for commissions. Of course, the Liberty *Tribune* endorsed Doniphan as one of the best men to organize citizen-soldiers in the crisis, but his personal choices and motivations were disputed then and later. In early May things were more desperate than only a few weeks earlier. Virginia had seceded on April 17, and secession conventions in Arkansas and Tennessee were ready to break those states' ties to the Union. North Carolina called a secession convention. Across the country Regular officers, veterans, and politicians scrambled for commissions in state or Federal or Confederate service; military outfits everywhere drilled with fresh urgency. The signs of widening war were unmistakable. Thomas Snead, Governor Jackson's aide, recalled that "everything indicated the opening of hostilities."[43]

Accepting an appointment as a brigadier general in Governor Jackson's militia meant committing to the Confederacy. Becoming a militia leader probably would mean leading pro-Confederate Missourians into combat with the state's Unionists. Many of Doniphan's friends, such as his old law partner, David Atchison, and several fellow veterans from Mexican War days, clearly supported the Confederacy. Momentarily, a truce of sorts between the U.S. Army and Price's militia seemed to offer the prospect of reducing the war fever in St. Louis. Seizing on this slender reed, Doniphan wrote Governor Jackson, explaining his refusal of the militia commission on a surprisingly sanguine assertion that "relations have been so adjusted [in Missouri] as to promise entire peace in the future." This was a remarkable claim given the political animosities engulfing the state. Doniphan then rounded out his refusal of the commission by falling back on the kinds of reasons he had used before when deciding the time was not right to do something: his wife was ill and he himself was not well. Doniphan also mentioned the deaths of his sons (eight and three years earlier), indicating that his most important reasons to decline the appointment were personal.[44]

By then it was clear that Doniphan would not draw his saber against the Union or fire upon the flag he had carried in the war with Mexico. Furthermore, in sharp contrast to Sterling Price, Doniphan could not raise his hand in anger against the men who had shared the dangers of the Santa Fe Trail and the march to Chihuahua—friends of twenty years or more. In the weeks to come, he made modest efforts on behalf of the Union, but he made them as a civilian, not as a soldier, not in the uniform of the Missouri militia or Federal volunteers. As anticipated, Reid and Atchison later received state commissions, and within a few weeks both were in Confederate service.[45]

Unquestionably, the crisis of the Union coincided with a crisis in Doniphan's personal life. During May, Jane Doniphan's health grew worse with each passing day. Doniphan's obligation to care for his wife may have overridden an offer of any civil post or military commission. If that was true, the Union would be deprived in any event of one of the best men who could have bolstered its cause in Missouri. Unionists realized that there were few Missourians who made a better symbol of nationalism and fewer who had such an established reputation for military leadership.[46]

Contemporaries disputed the exact reasons that Doniphan rejected a militia commission, but he left his wife's bedside and went to St. Louis on June 11 in an attempt to defuse the city's powder-charged atmosphere. His trip coincided with a tense meeting between General Lyon and Frank Blair, on one hand, and Governor Jackson and Sterling Price, on the other. Along with hundreds of concerned Missourians, Doniphan awaited the outcome of the meeting. The rival leaders discussed several ideas during a four-hour meeting at the Planter's House Hotel, with Jackson saying he favored Missouri's "neutrality" in the sectional crisis. Would each side continue to raise separate militias in Missouri? Would Jackson's state militia stand down if Federal troops made no moves to leave St. Louis and occupy other towns in the state? Could the governor promise to keep Confederate soldiers and munitions out of Missouri? If not, how long would Confederate forces wait before entering the state? Considering that such tradeoffs made bad bargains, General Lyon concluded that any accommodations to Jackson's "neutral" proposals meant giving ground, either figuratively or literally, to the secessionists. After all, Missouri was a state in the Union. Accordingly, Lyon abruptly terminated the meeting, dismissing Jackson and Price with the graphic phrase "This means war."[47]

With the state government writhing and divided, Doniphan again took his seat in the old secession convention, reconvening at Jefferson City. It was called back to order on July 22. Meanwhile, when Lyon had led his units toward the capital, Governor Jackson and pro-Confederate members of the legislature abandoned the city. In highly irregular proceedings, and with the convention now dominated by Unionists, Frank Blair and other pro-Union delegates proposed to name alternate state officials, announcing that Hamilton Gamble was willing to serve as governor and Willard Hall as lieutenant governor. The convention put their names on a ballot of a special election and constituted itself as a state legislature until a new one was elected. In an election on July 31 the convention voted for Gamble and Hall to fill their offices, forming a provisional government. Meanwhile, Claiborne Jackson still called himself Missouri's governor. The state had fallen to an ignominious low point. Two groups each claimed to be Missouri's legitimate government.[48]

Only a few days later, on August 10, 1861, General Lyon led Federal troops in the Battle of Wilson's Creek, against an army composed of Missourians and Confederates; one of their leaders was Sterling Price. Although Lyon was killed and Union forces were defeated, the battle so disrupted the Confederates that they were unable to march either against the state capital at Jefferson City or all the way to St. Louis. The mixed results of Wilson's Creek did not dissuade a faction of the old state legislature, which assembled at Neosho and on October 28 announced its support for an ordinance of secession. Governor Jackson, who had met with President Jefferson Davis in Richmond, recognized the ordinance, considered Missouri out of the Union, and moved to create ties with the Confederacy. The Confederate government ushered Missouri into its association on November 28. By such questionable procedures, without the state's voters casting ballots to indicate their views as stipulated by the prewar legislature, Missouri gained a star in the Confederacy's flag and seats in its congress, while maintaining its membership in the Union. It also experienced some of the worst internecine fighting of the Civil War.[49]

A few months later, in April 1862, Doniphan delivered a speech at Liberty, urging all those "caught by the Secession delusion to abandon that cause, to lay down their arms if they have been engaged in acts of disloyalty, and to show their sincerity by taking the oath of allegiance" to the Union. By then Sterling Price and many of Doniphan's former volunteers from Mexican War days, including John Hughes, Richard Weightman, John Reid, Mosby Parsons, Meriwether Clark, and Waldo Johnson, served the Confederacy. Recalling Missouri politics of the 1850s, reports speculated that Doniphan was being considered as a candidate for Congress, especially for the Senate, where both of Missouri's senators (Waldo Johnson and Trusten Polk) had been expelled for being pro-Confederate. Another time Doniphan declined to be considered for Congress.[50]

When Governor Gamble called the special state convention to meet again in Jefferson City on June 15, 1863, it addressed the possible emancipation of Missouri's slaves. Speeches given by the delegates delineated both pro-slavery and antislavery points of view. The delegates read several propositions, including ones prohibiting sale of slaves outside the state and submitting the question of emancipation to Missouri's voters. The debaters mentioned several dates for emancipation to take effect in Missouri, among them January 1, 1864, November 1, 1866, July 4, 1870, and July 4, 1876—or even as late as 1900. Doniphan at first preferred July 4, 1876. According to a complicated gradual emancipation scheme passed by the convention, young slaves would be restricted to serve their owners for several years in a kind of apprenticeship arrangement. In several ways unrealistic, these proposals recognized that the institution of slavery was on its last legs in the United States. Doniphan observed that slavery was not going to "survive the continuance of such a war carried on as this has been for the last year." He concluded that specifying a date for emancipation in such revolutionary times was like trying to "hold a live eel by the tail."[51]

In the summer of 1863 Doniphan returned to western Missouri to explain his votes in the convention, especially on the emancipation plan. At its final session, the majority of the State Convention, including Doniphan, voted to end slavery in Missouri by July 4, 1870. President Lincoln's Emancipation Proclamation, in effect since January 1, rang a death knell for slavery, but the institution's longevity in the border states remained uncertain. Doniphan reminded his listeners that he was a slave owner, but now the institution had to be viewed differently. Plainly put, the war jeopardized and undermined slavery. In an amazing step, unprecedented in its scale, the Union army was recruiting thousands of freedmen into units officially designated as United States Colored Troops. It was time for slave owners, even Unionists like Doniphan, to know that in order to "restore peace, prosperity, and security to the state and the nation," slavery was ending in the United States. Doniphan had opposed secession, and now it was clear that perpetuating the Union was more important than continuing slavery.[52]

Leaving war-torn western Missouri, Doniphan and his wife moved to the relative safety of St. Louis in late 1863. Governor Willard P. Hall selected Doniphan to serve as special claims agent, handling the cases of widows and children of soldiers. The next year he felt some discomfort by deciding to cast his first vote for a Democrat, supporting George B. McClellan in the 1864 presidential election. Lincoln overwhelmed McClellan in Missouri, with voters going for the Republican more than two to one. After taking that first step toward the Democratic party, the colonel settled into its fold for more than twenty years.[53]

Remaining a civilian during the Civil War, Alexander Doniphan refused to lend his name and military reputation to either the Federals or the Confederates. He rejected any prospect of a military appointment from either side. Although Doniphan's opposition to secession failed to persuade many of his former soldiers to follow his lead, his actions were among those by several Missouri leaders that helped keep the state in the Union.

EPILOGUE

After Doniphan's Wars

Members of Kearny's Army of the West and Doniphan's March to Chihuahua counted those military campaigns among the high points of their lives. The crisis of the Union divided veterans of the Doniphan Expedition, just as it split the nation. In response to the sectional split, some became devoted to the Confederate States. Others held with the Union and served in some way to reunite the continental America they had helped to win in 1846.

Delivering New Mexico to the United States was not the last accomplishment of Doniphan's mentor, Brigadier General Stephen W. Kearny, who went on to command American troops in the conquest of California. Kearny led his dragoons across the rough passage to the Pacific Coast, arriving there in early December 1846. In the next few weeks, Kearny found it difficult to work with U.S. Navy commodores, including John D. Sloat and Robert Stockton, who were supposed to cooperate with him to defeat the Mexican forces in California. That was easier said than done. On December 6 the Mexicans fought well in a skirmish at San Pasqual, near San Diego. There one hundred Mexicans, under General Andrés Pico, defeated Kearny's troops, numbering only about 150 men. After the engagement, the Mexicans could not consolidate their advantage and had to retreat, yielding the field to the Americans. Kearny commanded a small force to victory in another skirmish at the San Gabriel River, near Los Angeles. Those two small military engagements contributed significantly to the United States' conquest of California. The War Department awarded Kearny a brevet of major general for gallantry and meritorious conduct at San Pasqual. Like hundreds of other U.S. soldiers during the war, Kearny contracted yellow fever. He died at the home of Major Meriwether Clark in St. Louis in late 1848.[1]

Charles Wooster, lieutenant, 1st Dragoons, and one of Doniphan's Regular

Army advisers, was given a brevet of captain for his service at the Battle of Sacramento. He took sick leave for a year after the expedition returned to the United States, then resumed field duty in Florida against the Seminoles. He was promoted to captain and transferred to the 4th Artillery Regiment in 1850, subsequently serving at posts in the Northern states. Returning to the southwestern frontier, Wooster was stricken with yellow fever and died at Fort Brown, Texas, in early 1856.[2]

Philip R. Thompson, captain, 1st Dragoons, the most important of Doniphan's Regular Army advisers, earned a brevet of major for his service at the Battles of Brazito and Sacramento. The postwar years found him on duty in the territories, including Kansas, Dakota, New Mexico, and Colorado. Called as a witness in a court-martial, Thompson himself was court-martialed and cashiered on September 4, 1855, for "disrespect to a Court-Martial, before which he appeared in a state of intoxication." His army career ruined, Thompson sought employment as a filibuster. He went to Nicaragua in 1856 as part of the infamous expedition led by William Walker, signing on as Walker's adjutant. Thompson drowned in the Gulf of Mexico in the summer of 1857.[3]

David D. Mitchell, lieutenant colonel, 2nd Missouri Regiment of Mounted Volunteers, found himself embroiled in court battles resulting from the confiscation of Manuel X. Harmony's wagons and goods. Like many of his fellow veterans, Mitchell returned to St. Louis. Financially strapped by the demanding court cases, he cast about for gainful employment, reclaiming the office of superintendent of Indian affairs, the post he had held before the war. Mitchell served in that capacity from 1849 to 1853. In 1855 he helped organize the Missouri and California Overland Mail and Transportation Company, headquartered in St. Louis, and served as its president for six years.[4]

Richard H. Weightman, volunteer captain of artillery, held on to his commission, serving as an army paymaster until he was mustered out in August 1849. Captivated by Santa Fe, he settled there in 1851. He opened a law office, operated a newspaper, and served as an Indian agent. None of those vocations proved successful. Entering politics, Weightman won the seat as territorial delegate to the U.S. Congress, 1851–1853, where he pushed for New Mexico statehood. After a violent altercation, in which he killed a man in a Santa Fe saloon, Weightman moved back to Missouri. At the outbreak of the Civil War, he sought a commission in the Confederate forces, gaining the rank of colonel. While leading a brigade, Weightman was killed in action at the Battle of Wilson's Creek, Missouri, on August 10, 1861.[5]

John T. Hughes, chronicler of Doniphan's March, contacted a firm in Cincinnati, Ohio, for the publication of his book, *Doniphan's Expedition* (1847). It went through several printings. Hughes worked for the U.S. Land Office in Missouri and took a turn at politics, winning a seat in the state legislature in 1854. He purchased several slaves and a plantation north of Plattsburg, Missouri. During the secession crisis Hughes stood first for the Union, but his advocacy of states' rights and slavery prompted him to support the Confederacy. Serving as a colonel in Missouri state forces, Hughes fought at Wilson's Creek and at the Battle of Pea Ridge (Elkhorn Tavern), Arkansas, in March 1862. Hughes was killed in action during a skirmish with Federal troops near Independence, Missouri, on August 11, 1862.[6]

Mosby M. Parsons, captain of Doniphan's Company F, from Cole County, returned to his law practice in Jefferson City. Receiving public acclaim for his service in the Mexican War, he won seats in the Missouri state house and senate in the 1850s. In 1861 Parsons devoted himself to the Confederacy, eventually rising to the rank of major general in the Southern armies during the Civil War. Afterward, he was one of several former Confederate officers who fled the country and served with Maximilian's French forces in Mexico. Anti-French Mexicans killed Parsons in 1865.[7]

Sterling Price enjoyed having President Polk promote him to brigadier general of volunteers. Price led his 2nd Missouri Volunteers on a superfluous campaign that recaptured Chihuahua City in March 1848. By then diplomats of Mexico and the United States already had negotiated the Treaty of Guadalupe Hidalgo to officially end the war. In the 1850s, as a Democrat, Price returned to Missouri politics, winning election as governor and holding the office from 1853 to 1857. In 1860 he announced against secession and presided over the special state convention considering a break with the Union. He became commander of the Missouri state militia in June 1861 and shifted his support to the Confederacy. He was one of the Southern commanders at the Battle of Wilson's Creek, on August 10, 1861, a fruitless tactical victory that exhausted the Confederates and blunted their drive to gain control of Missouri. Serving under Major General Earl van Dorn, Price fought at the Battle of Pea Ridge (Elkhorn Tavern), Arkansas, on March 7–8, 1862, a Southern defeat that became one of a string of military disappointments for the Confederacy in the West. Nevertheless, Price was promoted to major general in the Confederate army and served in Arkansas and Mississippi for the next two years. He led a Confederate raid into Missouri in the fall of 1864, but his army was repulsed at the Battle of Westport (near modern Kansas City). Price sought employment and refuge in Mexico after the war. Following a year below the Rio Grande, he made his way back to Missouri. Destitute and exhausted by the rigors of campaigning, he died in St. Louis in 1867.[8]

Thomas B. Hudson, captain of the Leclede Rangers, resumed his law practice in St. Louis and also held the presidency of the North Missouri Railroad Company. Evidently in poor health, he retired from business and politics to a home outside the city in 1854.[9]

David Waldo, commanding Company A from Jackson County, hailed from western Virginia and had settled in Missouri in 1826. Making a major contribution to the expedition by assisting Doniphan in the preparation of the New Mexico territorial code, Waldo followed the colonel on the remainder of the march into Mexico. Returning to Missouri with the rest of the veterans, Waldo operated a freight-hauling business into the 1870s.[10]

Meriwether Lewis Clark, major of the St. Louis volunteer artillery battalion, sought a federal patronage position as surveyor general of Missouri, awarded by President Zachary Taylor. Clark held that job from 1848 to 1853. In 1861 he lent his fame from the war with Mexico to the Confederate cause. Obtaining the rank of general in the Missouri State Guard, Clark also got the rank of major in the Confederate forces. He was later promoted to colonel. Naturally, Clark wanted to serve with the artillery. An apparent disagreement with General Braxton Bragg cost Clark command of his artillery brigade in November 1862. He had also served as chief of artillery for the Confederate Army of the West. For the rest of the war he languished, taking duties with various military courts and boards in Richmond, Virginia. Following Robert E. Lee's surrender at Appomattox, Clark settled in Kentucky. Obtaining the post of professor of mathematics at the Kentucky Military Institute in Frankfort, Clark was also the school's commandant of cadets for several years.[11]

John W. Reid, commanding Company D, from Saline County, reestablished himself at his law office in Jefferson City. Strident in his support for a new slave state as Missouri's neighbor, Reid participated in the notorious violence of "Bleeding Kansas." He also sought political office, holding a seat in the Missouri legislature (1854–1856) and winning election to the U.S. Congress in 1860. He resigned in August 1861 after deciding to support the Confederacy and later served as an aide to General Sterling Price. After the war, Reid promoted the growth of Kansas City and maintained a law practice there.[12]

Willard P. Hall was an ardent Democrat, having served as an elector for the Polk presidential ticket in 1844, and he had been one of Doniphan's rivals in Missouri politics. Nevertheless, his cordial personality and skill as a lawyer prompted Kearny to choose him to help Doniphan write the New Mexico territorial code. In 1846, before the expedition moved south, Hall was elected to the U.S. House of Representatives, but rather than going back to Missouri right away he decided to accompany Captain Philip St. George Cooke to California. Representing Missouri, Hall served three terms in Congress (1847–1853) but failed to win election to the U.S. Senate in 1856. During the secession crisis he helped to hold Missouri for the Union, serving as lieutenant governor (1862–1863) and governor (1864–1865) of the state. Hall was a successful attorney in St. Joseph, Missouri, after the War between the States.[13]

Charles L. Ruff, former lieutenant colonel of the 1st Missouri Regiment, made a career in the U.S. Army. As a captain in the Regiment of Mounted Rifles in the Mexico City campaign, he fought at Contreras and Molino del Rey, where he was wounded and awarded a brevet of major. Returning to duty, he fought at Chapultepec on September 13, 1847. After the war he served in the Pacific Northwest territories. Later, Ruff became superintendent of cavalry recruiting and commanded the Cavalry School at Jefferson Barracks, Missouri, near St. Louis. Subsequent assignments included tours in Texas and New Mexico. Remaining loyal to the Union, Ruff was on recruiting duties during most of the Civil War. On March 30, 1864, a board of officers met to determine his fitness and decided to retire Ruff, for reasons of health, due to long-term effects of wounds received during the Mexican War. Toward the end of the Civil War, on March 13, 1865, he was breveted brigadier general of volunteers for meritorious service to the Union. Ruff was professor of military science at the University of Pennsylvania from 1868 to 1870.[14]

Waldo P. Johnson, private in Captain David Waldo's Company A, left Doniphan's regiment early, returning to Missouri in mid-December 1846 before Brazito, to hold a seat in the state legislature. Later he was a district judge. In 1861 he sat with Doniphan in the Peace Convention and the Missouri secession convention. As a Breckinridge Democrat, Johnson was elected by the Missouri legislature over Doniphan as U.S. senator, serving from March 17, 1861, to January 10, 1862, when the Senate expelled him upon learning that he had joined the Confederate army. As lieutenant colonel of the 4th Missouri Infantry Regiment, he was wounded at the Battle of Pea Ridge. Recovering from his wounds, in 1863 Johnson was appointed by Governor Thomas Reynolds to a seat in the Confederate Senate. Serving there for the rest of the war, Johnson expressed states' rights views and criticism for President Jefferson Davis. After the Civil War, Johnson resided in Canada for about a year before resettling in Missouri and returning to his law practice in Osceola.[15]

William Gilpin, major of the 1st Missouri Regiment, recruited and took command of his own battalion, filled with fresh Missouri enlistees, from 1847 to 1848. Gilpin and his "Indian Battalion" protected American wagon trains moving along the Santa Fe Trail, and he also led a campaign against the Apaches and Comanches. Gilpin saw great things in the lands the United States had gained from Mexico. As a Republican, Gilpin served as governor of Colorado

Territory from 1861 to 1862. He tirelessly promoted railroads and western settlement, writing several articles for newspapers and magazines as well as longer works, including *The Central Gold Region* (1860), *Mission of the North American People* (1873), and *The Cosmopolitan Railway* (1890). Based in Denver and always watching for the main chance, Gilpin speculated in land deals in Colorado into the 1890s.[16]

John D. Stevenson, commander of Company E from Franklin County, practiced law in the town of Union. His reputation as a fearless combat officer helped him in politics. Voters elected him to both houses of the Missouri legislature during the 1850s. Like Doniphan, Stevenson remained loyal to the Union. Wearing Federal blue, he served in a variety of assignments and finished the Civil War as brigadier general of volunteers. After the war, fierce competition for senior assignments characterized the Regular U.S. Army. Stevenson gained a commission as colonel of the 30th Infantry Regiment and served until 1870, when he resigned and set up a law office in St. Louis.[17]

Alexander William Doniphan moved from St. Louis to Richmond, Missouri, in 1868. Only a few miles from Liberty, and his beloved William Jewell College, he renewed his law practice and also established and served as president of the Ray County Savings Bank. Jane Doniphan died in 1873. The U.S. Congress passed the Mexican War Pension Act on January 29, 1887, and on February 22, 1887, Doniphan filed for a military pension and a bounty land claim for 160 acres. The Pension Office approved his land claim on May 7 and his pension on May 9. Three months later, on August 8, 1887, Doniphan died in Richmond. In 1912 the states of New Mexico and Arizona joined the Union. On July 29, 1918, at the courthouse square in Richmond, Missouri, a grateful public dedicated a heroic statue in Colonel Doniphan's honor. Armed with a dragoon's saber and standing ten feet tall atop a seven-foot-high red granite pedestal, a bronze Doniphan gazes to the southwest, across the western United States, toward Santa Fe and on to Chihuahua.[18]

NOTES

Prologue. Two Tall Men: A Legendary Meeting

1. The episode is related in William L. Webb, *Battles and Biographies of Missourians, or the Civil War Period in Our State* (Kansas City, 1900), 280–81. Slightly different wording of the same story is given in the pamphlet by D. C. Allen, *A Sketch of the Life and Character of Col. Alexander W. Doniphan* (Liberty, Mo., 1897), 27–28. Allen's sketch was reprinted in William E. Connelley, comp., *Doniphan's Expedition and the Conquest of New Mexico and California* (Topeka, 1907), quoted on 39; and in Allen, "Builders of the Great American West: Remarkable Experiences of Alexander Doniphan," *Journal of American History* 4 (1910), 511–24, quote on 524. See also Frank B. Latham, "Doniphan of Missouri: Soldier, Lawyer, and Statesman," *New York Westerners Brand Book* 2, no. 4 (1955), 75; and Raymond Settle, "Alexander William Doniphan: Zenophon [*sic*] of the West" (unpublished typescript, Charles F. Curry Library, William Jewell College, Liberty, Missouri), 600. A contemporary basis for the story comes from a report in Liberty, Mo., *Weekly Tribune*, March 8, 1861.

2. James W. Oberly, *Sixty Million Acres: American Veterans and the Public Lands before the Civil War* (Kent, Ohio, 1990), 10–13. As Oberly points out, these bounties were designed for soldiers who served as enlisted men, not for officers.

3. Philadelphia *North American*, June 26, 1847.

Chapter 1. Going Off to War

1. Jerry Cooper, *The Rise of the National Guard: The Evolution of the American Militia, 1865–1920* (Lincoln, Neb., 1997), 11–19; Richard Bruce Winders, *Mr. Polk's Army: The American Military Experience in the Mexican War* (College Station, Tex., 1997), 1–2, 9–13.

2. Alexis de Tocqueville, *Democracy in America*, 2 vols. (New York, 1898), 2:342.

3. "Sketch of Life [of Alexander W. Doniphan]," pp. 1–2, in Alexander W. Doniphan Papers, Missouri Historical Society (MHS), St. Louis; Roger D. Launius, *Alexander William Doniphan, Portrait of a Missouri Moderate* (Columbia, Mo., 1997), 1–2; André P. Duchateau,

"Missouri Colossus: Alexander William Doniphan, 1808–1887" (Ed.D. dissertation, Oklahoma State University, 1973), 1–8.

4. Doniphan, "Sketch of Life," pp. 1–2, in Doniphan Papers, MHS, St. Louis; Doniphan, Alexander William, Individual Service Record, Military Pension Records, Record Group (RG) 75, National Archives (NA), Washington, D.C.; D. C. Allen, "Col. Alexander W. Doniphan—His Life and Character," in William E. Connelley, comp., *Doniphan's Expedition and the Conquest of New Mexico and California* (Topeka, 1907), 19–20; Launius, *Doniphan, Missouri Moderate,* 1–3; Duchateau, "Missouri Colossus," 9–10.

5. Doniphan, "Sketch of Life," p. 2, Doniphan Papers, MHS, St. Louis; Launius, *Doniphan, Missouri Moderate,* 4; Duchateau, "Missouri Colossus," 10–11.

6. Perry McCandless, *A History of Missouri,* vol. 2, *1820–1860* (Columbia, Mo., 1972), 1–2, 4–5, 20–21, 41–46; Edwin C. McReynolds, *Missouri: A History of the Crossroads State* (Norman, Okla., 1962), 67–71; William E. Parrish et al., *Missouri: The Heart of the Nation* (St. Louis, 1980), 37, 41, 50–52, 58–59, 66–74.

7. Doniphan, "Sketch of Life," pp. 3–4, Doniphan Papers, MHS, St. Louis; Duchateau, "Missouri Colossus," 11–12, 16; William E. Parrish, *David Rice Atchison of Missouri, Border Politician* (Columbia, Mo., 1961), 1–5; Launius, *Doniphan, Missouri Moderate,* 8.

8. Henry C. McDougal, *Recollections, 1844–1909* (Kansas City, 1910), 37 (quote); *Portrait and Biographical Record of Clay, Ray, Carroll, Chariton and Linn Counties, Missouri* (Chicago, 1893), 649–50. See also Allen, "Col. Doniphan—His Life and Character," in Connelley, comp., *Doniphan's Expedition,* 39; Duchateau, "Missouri Colossus," 35–36; Launius, *Doniphan, Missouri Moderate,* 25–28.

9. Launius, *Doniphan, Missouri Moderate,* 28–32; McCandless, *History of Missouri,* 117, and map, 113.

10. Duchateau, "Missouri Colossus," 38, 40, 69; W. H. Woodson, *History of Clay County, Missouri* (Topeka, 1920), 117; Merrill D. Peterson, *The Great Triumvirate: Webster, Clay, and Calhoun* (New York, 1987), 235, 268–70; Launius, *Doniphan, Missouri Moderate,* 35–40.

11. Launius, *Doniphan, Missouri Moderate,* 11–22; Parrish et al., *Missouri,* 95–96.

12. Democratic governor Lilburn W. Boggs made Doniphan a general in the militia, indicating that Doniphan's father-in-law, John Thornton, a prominent Democrat, may have helped his son-in-law gain the appointment. For background on the "Mormon War," see McCandless, *History of Missouri,* 107–10; Parrish et al., *Missouri,* 95–96.

13. Launius, *Doniphan, Missouri Moderate,* 48–71, gives an excellent survey of the Mormon troubles and the best description of Doniphan's role in the crisis. See also Kenneth H. Winn, *Exiles in a Land of Liberty: Mormons in America, 1830–1846* (Chapel Hill, N.C., 1989), 103, 105, 142–43; Stephen C. LeSueur, *The 1838 Mormon War in Missouri* (Columbia, Mo., 1987), 90–93, 115–16, 130, 145–46, 158–60, 172, 182–83, 198, 212, 216; Duchateau, "Missouri Colossus," 21–27, 37, 44–67.

14. Launius, *Doniphan, Missouri Moderate,* esp. 61–65; LeSueur, *Mormon War,* 162–68. Doniphan's stand was favorably portrayed by actor Peter Lawford in an episode of the NBC television series *Profiles in Courage,* telecast in 1964.

15. Duchateau, "Missouri Colossus," 72–80, 89–90; Launius, *Doniphan, Missouri Moderate,* 76–78. Following a similar path to the General Assembly in 1840 was Sterling Price, leading Democrat and militia officer. Rather than defending the Mormons, Price took a hand in suppressing them. See Robert E. Shalhope, *Sterling Price, Portrait of a Southerner* (Columbia, Mo., 1971), 26–31.

16. William H. Paxton, *Annals of Platte County, Missouri* (Kansas City, 1897), 549–51; Launius, *Doniphan, Missouri Moderate,* 41–42; Duchateau, "Missouri Colossus," 16, 33–36, 40, 43.

17. A sturdy, brief summary of Manifest Destiny is found in Ray A. Billington, *Westward Expansion* (New York, 1949), 572; John O'Sullivan, "Annexation," *Democratic Review* 17 (July 1845), 5, 7. See also Albert K. Weinberg, *Manifest Destiny: A Study of Nationalist Expansionism in American History* (Baltimore, 1935), 112; Frederick Merk and Lois B. Merk, *Manifest Destiny and Mission in American History: A Reinterpretation* (New York, 1963), 24–27, 39–40, 58; Rush Welter, "The Frontier West as Image of American Society: Conservative Attitudes before the Civil War," *Mississippi Valley Historical Review* 46 (March 1960), 593–614, esp. 596–97, 601–7. Noting some Whig divisions on territorial expansion is Michael A. Morrison, *Slavery and the American West: The Eclipse of Manifest Destiny and the Coming of the Civil War* (Chapel Hill, N.C., 1997), 19, 21–26, 72–73, 81.

18. For a narrative covering national issues and results, see Charles G. Sellers, "The Election of 1844," in Arthur M. Schlesinger Jr., ed., *History of American Presidential Elections, 1789–1968,* 4 vols. (New York, 1971), 1:747–98, as well as the summary by Paul H. Bergeron, *The Presidency of James K. Polk* (Lawrence, Kans., 1987), 15–20.

19. An exposition of the attitudes of top Whig leaders on annexing Texas and expansion is found in Thomas Brown, *Politics and Statesmanship: Essays on the American Whig Party* (New York, 1985), esp. 77–79, 102, 145–47, 199–205. For a contemporary pejorative implication of "annexationist," see John R. Bartlett, *Dictionary of Americanisms: A Glossary of Words and Phrases* (Boston, 1859), 9. Jesús Velasco Márquez, *La guerra del 47 y la opinión pública (1845–1848)* (Mexico City, 1975), 71, concludes that the war "was, without a doubt, the product of the expansionism of the United States." However, he downplays the fact that Mexico had lost control of Texas for ten years prior to the outbreak of war. Josefina Zoraida Vázquez, "The Texas Question in Mexican Politics, 1836–1845," *Southwestern Historical Quarterly* 89 (January 1986), 309–44, provides a sound discussion; and a memoir of one of Doniphan's soldiers, Isaac George, *Heroes and Incidents of the Mexican War, Containing Doniphan's Expedition* (Greensburg, Pa., 1903), 12, emphasized that Texas was the primary bone of contention. See also Gene M. Brack, *Mexico Views Manifest Destiny, 1821–1846: An Essay on the Origins of the Mexican War* (Albuquerque, 1975), 116, 119.

20. Alexander W. Doniphan and Henry Routt to William L. Marcy, September 5, 1845, filed with Secretary of War Applications File, 1846–1848, Box 9, RG 107, NA. Several other letters from around the nation, containing comments of a similar tone, are filed in ibid., and Secretary Marcy replied to prospective volunteers from several states, including Georgia, Pennsylvania, Virginia, Ohio, North Carolina, Indiana, Alabama, Illinois, and Kentucky. See Marcy's correspondence in Letters Sent by the Secretary of War, Microcopy M-6, roll 26, RG 107, NA.

21. Columbia *Missouri Statesman,* April 12, 1846; Frank S. Edwards, *A Campaign in New Mexico with Colonel Doniphan* (Philadelphia, 1847), 93, used the term "Texians." William C. Binkley, *The Expansionist Movement in Texas, 1836–1850* (Berkeley, Calif., 1925), 173–75. Mexicans tried without success to contend that the Texan–Santa Anna treaty was invalid at the time it was signed because the general did not have official authority to make such a treaty. Brack, *Mexico Views Manifest Destiny,* 74.

22. Doniphan's quote on Henry Clay is from Doniphan to Cousin Emma Doniphan, May 3, 1876, in William B. McGroarty, ed., "Letters from Alexander W. Doniphan," *Missouri*

Historical Review 24 (October 1929), 27. On Jackson's hopes for expansion, see Robert V. Remini, *Andrew Jackson and the Course of American Empire* (New York, 1977), 305, 344, 384, 389; and Remini, *The Life of Andrew Jackson* (New York, 1988), 56–60, 62, 109, 309–14. Doniphan later reiterated his support for adding "an empire" to the United States in *Address by Col. Alexander W. Doniphan, Delivered in Liberty, Mo., June 5, 1872* (Liberty, Mo., 1883).

23. See D. W. Meinig, *The Shaping of America: A Geographical Perspective on 500 Years of History*, vol. 2, *Continental America, 1800–1867* (New Haven, Conn., 1993), 129–35, 138–43. Ward Alan Minge, "Frontier Problems in New Mexico Preceding the Mexican War, 1840–1846" (Ph.D. dissertation, University of New Mexico, 1965), 105, points out that New Mexico was not obligated to send taxes to the national treasury until 1845, so that funds collected by the province's governor, including a tax of five hundred dollars per wagon from Anglo traders, could be used to pay for the cost of militia employed against the Indians. Minge (ibid., 73, 80, 81 n. 64, 82, 98, 100, 106, 118, 120–23, 127, 135, 190, 211) also presents cogent analysis of Mexico's difficulties in administering New Mexico. For other aspects of military matters, see William A. DePalo Jr., *The Mexican National Army, 1822–1852* (College Station, Tex., 1997), 88–89. According to DePalo, "The failure (or inability) of the Mexican federal government to integrate New Mexico into the nation's political, social, and economic fabric, rendered that distant region easy pickings for the United States Army." Ibid., 107. For the development of the Santa Fe trade, see Minge, "Frontier Problems in New Mexico," 107, 116–77, 200, 236–44; David J. Weber, *The Mexican Frontier, 1821–1846* (Albuquerque, 1982), 97, 128–30; Howard R. Lamar, *The Far Southwest, 1846–1912, A Territorial History* (New Haven, Conn., 1966), 62. Leo E. Oliva, *Soldiers on the Santa Fe Trail* (Norman, Okla., 1967), 55, concludes that "the Santa Fe traders had helped to prepare the way for the conquest of New Mexico." Seymour V. Connor and Jimmy M. Skaggs, *Broadcloth and Britches: The Santa Fe Trade* (College Station, Tex., 1977), 126, reach a similar conclusion. See also the summary of the trade, ibid., 196–204. For observations by Doniphan's contemporaries see George, *Heroes and Incidents*, 24, and Edwards, *Campaign in New Mexico*, 18–19. Reports in the Philadelphia *Public Ledger* (September 1, 12, 1846) indicated that the Northern press also took note of the benefits of the Santa Fe trade.

24. Covering Texans' claims on Santa Fe, J. Milton Nance concludes that the failure of the expedition of 1841 "lessened the prowess of the Texans in the minds of the Mexicans." Nance, *After San Jacinto: The Texas-Mexican Frontier, 1836–1841* (Austin, 1963), 519. See also Brack, *Mexico Views Manifest Destiny*, 100–101, 107.

25. John T. Hughes, *Doniphan's Expedition; Containing an Account of the Conquest of New Mexico . . .* (Cincinnati, 1847; repr., Chicago, 1962), 386. For the venture to Mier see Sam W. Haynes, *Soldiers of Misfortune: The Somervell and Mier Expeditions* (Austin, 1990). See also Brack, *Mexico Views Manifest Destiny*, 108.

26. Michael P. Costeloe, *The Central Republic in Mexico, 1835–1846* (Cambridge, Mass., 1993), 209, 223, 240–43, 273–74; DePalo, *Mexican National Army*, 83–84; Vázquez, "The Texas Question in Mexican Politics," 309–44; Brack, *Mexico Views Manifest Destiny*, 97–98.

27. Norma Lois Peterson, *The Presidencies of William Henry Harrison and John Tyler* (Lawrence, Kans., 1989), 226–28, 251–52, 254–58; David M. Pletcher, *The Diplomacy of Annexation: Texas, Oregon, and the Mexican War* (Columbia, Mo., 1973), 76–79.

28. Edwards, *Campaign in New Mexico*, 18; Brack, *Mexico Views Manifest Destiny*, 119, 128–31, 137.

29. An excellent introduction to British interest in Texas is Sam W. Haynes, "Anglophobia

and the Annexation of Texas: The Quest for National Security," in Sam W. Haynes and Christopher Morris, eds., *Manifest Destiny and Empire: American Antebellum Expansionism* (College Station, Tex., 1997), 115–45.

30. Frederick Merk and Lois B. Merk, *The Monroe Doctrine and American Expansionism, 1843–1849* (New York, 1966), 10–39; Pletcher, *Diplomacy of Annexation*, 117–18, 134–35, 156–61, 186–91, 204–7; Vázquez, "The Texas Question in Mexican Politics," 327, 332, 335, 337, 339, 342–43, indicates how the British seemed willing to intercede in Mexican affairs and Mexican–U.S. relations; William W. Freehling, *The Road to Disunion: Secessionists at Bay, 1776–1854* (New York, 1990), 392, 410.

31. O'Sullivan, "Annexation," 5; James B. Bowlin, *Congressional Globe*, 29th Cong., 1st Sess. (January 6, 1846); Merk and Merk, *Monroe Doctrine and Expansionism*, 3–4, 65–68, 72–86, 103–4; Thomas R. Hietala, *Manifest Design: Anxious Aggrandizement in Late Jacksonian America* (Ithaca, N.Y., 1985), 71–83; Reginald C. Stuart, *United States Expansionism and British North America, 1775–1871* (Chapel Hill, N.C., 1988), 102–5; Pletcher, *Diplomacy of Annexation*, 102–5, 221–25, 413–15; Edwin A. Miles, "'Fifty-Four Forty or Fight'—An American Political Legend," *Mississippi Valley Historical Review* 44 (September 1957), 291–309.

32. For a careful exposition stressing how Americans' impressions of English actions from 1812 to the 1840s shaped their distrust of Britain, refer to Haynes, "Anglophobia and the Annexation of Texas," in Haynes and Morris, eds., *Manifest Destiny and Empire*, 115–45, esp. 117–20, 127, 133. See also Pletcher, *Diplomacy of Annexation*, 89, 95–97, 212–13, 294–96, 424–26, esp. 424 and 592–93; Merk and Merk, *Monroe Doctrine and Expansionism*, 66, 115, 181–84; and Josiah Royce, *California from the Conquest in 1846 to the Second Vigilance Committee in San Francisco: A Study of American Character* (Boston, 1886), 151–56.

33. Pletcher, *Diplomacy of Annexation*, 58–60. In 1862 France intervened in Mexico again, deploying thirty thousand soldiers and setting up a puppet monarch beholden to Emperor Napoleon III, an obvious attempt to sunder Mexican sovereignty and expand the French empire. Commodore Jones's actions are summarized in Kenneth J. Hagan, *This People's Navy: The Making of American Sea Power* (New York, 1991), 119–20. García Conde's failure to send the expedition north is mentioned briefly in Frank A. Knapp Jr., "The Mexican Fear of Manifest Destiny in California," in Thomas E. Cotner and Carlos E. Castañeda, eds., *Essays in Mexican History* (Austin, 1958), 207. Andrew Jackson to Francis P. Blair, May 11, 1844, John S. Basset, ed., *The Correspondence of Andrew Jackson*, 7 vols. (Washington, D.C., 1926–1935), 6:286.

34. Hans Kohn, *American Nationalism: An Interpretive Essay* (New York, 1957), 185; Welter, "Frontier West as Image," 593–614; Royce, *California from the Conquest in 1846*, 151–56; William R. Franklin to Editor, Liberty, Mo., *Weekly Tribune*, January 27, 1847, Robert Miller Papers, MHS, St. Louis; Hughes, *Doniphan's Expedition*, 40; J. W. Scott, "The Great West," *DeBow's Review* 15 (July 1853), 50. See also Merk and Merk, *Manifest Destiny and Mission*, 30–32.

35. Hughes, *Doniphan's Expedition*, 35–36. For a summary of the diplomatic imbroglios, see Brack, *Mexico Views Manifest Destiny*, 116–17.

36. Recollection of Oliver P. Moss, O. P. Moss Manuscript, Raymond Settle Collection, Charles F. Curry Library, William Jewell College, Liberty, Missouri; George, *Heroes and Incidents*, 35; William R. Franklin to Editor, Liberty *Weekly Tribune*, January 27, 1847, Miller Papers, MHS, St. Louis; Hughes, *Doniphan's Expedition*, 40.

37. The federal census taken prior to the Mexican War indicated that Doniphan's direct investment in slavery was modest. He owned three household slaves, a boy under age ten, a girl of about the same age, and another female between the ages of ten and twenty-four. Federal Population Census of the United States, Sixth Census, 1840, Missouri, Population Schedules for Clay County, Microcopy M-704, roll 222, RG 29, NA.

38. Brack, *Mexico Views Manifest Destiny*, 62; Daniel Webster, "The Admission of Texas" [December 22, 1845], in Charles M. Wiltse, ed., *The Papers of Daniel Webster*, series 4, *Speeches and Formal Writings, 1834–1852*, 2 vols. (Hanover, N.H., 1988), 2:357; Reginald Horsman, *Race and Manifest Destiny: The Origins of American Racial Anglo-Saxonism* (Cambridge, Mass., 1981), 236–37. See also Frederick Merk, *Slavery and the Annexation of Texas* (Cambridge, Mass., 1972); Gene M. Brack, "Mexican Opinion, American Racism, and the War of 1846," *Western Historical Quarterly* 1 (April 1970), 161–74.

39. The main work is Horsman, *Race and Manifest Destiny*, 208–48, esp. 217 (quoting Buchanan), 231–32, 237–38, 243 (quoting Houston); Francis Lieber to Karl Joseph Anton Mittermaier, May 7, 1847, in Thomas S. Perry, ed., *The Life and Letters of Francis Lieber* (Boston, 1882), 209. See also Weinberg, *Manifest Destiny*, 160–82.

40. Richard S. Elliott, *Notes Taken in Sixty Years* (St. Louis, 1883), 218; George, *Heroes and Incidents*, 41.

41. Missouri's congressional delegation, two senators and five representatives, all Democrats, voted unanimously for war. *Congressional Globe*, 29th Cong., 1st Sess., May 11, 1846, p. 795. Bergeron, *Presidency of Polk*, 76–77; Merk and Merk, *Manifest Destiny and Mission*, 91–92; St. Louis *Weekly Reveille*, May 11, 1846 (emphasis in the original). For general discussions see Norman A. Graebner, "The Mexican War: A Study in Causation," *Pacific Historical Review* 49 (August 1980), 405–26; and Peter T. Harstad and Richard W. Resh, "The Causes of the Mexican War: A Note on Changing Interpretations," *Arizona and the West* 6 (Winter 1964), 289–302.

42. Brack, *Mexico Views Manifest Destiny*, 135, 147–49.

43. John F. Callan, *The Military Laws of the United States, Relating to the Army, Volunteers, Militia, and to Bounty Lands and Pensions, from the Foundation of the Government to the Year 1863* (Philadelphia, 1863), 367; Winders, *Mr. Polk's Army*, 10, 69. Doniphan and Routt to Marcy, May 16, 1846, filed with Secretary of War Applications File, 1846–1848, Box 9, RG 107, NA (emphasis added). William H. Goetzmann contends that President Polk seemed "as much interested in the interior trade, with Santa Fe, the object of anxious clamor by his western constituents, as he was in the California ports." Goetzmann, *When the Eagle Screamed: The Romantic Horizon in American Diplomacy, 1800–1860* (New York, 1966), 60.

44. DePalo, *Mexican National Army*, 73–75, 88–90, 96–97; Russell F. Weigley, *History of the United States Army*, enl. ed. (Bloomington, Ind., 1984), 117–72.

45. Antoine Henri de Jomini, *The Art of War*, trans. G. H. Mendell and W. P. Craighill (Philadelphia, 1862; repr., Westport, Conn., 1971), 61; DePalo, *Mexican National Army*, 72, 87, 96; giving one account of strength in 1846 is Manuel Balbontín, *Estado Militar de la República Mexicana en 1846* (Mexico City, 1891), 13; Costeloe, *The Central Republic*, 168–69; Waddy Thompson, *Recollections of Mexico* (New York, 1846), 168; Brantz Mayer, *Mexico As It Was and As It Is* (Philadelphia, 1847), 285; Stephen L. Hardin, *Texian Iliad: A Military History of the Texas Revolution* (Austin, 1994), 160, 168–69, 203–5, 248.

The U.S. Army, on the other hand, failed to impress European observers and left some

Mexicans doubting America's military capabilities. The Regular Army was diminutive, averaging about ten thousand during the 1840s and standing at only eighty-five hundred in 1845, small for a nation of about seventeen million. In wartime Congress could authorize more Regulars, but it would take time to raise and train them. Selected American infantry and mounted units were good, and the horse-drawn batteries of mobile cannons were said to have great potential. Overall, however, the U.S. Army appeared unimpressive. See Weigley, *History of the United States Army*, 171–72, 597; K. Jack Bauer, "The Battles on the Rio Grande: Palo Alto and Resaca de la Palma," in Charles E. Heller and William A. Stofft, eds., *America's First Battles, 1776–1965* (Lawrence, Kans., 1986), 57–63.

46. F. N. Samponaro, "The Political Role of the Army in Mexico, 1821–1848" (Ph.D. dissertation, State University of New York at Stony Brook, 1974), 72; DePalo, *Mexican National Army*, 74–75, 78, 88–91, 97; Costeloe, *The Central Republic*, 7–8, 168, 245, 266; Stanley C. Green, *The Mexican Republic: The First Decade, 1823–1832* (Pittsburgh, 1987), 183–86; Thompson, *Recollections of Mexico*, 169, 172–73; Mayer, *Mexico As It Was*, 286 (quote); Otero, "Considerations of the Mexican Republic in 1847," quoted in Cecil Robinson, ed., *The View from Chapultepec: Mexican Writers on the Mexican-American War* (Tucson, 1989), 20; Thomas E. Cotner, *The Military and Political Career of José Joaquín de Herrera, 1792–1854* (Austin, 1949), 85.

In contrast with Mexico, the U.S. Army maintained a more efficient system. Although many soldiers came from the lower levels of society, U.S. Regulars enlisted on their own choice for five-year terms. Nearly one-half of U.S. Army recruits were recent immigrants from Europe (about 25 percent of the army was Irish immigrants). Sometimes involved in tactical drills, soldiers occupied most of their days on work details, building or repairing forts and roads. Receiving pay of a few dollars per month, most American soldiers guarded the frontier, where some deserted to start a new life; desertion ran to 20 percent or more in some U.S. units. In keeping with the American tradition of civilian control over the army, Congress passed tight military budgets, insisted on reliable army records, and demanded competent accounting for expenditures for everything, including pay, weapons, and construction. In general, see Edward M. Coffman, *The Old Army: A Portrait of the American Army in Peacetime, 1784–1898* (New York, 1986), 137–211; for pay procedure see U.S. War Department, *General Regulations for the Army of the United States, 1841* (Washington, D.C., 1841), 340.

47. Samponaro, "Political Role of the Army," 67, 78; Costeloe, *The Central Republic*, 7, 266, 303–4; Mayer, *Mexico As It Was*, 285–86; Thompson, *Recollections of Mexico*, 169; DePalo, *Mexican National Army*, passim, offers capsules of the careers of several officers; Cotner, *Career of Herrera*, 81; Donald F. Stevens, *Origins of Instability in Early Republican Mexico* (Durham, N.C., 1991), 56; Charles A. Hale, *Mexican Liberalism in the Age of Mora, 1821–1853* (New Haven, Conn., 1968), 14; Justo Sierra, *The Political Evolution of the Mexican People*, trans. Charles Ramsdell (Austin, 1969), 235; Francisco Bulnes, *The Great Lies of Our History* [1904], excerpt in Robinson, ed., *View from Chapultepec*, 122–23; Otero, "Considerations of the Mexican Republic in 1847," ibid., 20, 22–23.

In 1846, unlike the Mexican army, the number of officers in the U.S. Army was limited to what was needed by units and a small staff. The American officer corps demonstrably included officers who relied on merit, though sometimes playing favorites, helping friends, or assisting relatives played a part in promotions or assignments. Many American lieutenants and captains were graduates of the Military Academy, and those who were not had been inculcated in the requirements of officership by their fellows. Coffman, *The Old Army*, 47–58, 90–93; William B. Skelton, *An American Profession of Arms: The Army Officer Corps, 1784–1861* (Lawrence, Kans., 1992), 137–345, passim.

48. DePalo, *Mexican National Army*, 89; Costeloe, *The Central Republic*, 266; Donald F. Stevens, *Instability in Early Mexico*, 34; Pedro Santoni, "A Fear of the People: The Civic Militia of Mexico in 1845," *Hispanic-American Historical Review* 68 (May 1988), 269–88. See also Launius, *Doniphan, Missouri Moderate*, 197–98.

49. DePalo contends that some Mexican leaders "believed that the US Army was weak, that American volunteers would not fight outside their own borders." DePalo, "Praetorians and Patriots: The Mexican National Army, 1822–1852" (Ph.D. dissertation, University of New Mexico, 1994), 247. On the problems of the American militia, see John K. Mahon, *History of the Militia and the National Guard* (New York, 1983), 67–73, 83–90. Along these same lines, Mexicans were aware that Texans also had failed to capture Santa Fe with militia-style units.

50. Governor John C. Edwards, First Biennial Address, November 16, 1846, in Buel Leopard and Floyd C. Shoemaker, eds., *The Messages and Proclamations of the Governors of the State of Missouri*, 2 vols. (Columbia, Mo., 1922), 2:69; Mahon, *History of the Militia*, 78–94; Winders, *Mr. Polk's Army*, 67–69.

51. According to Stephen Peter Rosen, "Offensive military power is defined as the surplus of military power, beyond what is needed to maintain domestic order, that can be projected beyond the boundaries of a country. Defensive military power is the ability to resist foreign military invasion." Rosen's study discusses concepts that can be applied to many international conflicts. As became clear, in 1846 the United States possessed both offensive and defensive military power to fight a war in North America. On the other hand, Mexico was deficient in both offensive and defensive means of war making. See Stephen Peter Rosen, *Societies and Military Power: India and Her Armies* (Ithaca, N.Y., 1996), viii–ix.

52. "Maxims of Napoleon," in Thomas R. Phillips, ed., *Roots of Strategy* (Harrisburg, Pa., 1940), 425. DePalo, *Mexican National Army*, 91, concludes that "the endemic and enervating political chaos of the decade of centralism had rendered the nation's military establishment incapable of preserving territorial integrity." See also Samponaro, "Political Role of the Army," 67; and Minge, "Frontier Problems in New Mexico," 190.

53. Stevens, *Instability in Early Mexico*, 116–17; Samponaro, "Political Role of the Army," 61, 64–65; Minge, "Frontier Problems in New Mexico," 48–100, 176–85, 198–99, 272–75, 283–93; James E. Officer, *Hispanic Arizona, 1536–1856* (Tucson, 1987), 150–54, 158–71; Costeloe, *The Central Republic*, 8–9, 242.

54. Samuel E. Morison, Frederick Merk, and Frank Freidel, *Dissent in Three American Wars* (Cambridge, Mass., 1970), 39–43, 45–46, 49–51, 62; Russell F. Weigley, "Dissent in Wars," in Alexander DeConde, ed., *Encyclopedia of American Foreign Policy*, 3 vols. (New York, 1978), 1:259; Robert Johannsen, *To the Halls of the Montezumas: The Mexican War in the American Imagination* (New York, 1985), 72, 215; Francis Lieber to Karl J. A. Mittermaier, May 7, 1847, in Perry, ed., *Life and Letters of Lieber*, 209–10; John H. Schroeder, *Mr. Polk's War: American Opposition and Dissent, 1846–1848* (Madison, Wis., 1973), 27–30, 125, 139–41, 143–45. Abraham Lincoln did not introduce his controversial "spot resolutions" until January 1848, when the war was almost over. Mark E. Neely, "Lincoln and the Mexican War: An Argument by Analogy," *Civil War History* 24 (March 1978), 5–24. While many Whigs opposed the war for various reasons, a minority of Whigs, like Doniphan, heartily sup-

ported expansion and the war. Like Doniphan, some Whigs became officers in volunteer units.

55. Merk, *Dissent in Three American Wars,* 55; Weigley, "Dissent in Wars," 259; Kohn, *American Nationalism,* 60, 179; Schroeder, *Mr. Polk's War,* 37–40, 102–4, 113–15.

56. Brack, *Mexico Views Manifest Destiny,* 179; Minge, "Frontier Problems in New Mexico," 321.

57. Brack, *Mexico Views Manifest Destiny,* 179. Mexican historian Josefina Zoraida Vázquez concluded that it was "The Inevitable War." Vázquez, *Mexicans and North Americans on the War of 47* [1977], excerpt in Robinson, ed., *View from Chapultepec,* 198, 207.

58. Norman A. Graebner, *Empire on the Pacific: A Study in American Continental Expansion* (New York, 1955; repr., Santa Barbara, Calif., 1983), 70–82, 119–20, 157–58, 218–24, 227, advances the concept that commercial expansionism and seeking harbors propelled the United States to acquire the Pacific Coast. William L. Marcy to Zachary Taylor, July 9, 1846, William L. Marcy Papers, Manuscript Division, Library of Congress; Pletcher, *Diplomacy of Annexation,* 31; the important phrase "national patrimony" is used by Vázquez, *Mexicans and North Americans on the War of 47,* excerpt in Robinson, ed., *View from Chapultepec,* 205.

59. Geoffrey Blainey, *The Causes of War,* 3rd ed. (New York, 1988), 112–14, 144 (first quote), asserts that a main cause of war is the failure of belligerents to agree on how to measure their respective strengths. The second quote, with original emphasis, is from Allan R. Millett and Williamson Murray, "Lessons of War," *The National Interest* 14 (Winter 1988), 83. "Origin of the War with Mexico," *Southern Quarterly Review* 15 (April 1849), 83–113; Vázquez, *Mexicans and North Americans on the War of 47,* excerpt in Robinson, ed., *View from Chapultepec,* 196; Doniphan and Routt to Sec. of War Marcy, May 16, 1846, filed with Secretary of War Applications File, 1846–1848, Box 9, RG 107, NA.

Chapter 2. Assembly at Fort Leavenworth

1. Missouri newspapers carried Edwards's proclamation. For examples, see Jefferson City, Mo., *Weekly Inquirer* (hereafter Jefferson City *Inquirer*), May 20, 1846, with emphasis in the original about the number of volunteers in the *Inquirer,* and St. Louis *Weekly Reveille,* May 18, 1846 (emphasis added on territorial claims). According to George R. Gibson, *Journal of a Soldier under Kearny and Doniphan, 1846–1847,* ed. Ralph P. Bieber (Glendale, Calif., 1935), 32, Edwards was visiting Washington, D.C., when the announcement was issued.

2. For Doniphan making speeches, John T. Hughes, *Doniphan's Expedition; Containing an Account of the Conquest of New Mexico . . .* (Cincinnati, 1847; repr., Chicago, 1962), 19; Democrats David D. Mitchell and William Gilpin were also singled out as potential officers of Missouri volunteers: William L. Marcy to Gov. John Edwards, June 3, 1846, in *Senate Doc. No. 439,* Serial 478, 29th Cong., 1st Sess., p. 2. The volunteers' kit is described in St. Louis *Weekly Reveille,* June 1, 8, 1846. See also Frank S. Edwards, *A Campaign in New Mexico with Colonel Doniphan* (Philadelphia, 1847), 21; Isaac George, *Heroes and Incidents of the Mexican War, Containing Doniphan's Expedition* (Greensburg, Pa., 1903), 23; Robert E. Shalhope, *Sterling Price, Portrait of a Southerner* (Columbia, Mo., 1971), 14–45, 55.

3. Alexis de Tocqueville, *Democracy in America,* 2 vols. (New York, 1898), 2:329; "Sketch of Life [of Alexander W. Doniphan]," p. 6, in Alexander W. Doniphan Papers, Missouri Historical Society (MHS), St. Louis; A. W. Doniphan, *Address by Col. Alexander W. Doniphan,*

Delivered in Liberty, Mo., June 5, 1872 [pamphlet] (Liberty, Mo., 1883); Waldo Johnson to Mortimer Johnson, November 15, 1846, Waldo P. Johnson Papers, Joint Collection, Western Historical Manuscript Collection–State Historical Society of Missouri, University of Missouri–Columbia; on Johnson's background see *Biographical Directory of the American Congress, 1774–1989* (Washington, D.C., 1989), 1272; Richard S. Elliott, *Notes Taken in Sixty Years* (St. Louis, 1883), 217, 221; Edwards, *Campaign in New Mexico,* 20–21; John Hughes to Editors, September 25, 1846, Liberty, Mo., *Weekly Tribune* (hereafter Liberty *Tribune*), November 14, 1846 (original capitalization).

4. Twenty of twenty-nine states in the Union in 1846 raised regiments with volunteer colonels. States without units included Connecticut, Maine, New Hampshire, Rhode Island, Vermont, and Delaware. Florida, New Jersey, and Iowa recruited companies or battalions but did not put full regiments on active service. See Charles K. Gardner, *A Dictionary of All Officers Who Have Been Commissioned, or Have Been Appointed and Served in the Army of the United States* (New York, 1853), 527–63; Cadmus M. Wilcox, *History of the Mexican War* (Washington, D.C., 1892), 653–95. The best explanation for total volunteers in service is in Richard Bruce Winders, *Mr. Polk's Army: The American Military Experience in the Mexican War* (College Station, Tex., 1997), 72. An excellent introduction is Winders's essay "U.S. Army," in Donald Frazier, ed., *The United States and Mexico at War: Nineteenth-Century Expansion and Conflict* (New York, 1998), 24–26; and the chart "U.S. Forces Employed in the War with Mexico," ibid., 495–97.

5. Muster Rolls, 1st Missouri Regiment, June 1846, Volunteer Organizations, Mexican War, Records of the Army Adjutant General's Office, Record Group (RG) 94, National Archives (NA), Washington, D.C., and individual service cards, with soldiers' ages, microfilm copy, based on National Archives files, at Missouri State Archives, Jefferson City. See also muster lists in William E. Connelley, comp., *Doniphan's Expedition and the Conquest of New Mexico and California* (Topeka, 1907), 530–81, 649, with background on captains, 133 n, 134 n, 135–36 n, 136–37 n; William Young, *Young's History of Lafayette County, Missouri*, 2 vols. (Indianapolis, 1910), 2:430; William Hyde and Howard L. Conrad, eds., *Encyclopedia of the History of St. Louis,* 4 vols. (St. Louis, 1899), 4:2137; St. Louis *Daily Missouri Republican*, November 14, 1885.

6. An excellent contemporary description of the fort at the time Doniphan and his men trained there is in the Columbia *Missouri Statesman*, July 31, 1846 (hereafter Columbia *Statesman*). See also Elvid Hunt, *History of Fort Leavenworth, 1827–1927* (Fort Leavenworth, Kans., 1926), 86–87; and Percival Lowe, *Five Years a Dragoon: ('49 to '54) and Other Adventures on the Great Plains* (Kansas City, 1906; repr., Norman, Okla., 1965), 24–26.

7. Individual Service Record of Alexander William Doniphan, Military Pension Records, RG 75, NA; Supplementary Report for Doniphan's Regiment, June 29, 1846, at Fort Leavenworth, Muster Rolls, Volunteer Organizations, Mexican War, RG 94, NA. An informative examination and analysis of American volunteer soldiering in the Civil War is Reid Mitchell, *The Vacant Chair: The Northern Soldier Leaves Home* (New York, 1993), esp. chap. 2, pp. 19–37, on the influence of their community on the soldiers. Columbia *Statesman*, May 29, 1846.

8. William L. Marcy to Gov. John Edwards, May 13, 1846, Secretary of War, Letters Sent Relating to Military Affairs, 1800–1889, Microcopy M-6, RG 107, roll 26, NA; Federal Population Census of the United States, Sixth Census, 1840, Missouri, Population Schedule for Clay County, Microcopy M-704, roll 222, RG 29, NA. Procedures varied from state to

state. Some governors appointed colonels, and a few states used a combination of appointments and elections.

9. Information about Price, Gilpin, and Ruff can be found in Connelley, comp., *Doniphan's Expedition*, 133 n, 144–48 n; Thomas L. Karnes, *William Gilpin, Western Nationalist* (Austin, 1970), 19–21, 28–45; Francis B. Heitman, *Historical Register and Dictionary of the United States Army*, 2 vols. (Washington, D.C., 1903), 1:458, 850; George W. Cullum, *Biographical Register of the Officers and Graduates of the United States Military Academy*, 2 vols. (New York, 1868), 1:570–71; Liberty *Tribune*, June 20, 27, 1846. Notable fellow graduates in Ruff's Class of 1838 included Irvin McDowell, a future Union general, and P.G.T. Beauregard, William J. Hardee, and Henry Hopkins Sibley, future Confederate generals.

10. Private Marcellus Edwards, of Captain John Reid's Company D from Saline County, claimed that Doniphan was elected "almost unanimously." Abraham R. Johnston, Marcellus Ball Edwards, and Philip G. Ferguson, *Marching with the Army of the West, 1846–1848*, ed. Ralph P. Bieber (Glendale, Calif., 1936), 115 (hereafter [soldier's name], *Marching with the Army*). Neither the Liberty *Tribune*, June 20, 1846, nor Hughes, *Doniphan's Expedition*, 19–20, 26, gave exact vote totals, but Hughes related that Doniphan won by a "respectable majority" (20).

11. The former Regulars serving as volunteer regimental commanders included: Ward Burnett (2nd New York Infantry; graduate of the U.S. Military Academy, 1832, served on active duty 1832–1836); Pierce Butler (1st South Carolina Infantry; appointed a Regular captain, 1819–1829, but not a USMA graduate); Samuel R. Curtis (3rd Ohio Infantry; USMA, 1831, served 1831–1832); Horatio Davis (4th Louisiana Infantry; former Regular captain, 1813–1815); Jefferson Davis (1st Mississippi Rifles; USMA, 1828, served 1828–1835); Lewis DeRussy (DeRussy's Louisiana Infantry; USMA, 1814, served 1814–1842); John F. Hamtramck (1st Virginia Infantry; USMA, 1819, served 1819–1822); George Hughes (Maryland and D.C. Infantry; USMA cadet 1823–1827 but not a graduate, served 1827–1847); William Irvin (5th Ohio Infantry; USMA, 1839, served 1839–1841); Albert Sidney Johnston (Johnston's Texas Regiment; USMA, 1826, served 1826–1834); William McKee (2nd Kentucky Infantry; USMA, 1829, served 1829–1836); Humphrey Marshall (1st Kentucky Cavalry; USMA, 1832, served 1832–1833); Alexander M. Mitchell (1st Ohio Infantry; USMA, 1835, served 1835–1837); George W. Morgan (2nd Ohio Infantry; USMA cadet 1841–1843 but not a graduate); Thomas B. W. Stockton (1st Michigan Infantry; USMA, 1827, served 1827–1836). See Gardner, *Dictionary of All Officers*; Cullum, *Biographical Register*; Heitman, *Historical Register*. Heitman lists officers alphabetically; Cullum lists by class rank within West Point class; Gardner lists alphabetically by last name, but then by years of service.

12. On the status of the militia and attitudes toward military service, see Jerry Cooper, *The Rise of the National Guard: The Evolution of the American Militia, 1865–1920* (Lincoln, Neb., 1997), chap. 1. See also Robert Johannsen, *To the Halls of the Montezumas: The Mexican War in the American Imagination* (New York, 1985), 41; and Winders, *Mr. Polk's Army*, 81–85.

13. A wide range of nineteenth-century state biographical encyclopedias as well as modern reference works yielded background information on the colonels.

14. On the Democratic generals, the best assessment is Winders, *Mr. Polk's Army*, esp. 36–37, 75–76. On the colonels, see ibid., 78–79. Other colonels who were Democrats or probable Democrats, and their regiments (all infantry, unless cavalry specified) included Pierce M. Butler, 1st South Carolina; George W. Morgan, 2nd Ohio; Charles H. Brough, 4th

Ohio; John S. Roane, 1st Arkansas; Isaac H. Wright, 1st Massachusetts; Henry R. Jackson, 1st Georgia; William H. Bissell, 2nd Illinois; Ferris Foreman, 3rd Illinois; James P. Drake, 1st Indiana; William A. Bowles, 3rd Indiana; James H. Lane, 4th Indiana; Willis Gorman, 5th Indiana; Samuel F. Marks, 3rd Louisiana; and Horatio Davis, 4th Louisiana; George Hughes was directly appointed to command the Maryland and D.C. Regiment by President Polk; James S. Williams, 4th Kentucky; Reuben Davis, 2nd Mississippi; John Ralls, 3rd Missouri Mounted; Ward Burnett, 2nd New York; Texans Peter H. Bell (Bell's Regiment), John C. Hays (Hays' Regiment), and George T. Wood (Wood's Regiment); Benjamin F. Cheatham, 3rd Tennessee; Richard Waterhouse, 4th Tennessee; George R. McClelland, 5th Tennessee; Jonas E. Thomas, 1st Tennessee Cavalry; Francis M. Wynkoop, 1st Pennsylvania; John Geary, also 1st Pennsylvania; William B. Roberts, 2nd Pennsylvania; and Thomas B. W. Stockton, 1st Michigan. Caleb Cushing and Joseph Lane were also appointed by Polk as brigadier generals of volunteers.

15. Other Whigs and their regiments (infantry unless cavalry specified) included Lewis DeRussy, DeRussy's Louisiana; William Haskell, 2nd Tennessee; Humphrey Marshall, 1st Kentucky Cavalry; Manilus V. Thomson, 3rd Kentucky; and Robert T. Paine, 1st North Carolina. Other probable Whigs were Alexander Mitchell, 1st Ohio; Samuel R. Curtis, 3rd Ohio; John Hamtramck, 1st Virginia; and Stephen Ormsby, 1st Kentucky.

Other state colonels, political parties not confirmed, included John R. Coffey, 1st Alabama; James Collins, 6th Illinois; James H. Dakin, 2nd Louisiana; William Irvin, 2nd Ohio; Edward Newby, Newby's Illinois; William Weatherford, 1st Illinois (replacing Hardin); James B. Walton, 1st Louisiana; William B. Young, Young's Texas Regiment; and Edward Featherston, 6th Louisiana.

16. Edwards, *Marching with the Army*, 115, indicated a close election for Ruff but provided no tabulations. See also Liberty *Tribune*, June 20, 1846; Hughes, *Doniphan's Expedition*, 26; Army of the West, Order No. 1, June 19, 1846, in Orders of Brig. Gen. Stephen W. Kearny and Brig. Gen. Sterling Price, Army of the West, Microcopy T-1115, roll 1, RG 94, NA.

Only six (including Ruff) of more than sixty regimental lieutenant colonels were former Regulars. These included Henry Clay Jr. (USMA 1831, resigned 1831), with the 2nd Kentucky Cavalry (Gardner, *Dictionary of All Officers*, 119; Heitman, *Historical Register*, 1:308); Henry S. Burton (USMA 1839, served 1839–1846), on active duty when selected for lieutenant colonel in Stevenson's New York regiment (Gardner, 97; Heitman, 1:267; Cullum, *Biographical Register*, 1:577–78); William H. Emory (USMA 1831, served 1831–1846), on active duty when selected as lieutenant colonel of the Maryland and District of Columbia Infantry (Gardner, 165; Heitman, 1:405); Thomas B. Randolph (USMA 1812, served 1812–1815), 1st Virginia Infantry (Gardner, 372; Heitman, 1:815); Jason Rogers (USMA 1821, served 1821–1836), 1st Kentucky Infantry (Gardner, 386; Heitman, 1:843; Cullum, 1:219).

17. First quotation from Edwards, *Campaign in New Mexico*, 20; Doniphan's recollection of Kearny in Doniphan to D. C. Allen, September 19, 1883, Doniphan Papers, MHS, St. Louis; and Doniphan, "Graduation Address to Cadets at the U.S. Military Academy, June 15, 1848," in *Addresses Delivered in the Chapel at West Point . . . by the Hon. Ashbel Smith, of Texas, and Col. A. W. Doniphan, of Missouri, June 16, 1848* (New York, 1848), 19 (Doniphan's quotation). The durable biography is Dwight L. Clarke, *Stephen Watts Kearny, Soldier of the West* (Norman, Okla., 1961), esp. 43, 72–73.

18. Edwards, *Campaign in New Mexico*, 22. The "Model 1841" is described in K. Jack Bauer, "The Battles on the Rio Grande: Palo Alto and Resaca de la Palma," in Charles E.

Heller and William A. Stofft, eds., *America's First Battles, 1776–1965* (Lawrence, Kans., 1986), 59; Russell F. Weigley, *History of the United States Army*, enl. ed. (Bloomington, Ind., 1984), 172; and David Nevin, *The Mexican War* (Alexandria, Va., 1978), 186–87. A more detailed description, calling it the "Model 1842" musket, is in Louis A. Garavaglia and Charles G. Worman, *Firearms of the American West, 1803–1865* (Albuquerque, 1984), 110–12. See also Allan R. Millett and Peter Maslowski, *For the Common Defense*, rev. ed. (New York, 1994), 129.

19. An early report in the St. Louis *Weekly Reveille* (June 1, 1846) predicted that Missouri's volunteers would receive federal arms at Fort Leavenworth. Quarterly Summary Statements of Ordnance and Ordnance Stores on Hand at Forts and Batteries, 1838–1853, vol. 2, Records of the Office of the Chief of Ordnance, RG 156, NA, did not indicate specifically which weapons were on hand at Fort Leavenworth. Ordnance correspondence indicated that Capt. William H. Bell "supplied . . . Gen. Kearney's [*sic*] command spare parts for repairing *small arms of different kinds*" (emphasis added), without revealing the types of rifles, muskets, or carbines issued to the companies of Doniphan's regiment. See Lt. Col. George Talcott, Office of the Chief of Ordnance, to Lt. Alexander B. Dyer, Fort Leavenworth, July 15, 1846, in Letters, Telegrams, and Endorsements Sent to Ordnance Officers and Military Storekeepers, 1839–1889, vol. 8, RG 156, NA.

20. For Company E, see [John Stevenson?] to wife, August 22, 1846 (who wrote: "My company being armed with the Hall Rifle . . ."), Getty Family Papers, New Mexico State Archives, Santa Fe; see also Muster Rolls, Capt. John D. Stevenson, Company E, 1st Missouri Regiment, Volunteer Organizations, Mexican War, Records of the U.S. Army Adjutant General's Office, RG 94, NA; Edwards, *Marching with the Army*, 256. On the return march from Santa Fe to Leavenworth in 1848, Lieutenant George Gibson noted that his companions were "well armed and in fine spirits. Swift has a musket, Raymond my carbine, and Smith and myself Halls [*sic*] Patent Rifles." See George R. Gibson, *Over the Chihuahua and Santa Fe Trails, 1847–1848*, ed. Robert W. Frazer (Albuquerque, 1981), 66. For other mentions of rifles, see, for example, William B. McGroarty, ed., "William H. Richardson's Journal of Doniphan's Expedition," *Missouri Historical Review* (*MHR*) 22 (July 1928), 513; Doniphan to Adj. Gen. Roger Jones, March 4, 1847, *Senate Exec. Doc. No. 1*, Serial 503, 30th Cong., 1st Sess., p. 500 (also quoted in Connelley, comp., *Doniphan's Expedition*, 431, 432); St. Louis *Daily Union*, June 26, 1847. The Hall's rifle is described in Carl P. Russell, *Guns on the Early Frontiers* (Berkeley, Calif., 1957), 183–87; and Garavaglia and Worman, *Firearms of the West*, 120–22.

21. Doniphan reported to the army's adjutant general that his "whole force was . . . armed with rifles." Doniphan to Adj. Gen. Roger Jones, March 4, 1847, *Senate Exec. Doc. No. 1*, Serial 503, 30th Cong., 1st Sess., p. 497. Private William Richardson complimented the Mississippi Rifle, McGroarty, ed., "Richardson's Journal," *MHR* 22 (July 1928), 513, and mentioned that his company carried rifles in the skirmish at Brazito: ibid. (April 1928), 347. Private Frank Edwards, *Campaign in New Mexico*, 139, used the phrase "Yankee rifles" to describe their weapons. Several Regular Army units also carried the Model 1841 after the war, adding to its reputation. M. B. Edwards, *Marching with the Army*, 132–33, mentioned cleaning his "rifle" lock. See Garavaglia and Worman, *Firearms of the West*, 121–22.

22. St. Louis *Daily Missouri Republican*, June 8, 1846 (hereafter St. Louis *Republican*); St. Louis *Weekly Reveille*, June 1, 8, 1846; J. Thomas Scharf, *History of Saint Louis City and County*, 2 vols. (Philadelphia, 1883), 2:1487; Mark L. Gardner and Marc Simmons, eds., *The Mexican War Correspondence of Richard Smith Elliott* (Norman, Okla., 1997), 3–7.

23. St. Louis *Weekly Reveille*, June 8, 29, 1846; St. Louis *Republican*, July 2, 1846; artillery uniforms briefly described by William C. Kennerly, *Persimmon Hill: A Narrative of Old St. Louis and the Far West* (Norman, Okla., 1948), 191; Heitman, *Historical Register*, 1:305, 1041; Cullum, *Biographical Register*, 1:370. Bruce Allardice, *More Generals in Gray* (Baton Rouge, La., 1995), 61, mentions that President Zachary Taylor later appointed Clark as federal surveyor general for Illinois and Missouri, indicating that Clark was probably a Whig. On Weightman see *Biographical Directory of the American Congress, 1774–1989*, 2023–24. Fischer's background in Justin H. Smith, *The War with Mexico*, 2 vols. (New York, 1919), 1:288; Hyde and Conrad, eds., *Encyclopedia of the History of St. Louis*, 2:785.

24. *Addresses Delivered in the Chapel at West Point*, 20.

25. Fayette, Mo., *Boon's Lick Times*, June 27, 1846; St. Louis *Republican*, June 20, 1846 (quote).

26. Elliott, *Notes Taken*, 222; Johnston, *Marching with the Army*, 73.

27. Hughes, *Doniphan's Expedition*, 26 (first and last quotes); Edwards, *Marching with the Army*, 113; "John Brown" [Lt. Elliott] to St. Louis *Reveille*, June 10, 12, 1846, in Gardner and Simmons, eds., *Correspondence of Elliott*, 26–28.

28. Quotes, Hughes, *Doniphan's Expedition*, 26 (first and last quotes); "John Brown" [Lt. Elliott] to St. Louis *Reveille*, June 20, 1846, in Gardner and Simmons, eds., *Correspondence of Elliott*, 32; Edwards, *Marching with the Army*, 115. See also "John Brown" [Lt. Elliott] to St. Louis *Reveille*, June 12, 23, 25, 1846, in Gardner and Simmons, eds., *Correspondence of Elliott*, 27–28, 35–39.

29. "John Brown" [Lt. Elliott] to St. Louis *Reveille*, June 22, 25, 1846, in Gardner and Simmons, eds., *Correspondence of Elliott*, 33–34, 37–39, quoting Kearny's original emphasis (34); Message of Gov. John C. Edwards to the General Assembly, January 10, 1847, in Buel Leopard and Floyd C. Shoemaker, eds., *The Messages and Proclamations of the Governors of the State of Missouri*, 2 vols. (Columbia, Mo., 1922), 208; Hughes, *Doniphan's Expedition*, 26. See also St. Louis *Republican*, June 15, July 2, 1846.

30. One of the lieutenants from Platte County wrote a chronicle of the expedition. See Gibson, *Journal of a Soldier*, 120–23. Angney's background in Connelley, comp., *Doniphan's Expedition*, 514–15 note; and *History of Cole, Moniteau, Morgan, Benton, Miller, Maries and Osage Counties, Missouri* (Chicago, 1889), 250.

31. Edwards, *Marching with the Army*, 109–11; Jefferson City *Inquirer*, June 10, 12, July 1, 1846.

32. James M. Cutts, *The Conquest of California and New Mexico by the Forces of the United States in the Years 1846 and 1847* (Philadelphia, 1847), 35–36; Hughes, *Doniphan's Expedition*, 28–29, 36; Edwards, *Marching with the Army*, 242. See also Mitchell, *Vacant Chair*, 26.

33. Reid Mitchell points out the same effect of soldier-reporters on enlistees in their units during the Civil War. See Mitchell, *Vacant Chair*, 27.

34. "John Brown" [Lt. Elliott] to St. Louis *Reveille*, July 7, 1846, in Gardner and Simmons, eds., *Correspondence of Elliott*, 46–49; *House Exec. Doc. No. 41*, Serial 517, 30th Cong., 1st Sess., "Reports and Journals of Army Officers"; Adrian G. Trass, *From the Golden Gate to Mexico City: The U.S. Army Topographical Engineers in the Mexican War, 1846–1848* (Washington, D.C., 1993), 63, 66.

35. While contemporary sources differ on strengths of the units in the Army of the West, they basically agree on the total number of soldiers (1,657 or 1,658). See St. Louis *Weekly Reveille*, July 27, 1846; Hughes, *Doniphan's Expedition*, 26–27; Gibson, *Journal of a Soldier*,

125; and Edwards, *Campaign in New Mexico*, 23. See also Clarke, *Kearny*, 111–13. Brief mention of the slaves can be found in Edwards, *Campaign in New Mexico*, 126–27; Gibson, *Journal of a Soldier*, 140, 153, 330; and Edwards, *Marching with the Army*, 133. See also Phillip T. Tucker, "Above and Beyond: African-American Missourians of Colonel Alexander Doniphan's Expedition," *Password: The Quarterly Journal of the El Paso County Historical Society* 35 (Fall 1990), 133–37. Number of animals given in QM Gen. Thomas Jesup to Sec. of War William Marcy, November 24, 1847, *House Exec. Doc. No.* 8, Serial 515, 30th Cong., 1st Sess., p. 545. Quotation from Maj. Swords to Gen. Jesup, July 12, 1846, Office of the Quartermaster General, Consolidated Correspondence File, Box 50, RG 92, NA. Reid's background in *Biographical Directory of the American Congress*, 1704–5; Rodgers's in Connelley, comp., *Doniphan's Expedition*, 138 n, and *History of Callaway County, Missouri* (St. Louis, 1884), 380–82.

36. B. H. Liddell Hart, *Strategy*, 2nd rev. ed. (New York, 1967), 335.

37. Milo M. Quaife, ed., *The Diary of James K. Polk, 1845–1849*, 4 vols. (Chicago, 1910), 1:399–401. Polk observed that he "did not think that so many as 20,000 volunteers besides the regular army was necessary" for these ambitious operations (ibid., 1:401). See also Oakah L. Jones Jr., "The Pacific Squadron off California," *Journal of the West* 5 (April 1966), 187–202; D. E. Livingston-Little, "U.S. Military Forces in California," *Journal of the West* 11 (April 1972), 299–306; K. Jack Bauer, *The Mexican War, 1846–1848* (New York, 1974), 127–30; Donald C. Biggs, *Conquer and Colonize: Stevenson's Regiment and California* (San Rafael, Calif., 1977). None of the secondary sources reaches the conclusion or stresses the point regarding the small size of U.S. forces and the breadth of the strategic tasks that Polk gave them. However, in *The Year of Decision, 1846* (Boston, 1943), Bernard DeVoto contends that an American invasion to capture Santa Fe was "Polk's fantasy" (235) and an "expedition against . . . New Mexico, was [almost] preposterous as a military conception but it did not fail" (229). Although President Polk and others had been informed by American chargé Thomas O. Larkin and others as to Mexico's lack of defenses and the absence of Mexican regular army units in California, Don E. Fehrenbacher downplays the scope of the United States plan, writing that "the conquest [of California] itself required no great expenditure of military effort" without measuring such an effort against troops and military resources on hand in 1846, the distances to be traveled, and the possibility that even a modest resistance by Mexicans living in California and New Mexico might block the American effort. See Don E. Fehrenbacher, "The Mexican War and the Conquest of California," in George H. Knoles, ed., *Essays and Assays: California History Reappraised* (San Francisco, 1973), 62.

38. Quaife, ed., *Diary of James K. Polk*, 1:403–44. Polk added the specific about an expedition to Upper California to the cabinet on May 26. Ibid., 1:429. On May 30, at another cabinet meeting, the president summarized his objectives. Polk "declared my purpose to be to acquire for the United States, California, New Mexico, and perhaps some others of the Northern Provinces of Mexico," and he had related such a design to his special representative, John Slidell, in the fall of 1845. Now he specifically gave the mission to Kearny's expedition. Ibid., 1:438–39. In *James K. Polk, Continentalist, 1843–1846* (Princeton, 1966), Charles Sellers discusses Polk's "continental vision" (213) and the audacity of Polk's plans (422–23), while at the same time saying that the president expected to use the "military and naval might" (229) of the United States. A few ships and a few thousand soldiers hardly constituted a mighty force. Wool's expedition was not ready to invade Mexico until October. Bauer, *Mexican War*, 146.

39. Orders to Kearny were relayed in U.S. Army Adj. Gen. Roger Jones, Washington, D.C., to Col. S. W. Kearny, Fort Leavenworth, May 13, 14, 1846; and Sec. of War William Marcy to Kearny, May 27, 1846; copies of both in Justin H. Smith Papers, Benson Latin American Collection, University of Texas, Austin.

40. Roswell S. Ripley, *The War with Mexico,* 2 vols. (New York, 1849), 1:281.

41. Russell Weigley asserts that "Kearny dropped off enough garrisons between Texas and California to terminate Mexican sovereignty in the intervening territory, especially when shielded by the anabasis of Colonel Alexander Doniphan's one thousand across Chihuahua." Russell F. Weigley, *The American Way of War: A History of United States Military Strategy and Policy* (New York, 1973), 73–74.

42. Bauer, *Mexican War,* 127–28.

43. For reports of Mexicans, see, for example, St. Louis *Republican,* June 26, 1846; and Gibson, *Journal of a Soldier,* 165–66 n. Scott's views are on an endorsement, dated July 17, 1846, of a letter from Gov. Edwards to Sec. of War Marcy, in *House Exec. Doc. No. 60,* Serial 520, 30th Cong., 1st Sess., pp. 1262–63 (quote on 1263). See also William Y. Chalfant, *Dangerous Passage: The Santa Fe Trail and the Mexican War* (Norman, Okla., 1994), 6.

44. Carl von Clausewitz emphasized that many observers could not understand or "distinguish real war from war on paper." Carl von Clausewitz, *On War,* trans. Michael Howard and Peter Paret (Princeton, 1984), 119.

45. Clausewitz postulated, "Everything in war is very simple, but the simplist thing is difficult." He concluded: "Countless minor incidents—the kind you can never really foresee—combine to lower the general level of performance [of soldiers], so that one always falls far short of the intended goal." Ibid., 113–16, 119–21 (quotes on 119).

46. A parallel is the Confederate invasion of New Mexico in 1862 during the Civil War. General Henry H. Sibley's invading Confederates won tactical victories at the Battles of Valverde and Glorieta Pass, New Mexico, and captured Santa Fe. However, during the campaign the Confederates suffered extensive losses to their supplies, wagons, and animals. Unable to replenish his column by capturing any Union strongholds or supplies, Sibley was forced to retreat, and the expedition failed. Thomas S. Edrington and John Taylor, *The Battle of Glorieta Pass* (Albuquerque, 1998), 22–26, 105–9, 114–16, 121–22.

47. Moreover, it was easy to make assumptions about the individual soldiers themselves. As Clausewitz wrote, "A battalion is made up of individuals, the least important of whom may chance to delay things or somehow make them go wrong." Clausewitz, *On War,* 119.

48. Army of the West, Order No. 4, June 27, 1846, Microcopy T-1115, roll 1, RG 94, NA; Elliott, *Notes Taken,* 227.

49. Hughes, *Doniphan's Expedition,* 35–36. The expedition was actually to make the journey in fifty-six days, still a remarkable example of marching considering the natural obstacles.

50. St. Louis *Weekly Reveille,* June 1, 1846 (all emphasis in the original); Fayette, Mo., *Boon's Lick Times,* May 23, 1846.

Chapter 3. Down the Santa Fe Trail to Invade Mexico

1. Army of the West, Order No. 4, June 27, 1846, Orders of Brig. Gen. Stephen W. Kearny and Brig. Gen. Sterling Price, Army of the West, Microcopy T-1115, roll 1, Record Group (RG) 94, National Archives (NA), Washington, D.C.; June 26, 1846, Notebook,

Notes of the Expedition to Santa Fe, by One of the B Co. Boys, Charles F. Ruff Papers, Missouri Historical Society (MHS), St. Louis (hereafter cited as B Co. Notebook, Ruff Papers); Dwight L. Clarke, *Stephen Watts Kearny, Soldier of the West* (Norman, Okla., 1961), 117.

2. A summary of the march is found in William Y. Chalfant, *Dangerous Passage: The Santa Fe Trail and the Mexican War* (Norman, Okla., 1994), 3–20, esp. 4–7. See also John T. Hughes, *Doniphan's Expedition; Containing an Account of the Conquest of New Mexico* (Cincinnati, 1847; repr., Chicago, 1962), 29–30, 35; Abraham R. Johnston, Marcellus B. Edwards, and Philip G. Ferguson, *Marching with the Army of the West, 1846–1848*, ed. Ralph P. Bieber (Glendale, Calif., 1936), 73 (hereafter cited as [soldier's name] *Marching with the Army*); Jacob S. Robinson, *A Journal of the Santa Fe Expedition under Colonel Doniphan*, ed. Carl L. Cannon (Princeton, 1932), 1.

3. "John Brown" [Lt. Richard S. Elliott], St. Louis *Reveille*, July 1, 1846, in Mark L. Gardner and Marc Simmons, eds., *The Mexican War Correspondence of Richard Smith Elliott* (Norman, Okla., 1997), 43–44; Hughes, *Doniphan's Expedition*, 36; Frank S. Edwards, *A Campaign in New Mexico with Colonel Doniphan* (Philadelphia, 1847), 23; George R. Gibson, *Journal of a Soldier under Kearny and Doniphan, 1846–1847*, ed. Ralph P. Bieber (Glendale, Calif., 1935), 126–27, 130; Dwight L. Clarke, ed., *The Original Journals of Henry Smith Turner with Stephen Watts Kearny to New Mexico and California, 1846–1847* (Norman, Okla., 1966), 58.

4. Hughes, *Doniphan's Expedition*, 33–34.

5. Robinson, *Journal*, 6 (first quote); Hughes, *Doniphan's Expedition*, 30 (second quote); Lt. Lucian J. Eastin to Editors, June 30, 1846, Jefferson City, Mo., *Weekly Inquirer* (hereafter Jefferson City *Inquirer*), July 15, 1846 (third quote); Edwards, *Campaign in New Mexico*, 24 (last quote).

6. Johnston, *Marching with the Army*, 74–75 (first quote), 77, 79–81; Edwards, *Marching with the Army*, 120–21, 134 (second quote); Hughes, *Doniphan's Expedition*, 31 (third quote); Robinson, *Journal*, 3 (fourth quote), 6; Gibson, *Journal of a Soldier*, 128–33; Edwards, *Campaign in New Mexico*, 23–24; Clarke, ed., *Turner Journal*, 59; M. B. Edwards to Joe Edwards, July 9, 1846, Mexican War Papers, MHS, St. Louis. See also Chalfant, *Dangerous Passage*, 12–13.

7. José María Roa Bárcena, *Memories of the North American Invasion* [1902], quoted in Cecil Robinson, ed., *The View from Chapultepec: Mexican Writers on the Mexican-American War* (Tucson, 1989), 47. In *Las invasiones norteamericanas en Mexico* (Mexico City, 1971), 160, Gastón García Cantú labeled the movement from Fort Leavenworth as the "Invasion of New Mexico by the soldiers of Colonel Doniphan."

8. "John Brown" [Lt. Elliott] to St. Louis *Reveille*, July 10, 1846, in Gardner and Simmons, eds., *Correspondence of Elliott*, 49–51 (quote on 50). Lt. Christian Kribben also emphasized Kearny's intent to travel twenty-five to thirty miles per day. "bb" [Lt. Kribben] to Editor, July 16, 1846, St. Louis *Republican*, August 6, 1846, also in Christian Kribben Typescript Letters, Mexican War Papers, MHS, St. Louis. See also Clarke, ed., *Turner Journal*, passim; Gibson, *Journal of a Soldier*, 159 n; Chalfant, *Dangerous Passage*, 4.

9. Hughes, *Doniphan's Expedition*, 50 (first quote); Edwards, *Marching with the Army*, 118, 123 (second quote); see also Johnston, *Marching with the Army*, 78; Gibson, *Journal of a Soldier*, 133–36, 139; Clarke, ed., *Turner Journal*, 59; B Co. Notebook, July 1 and 2, 1846, Ruff Papers, MHS, St. Louis.

10. Meanwhile, on July 7, about the time that detachments of the Army of the West were

passing through Council Grove, off the California coast Commodore John Sloat sent a landing force ashore from a U.S. naval squadron and proclaimed the occupation of Monterey. The landing was unopposed by any Mexican military units. See K. Jack Bauer, *The Mexican War, 1846–1848* (New York, 1974), 170–73.

11. Robinson, *Journal*, 7 (quote), 8; Johnston, *Marching with the Army*, 79–81; B Co. Notebook, July 5, 1846, Ruff Papers, MHS, St. Louis; Hughes, *Doniphan's Expedition*, 41; Gibson, *Journal of a Soldier*, 136, 139, 144; Edwards, *Campaign in New Mexico*, 27.

12. Edwards, *Campaign in New Mexico*, 25 (first quote); Hughes, *Doniphan's Expedition*, 39.

13. Hughes, *Doniphan's Expedition*, 41–45, 81 (Hughes's original emphasis); Robinson, *Journal*, 9, 13; Clarke, ed., *Turner Journal*, 59–61; Edwards, *Marching with the Army*, 110; Gibson, *Journal of a Soldier*, 141, 148; Dragoon Sgt. M. L. Baker to M. P. Baker, December 1846, Mexican War Papers, MHS, St. Louis. See also Chalfant, *Dangerous Passage*, 11–12.

14. Hughes, *Doniphan's Expedition*, 43 (first quote); Gibson, *Journal of a Soldier*, 147 (second and fourth quotes); Robinson, *Journal*, 9, 13 (third quote); Edwards, *Campaign in New Mexico*, 29 (fifth quote), 36; Edwards, *Marching with the Army*, 138 (last quote). Other complaints about half rations are found in Thomas Edwards to Joe Edwards, September 15, 1846, Mexican War Papers, MHS, St. Louis; Oliver P. Moss Manuscript, Raymond Settle Collection, Charles F. Curry Library, William Jewell College, Liberty, Missouri.

15. Lt. Lucian J. Eastin to Editors, Jefferson City *Inquirer*, August 11, 1846 (first quote); Gibson, *Journal of a Soldier*, 140–41 (second quote), 162 (last quote); Edwards, *Campaign in New Mexico*, 26, 30–31 (third quote). See also Robinson, *Journal*, 3; Edwards, *Marching with the Army*, 136–37; Johnston, *Marching with the Army*, 88.

16. Robinson, *Journal*, 11; Edwards, *Campaign in New Mexico*, 30.

17. Edwards, *Campaign in New Mexico*, 28; Gibson, *Journal of a Soldier*, 142–43, 153 (quote). See also Johnston, *Marching with the Army*, 82–83; Edwards, *Marching with the Army*, 127; Hughes, *Doniphan's Expedition*, 43, 45.

18. Hughes, *Doniphan's Expedition*, 45–47 (quote on 47); Gibson, *Journal of a Soldier*, 145–46 (quote on 145).

19. Robinson, *Journal*, 11–12; Edwards, *Campaign in New Mexico*, 28 (second quote); Marcellus B. Edwards to Joe Edwards, July 9, 1846, Mexican War Papers, MHS, St. Louis (third quote); Edwards, *Marching with the Army*, 129–30 (last quote), 133. See also Hughes, *Doniphan's Expedition*, 47–48; Clarke, *Kearny*, 119.

20. Hughes, *Doniphan's Expedition*, 43–44, 48–49; Robinson, *Journal*, 13; Edwards, *Campaign in New Mexico*, 28, 30; Clarke, ed., *Turner Journal*, 61; Gibson, *Journal of a Soldier*, 148–49; "bb" [Lt. Kribben] to Editor, July 16, 1846, St. Louis *Republican*, August 6, 1846.

21. Clarke, ed., *Turner Journal*, 63; Johnston, *Marching with the Army*, 85; Hughes, *Doniphan's Expedition*, 48–49; Gibson, *Journal of a Soldier*, 151.

22. Doniphan's recollection of the conversation is in Doniphan to D. C. Allen, September 20, 1883, Doniphan Papers, MHS, St. Louis; Henry S. Turner to wife [Mrs. Julia Turner], August 5, 1846, Henry S. Turner Collection, MHS, St. Louis.

23. Clarke, ed., *Turner Journal*, 61, 63–64; Johnston, *Marching with the Army*, 87; Gibson, *Journal of a Soldier*, 146 (quote), 149, 153–56, 158, 160–61; Robinson, *Journal*, 2; B Co. Notebook, July 14, 1846, Ruff Papers, MHS, St. Louis.

24. Hughes, *Doniphan's Expedition*, 50–51; Robinson, *Journal*, 14; Clarke, ed., *Turner Journal*, 63; Edwards, *Marching with the Army*, 133; Gibson, *Journal of a Soldier*, 161. Similar

indication of Missourians' high morale and rumors about resistance in New Mexico are in "bb" [Lt. Kribben] to Editor, St. Louis *Republican*, July 16, 23, 1846, Mexican War Papers, MHS, St. Louis. About that time President Polk gave some credence to rumors that "a larger Mexican force than had been anticipated were assembled in New Mexico to resist the approach of Gen'l Kearney [*sic*]." Polk ordered Secretary of War Marcy to send a regiment of Illinois volunteers down the Santa Fe Trail and also authorized the enlistment of a third regiment of Missouri volunteers. Milo M. Quaife, ed., *The Diary of James K. Polk, 1845–1849*, 4 vols. (Chicago, 1910), 2:31, entry for July 18, 1846.

25. Lt. William H. Emory, "Notes of a Military Reconnoissance [*sic*] from Fort Leavenworth . . . to San Diego . . . ," *Senate Executive Doc. No. 7*, Serial 505, 30th Cong., 1st Sess., p. 13, also in Ross Calvin, ed., *Lieutenant Emory Reports* (Albuquerque, 1951), 29; Gibson, *Journal of a Soldier*, 151–53; Robinson, *Journal*, 10; Hughes, *Doniphan's Expedition*, 54–55 (quote on 55).

26. Calvin, ed., *Emory Reports*, 32; Robinson, *Journal*, 16; Edwards, *Campaign in New Mexico*, 36–37; Gibson, *Journal of a Soldier*, 165; Clarke, ed., *Turner Journal*, 65; Hughes, *Doniphan's Expedition*, 55–56. Elevation above sea level at the fort was 4,523 feet, according to Lieutenant Emory. Calvin, ed., *Emory Reports*, 33.

27. Hughes, *Doniphan's Expedition*, 59; Robinson, *Journal*, 16–17; "John Brown" [Lt. Elliott] to St. Louis *Reveille*, July 31, 1846, in Gardner and Simmons, eds., *Correspondence of Elliott*, 58; Edwards, *Campaign in New Mexico*, 38; Gibson, *Journal of a Soldier*, 168; Edwards, *Marching with the Army*, 141. For a comprehensive study, see David Lavender, *Bent's Fort* (Garden City, N.Y., 1954), esp. 146–47, 275. It appears that several of Kearny's civilian teamsters strictly interpreted their contracts, which they said called for them to deliver military supplies only as far as Bent's Fort. Therefore, many of the army's contract wagons left the expedition and returned to Fort Leavenworth. See the explanation by Chalfant, *Dangerous Passage*, 18.

28. Hughes, *Doniphan's Expedition*, 56; LeRoy R. Hafen and William J. Ghent, *Broken Hand: The Life Story of Thomas Fitzpatrick, Chief of the Mountain Men* (Denver, 1931), 183; Clarke, ed., *Turner Journal*, 65; Gibson, *Journal of a Soldier*, 166–67, 166 n; "E" (at Bent's Fort) to Jefferson City *Inquirer*, September 15, 1846; "P" to Editor, July 31, 1846, ibid.; Richard S. Elliott, *Notes Taken in Sixty Years* (St. Louis, 1883), 224.

29. Hughes, *Doniphan's Expedition*, 56; Johnston, *Marching with the Army*, 91 (quotes); Johnston recalled that one of the traders, "a Mr. Harmony of New York[,] obtained permission to go to Santa Fe with the released prisoners." "John Brown" [Lt. Elliott] to St. Louis *Reveille*, July 7, 1846, in Gardner and Simmons, eds., *Correspondence of Elliott*, 48 (emphasis in the original); Edwards, *Campaign in New Mexico*, 37; Gibson, *Journal of a Soldier*, 167; Clarke, ed., *Turner Journal*, 66–67; Kearny Proclamation, July 31, 1846, Special Order No. 2, July 31, 1846, Microcopy T-1115, roll 1, RG 94, NA, also found in William E. Connelley, comp., *Doniphan's Expedition and the Conquest of New Mexico and California* (Topeka, 1907), 181 n.

30. Clarke, ed., *Turner Journal*, 67–68; Stella M. Drumm, ed., *Down the Santa Fe Trail and into Mexico: The Diary of Susan Shelby Magoffin 1846–1847* (New Haven, Conn., 1926), xi–xxv; Clarke, *Kearny*, 126–27; Kearny to Armijo, August 1, 1846, in Max L. Moorhead, ed., "Notes and Documents," *New Mexico Historical Review* 26 (January 1951), 80, original in Microcopy M-567, roll 319, RG 94, NA, also quoted in Connelley, comp., *Doniphan's Expedition*, 181–82 n.

31. Background on Magoffin in Connelley, comp., *Doniphan's Expedition*, 196–98 n;

Drumm, ed., *Down the Santa Fe Trail*, xi–xxv; Clarke, *Kearny*, 126–27; William E. Connelley, ed., "The Magoffin Papers," *Publications of the Historical Society of New Mexico*, no. 24 (1921), 42–63; Kearny to AG Jones, August 1, 1846, Records of the Adjutant General's Office, Letters Received by the Office of the Adjutant General (Main Series), Microcopy M-567, roll 319, RG 94, NA; Otis E. Young, *The West of Philip St. George Cooke, 1809–1895* (Glendale, Calif., 1955), 177; Sec. of War William Marcy to Kearny, June 18, 1846, Secretary of War, Letters Sent Relating to Military Affairs, 1800–1889, Microcopy M-6, roll 26, RG 107, NA. One of Bent's associates who joined the expedition at that point was Francis P. "Frank" Blair Jr.; "John Brown" [Lt. Elliott] to St. Louis *Reveille*, July 29, 1846, in Gardner and Simmons, eds., *Correspondence of Elliott*, 53.

32. Hughes, *Doniphan's Expedition*, 58–59; Johnston, *Marching with the Army*, 90; Edwards, *Marching with the Army*, 141; Robinson, *Journal*, 19; "P" to Editor, July 31, 1846, Jefferson City *Inquirer*, September 15, 1846.

33. Headquarters, Army of the West, Order No. 10, July 31, 1846, Microcopy T-1115, roll 1, RG 94, NA; Hughes, *Doniphan's Expedition*, 53, 60; Robinson, *Journal*, 18; Johnston, *Marching with the Army*, 92; Clarke, ed., *Turner Journal*, 64–65; Edwards, *Marching with the Army*, 141; St. Louis *Republican*, July 23, 1846, reported the problem with diarrhea. B. B. Durrett and a Mr. Long were the surgeons' assistants.

34. Edwards, *Marching with the Army*, 141; Johnston, *Marching with the Army*, 91; Gibson, *Journal of a Soldier*, 173; Edwards, *Campaign in New Mexico*, 39; Clarke, ed., *Turner Journal*, 67; Hughes, *Doniphan's Expedition*, 59–60; García Cantú, *Las invasiones norteamericanas en México*, 160.

35. Josiah Gregg, *Commerce of the Prairies*, 2 vols. (New York, 1844), 1:134. A good overview is Ward Alan Minge, "Frontier Problems in New Mexico Preceding the Mexican War, 1840–1846" (Ph.D. dissertation, University of New Mexico, 1965), passim. See David J. Weber, *The Mexican Frontier, 1821–1846* (Albuquerque, 1982), 98, regarding selling guns to the Indians.

36. "Report of the Citizens of New Mexico to the President of Mexico," in Moorhead, ed., "Notes and Documents," 70–71.

37. Ibid.; Armijo's proclamation, August 1846, in Benjamin M. Read Collection, New Mexico State Records Center, Santa Fe, also in Ralph E. Twitchell, *The History of the Military Occupation of the Territory of New Mexico from 1846 to 1851* (Denver, 1909), 62–63; Mexicans showed copies of Armijo's proclamation to the Americans, according to Emory, Calvin, ed., *Emory Reports*, 42; Proclamation, Governor of Chihuahua to the Inhabitants of Chihuahua, July 11, 1846, Governor of Chihuahua to Governor of Yucatán, July 18, 1846, Western Americana Manuscripts,—Mexican War, Beinecke Library, Yale University, New Haven, Conn.

38. "Citizens [of New Mexico] to the President of Mexico," in Moorhead, ed., "Notes and Documents," 71–73, indicates that as many as four thousand New Mexico militia had reported for duty, but Armijo himself, in "Report of Gov. Manuel Armijo to the Minister of Foreign Relations," September 8, 1846, ibid., 76–77, put the total at eighteen hundred. The militia and their leaders appeared reluctant to act. Edwards, *Campaign in New Mexico*, 44–45; Hughes, *Doniphan's Expedition*, 77–78; Clarke, *Kearny*, 136; Young, *Philip St. George Cooke*, 179–80. See also Connelley, ed., "The Magoffin Papers," 42–63.

39. The types of preparations Armijo made for a defense at Apache Canyon were delineated in a sketch map, published in the Jefferson City *Weekly Inquirer*, September 29, 1846,

reproduced in Gardner and Simmons, eds., *Correspondence of Elliott*, 69. Armijo's letter to Kearny, August 12, 1846, in Moorhead, ed., "Notes and Documents," 80–81; Headquarters, Army of the West, Special Order No. 4 [listing captured Mexican weapons and ammunition], Records of the U.S. Army, Adjutant General's Office, Letters Received by the Office of the Adjutant General (Main Series), 1822–1860, Microcopy M-567, roll 319, RG 94, NA; Daniel Tyler, "Gringo Views of Governor Manuel Armijo," *New Mexico Historical Review* 45 (January 1970), 23, 27, 38–39. See also Tyler, "Governor Armijo's Moment of Truth," *Journal of the West* 11 (April 1972), 307–16.

40. Edwards, *Marching with the Army*, 143; Calvin, ed., *Emory Reports*, 35; "bb" [Lt. Kribben] to Editor, St. Louis *Republican*, August 24, 1846, Mexican War Papers, MHS, St. Louis (first quote); Robinson, *Journal*, 20 (second quote); Hughes, *Doniphan's Expedition*, 62 (other quotes). Hughes made a reference to the Roman general Caecilius Metellus, who led Roman forces during a campaign in Numidia, North Africa, winning a victory at the battle of the Muthul in 108 B.C.; Calvin, ed., *Emory Reports*, 37.

41. Robinson, *Journal*, 20; Edwards, *Marching with the Army*, 143, 144–45 (quotes); Gibson, *Journal of a Soldier*, 174–75; Johnston, *Marching with the Army*, 93–94; Clarke, ed., *Turner Journal*, 68; Hughes, *Doniphan's Expedition*, 63.

42. Clarke, ed., *Turner Journal*, 68–69; Calvin, ed., *Emory Reports*, 35, 39; Gibson, *Journal of a Soldier*, 180, 183–84; Edwards, *Marching with the Army*, 146–49; Drumm, ed., *Down the Santa Fe Trail*, 67 (quote on Ratón); Hughes, *Doniphan's Expedition*, 63–66; Elliott, *Notes Taken*, 227.

43. Hughes, *Doniphan's Expedition*, 66–67; Edwards, *Marching with the Army*, 147–48; Calvin, ed., *Emory Reports*, 40.

44. Doniphan to D. C. Allen, September 19, 1883, Doniphan Papers, MHS, St. Louis; Roger D. Launius, *Alexander William Doniphan, Portrait of a Missouri Moderate* (Columbia, Mo., 1997), 102.

45. Calvin, ed., *Emory Reports*, 31.

46. Gibson, *Journal of a Soldier*, 188; Edwards, *Marching with the Army*, 150; Calvin, ed., *Emory Reports*, 42; Hughes, *Doniphan's Expedition*, 67 (emphasis in the original).

47. Gibson, *Journal of a Soldier*, 187; Hughes, *Doniphan's Expedition*, 67; Calvin, ed., *Emory Reports*, 42; Edwards, *Marching with the Army*, 149; Clarke, ed., *Turner Journal*, 70.

48. Gibson, *Journal of a Soldier*, 188; Edwards, *Marching with the Army*, 148–49; Hughes, *Doniphan's Expedition*, 68–69. Regarding nineteenth-century American soldiers' attitudes toward disease, see Gerald E. Linderman, *Embattled Courage: The Experience of Combat in the American Civil War* (New York, 1987), 115–17; Reid Mitchell, *Civil War Soldiers: Their Expectations and Their Experiences* (New York, 1988), 60–61; and James M. McCaffrey, *Army of Manifest Destiny: The American Soldier in the Mexican War, 1846–1848* (New York, 1992), 52–65.

49. Edwards, *Marching with the Army*, 150–51; Doniphan paraphrased by Hughes, *Doniphan's Expedition*, 69–70.

50. It turned out that all of the rumors had a basis in fact, but the Mexican actions were uncoordinated and incomplete. Edwards, *Marching with the Army*, 149; Johnston, *Marching with the Army*, 98; Clarke, ed., *Turner Journal*, 70; Gibson, *Journal of a Soldier*, 192; Calvin, ed., *Emory Reports*, 47. The northward movement of Mexican dragoons was mentioned briefly by Emory ("Notes of a Military Reconnoissance [*sic*]," *Senate Executive Doc. No. 7*, Serial 505, p. 33) and is described in William A. DePalo Jr., *The Mexican National Army*,

1822–1852 (College Station, Tex., 1997), 107. Hughes's description of the countryside is in *Doniphan's Expedition*, 70.

51. Daniel Hastings Diary, August 14, 1846, Justin H. Smith Papers, Benson Latin American Collection, University of Texas–Austin (first quote); Gibson, *Journal of a Soldier*, 192 (second quote); Edwards, *Marching with the Army*, 153 (third quote); "E" to Friend James, August 24, 1846, Jefferson City *Inquirer*, September 29, 1846. See also St. Louis *Daily Missouri Republican*, September 24, 1846.

52. "bb" [Lt. Kribben] to Editor, St. Louis *Republican*, August 24, 1846, Mexican War Papers, MHS, St. Louis; Johnston, *Marching with the Army*, 98 (quote); Hughes, *Doniphan's Expedition*, 71.

53. Doniphan to D. C. Allen, September 19, 1883, Doniphan Papers, MHS, St. Louis; Henry Turner to wife [Julia Turner], August 14, 1846, Turner Collection, MHS, St. Louis; Johnston, *Marching with the Army*, 99; M. B. Edwards to Joe Edwards, August 23, 1846, Mexican War Papers, MHS, St. Louis.

54. Doniphan to D. C. Allen, September 19, 1883, Doniphan Papers, MHS, St. Louis; Calvin, ed., *Emory Reports*, 49.

55. Doniphan to Allen, September 19, 1883, Doniphan Papers, MHS, St. Louis; Launius, *Doniphan, Missouri Moderate*, 103.

56. Conversation recalled by Doniphan in Doniphan to D. C. Allen, September 20, 1883, Doniphan Papers, MHS, St. Louis. See also Hughes, *Doniphan's Expedition*, 69–71.

57. Doniphan recalled the matter of the proclamation in Doniphan to D. C. Allen, September 20, 1883, Doniphan Papers, MHS, St. Louis; Johnston, *Marching with the Army*, 100–101; Elliott, *Notes Taken*, 233; Hughes, *Doniphan's Expedition*, 71; Calvin, ed., *Emory Reports*, 49.

58. "bb" [Lt. Kribben] to Editor, St. Louis *Republican*, August 24, 1846, Mexican War Papers, MHS, St. Louis; Clarke, ed., *Turner Journal*, 72 n; Calvin, ed., *Emory Reports*, 53; Elliott, *Notes Taken*, 234–35; Johnston, *Marching with the Army*, 99; Hughes, *Doniphan's Expedition*, 75, 77–78; Waldo P. Johnson to William Waldo, August 24, 1846, in Waldo P. Johnson Papers, Joint Collection, Western Historical Manuscript Collection–State Historical Society of Missouri, University of Missouri–Columbia.

59. Hughes, *Doniphan's Expedition*, 69–70, 72, 76 (selling food); Edwards, *Marching with the Army*, 153; Johnston, *Marching with the Army*, 101–2. See also Robinson, *Journal*, 23, and Elliott, *Notes Taken*, 233, 237.

60. "E" to James Lusk, August 24? 1846, Jefferson City *Inquirer*, September 29, 1846 (first quote); "F" to Editor, September 2, 1846, ibid., October 13, 1846 (second quote); Thomas Edwards to Joe Edwards, September 15, 1846, Mexican War Papers, MHS, St. Louis (last quote). See also "M" to Editor, August 22, 1846, Jefferson City *Inquirer*, October 6, 1846; B. E. Lackland to T. Lackland, November 8, 1846, James C. Lackland Papers, MHS, St. Louis.

61. M. B. Edwards to Joe Edwards, August 23, 1846, Mexican War Papers, MHS, St. Louis; Hughes, *Doniphan's Expedition*, 78–79.

62. "Citizens of New Mexico to the President of Mexico [Regarding Gov. Armijo's Retreat]," in Moorhead, ed., "Notes and Documents," 74–75 (quote on 74); Manuel Armijo quoted in LeRoy R. Hafen et al., eds., *Ruxton of the Rockies* (Norman, Okla., 1950), 133; Calvin, ed., *Emory Reports*, 58. Within days of the fall of Santa Fe, Major General Pedro de Ampudia, commander of Mexico's Military Division of the North, urged the mayor of

Monterrey to join with him to fight General Zachary Taylor's army in order to prevent the national disgrace of failing to respond to another American invasion.

63. Johnston, *Marching with the Army*, 103; Elliott, *Notes Taken*, 237; Minge, "Frontier Problems in New Mexico," 330. See also the analysis by Howard Lamar, *The Far Southwest, 1846–1912, A Territorial History* (New Haven, Conn., 1966), 62; Launius, *Doniphan, Missouri Moderate*, 106 n. 20, 107.

Chapter 4. Military Government in Santa Fe and the Indian Treaties

1. Baltimore *Daily Republican & Argus*, September 9, 1846; Milwaukee *Daily Sentinel and Gazette*, September 14, 1846; Richmond, Va., *Enquirer*, October 6, 1846; Baltimore *Sun*, October 2, 5, 1846; Hartford, Conn., *Weekly Times*, September 12, October 10, 31, 1846; Washington *Daily Union*, October 3, 1846. See also Cincinnati *Daily Commercial*, September 30, October 1, 1846; New Orleans *Daily Picayune*, October 3, 1846; New York *Herald*, October 3, 1846; Philadelphia *North American*, October 19, 1846; New York *Tribune*, October 2, 1846.

2. An outstanding treatment of the U.S. Army's officer corps in the early nineteenth century, including its activities in the territories, is William B. Skelton, *An American Profession of Arms: The Army Officer Corps, 1784–1861* (Lawrence, Kans., 1992), esp. 68–86, 300–301; Robert V. Remini, *Andrew Jackson and the Course of American Empire* (New York, 1977), 308–15; Theodore Grivas, *Military Governments in California, 1846–1850* (Glendale, Calif., 1963), 30–31.

3. Grivas, *Military Governments*, 13–16 (quote on 16).

4. As Private John Hughes recorded in his diary: "Col. Doniphan left as Governor of the Territory of New Mexico." "Hughes Diary," August 31, 1846, in William E. Connelley, comp., *Doniphan's Expedition and the Conquest of New Mexico and California* (Topeka, 1907), 65. During the Mexican-American War, U.S. military officers served as interim administrators of martial law in occupied cities, such as Matamoros, Veracruz, and Mexico City, and military governors of another large conquered province, California.

5. Proclamation by Stephen W. Kearny, with same announcement in both English and Spanish, August 22, 1846 (emphasis added), filed in Benjamin M. Read Collection, New Mexico State Records Center, Santa Fe, also quoted in Ralph E. Twitchell, *The History of the Military Occupation of the Territory of New Mexico from 1846 to 1851* (Denver, 1909), 73–74; Army of the West, Order No. 13, August 17, 1846, Orders issued by Brig. Gen. Stephen Kearny and Brig. Gen. Sterling Price, 1846–1848, Microcopy T-1115, roll 1, Record Group (RG) 94, National Archives (NA); Kearny's Order No. 20, August 30, 1846, in Letters Received by the Office of the Adjutant General, Main Series, 1822–1860, Microcopy M-567, roll 319, RG 94, NA. See also Dwight L. Clarke, *Stephen Watts Kearny, Soldier of the West* (Norman, Okla., 1961), 146, 148.

6. Kearny to Sec. of War William L. Marcy, September 22, 1846, and Kearny to Adj. Gen. Roger Jones, August 24, 1846, in Letters Received by the Office of the Adjutant General, Main Series, 1822–1860, Microcopy M-567, roll 319, RG 94, NA; Milo M. Quaife, ed., *The Diary of James K. Polk 1845–1849*, 4 vols. (Chicago, 1910), 2:169, entry for October 2, 1846.

7. On Bent's background, see Harold H. Dunham, "Charles Bent," in LeRoy Hafen, ed., *The Mountain Men and the Fur Trade of the Far West: Biographical Sketches of the Participants*,

10 vols. (Glendale, Calif., 1965–1972), 2:27–48. Howard R. Lamar, *The Far Southwest, 1846–1912, A Territorial History* (New Haven, Conn., 1966), 64–65, 67; Kearny's announcement appointing Rivera, August 29, 1846, Kearny to Adj. Gen. Jones, September 1 and 22, 1846, Microcopy M-567, roll 319, RG 94, NA; John T. Hughes to Editor, September 25, 1846, Liberty, Mo., *Weekly Tribune* (hereafter Liberty *Tribune*), November 14, 1846; Isaac George, *Heroes and Incidents of the Mexican War, Containing Doniphan's Expedition* (Greensburg, Pa., 1903), 45.

8. Kearny to Adj. Gen. Jones, September 16, 1846, Microcopy M-567, roll 319, RG 94, NA; St. Louis *Daily Missouri Republican*, November 9, 1846 (hereafter St. Louis *Republican*); Liberty *Tribune*, September 26, 1846 (emphasis in the original). The overlapping combination of military government along with some civil officials would be duplicated during the 1860s in the federal army's Reconstruction duties in the Southern states and also in governing the island possessions of America's new empire of the 1890s. This sort of dual administration was another of the firsts of military government under Doniphan's direction that would be followed, though not acknowledged, in the years to come.

9. Waldo P. Johnson to William Waldo, August 24, 1846, Waldo P. Johnson Papers, Joint Collection, Western Historical Manuscript Collection–State Historical Society of Missouri, University of Missouri, Columbia (hereafter Joint Collection, WHMC–SHSM, UM–Columbia; emphasis added); Army of the West, Order No. 30, September 23, 1846, Microcopy T-1115, roll 1, RG 94, NA. Regarding Kearny's outlook and Wool's invasion plans, see K. Jack Bauer, *The Mexican War, 1846–1848* (New York, 1974), 136, 145–46. Although Polk outlined Wool's purpose in June, the expedition did not begin to take shape until August, about the time that Kearny and Doniphan entered Santa Fe.

10. Backgrounds: on Hall, see Connelley, comp., *Doniphan's Expedition*, 238–39 n, and *Biographical Directory of the American Congress, 1774–1989* (Washington, D.C., 1989), 1116; on Waldo, see Connelley, comp., *Doniphan's Expedition*, 133–34 n; on Blair, see Ezra J. Warner, *Generals in Blue: Lives of the Union Commanders* (Baton Rouge, La., 1964), 35–36.

11. Doniphan to Editor, September 4, 1846, Liberty *Tribune*, October 10, 1846.

12. Alexander W. Doniphan and Willard P. Hall, *Organic Law of the Territory of New Mexico* (Santa Fe, 1846; repr., Santa Fe, 1970), 4–5, 8–9, 11, 13. The booklet was also reprinted in *House Exec. Doc. No. 19*, Serial 499, 29th Cong., 2nd Sess., pp. 18–73. See also Lamar, *Far Southwest*, 64; Roger D. Launius, *Alexander William Doniphan, Portrait of a Missouri Moderate* (Columbia, Mo., 1997), 115.

13. Doniphan and Hall, *Organic Law of New Mexico*, 13 (capitalization in the original), 14–15, 79–80, and passim. See also Lamar, *Far Southwest*, 66; Twitchell, *Military Occupation of New Mexico*, 84; Doniphan interview, Santa Fe *Era Southwestern*, August 7, 1880; Grivas, *Military Governments*, 35–36; Army of the West, Order No. 20, August 30, 1846, Microcopy T-1115, roll 1, RG 94, NA; André P. Duchateau, "Missouri Colossus: Alexander William Doniphan, 1808–1887" (Ed.D. dissertation, Oklahoma State University, 1973), 142–44; David Y. Thomas, *A History of Military Government in Newly Acquired Territory of the United States* (New York, 1904), 105; William E. Daugherty and Marshall Andrews, *A Review of U.S. Historical Experience with Civil Affairs, 1776–1954* (Bethesda, Md., 1961), 56; John T. Hughes, *Doniphan's Expedition; Containing an Account of the Conquest of New Mexico . . .* (Cincinnati, 1847; repr., Chicago, 1962) 120–21; Kearny to Adjutant General, Washington, D.C., September 22, 1846, Microcopy M-567, roll 319, RG 94, NA.

14. Doniphan and Hall, *Organic Law of New Mexico,* 5 (emphasis added), 6, 7.

15. Kearny to Adjutant General, Washington, D.C., September 22, 1846 (emphasis added), Kearny to Adj. Gen. Jones, September 24, 1846, in Microcopy M-567, roll 319, RG 94, NA; William L. Marcy to Zachary Taylor, September 22, 1846, William L. Marcy Papers, Library of Congress; Baltimore *Niles National Register,* November 28, 1846; Richmond, Va., *Enquirer,* October 13, 1846. Most newspaper reports of events in Santa Fe naturally highlighted Kearny's role until his departure for California. The Detroit *Free Press* (October 24, 1846) noted that Kearny was leaving Doniphan in command in New Mexico.

16. Grivas, *Military Governments,* 35–36, called the code a "notable and lasting achievement." Writing from Kearny's point of view, Clarke, *Kearny,* 149–50, complimented the code for its practical utility and longevity and concluded that merely by signing the code, Kearny rose "above the plane of mere military command to the stature of statesmanship." See also Duchateau, "Missouri Colossus," 151; Launius, *Doniphan, Missouri Moderate,* 113–16.

17. St. Louis *Republican,* September 28, 1846; Detroit *Free Press,* October 28, 1846; Newark, N.J., *Daily Advertiser,* October 5, 1846; Richmond, Va., *Enquirer,* October 13, 1846.

18. *Congressional Globe,* 29th Cong., 2nd Sess., December 9–10, 1846, pp. 13–18, 20–23, December 17 (quotes on p. 33).

19. Marcy to Kearny, January 11, 1847, William L. Marcy Papers, Library of Congress; Quaife, ed., *Diary of James K. Polk,* 2:281–82, entry for December 19, 1846; James K. Polk, message to Congress, December 22, 1846, in James D. Richardson, *Messages and Papers of the Presidents, 1789–1897,* 10 vols. (Washington, D.C., 1897), 4:506–7. See also Twitchell, *Military Occupation of New Mexico,* 91; Thomas, *History of Military Government,* 106; Robert W. Larson, *New Mexico's Quest for Statehood, 1848–1912* (Albuquerque, 1968), 5–6. Political rights for residents of New Mexico were confirmed several months later when the United States officially acquired the conquered province by the terms of the Treaty of Guadalupe Hidalgo.

20. For a view indicating the arbitrariness of the military government in New Mexico, under both volunteers and Regulars, see Lamar, *Far Southwest,* 70–76. See also Larson, *New Mexico's Quest for Statehood,* 18–40; Robert W. Frazer, ed., *New Mexico in 1850: A Military View* (Norman, Okla., 1968).

21. Army of the West, Order No. 25, September 25, 1846, Microcopy T-1115, roll 1, RG 94, NA, detailed Ruff to the Regulars; William Hayter to H. Colman & Family, October 19, 1846, Colman-Hayter Collection, Joint Collection, WHMC–SHSM, UM–Columbia; Connelley, comp., *Doniphan's Expedition,* 249 n; Maj. Meriwether L. Clark to Kearny, September 21, 1846, in Meriwether Lewis Clark Letterbook, Beinecke Library, Yale University, New Haven, Conn.; Thomas L. Karnes, *William Gilpin, Western Nationalist* (Austin, 1970), 154–55; Hughes to Editor, September 25, 1846, Liberty *Tribune,* November 14, 1846; Hughes, *Doniphan's Expedition,* 255–56; Hughes to Editor William Switzer, October 8, 1846, Columbia *Missouri Statesman,* November 13, 1846 (hereafter cited as Columbia *Statesman*); *House Exec. Doc. No. 23,* Serial 599, 31st Cong., 2nd Sess., p. 6, refers to the appointment of Dr. J. F. Morton.

22. Thomas B. Hudson to James Clemens Jr. in St. Louis, August 24, 1846, in Mary C. Clemens Collection, Missouri Historical Society (MHS), St. Louis; Army of the West, Order No. 20, August 30, 1846, Order No. 25, September 17, 1846, Order No. 26, September 18, Order No. 30, September 23, 1846, Microcopy T-1115, roll 1, RG 94, NA; Hughes to Editor,

September 25, 1846, Liberty *Tribune*, November 14, 1846; Hughes, *Doniphan's Expedition*, 256–57; M. L. Clark to Gov. John Edwards, September 26, 1846, Clark Letterbook, Beinecke Library, Yale; Asst. Adj. Gen. Henry Turner to Sterling Price, October 2, 1846, Microcopy M-567, roll 319, RG 94, NA; Kearny to Adj. Gen. Jones, September 24, 1846, ibid.; Johnson to Waldo, August 24, 1846, Johnson Papers, Joint Collection, WHMC–SHSM, UM–Columbia; New Orleans *Daily Picayune*, November 17, 1846. It turned out that Wool left San Antonio in October, later than expected, and never pressed all the way to Chihuahua, but Doniphan was not sure of the general's location. Bauer, *Mexican War*, 146–49.

23. Kearny to Adj. Gen. Jones, September 24, 1846, Microcopy M-567, roll 319, RG 94, NA; Kearny Proclamation, October 5, 1846, ibid.; Anonymous soldier to Editors, November 25, 1846, St. Louis *Republican*, December 5, 1846; Daniel Hastings Diary, n.d. [November 1846?], Justin H. Smith Papers, Benson Latin American Collection, University of Texas–Austin (UT–Austin).

24. Hughes to Editors, September 25, 1846, Liberty *Tribune*, November 14, 1846; William C. Kennerly, *Persimmon Hill: A Narrative of Old St. Louis and the Far West* (Norman, Okla., 1948), 190; Ralph E. Twitchell, *The Story of the Conquest of Santa Fe, New Mexico, and the Building of Old Fort Marcy* (Albuquerque, 1922), 35–38; Hughes, *Doniphan's Expedition*, 122–23; Ross Calvin, ed., *Lieutenant Emory Reports* (Albuquerque, 1951), 57.

25. Hughes to Editors, September 25, 1846, Liberty *Tribune*, November 14, 1846; Santa Fe *Republican*, September 24, 1847; Thomas Fitzpatrick to "Dear Campbell" (Col. Robert Campbell, aide to Gov. Edwards), September 3, 1846, St. Louis *Weekly Reveille*, October 26, 1846; "F" to Editor, September 2, 1846, Jefferson City, Mo., *Weekly Inquirer* (hereafter Jefferson City *Inquirer*), October 13, 1846 (food quote); Hughes to Editor William Switzler, Columbia *Statesman*, October, 8, 1846; "John Brown" [Lt. Richard S. Elliott] to St. Louis *Reveille*, October 30, 1846, in Mark L. Gardner and Marc Simmons, eds., *The Mexican War Correspondence of Richard Smith Elliott* (Norman, Okla., 1997), 87–90.

26. "John Brown" [Lt. Elliott] to St. Louis *Reveille*, September 4, 1846, in Gardner and Simmons, eds., *Correspondence of Elliott*, 80; Hastings Diary, n.d. [August 1846?], Justin Smith Papers, Benson Collection, UT–Austin; "F" to Editor, September 2, 1846, Jefferson City *Inquirer*, October 13, 1846; "E" to James Lusk, October ? 1846, ibid., November 17, 1846; "E" to Lusk, August 24? 1846, ibid., September 29, 1846; Thomas Hudson to James Clemens, August 24, 1846, Clemens Collection, MHS, St. Louis.

27. Hudson to Clemens, August 24, 1846, Clemens Collection, MHS, St. Louis; Hughes to Editors, October 29, 1846, Liberty *Tribune*, January 2, 1847; "John Brown" [Lt. Elliott] to St. Louis *Reveille*, October 25, November 1, 10, 15, 1846, in Gardner and Simmons, eds., *Correspondence of Elliott*, 83, 92–93, 107–8, 109–10.

28. Philip St. George Cooke, *The Conquest of New Mexico and California: An Historical and Personal Narrative* (New York, 1878; repr., Oakland, Calif., 1942), 39.

29. Hastings Diary, August 14, 1846, and n.d. [September 1846?], Justin Smith Papers, Benson Collection, UT–Austin; New Orleans *Daily Picayune*, June 23, 1847.

30. George R. Gibson, *Journal of a Soldier under Kearny and Doniphan, 1846–1847*, ed. Ralph P. Bieber (Glendale, Calif., 1935), 370; George F. Ruxton, *Adventures in Mexico and the Rocky Mountains* (New York, 1855), 197; "bb" [Lt. Christian Kribben] to Editor, September 26, 1846, St. Louis *Republican*, November 17, 1846. Other criticisms of the volunteers' behavior can be found in Roswell S. Ripley, *The War with Mexico*, 2 vols. (New York, 1849), 1:447; Justin H. Smith, *The War with Mexico*, 2 vols. (New York, 1919), 2:216–17; Thomas,

History of Military Government, 158. See also Hubert H. Bancroft, *History of Arizona and New Mexico, 1530–1888* (San Francisco, 1889; repr., Albuquerque, 1962), 431.

31. Hughes to Editor, September 25, 1846, Liberty *Tribune*, November 14, 1846; Hughes to Editor William Switzler, Columbia *Statesman*, October 8, 1846; Kennerly, *Persimmon Hill*, 191; Hastings Diary, August 21, 1846, Justin Smith Papers, Benson Collection, UT–Austin; Richard S. Elliott, *Notes Taken in Sixty Years* (St. Louis, 1883), 249–50.

32. Hughes to Editors, September 25, 1846, Liberty *Tribune*, November 14, 1846; Hastings Diary, n.d. [August–September 1846], Justin Smith Papers, Benson Collection, UT–Austin; Kennerly, *Persimmon Hill*, 191.

33. Hughes to Editor, October 14, 1846, Liberty *Tribune*, November 14, 1846; Twitchell, *Military Occupation of New Mexico*, 95. See also Robert E. Shalhope, *Sterling Price: Portrait of a Southerner* (Columbia, Mo., 1971), 59, 62; "bb" [Lt. Kribben] to Editor, September 26, 1846, St. Louis *Republican*, November 17, 1846; and Kennerly, *Persimmon Hill*, 190, 193. For the Mormon Battalion in Santa Fe see Norma B. Ricketts, *The Mormon Battalion, U.S. Army of the West, 1846–1848* (Logan, Utah, 1996), 62–71.

34. Clarke, *Kearny*, 155; Headquarters, Army of the West, Orders No. 15, 17, August 19, 26, 1846, Microcopy T-1115, roll 1, RG 94, NA; Hughes to Editors, September 25, 1846, Liberty *Tribune*, November 14, 1846.

35. Headquarters, Army of the West, Order No. 28, September 19, 1846, Microcopy T-1115, roll 1, RG 94, NA.

36. Army of the West, Orders No. 23 and 30, September 15 and 23, 1846, Special Order No. 7, September 16, 1846, Microcopy T-1115, roll 1, RG 94, NA; Doniphan to Editor, September 4, 1846, and January 4, 1847, in Liberty *Tribune*, October 10, 1846, and April 10, 1847, respectively; Doniphan to Sec. of War William Marcy, October 20, 1846, filed with U.S. Army, Adjutant General's Office, Letters Received, 1805–1889, Microcopy M-567, roll 314, RG 94, NA; Bent's estimate in "Indians in Oregon, California, and New Mexico," *House Executive Document No. 76*, Serial 521, 30th Cong., 1st Sess., p. 11. An excellent overview of Doniphan and the Indians is Launius, *Doniphan, Missouri Moderate*, 118–33.

37. Hughes to Editor, September 20, 1846, Liberty *Tribune*, November 14, 1846; Hughes to Editor, October 20, 1846, ibid., December 5, 1846. "E" to James Lusk, October 12, 1846, Jefferson City *Inquirer*, November 24, 1846, shared Hughes's view that the Indians would "give us more trouble than the Mexicans." See also the analysis in Frank McNitt, *Navajo Wars: Military Campaigns, Slave Raids, and Reprisals* (Albuquerque, 1972), 120.

38. Kearny to Doniphan, Army of the West, Order No. 32, October 2, 1846, Microcopy T-1115, roll 1, RG 94, NA; Hughes to Editor William Switzler, October 8, 1846, Columbia *Statesman*, November 13, 1846; Captain of Volunteers, *The Conquest of Santa Fe and Subjugation of New Mexico* (Philadelphia, 1847), 25–26. See also James M. Cutts, *The Conquest of California and New Mexico* (Philadelphia, 1847; repr., Albuquerque, 1965), 67; Twitchell, *Military Occupation of New Mexico*, 96, 98, 100; William A. Keleher, *Turmoil in New Mexico, 1846–1848* (Santa Fe, 1952), 25; McNitt, *Navajo Wars*, 100, 117.

39. Doniphan to Sec. of War William Marcy, October 20, 1846, Microcopy M-567, roll 314, RG 94, NA; Capt. William McKissack to QM Gen. Thomas Jesup, October 6, 1846, Records of the Office of the Quartermaster General, Consolidated Correspondence File, 1794–1915, RG 92, NA, also quoted in McNitt, *Navajo Wars*, 106; Hughes, *Doniphan's Expedition*, 163. See also Launius, *Doniphan, Missouri Moderate*, 123–25. Bear Spring is near modern Gallup, New Mexico.

40. Doniphan to Sec. of War William Marcy, October 20, 1846, Microcopy M-567, roll 314, RG 94, NA; Hughes, *Doniphan's Expedition*, 176; Karnes, *William Gilpin*, 157–63; and Duchateau, "Missouri Colossus," 157–64.

41. Hughes, *Doniphan's Expedition*, 145–46, 150, 179–80, summarizes soldiers' complaints; Jacob S. Robinson, *A Journal of the Santa Fe Expedition under Colonel Doniphan*, ed. Carl L. Cannon (Princeton, 1932), 59; McNitt, *Navajo Wars*, 113–16; Launius, *Doniphan, Missouri Moderate*, 125–26.

42. Hughes, *Doniphan's Expedition*, 181–85; Launius, *Doniphan, Missouri Moderate*, 126–27.

43. Doniphan, quoted in Hughes, *Doniphan's Expedition*, 186.

44. Quoted in Hughes, *Doniphan's Expedition* (quotes on 187–88; original emphasis ["our war"], but emphasis added ["If New Mexico be really in your possession"]); also quoted in McNitt, *Navajo Wars*, 118. The scene is also portrayed by Launius, *Doniphan, Missouri Moderate*, 128–30.

45. Doniphan to Adj. Gen. Roger Jones, n.d., *Senate Exec. Doc. No. 1*, Serial 503, 30th Cong., 1st Sess., p. 496. A summary of the treaty is found in McNitt, *Navajo Wars*, 119. The treaty is neither included in the comprehensive *Indian Affairs. Laws and Treaties*, Charles J. Kappler, comp. and ed., *Senate Doc. No. 319*, Serial 4624, 58th Cong., 2nd Sess., nor discussed in Francis P. Prucha, *American Indian Treaties: A History of a Political Anomaly* (Berkeley, Calif., 1994).

46. New York *Evening Post*, March 4, 1847; "John Brown" [Lt. Elliott] to St. Louis *Reveille*, December 6, 1846, in Gardner and Simmons, eds., *Correspondence of Elliott*, 121–22; the ambush is described in Hughes, *Doniphan's Expedition*, 155–56. See also Major Clark's report of the campaign to Governor Edwards of Missouri, November 14, 1846, in Clark Letterbook, Beinecke Library, Yale. Writing after the war, and issuing one of his few compliments to volunteers, Lieutenant Roswell Ripley concluded that Doniphan's Indian campaign had produced a "useful" treaty. Indeed, Ripley contended that the best result of the entire Doniphan expedition "was the [U.S.] display of force in the Navajoe [*sic*] country." Ripley, *War with Mexico*, 2:247.

47. While a number of scholars have covered aspects of Doniphan's Navajo campaign, none have considered it in relation to his being an officer with responsibilities in a de facto military government. Historians have pointed out that Doniphan's Navajo treaty carried no long-term success. Both Hubert Howe Bancroft and Justin H. Smith saw no benefits from Doniphan's diplomacy among the Indians. Bancroft contended that the treaty "had no effect whatever," and that the Navajos soon renewed their raiding (Bancroft, *History of Arizona and New Mexico*, 463). Smith maintained that the "Indians continued their depredations as if no treaties had been made." Smith, *War with Mexico*, 2:217. Francis P. Prucha, *The Great Father: The United States Government and the American Indians*, 2 vols. (Lincoln, 1984), 1:367, noted, "It did not take long for Indian unrest to reappear." See also Robert A. Trennert, *Alternative to Extinction: Federal Indian Policy and the Beginnings of the Reservation System, 1846–1851* (Philadelphia, 1975), 103; Edward H. Spicer, *Cycles of Conquest: The Impact of Spain, Mexico, and the United States on the Indians of the Southwest, 1533–1960* (Tucson, 1962), 214–16; Keleher, *Turmoil*, 26.

48. Charles Bent to James Buchanan, December 26, 1846, *House Exec. Doc. No. 70*, Serial 521, 30th Cong., 1st Sess., p. 17. A soldier in Sterling Price's 2nd Missouri Regiment noted: "Rumors are rife here of an intended insurrection among the [Mexican] people . . . and we are

preparing to meet it in case it should happen, but I believe that there is no foundation for the report." "T" [Robert B. Todd] to Editor William Switzler, Columbia *Statesman*, October 25, 1846. Col. George A. McCall, writing a postwar report, recommended a significant allocation of the Regular Army (about three regiments) as a minimum garrison for New Mexico—about 2,450 of the army's 10,950 soldiers in 1850. Frazer, ed., *New Mexico in 1850*, 183.

49. Robert E. May, *John A. Quitman, Old South Crusader* (Baton Rouge, La., 1985), 187, 194–98; Smith, *War with Mexico*, 2:164, 166–68, 223–32.

50. See Neal Harlow, *California Conquered: War and Peace on the Pacific, 1846–1850* (Berkeley, Calif., 1982), passim. See also Frazer, ed., *New Mexico in 1850*, passim. Half a century later, the United States became embroiled in another overseas war that required the army to operate military governments in conquered enemy lands. U.S. administrators searched through the army's experience in civil affairs and rediscovered the actions of Kearny, Doniphan, and other officers who had served in military government during and after the Mexican-American War. Americans, especially army officers, saw value in studying the events of the 1840s for the military responsibilities of the 1890s and the early twentieth century. Taking a more professional attitude toward the operation of military government in conquered territory indicated the maturing of the U.S. Army. Charles Magoon, a civilian lawyer with the Bureau of Insular Affairs, assembled a remarkable seven-hundred-page tome entitled *Reports of the Law of Civil Government in Territory Subject to Military Occupation by the Military Forces of the United States*, known informally as *Magoon's Reports*. Magoon reached back more than fifty years to cite historical examples of military government in New Mexico and California to provide guidance for officials of U.S. military governments operating after the Spanish-American War in Cuba, Puerto Rico, the Philippines, and Guam. Magoon noted that the new "military governments under consideration [in America's new island possessions] were established to deal with conditions resulting from successful invasion" of enemy territory during wartime, exactly as had been the case with the wartime governments established in Santa Fe and California. Magoon's references to New Mexico and California clearly pointed out to U.S. Army officers that their predecessors had taken similar steps prior to 1898–1899, and those initial steps bolstered the legal foundation for writing colonial regulations and laws, administering individual cities and entire colonies, and negotiating with indigenous peoples. Doniphan's example instructed a new generation of American military officers. See Charles E. Magoon, *Reports on the Law of Civil Government in Territory Subject to Military Occupation by the Military Forces of the United States* (Washington, D.C., 1903), 16. See also Daugherty and Andrews, *Review of U.S. Historical Experience with Civil Affairs*, 54–59, who indicate that the actions of Kearny and Doniphan in New Mexico provided the early building blocks in the American experience with military government.

51. "bb" [Lt. Kribben] to Editor, September 26, 1846, St. Louis *Republican*, November 17, 1846; "John Brown" [Lt. Elliott] to St. Louis *Reveille*, November 7, 1846, in Gardner and Simmons, eds., *Correspondence of Elliott*, 106; Doniphan to Brig. Gen. John Wool, March 20, 1847, quoted in Connelley, comp., *Doniphan's Expedition*, 454.

52. "bb" [Lt. Kribben] to Editor, October 20, 1846, St. Louis *Republican*, November 28, 1846; [Samuel C.] Owens and [James] Aull to Editor, Independence, Mo., *Expositor*, quoted in Fayette, Mo., *Boon's Lick Times*, December 12, 1846; Chicago *Daily Journal*, March 4, 1847. See also St. Louis *Republican*, December 5, 1846; Hughes to Editors, September 25, 1846, Liberty *Tribune*, November 14, 1846.

Chapter 5. The Battle at Brazito

1. Army of the West, Order No. 30, September 23, 1846, Orders of Brig. Gen. Stephen W. Kearny and Brig. Gen. Sterling Price, Microcopy T-1115, roll 1, Record Group (RG) 94, National Archives (NA), Washington, D.C.

2. A Georgian, Thompson graduated from the U.S. Military Academy thirty-sixth of fifty-six cadets in 1835, but he had been delayed one year for academic deficiencies. He went into the dragoons and did well to reach the rank of captain eleven years after graduation. Wooster, from New York, graduated from West Point thirty-first of fifty members of the Class of 1837. He served with artillery units and was promoted to first lieutenant in 1842. Armstrong, from Ohio, graduated twenty-second of forty-one cadets in the Academy Class of 1845, becoming an officer only a few months before the war began. George W. Cullum, *Biographical Register of the Officers and Graduates of the United States Military Academy*, 3 vols., 3rd ed. (Boston, 1891), 1:126, 616, 687; Francis B. Heitman, *Historical Register and Dictionary of the United States Army*, 2 vols. (Washington, D.C., 1903), 1:169, 957, 1060.

3. This analysis is based partly on the appraisal of Civil War volunteer colonels by T. Harry Williams, *Hayes of the Twenty-third: The Civil War Volunteer Officer* (New York, 1965), 18–38. Williams's applicable chapter is entitled "The Good Colonels," and his discussion is applicable to volunteer officers throughout the nineteenth century. For the Mexican War, see Richard Bruce Winders, *Mr. Polk's Army: The American Military Experience in the Mexican War* (College Station, Tex., 1997), 61, 81–82, 84–87. The first soldier quotation is from Frank S. Edwards, *A Campaign in New Mexico with Colonel Doniphan* (Philadelphia, 1847), 76; the second is from William B. McGroarty, ed., "William H. Richardson's Journal of Doniphan's Expedition," *Missouri Historical Review (MHR)* 22 (July 1928), 535.

4. By the summer of 1847 Doniphan was exhausted, and his poor health was probably the major reason he did not sign on to fight for the duration of the war. See chapter 10 regarding Doniphan's health in the postwar years.

5. "Hughes Diary," in William E. Connelley, comp., *Doniphan's Expedition and the Conquest of New Mexico and California* (Topeka, 1907), 91; John T. Hughes, *Doniphan's Expedition; Containing an Account of the Conquest of New Mexico . . .* (Cincinnati, 1847; repr., Chicago, 1962), 255–56, 281 n.

6. El Paso del Norte is modern Juaréz, Mexico. "Grumbling" noted by Jacob S. Robinson, *A Journal of the Santa Fe Expedition under Colonel Doniphan*, ed. Carl Cannon (Princeton, 1932), 65; Doniphan to Adj. Gen. Roger Jones, March 4, 1847, *Senate Exec. Doc. No. 1*, Serial 503, 30th Cong., 1st Sess., p. 497; Maj. Meriwether L. Clark to Doniphan, December 14, 1846, in M. L. Clark Letterbook, Western Manuscripts Collection, Beinecke Library, Yale University, New Haven, Conn.; the expression of confidence is in an anonymous letter, December 14, 1846, in St. Louis *Daily Missouri Republican*, February 20, 1847. See also Capt. W.M.D. McKissack, QM at Santa Fe, to Maj. Gen. Thomas Jesup, QM Gen., Washington, D.C., January 9, 1847, who alludes to Major Clark's preparations making him ready by December 26, but Colonel Sterling Price delayed Clark's departure due to the threat of unrest in New Mexico. Office of the Quartermaster Gen., Quartermaster Consolidated Correspondence File, Box 515, RG 92, NA; and George R. Gibson, *Journal of a Soldier under Kearny and Doniphan, 1846–1847*, ed. Ralph P. Bieber (Glendale, Calif., 1935), 323.

7. James Glasgow to sister Sue, December 10, 1846, in Mark L. Gardner, ed., *Brothers on the Santa Fe and Chihuahua Trails* (Niwot, Colo., 1993), 101; Connelley, comp., *Doniphan's*

Expedition, 196–98 n; Hughes, *Doniphan's Expedition*, 256; Stella M. Drumm, ed., *Down the Santa Fe Trail and into Mexico: The Diary of Susan Shelby Magoffin, 1846–1847* (New Haven, Conn., 1926), 161, 169.

8. Copy of Trías Proclamation of November 9, 1846, in John T. Hughes to Robert H. Miller, Robert H. Miller Papers, Missouri Historical Society (MHS), St. Louis. The proclamation was printed in American newspapers; see, for example, New Orleans *Daily Picayune*, January 9, 1847.

9. Price's order in appendix, Gibson, *Journal of a Soldier*, 371; departure date in McGroarty, ed., "Richardson's Journal," *MHR* (April 1928), 340; Hughes, *Doniphan's Expedition*, 256–57. On Mitchell's background see Ray H. Mattison, "David Dawson Mitchell," in LeRoy R. Hafen, ed., *The Mountain Men and the Fur Trade of the Far West*, 10 vols. (Glendale, Calif., 1965–1972), 2:241–46.

10. "John Brown" [Lt. Elliott] to St. Louis *Reveille*, December 3, 1846, in Mark L. Gardner and Marc Simmons, eds., *The Mexcian War Correspondence of Richard Smith Elliott* (Norman, Okla., 1997), 114–16; Connelley, comp., *Doniphan's Expedition*, 365–68 n; McGroarty, ed., "Richardson's Journal," *MHR* (April 1928), 341; Gibson, *Journal of a Soldier*, 292.

11. Brodie Crouch, *Jornada Del Muerto: A Pageant of the Desert* (Spokane, Wash., 1989), 44–45, 48–49; Hughes, *Doniphan's Expedition*, 257; Edwards, *Campaign in New Mexico*, 76. The mention of snow is in ibid., 72; McGroarty, ed., "Richardson's Journal," *MHR* (April 1928), 341; Gibson, *Journal of a Soldier*, 282, 296. Another contemporary, Dr. Frederick Wislizenus, related that "Jornada del Muerto means, literally, the day's journey of the dead man, and refers to an old tradition that the first traveller who attempted to cross it in one day perished in it." Frederick A. Wislizenus, *Memoir of a Tour to Northern Mexico Connected with Col. Doniphan's Expedition in 1846 and 1847 (Senate Misc. Doc. No. 26*, Serial 511, 30th Cong., 1st Sess.; repr., Glorieta, N.M., 1969), 38. See also Roger D. Launius, *Alexander William Doniphan, Portrait of a Missouri Moderate* (Columbia, Mo., 1997), 137, 139.

12. Hughes, *Doniphan's Expedition*, 257–58; "Hughes Diary," in Connelley, comp., *Doniphan's Expedition*, 86–87; Doniphan to Adj. Gen. Roger Jones, March 4, 1847, *Senate Exec. Doc. No. 1*, Serial 503, 30th Cong., 1st Sess., p. 497; McGroarty, ed., "Richardson's Journal," *MHR* (April 1928), 343–44; Gibson, *Journal of a Soldier*, 292–94.

13. Hughes, *Doniphan's Expedition*, 257–58 (first quote); William R. Franklin to Editor, January 27, 1847, Liberty *Weekly Tribune*, April 10, 1847 (second quote); McGroarty, ed., "Richardson's Journal," *MHR* (April 1928), 341–42; Abraham R. Johnston, Marcellus B. Edwards, and Philip G. Ferguson, *Marching with the Army of the West, 1846–1848*, ed. Ralph P. Beiber (Glendale, Calif., 1936), 216–22 (hereafter [soldier's name], *Marching with the Army*).

14. Edwards, *Marching with the Army*, 223–25; Edwards, *Campaign in New Mexico*, 76–79, 81; Robinson, *Journal*, 64–65; Gibson, *Journal of a Soldier*, 297–98; Hughes, *Doniphan's Expedition*, 258.

15. Gibson, *Journal of a Soldier*, 298 (quote); see also Edwards, *Marching with the Army*, 227–28; Robinson, *Journal*, 46; LeRoy R. Hafen, Clyde Porter, and Mae Reed Porter, eds., *Ruxton of the Rockies* (Norman, Okla., 1950), 168.

16. Hafen, Porter, and Porter, eds., *Ruxton of the Rockies*, 169–70, 168 (concluding quote). While Ruxton appropriately criticized the volunteers' indiscipline, he also acknowledged their morale, a crucial element in their campaign's success. Of course, morale, what Clausewitz called "military spirit," is a vital factor for all military units. Likewise, Jomini placed great

weight on morale, agreeing that "it is the morale of armies, as well as of nations, more than anything else, which makes victories and their results decisive." Antoine Henri de Jomini, *The Art of War*, trans. G. H. Mendell and W. P. Craighill (Philadelphia, 1862; repr., Westport, Conn., 1971), 178. Clausewitz calculated that the elements of "bravery, adaptability, stamina, and enthusiasm" melded into the compound of "military spirit"; during the war so far, Doniphan and his volunteers had demonstrated each of these elements, and they would be called upon to show them more often in the future. Various factors went into calculating and affecting national military spirit, of course, but Clausewitz considered that two were paramount: "The first is a series of victorious wars; the second, frequent exertions of the army to the utmost limits of its strength." By this stage of American national development, the U.S. military had not posted a "series of victorious wars," but during 1846, at least, American arms had scored a series of individual victories over Mexican forces, and this spirit of victory contributed to the Missourians' morale during their invasion of Mexico. Moreover, the 1st Missouri Regiment had demonstrated its strength and stamina by marching across the Plains and mountains to Santa Fe, a physical accomplishment that certainly built the regiment's feeling of unity and success. As Clausewitz termed it, "A soldier is just as proud of the hardships he has overcome as of the dangers he has faced." Carl von Clausewitz, *On War*, ed. and trans. Michael Howard and Peter Paret (Princeton, 1976), 188–89.

17. Hughes, *Doniphan's Expedition*, 258–59; Edwards, *Campaign in New Mexico*, 80–81; Gibson, *Journal of a Soldier*, 299.

18. Colonel Antonio Ponce de León's name is rendered in different ways by different authors. The style followed here is based on *Diccionario Porrua: De história, biografía y geografía de México* (Mexico, D.F., 1964), 817.

19. Isaac George, *Heroes and Incidents of the Mexican War* (Greensburg, Pa., 1903), 67. The strength of the Mexican force varies with the source. Putting it at about 1,200 were Robinson, *Journal*, 67; Edwards, *Campaign in New Mexico*, 87; and Mr. Murray to Editor, Liberty *Tribune*, March 13, 1847. Lieutenant Christian Kribben estimated 1,100 Mexicans (Kribben to Maj. M. L. Clark, December 26, 1846, in Clark Letterbook, Beinecke Library, Yale, quoted in Gibson, *Journal of a Soldier*, 303). Gibson himself put the number of Mexicans somewhat lower than the others, between 800 and 1,000 (ibid., 308). Doniphan recalled a figure of about 1,300 (Doniphan interview, Santa Fe *Era Southwestern*, August 5, 1880), an estimate supported by John Hughes (Hughes, *Doniphan's Expedition*, 261). Most of those making estimates split the Mexican force between regulars (around 500 to 600) and militia or National Guard (the remainder). The quotation on the Mexican observation is from Ramón Alcaraz et al., *The Other Side; or Notes for the History of the War between Mexico and the United States*, trans. Albert C. Ramsey (New York, 1850; repr., New York, 1970), 169, but the colonel had stated a total of 1,220 in his postbattle report to Adjutant General Jones (Doniphan to Jones, March 4, 1847, *Senate Exec. Doc. No. 1*, Serial 503, 30th Cong., 1st Sess., p. 498). The Missouri scouts and inspection are mentioned by Edwards, *Marching with the Army*, 227, and Gibson, *Journal of a Soldier*, 299. Gibson seemed to offer contradictory observations that although "all things have been made ready for a fight" the return to a loose line of march after the inspection meant that the Missourians were "not expecting to meet the enemy" (ibid., 299, 300). The claim of killing two Mexican scouts is from William Gilpin to T. Tasker Gantt, January 12, 1847, in St. Louis *Weekly Reveille*, May 10, 1847. See also John Hughes to Editor, January 4, 1847, Liberty *Tribune*, April 10, 1847; and Lt. Robert B. Todd to Editor

William Switzler, February 2, 1847, in Columbia *Missouri Statesman*, April 16, 1847 (hereafter Columbia *Statesman*).

20. George, *Heroes and Incidents*, 67–68; Hughes to Editor, January 4, 1847, Liberty *Tribune*, April 10, 1847; Edwards, *Marching with the Army*, 228–29; McGroarty, ed., "Richardson's Journal," *MHR* (April 1928), 346; T. L. Edwards to Joe Edwards, January 26, 1847, Mexican War Papers, MHS, St. Louis; Lt. Robert Todd to Editor William Switzler, February 2, 1847, in Columbia *Statesman*, April 16, 1847.

21. The difficulty of locating the Brazito battlefield is addressed in George Ruhlen, "Brazito—The Only Battle in the Southwest between American and Foreign Troops," *Password: The Quarterly Journal of the El Paso County Historical Society* 2 (February 1957), 4–13; Ruhlen, "The Battle of Brazito: Where Was It Fought?" ibid., 2 (May 1957), 53–60; Andrew Armstrong, "The Brazito Battlefield," *New Mexico Historical Review* 35 (January 1960), 63–74; and Charles M. Haecker, "Brazito Battlefield: Once Lost, Now Found," *New Mexico Historical Review* 72 (July 1997), 229–38. The "potato patch" description is from "A Lieutenant" [Lucian J. Eastin?] to Jefferson City, Mo., *Weekly Inquirer* (hereafter Jefferson City *Inquirer*), April 17, 1847. Versions of the card game are in Edwards, *Marching with the Army*, 229, and Hughes, *Doniphan's Expedition*, 261 (quote).

22. George, *Heroes and Incidents*, 68; Edwards, *Campaign in New Mexico*, 82–83; Edwards, *Marching with the Army*, 229–31; McGroarty, ed., "Richardson's Journal," *MHR* (April 1928), 346; Gibson, *Journal of a Soldier*, 298. Under the pressure of the moment, a few of the slaves with the regiment may have been armed and pressed into service. See Phillip T. Tucker, "Above and Beyond: African-American Missourians of Colonel Alexander Doniphan's Expedition," *Password: The Quarterly Journal of the El Paso County Historical Society* 35 (Fall 1990), 135.

23. The Mexican order of battle is described in Alcaraz, *Other Side*, 170. Quotes, in order, Edwards, *Campaign in New Mexico*, 83; Edwards, *Marching with the Army*, 230–32; Hughes, *Doniphan's Expedition*, 261; Lieutenant Kribben, quoted in Liberty *Tribune*, February 27, 1847. See also Hughes to Editor, January 4, 1847, ibid., April 10, 1847.

24. Lieutenant Lara is identified by name in "bb" [Lt. Kribben] to Editor, March 5, 1847, St. Louis *Republican*, May 19, 1847. Several Missouri veterans recalled the "Black Flag incident," each using somewhat different reconstructed dialogue to relate the exchange between the officers. Doniphan's view is presented in his report to Adj. Gen. Roger Jones, March 4, 1847, *Senate Exec. Doc. No. 1*, Serial 503, 30th Cong., 1st Sess., p. 497. See also Edwards, *Campaign in New Mexico*, 84; Edwards, *Marching with the Army*, 230; Gibson, *Journal of a Soldier*, 304 (picture of flag opposite p. 300); Hughes, *Doniphan's Expedition*, 262; McGroarty, ed., "Richardson's Journal," *MHR* (April 1928), 346; George, *Heroes and Incidents*, 69–70; Lt. Kribben to Maj. Clark, December 26, 1846, Clark Letterbook, Yale; Mr. Murray to Editor, Liberty *Tribune*, March 13, 1847. Major Gilpin summarized the confrontation succinctly: the Mexicans pledged, "We will destroy you and give you no quarter." Gilpin to T. Tasker Gantt, January 12, 1847, in St. Louis *Weekly Reveille*, May 10, 1847. Another sketch of the Black Flag itself is found in Valentine M. Porter, "A History of Battery 'A' of St. Louis: With an Account of the Early Artillery Companies from Which It Is Descended," *Missouri Historical Society Collections* 2 (1905), 15. See also Launius, *Doniphan, Missouri Moderate*, 146.

25. In his report of the battle, Doniphan acknowledged that Captain Thompson "acted as my aid [*sic*] and advisor, and was of the most essential service in forming the line during the

engagement." Doniphan to U.S. Army Adj. Gen. Roger Jones, March 4, 1847, *Senate Exec. Doc. No. 1*, Serial 503, 30th Cong., 1st Sess., p. 498, also quoted in Connelley, comp., *Doniphan's Expedition*, 378 n. Gibson was more emphatic: "Thompson was consulted upon all occasions, and his opinion followed throughout." *Journal of a Soldier*, 307. Gilpin to Gantt, January 12, 1847, in St. Louis *Weekly Reveille*, May 10, 1847, indicates that it took twenty minutes to form the Missouri companies.

26. F. M. Gallaher, ed., "Official [Mexican] Report of the Battle of Temascalitos (Brazito)," *New Mexico Historical Review* 3 (October 1928), 387, gives the perspective of Colonel León (hereafter Gallaher, ed., "Official Report of Temascalitos"). See also Hughes, *Doniphan's Expedition*, 265; McGroarty, ed., "Richardson's Journal," *MHR* (April 1928), 347; and Doniphan's report to Adj. Gen. Jones, March 4, 1847, *Senate Exec. Doc. No. 1*, Serial 503, 30th Cong., 1st Sess., pp. 497–98.

27. How the battle at Brazito developed from the American point of view is drawn from Doniphan to Adj. Gen. Jones, March 4, 1847, also in Connelley, comp., *Doniphan's Expedition*, 377 n; Gibson, *Journal of a Soldier*, 300, 305; Edwards, *Campaign in New Mexico*, 84–85; Mr. Murray to Liberty *Tribune*, March 13, 1847; Doniphan interview, Santa Fe *Era Southwestern*, August 5, 1880; Edwards, *Marching with the Army*, 231–33; McGroarty, ed., "Richardson's Journal," *MHR* (April 1928), 347; William Franklin to Editor, January 29, 1847, Liberty *Tribune*, April 10, 1847.

28. Gibson, *Journal of a Soldier*, 305, mentions that Doniphan, Thompson, and Mitchell gathered in a command cluster, but he makes no mention of Lieutenant Wooster being with them. In an interview two days after the battle, a civilian revealed that the lack of American gunfire made the Mexicans believe the Americans might be surrendering. Ibid., 310. Making the elbow, the Mexican shouts, and faltering infantry, see Edwards, *Marching with the Army*, 232–33; and Lt. Robert Todd to Editor William Switzler, Columbia *Statesman*, April 16, 1847.

29. Edwards, *Marching with the Army*, 233–34; Lt. Kribben to Maj. Clark, quoted in Gibson, *Journal of a Soldier*, 303; Maj. Gilpin's description in St. Louis *Weekly Reveille*, May 10, 1847; Francisco R. Almada, *Resumen de Historia del Estado de Chihuahua* (Mexico City, 1955), 224; León's view is in Gallahar, ed., "Official Report of Temascalitos," 388. After the battle some Mexican regulars contended that militia and volunteers from El Paso del Norte were the first to break ranks and leave the field, making the regulars' position untenable. However, based on the descriptions by American veterans, it appears that the losses among Mexican regular units discouraged the militia. See Carlos María de Bustamente, *El Nuevo Bernal Díaz del Castillo o Sea, História de la Invasión de los Anglo-Americanos en México, compuesta en 1847*, 2 vols. (Mexico, 1949), 2:224. On the other hand, Colonel León related that some of the "National Guard took no part in the combat, but on the contrary, some of them were already running away" when the regulars suffered serious casualties. Gallahar, ed., "Official Report of Temascalitos," 388.

30. Doniphan to Adj. Gen. Jones, March 4, 1847, *Senate Exec. Doc. No. 1*, Serial 503, 30th Cong., 1st Sess., p. 498, also in Connelley, comp., *Doniphan's Expedition*, 377 n; Gibson, *Journal of a Soldier*, 305, 307; Edwards, *Campaign in New Mexico*, 85; Gilpin in St. Louis *Weekly Reveille*, May 10, 1847; Edwards, *Marching with the Army*, 233; McGroarty, ed., "Richardson's Journal," *MHR* (April 1928), 347; William Franklin to Editor, January 29, 1847, Liberty *Tribune*, April 10, 1847; Gallahar, ed., "Official Report of Temascalitos," 389.

31. Doniphan's estimate of the Mexican casualties was 43 killed and 150 wounded. Doni-

phan to Adj. Gen. Jones, March 4, 1847, *Senate Exec. Doc. No. 1*, Serial 503, 30th Cong., 1st Sess., p. 498, also in Connelley, comp., *Doniphan's Expedition*, 378 n. Other variations on the casualty reports and captured goods are found in Gibson, *Journal of a Soldier*, 308–9; Edwards, *Campaign in New Mexico*, 87–88; Edwards, *Marching with the Army*, 234–36; Lt. Robert Todd to Editor William Switzler, Columbia *Statesman*, April 16, 1847. León's report is in Gallahar, ed., "Official Report of Temascalitos," 386. Subsequently, León led a brigade against Winfield Scott's army and died of wounds received at the Battle of El Molino Del Rey, September 8, 1847. K. Jack Bauer, *The Mexican War, 1846–1848* (New York, 1974), 308, 310.

32. An excellent summary of how journalists filed their reports is Martha A. Sandweiss et al., *Eyewitness to War: Prints and Daguerreotypes of the Mexican War, 1846–1848* (Washington, D.C., 1989), 17–18. More comprehensive is Fayette Copeland, *Kendall of the Picayune* (Norman, Okla., 1943), 140–202. Sample contemporary newspaper accounts of Brazito include New Orleans *Daily Delta*, March 5, 1847; Cincinnati *Daily Enquirer*, March 4, 1847; Charleston, S.C., *Mercury*, March 11, 16, 31, 1847; New York *Herald*, March 9, 1847; Natchez *Mississippi Free Trader*, March 10, 1847; Milledgeville, Ga., *Federal Union*, March 16, 1847; Vicksburg *Daily Whig*, March 5, 1847; Richmond, Va., *Whig and Public Advertiser*, March 30, 1847; New Orleans *Daily Picayune*, March 18, 1847; Augusta, Ga., *Constitutionalist*, April 2, 1847; Washington, D.C., *Daily Union*, March 17, 1847; New York *Tribune*, February 26, 27, 1847; New York *Weekly Evening Post*, March 18, 1847; Savannah, Ga., *Daily Republican*, March 12, 1847; Hartford, Conn., *Weekly Times*, March 13, 1847; Milwaukee *Daily Sentinel and Gazette*, March 9, 1847; Chicago *Daily Journal*, March 5, 1847. The Baltimore *Niles National Register* (February 27; April 3, 1847) offered two reports of the battle, including the Black Flag incident, but gave no special notice to Colonel Doniphan.

33. St. Louis *Daily Missouri Republican*, February 26, 1847; Fayette, Mo., *Boon's Lick Times*, February 27, 1847; Columbia *Statesman*, February 26, 1847; Jefferson City *Inquirer*, February 25, 1847; Springfield *Advertiser*, March 9, 1847; St. Louis *Weekly Reveille*, March 1, 1847; Liberty *Weekly Tribune*, February 27, 1847.

34. Roswell S. Ripley, *The War with Mexico*, 2 vols. (New York, 1849), 1:457. Although Ripley may have been offering his own opinion, he seems to have represented much about Regular Army views of volunteers in the 1840s.

35. Lewis Garrard, an American trader in the Southwest, recalled on February 11, 1847, that "we . . . felt badly indeed—Doniphan's regiment was in [the state of] Chihuahua, with no force to support it, and its certain defeat would have given the Santa Féans additional courage." Lewis H. Garrard, *Wah-to-Yah and the Taos Trail*, ed. Ralph P. Bieber (Philadelphia, 1850; repr., Glendale, Calif., 1938), 137; Hughes, *Doniphan's Expedition*, 266. An unnamed correspondent ("Cibola") to St. Louis *Daily Missouri Republican*, January 6, 1847, in *Republican*, March 3, 1847, postulated that the Mexican army had Santa Fe as its objective.

Chapter 6. *"In the Midst of the Enemy's Country"*

1. Quotes in order are from George R. Gibson, *Journal of a Soldier under Kearny and Doniphan, 1846–1847*, ed. Ralph P. Bieber (Glendale, Calif., 1935), 310; "bb" [Lt. Christian Kribben] to Editor, February 2, 1847, St. Louis *Daily Missouri Republican*, (hereafter St. Louis *Republican*), April 9, 1847; Doniphan interview, Santa Fe *Era Southwestern*, August 4, 1880;

John Hughes to Editors, January 4, 1847, Liberty, Mo., *Weekly Tribune* (hereafter Liberty *Tribune*), April 10, 1847. See also William B. McGroarty, ed., "William H. Richardson's Journal of Doniphan's Expedition," *Missouri Historical Review (MHR)* 22 (April 1928), 348, 354; Lt. Robert B. Todd to Editor William Switzler, February 2, 1847, Columbia *Missouri Statesman* (hereafter Columbia *Statesman*), April 16, 1847; Abraham R. Johnston, Marcellus B. Edward, and Philip G. Ferguson, *Marching with the Army of the West, 1846–1848*, ed. Ralph P. Bieber (Glendale, Calif., 1936), 238 (hereafter [soldier's name], *Marching with the Army*).

2. Quotes, in order, are from Jacob S. Robinson, *A Journal of the Santa Fe Expedition, under Colonel Doniphan*, ed. Carl L. Cannon (Princeton, 1932), 68; Frederick A. Wislizenus, *Memoir of a Tour to Northern Mexico Connected with Col. Doniphan's Expedition in 1846 and 1847* (*Senate Misc. Doc. No.* 26, Serial 511, 30th Cong., 1st Sess.; repr., Glorieta, N.M., 1969), 41; Edwards, *Marching with the Army*, 245. Other information from Gibson, *Journal of a Soldier*, 312, 316; McGroarty, ed. "Richardson's Journal," *MHR* (April 1928), 348, 350; Daniel Hastings Diary, February 2, 1847, Justin H. Smith Papers, Benson Latin American Collection, University of Texas–Austin (UT–Austin). Lt. Robert Todd to Editor William Switzler, February 2, 1847, Columbia *Statesman*, April 16, 1847.

3. Gibson, *Journal of a Soldier*, 323; Robinson, *Journal*, 68; John T. Hughes, *Doniphan's Expedition; Containing an Account of the Conquest of New Mexico . . .* (Cincinnati, 1847; repr., Chicago, 1962), 279 (last quote). Several soldiers made their own estimates of the population of El Paso, ranging from seven thousand (McGroarty, ed., "Richardson's Journal," *MHR* [April 1928], 348) to eleven thousand ("bb" [Lt. Kribben] to Editor, February 2, 1847, St. Louis *Republican*, April 9, 1847). See also Wislizenus, *Memoir of a Tour*, 40; Frank S. Edwards, *A Campaign in New Mexico with Colonel Doniphan* (Philadelphia, 1847), 98.

4. Robinson, *Journal*, 68–69; "bb" [Lt. Kribben] to Editor, February 2, 1847, St. Louis *Republican*, April 9, 1847; McGroarty, ed., "Richardson's Journal," *MHR* (April 1928), 350; Hastings Diary, February 2, 1847, Justin Smith Papers, Benson Collection, UT–Austin; Gibson, *Journal of a Soldier*, 315–16; Edwards, *Marching with the Army*, 245; Hughes, *Doniphan's Expedition*, 274, 277.

5. Gibson, *Journal of a Soldier*, 314, 316; Robinson, *Journal*, 69.

6. McGroarty, ed., "Richardson's Journal," *MHR* (April 1928), 350; Gibson, *Journal of a Soldier*, 312, 322–23; Robinson, *Journal*, 69; Edwards, *Campaign in New Mexico*, 91, 96–98; Hughes, *Doniphan's Expedition*, 271, 276; Edwards, *Marching with the Army*, 240.

7. Gibson, *Journal of a Soldier*, 322; Edwards, *Campaign in New Mexico*, 91; Hughes, *Doniphan's Expedition*, 276.

8. On the troops' drills see Hughes, *Doniphan's Expedition*, 282; Hughes to Editors, January 27, 1847, Liberty *Tribune*, April 10, 1847 (Hughes's letter is also in Alvord Collection, Joint Collection, Western Historical Manuscript Collection and State Historical Society of Missouri Manuscripts, University of Missouri–Columbia [hereafter Joint Collection, WHMC–SHSM, UM–Columbia]); "Hughes Diary," January 2, 10, 16, 31, 1847, in William E. Connelley, comp., *Doniphan's Expedition and the Conquest of New Mexico and California* (Topeka, 1907), 89, 90, 92, 95; and McGroarty, ed., "Richardson's Journal," *MHR* (April 1928), 348–49. Quotations, in order, Edwards, *Campaign in New Mexico*, 99 (two quotes, and last quote); Gibson, *Journal of a Soldier*, 309.

9. Quotes, Hughes, *Doniphan's Expedition*, 275–76; McGroarty, ed., "Richardson's Jour-

nal," *MHR* (April 1928), 349. See also Hughes to Editors, January 4, 1847, Liberty *Tribune*, April 10, 1847; Robinson, *Journal*, 68; "bb" [Lt. Kribben] to Editor, February 2, 1847, St. Louis *Republican*, April 9, 1847; Edwards, *Marching with the Army*, 240; Edwards, *Campaign in New Mexico*, 92.

10. Hughes to Editors, January 25 (first quote), 27 (second quote), 1847, Liberty *Tribune*, April 10, 1847; Thomas J. Bartholow to Editors, January 30, 1847, Fayette, Mo., *Boon's Lick Times*, April 10, 1847; and McGroarty, ed., "Richardson's Journal," *MHR* (April 1928), 351; Edwards, *Marching with the Army*, 242.

11. New York *Herald*, April 8, 1847, and Hartford, Conn., *Weekly Times*, April 3, 1847, *Times* headlines in all capitals; Detroit *Democratic Free Press*, March 22, 1847; Cincinnati *Daily Commercial*, March 15, 1847; see also Philadelphia *North American*, March 17, 1847; Milwaukee *Daily Sentinel and Gazette*, March 17, 1847; New York *Weekly Evening Post*, March 18, 25, 1847; Cincinnati *Daily Enquirer*, March 24, 1847; Montgomery, Ala., *Triweekly & Flag Advertiser*, March 20, 1847; James Glasgow to William Glasgow, Jr., Liverpool, England, March 18, 1847, in William C. Lane Collection, Missouri Historical Society (MHS), St. Louis; J. M. to St. Louis *Republican*, March 1, 1847, in issue of March 6, 1847; George C. Bingham to J. S. Rollins, March 10, 1847, in C. B. Rollins, ed., "Letters of George Caleb Bingham," *Missouri Historical Review* 32 (October 1937), 17.

12. Edwards, *Campaign in New Mexico*, 95–96; Hughes, *Doniphan's Expedition*, 277–78; William C. McGaw, *Savage Scene: The Life and Times of James Kirker* (New York, 1972), passim; Ralph A. Smith, "The 'King of New Mexico' and the Doniphan Expedition," *New Mexico Historical Review* 38 (January 1963), 29–31.

13. Lt. Robert Todd to Editor William Switzler, February 2, 1847, Columbia *Statesman*, April 16, 1847; Edwards, *Campaign in New Mexico*, 92; Edwards, *Marching with the Army*, 240.

14. Edwards, *Campaign in New Mexico*, 92–93; Gibson, *Journal of a Soldier*, 313–14, 323; Edwards, *Marching with the Army*, 243; Angelico Chavez, ed., "Ramon Ortiz (1813–1896): Priest and Patriot," *New Mexico Historical Review* 25 (October 1950), 265–95.

15. M. L. Kritter, quoted in St. Louis *Republican*, February 26, 1847.

16. Hughes, *Doniphan's Expedition*, 287 (emphasis in the original); "Maxims of Napoleon," in Thomas R. Phillips, ed., *Roots of Strategy* (Harrisburg, Pa., 1940), 407.

17. Maj. M. L. Clark to Doniphan, December 31, 1846, January 3, 1847, M. L. Clark Letterbook, Beinecke Library, Yale University, New Haven, Conn. Justin H. Smith, *The War with Mexico*, 2 vols. (New York, 1919), 1:303. Doniphan also coincidentally took the option that could have been recommended by Clausewitz. According to an observation by Clausewitz, "It is one of the most important and effective principles of strategy: *a success gained somewhere must be exploited on the spot as far as the circumstances permit it*; for all efforts made whilst the enemy is involved in that crisis have a much greater effect and it is a bad economy of force to let this opportunity slip away [emphasis added]." Quoted in Jehuda L. Wallach, *The Dogma of the Battle of Annihilation* (Westport, Conn., 1986), 189. For this quotation, Wallach draws from *Works of Clausewitz*, vol. 8, *Der Feldzug von 1815 in Frankreich* (1862), 149–50. See also Roger D. Launius, *Alexander William Doniphan, Portrait of a Missouri Moderate* (Columbia, Mo., 1997), 153.

18. For example, Brooklyn *Daily Eagle*, April 8, 1847; Boston *Evening Transcript*, April 9, 1847; Hartford, Conn., *Weekly Times*, April 10, 1847; New York *Herald*, April 8, 1847; New

York *Weekly Evening Post*, April 8, 15, 1847; Indianapolis *Indiana State Sentinel*, April 10, 1847; McGroarty, ed., "Richardson's Journal," *MHR* (April 1928), 352; Hughes, *Doniphan's Expedition*, 273.

19. Isaac George, *Heroes and Incidents of the Mexican War, Containing Doniphan's Expedition* (Greensburg, Pa., 1903), 75–76; Hastings Diary, January 16, 1847, Justin Smith Papers, Benson Collection, UT–Austin.

20. William C. Kennerly, *Persimmon Hill: A Narrative of Old St. Louis and the Far West* (Norman, Okla., 1948), 195; Hastings Diary, January 16, 1847, Justin Smith Papers, Benson Collection, UT–Austin; Edwards, *Marching with the Army*, 243.

21. Quotes, in order, Hastings Diary, February 1, 1847, Justin Smith Papers, Benson Collection, UT–Austin; McGroarty, ed., "Richardson's Journal," *MHR* (April 1928), 352–53; "bb" [Lt. Kribben] to Editor, February 2, 1847, St. Louis *Republican*, April 9, 1847; see also Edwards, *Campaign in New Mexico*, 99; Edwards, *Marching with the Army*, 243–44;

22. Hastings Diary, February 2, 1847, Justin Smith Papers, Benson Collection, UT–Austin.

23. Kennerly, *Persimmon Hill*, 196.

24. On the Taos Revolt in general see Seymour V. Connor and Odie B. Faulk, *North America Divided: The Mexican War, 1846–1848* (New York, 1971), 72–74. Hughes mentions the incomplete information about some sort of "conspiracy or rebellion" in his letter to Editor of the Liberty *Tribune*, January 27, 1847, Alvord Collection, Joint Collection, WHMC–SHSM, UM–Columbia.

25. Edwards, *Marching with the Army*, 241, 244, 245 (first quote), 246 (second quote). See also Edwards, *Campaign in New Mexico*, 103, for a different date of news arriving about the Taos Revolt—February 12. Doniphan's prospects for advancing into the state of Chihuahua differed from those of the upcoming expedition led by Major General Winfield Scott. Scott's army was much larger (around twelve thousand versus one thousand), and Scott aimed to march through states that generally had better water and a higher density of population.

26. Hughes, *Doniphan's Expedition*, 287; McGroarty, ed., "Richardson's Journal," *MHR* (April 1928), 352; Gibson, *Journal of a Soldier*, 324; Robinson, *Journal*, 69–70; Edwards, *Marching with the Army*, 241 (mutiny), 248 (last quote).

27. "Hughes Diary," January 13, 1847, in Connelley, comp., *Doniphan's Expedition*, 92; Edwards, *Marching with the Army*, 244; Hughes, *Doniphan's Expedition*, 278–79.

28. Quote in Edwards, *Campaign in New Mexico*, 104. See also Edwards, *Marching with the Army*, 247; Gibson, *Journal of a Soldier*, 327–28; McGroarty, ed., "Richardson's Journal," *MHR* (April 1928), 353.

29. Robinson, *Journal*, 70; Hastings Diary, February 8, 1847, Justin Smith Papers, Benson Collection, UT–Austin; Edwards, *Marching with the Army*, 247. According to Edwards (ibid.), one of these Mexicans was captured again at Sacramento.

30. Ramón Alcaraz et al., *The Other Side; or Notes for the History of the War between Mexico and the United States*, trans. Albert C. Ramsey (New York, 1850; repr., New York, 1970), 171–72.

31. Quotes, in order, are *Senate Exec. Doc No. 1*, Serial 503, 30th Cong., 1st Sess., pp. 498–99; Hastings Diary, February 10, 1847, Justin Smith Papers, Benson Collection, UT–Austin; McGroarty, ed., "Richardson's Journal," *MHR* (April 1928), 354.

32. Edwards, *Marching with the Army*, 238; Gibson, *Journal of a Soldier*, 332; Hastings Diary, February 9, 1847, Justin Smith Papers, Benson Collection, UT–Austin. On the elections of merchants, see also *House Report No. 458*, Serial 525, 30th Cong., 1st Sess., pp.

31–32; Mark L. Gardner, ed., *Brothers on the Santa Fe and Chihuahua Trails* (Niwot, Colo., 1993), 176 n. 5; Edwards, *Campaign in New Mexico,* 110; Hughes, *Doniphan's Expedition,* 289. Hughes estimated that there were about 150 merchants in the unofficial "battalion."

33. McGroarty, ed., "Richardson's Journal," *MHR* (April 1928), 354; Edwards, *Campaign in New Mexico,* 99; Hastings Diary, February 9, 1847, Justin Smith Papers, Benson Collection, UT–Austin.

34. Kennerly, *Persimmon Hill,* 196; "Hughes Diary," in Connelley, comp., *Doniphan's Expedition,* 98; Edwards, *Marching with the Army,* 253; McGroarty, ed., "Richardson's Journal," *MHR* (April 1928), 357.

35. Kennerly, *Persimmon Hill,* 196; Edwards, *Campaign in New Mexico,* 108; Gibson, *Journal of a Soldier,* 329. See also Hastings Diary, February 10, 1847, Justin Smith Papers, Benson Collection, UT–Austin; McGroarty, ed., "Richardson's Journal," *MHR* (April 1928), 355; Edwards, *Marching with the Army,* 248–49.

36. McGroarty, ed., "Richardson's Journal," *MHR* (April 1928), 357; Edwards, *Marching with the Army,* 249–50 (deserters); Connelley, comp., *Doniphan's Expedition,* 288, 291; Gibson, *Journal of a Soldier,* 332; quote on game from Hastings Diary, February 11, 1847, Justin Smith Papers, Benson Collection, UT–Austin.

37. Edwards, *Marching with the Army,* 249–50; Hughes, *Doniphan's Expedition,* 289–90; Edwards, *Campaign in New Mexico,* 104; *House Report No. 458,* Serial 525, 30th Cong., 1st Sess.; *Mitchell v. Harmony,* 13 Howard 122; New York Circuit, 11 Federal Cases 559, 1 Blatchford 562; Doniphan to Harmony, June 22, 1848, *Senate Misc. Doc. No. 11,* Serial 533, 30th Cong., 2nd Sess., p. 1.

38. Hughes, *Doniphan's Expedition,* 290; William E. Birkhimer, *Military Government and Martial Law,* 3rd ed. (Kansas City, Mo., 1914), 251–52; Gardner, ed., *Brothers on the Santa Fe and Chihuahua Trails,* 78, 81; *Mitchell v. Harmony,* 13 Howard 119, 124, 136, 140; Doniphan, unnumbered order, February 9, 1847, quoted in *House Report No. 458,* Serial 525, 30th Cong., 1st Sess., pp. 15–16; Mitchell's order to Harmony, ibid., p. 4; Reid's recollection in his deposition, January 4, 1848, *Senate Misc. Doc. No. 11,* Serial 533, 30th Cong., 2nd Sess., p. 11.

39. McGroarty, ed., "Richardson's Journal," *MHR* (April 1928), 355–56; Hughes, *Doniphan's Expedition,* 291; Gibson, *Journal of a Soldier,* 334.

40. Hughes, *Doniphan's Expedition,* 291–92; Robinson, *Journal,* 71; Edwards, *Campaign in New Mexico,* 102–3.

41. Edwards, *Campaign in New Mexico,* 105; Edwards, *Marching with the Army,* 253; McGroarty, ed., "Richardson's Journal," *MHR* (April 1928), 355–56; Gibson, *Journal of a Soldier,* 334.

42. Hughes, *Doniphan's Expedition,* 295; Gibson, *Journal of a Soldier,* 335, 337; Edwards, *Marching with the Army,* 253; Edwards, *Campaign in New Mexico,* 106.

43. McGroarty, ed., "Richardson's Journal," *MHR* (April 1928), 356; Hughes, *Doniphan's Expedition,* 293–94; Robinson, *Journal,* 71; *Edwards, Marching with the Army,* 253.

44. Robinson, *Journal,* 71; Hughes, *Doniphan's Expedition,* 293–94; Gibson, *Journal of a Soldier,* 337; McGroarty, ed., "Richardson's Journal," *MHR* (April 1928), 356–57; Edwards, *Campaign in New Mexico,* 106; Hastings Diary, February 19–20, 1847, Justin Smith Papers, Benson Collection, UT–Austin.

45. McGroarty, ed., "Richardson's Journal," *MHR* (April 1928), 357; Gibson, *Journal of a Soldier,* 338.

46. Quotes: Edwards, *Campaign in New Mexico,* 106–7; McGroarty, ed., "Richardson's Journal," *MHR* (April 1928), 357; Edwards, *Marching with the Army,* 252, 254, 255 (quotes). See also Robinson, *Journal,* 72.

47. Quotes: McGroarty, ed., "Richardson's Journal," *MHR* (April 1928), 357; Hughes, *Doniphan's Expedition,* 296. See also Hastings Diary, February 22, 1847, Justin Smith Papers, Benson Collection, UT–Austin; Edwards, *Marching with the Army,* 256.

48. McGroarty, ed., "Richardson's Journal," *MHR* (April 1928), 358; Hastings Diary, February 23, 1847, Justin Smith Papers, Benson Collection, UT–Austin; Gibson, *Journal of a Soldier,* 339; Hughes, *Doniphan's Expedition,* 297.

49. McGroarty, ed., "Richardson's Journal," *MHR* (April 1928), 358; Edwards, *Marching with the Army,* 256.

50. Quotes, in order, Kennerly, *Persimmon Hill,* 196 (first and last quotes); Hughes, *Doniphan's Expedition,* 298; Robinson, *Journal,* 72–73; Gibson, *Journal of a Soldier,* 341; Hastings Diary, February 25, 1847, Justin Smith Papers, Benson Collection, UT–Austin; McGroarty, ed., "Richardson's Journal," *MHR* (April 1928), 358–59; Robinson, *Journal,* 73.

51. Edwards, *Marching with the Army,* 258; Kennerly, *Persimmon Hill,* 196; Robinson, *Journal,* 74; McGroarty, ed., "Richardson's Journal," *MHR* (April 1928), 359.

52. Edwards, *Marching with the Army,* 258–59; McGroarty, ed., "Richardson's Journal," *MHR* (April 1928), 359.

53. Kennerly, *Persimmon Hill,* 196 (first quote); John D. Stevenson to wife, March 4, 1847, John D. Stevenson Papers, MHS, St. Louis (second quote); McGroarty, ed., "Richardson's Journal," *MHR* (April 1928), 360; Edwards, *Marching with the Army,* 259; Hughes, *Doniphan's Expedition,* 301.

Chapter 7. The Battle of Sacramento

1. Trías's role is indicated in Rómulo Jaurrieta, "Batalla de Sacramento 28 de Febrero de 1847," *Boletín de la Sociedad Chihuahuense de Estuidos Históricos* 7 (1950), 414 (hereafter Jaurrieta, "Batalla de Sacramento"). Jaurrieta wrote his essay in 1895, forty-eight years after the battle. Heredia's background is summarized in Alberto M. Carreño, ed., *Jefes del Ejército Mexicano en 1847: Biografías de generales . . .* (Mexico City, 1914), 128–29; Ramón Alcaraz et al., *The Other Side; or Notes for the History of the War between Mexico and the United States,* trans. and ed. Albert C. Ramsey (New York, 1850; repr., New York, 1970), 172; "bb" [Lt. Christian Kribben] to Editor, March 5, 1847, St. Louis *Daily Missouri Republican* (hereafter St. Louis *Republican*), May 19, 1847; John T. Hughes, *Doniphan's Expedition; Containing an Account of the Conquest of New Mexico . . .* (Cincinnati, 1847; repr., Chicago, 1962), 305.

2. For Doniphan's personal reconnaissance see William B. McGroarty, ed., "William H. Richardson's Journal of Doniphan's Expedition," *Missouri Historical Review (MHR)* 22 (July 1928), 511. Hughes, *Doniphan's Expedition,* 301; postbattle report, Doniphan to Adj. Gen. Roger Jones, March 4, 1847, in *Senate Exec. Doc. No. 1,* Serial 503, 30th Cong., 1st Sess., pp. 499, 501; Maj. M. L. Clark to Doniphan, March 2, 1847, ibid., 508–13, hereafter quoted in Frank S. Edwards, *A Campaign in New Mexico with Colonel Doniphan* (Philadelphia, 1847), 172–73. Mitchell's reconnaissance is mentioned favorably in Lt. Robert B. Todd to Editor William Switzler, March 4, 1847, in Columbia *Missouri Statesman* (hereafter Columbia *Statesman*), June 4, 1847; by St. Louis *Weekly Reveille,* May 24, 1847; and by Abraham R.

Johnston, Marcellus B. Edwards, and Philip G. Ferguson, *Marching with the Army of the West, 1846–1848*, ed. Ralph P. Bieber (Glendale, Calif., 1936), 259 (hereafter [soldier's name], *Marching with the Army*). Mexican livestock is described in St. Louis *Daily Union*, June 26, 1847. A detailed postbattle tabulation of the Mexican forces is "bb" [Lt. Kribben] to Editor, March 5, 1847, St. Louis *Republican*, May 19, 1847. See also William C. McGaw, *Savage Scene: The Life and Times of James Kirker* (New York, 1972), 171.

3. García Conde's background is in Carreño, ed., *Jefes del Ejército Mexicano*, 161; Alcaraz et al., *Other Side*, 172–73; Doniphan to Adj. Gen. Jones, March 4, 1847, in *Senate Exec. Doc. 1*, Serial 503, 30th Cong., 1st Sess., p. 499; personal impression of Mexican defenses by "bb" [Lt. Kribben] to Editor, March 5, 1847, St. Louis *Republican*, May 19, 1847. Diagrams of García Conde's lines are in Hughes, *Doniphan's Expedition*, 303; William E. Connelley, comp., *Doniphan's Expedition and the Conquest of New Mexico and California* (Topeka, 1907), 412; *Senate Exec. Doc. No. 1*, Serial 503, 30th Cong., 1st Sess., map section at end of document; and Alcaraz et al., *Other Side*, map insert between pages 166 and 167.

4. Alcaraz et al., *Other Side*, 172–73; Heredia's postbattle report to General Antonio Lopéz de Santa Anna, March 2, 1847, was reprinted in many U.S. newspapers; see, for examples, Baltimore *Niles National Register*, May 1, 1847, 132, and New Orleans *Daily Picayune*, April 10, 1847. About the rancheros see Sgt. William C. Kennerly to Justin H. Smith, ca. 1900, in William C. Kennerly Papers, Missouri Historical Society (MHS); St. Louis, and *The Anglo Saxon*, American occupation newspaper in Chihuahua, dated March 18, 1847, copy at Barker Texas History Center, University of Texas–Austin (Barker/UT–Austin); and Lt. Robert Todd to Editor William Switzler, March 4, 1847, Columbia *Statesman*, June 4, 1847. Most of the American sources put their estimates at more than 1,000 rancheros. In summary, it is important to point out that the American estimates of Mexican forces rounded out to more than 3,000; General Heredia placed his strength at about 2,000; and Doniphan claimed to have found the Mexican adjutant's report fixing Heredia's total at 4,220. Rómulo Jaurrieta concluded that 1,180 Mexican troops were in the units that first reached the defenses. They were supplemented by another 1,000 men, giving a total of more than 2,000 men "of the three arms" (infantry, cavalry, and artillery) present for duty. Jaurrieta, "Batalla de Sacramento," 415, 416.

5. The Mexican plans are given in Alcaraz et al., *Other Side*, 174; Daniel H. Hastings Diary, February 28, 1847, Justin H. Smith Papers, Benson Latin American Collection, University of Texas–Austin (UT–Austin), reported finding the ropes and handcuffs after the battle, as did Hughes, *Doniphan's Expedition*, 305. The conversations with merchants are mentioned in Columbia *Statesman*, April 30, 1847. Description of the evening of February 27 in Jaurrieta, "Batalla de Sacramento," 417.

6. Connelley presents the breakdown of soldiers in the regiment's units in *Doniphan's Expedition*, 407; Daniel Hastings Diary, February 28, 1847, Justin Smith Papers, Benson Collection, UT–Austin (first two quotes). Slightly different accounting of the Americans (total of 924), not including the merchants and teamsters, is Doniphan to Adj. Gen. Roger Jones, March 4, 1847, *Senate Exec. Doc. No. 1*, Serial 503, 30th Cong., 1st Sess., p. 499. George R. Gibson, *Journal of a Soldier under Kearny and Doniphan 1846–1847*, ed. Ralph P. Bieber (Glendale, Calif., 1935), 343 (third quote). Jaurrieta's estimate of the total American force, including teamsters, was 1,300, in "Batalla de Sacramento," 417.

7. Jaurrieta, "Batalla de Sacramento," 417; Hastings Diary, February 28, 1847, Justin Smith Papers, Benson Collection, UT–Austin; Edwards, *Marching with the Army*, 261; St.

Louis *Weekly Reveille*, May 24, 1847; Alcaraz et al., *Other Side*, 174; "bb" [Lt. Kribben] to Editor, March 5, 1847, St. Louis *Republican*, May 19, 1847; McGaw, *Savage Scene*, 171; Connelley, comp., *Doniphan's Expedition*, 388 n.

8. First quotation from Hastings Diary, February 28, 1847, Justin Smith Papers, Benson Collection, UT–Austin. Weightman's quotation from a postwar statement, quoted in *House Report No. 458*, Serial 525, 30th Cong., 1st Sess., p. 36. See also Gibson, *Journal of a Soldier*, 343; Doniphan to Adj. Gen. Jones, March 4, 1847, in *Senate Exec. Doc. No. 1*, Serial 503, 30th Cong., 1st Sess., p. 500. McGaw, *Savage Scene*, 180, attributes the American tactical approach to Kirker's advice to Doniphan.

9. Edwards, *Campaign in New Mexico*, 111 (first and second quotes), 113; measurement for the gully and third quote from Hastings Diary, February 28, 1847, Justin Smith Papers, Benson Collection, UT–Austin; Edwards, *Marching with the Army*, 261. Hughes asserted that there were as many as "one thousand [civilian] spectators" (*Doniphan's Expedition*, 307).

10. Heredia admitted his surprise at the direction of the American attack in his report, Heredia to Santa Anna, March 2, 1847, in Baltimore *Niles National Register*, May 1, 1847; Alcaraz et al., *Other Side*, 174–75. Jacob S. Robinson, *A Journal of the Santa Fe Expedition under Colonel Doniphan*, ed. Carl L. Cannon (Princeton, 1932),74; Hastings Diary, February 28, 1847, Justin Smith Papers, Benson Collection, UT–Austin; Gibson, *Journal of a Soldier*, 345; "bb" [Lt. Kribben] to Editor, March 5, 1847, St. Louis *Republican*, May 19, 1847.

11. Doniphan's order to Weightman mentioned by an unidentified Cole County officer in Jefferson City, Mo., *Weekly Inquirer* (hereafter Jefferson City *Inquirer*), May 15, 1847; Clark to Doniphan, March 2, 1847, quoted in Edwards, *Campaign in New Mexico*, 174; ibid., 111–12; Robinson, *Journal*, 74–75; Doniphan to Adj. Gen. Jones, March 4, 1847, in *Senate Exec. Doc. No. 1*, Serial 503, 30th Cong., 1st Sess., p. 500. Artillery firing procedures are delineated in U.S. War Department, *System of Exercise and Instruction of Field-Artillery, Including Manoeuvres for Light or Horse-Artillery* (Boston, 1829), esp. 13–16.

12. Hastings Diary, February 28, 1847, Justin Smith Papers, Benson Collection, UT–Austin (first two quotes); William C. Kennerly, *Persimmon Hill: A Narrative of Old St. Louis and the Far West* (Norman, Okla., 1948), 197–98 (third quote); Heredia to Santa Anna, March 2, 1847, Baltimore *Niles National Register*, May 1, 1847; Hughes to Editor, March 4, 1847, Liberty *Weekly Tribune*, May 29, 1847; "bb" [Lt. Kribben] to Editor, March 5, 1847, St. Louis *Republican*, May 19, 1847; Jaurrieta, "Batalla de Sacramento," 418.

13. Kennerly to Smith, ca. 1900, Kennerly Papers, MHS, St. Louis; Doniphan to Adj. Gen. Jones, March 4, 1847, in *Senate Exec. Doc. No. 1*, Serial 503, 30th Cong., 1st Sess., pp. 500–501; Clark to Doniphan, March 2, 1847, in Edwards, *Campaign in New Mexico*, 175.

14. Doniphan to Adj. Gen. Jones, March 4, 1847, *Senate Exec. Doc. No. 1*, Serial 503, 30th Cong., 1st Sess., pp. 500–501, acknowledges Captain Thompson's advice in forming the battle line; Robinson, *Journal*, 74; "bb" [Lt. Kribben] to Editor, March 5, 1847, St. Louis *Republican*, May 19, 1847; Edwards, *Campaign in New Mexico*, 112 (quote), 113; Hughes, *Doniphan's Expedition*, 306–7; Connelley, comp., *Doniphan's Expedition*, 416 n.

15. Hughes, *Doniphan's Expedition*, 307; Alcaraz et al., *Other Side*, 176; Heredia to Santa Anna, March 2, 1847, Baltimore *Niles National Register*, May 1, 1847; Edwards, *Campaign in New Mexico*, 126–27; Jaurrieta, "Batalla de Sacramento," 418.

16. Edwards, *Campaign in New Mexico*, 114 (quote); Hughes, *Doniphan's Expedition*, 307–11; Connelley, comp., *Doniphan's Expedition*, 418 n; Edwards, *Marching with the Army*, 264; McGaw, *Savage Scene*, 179; Juarrieta, "Batalla de Sacramento," 419.

17. Edwards, *Marching with the Army*, 263 (first quote); Hughes, *Doniphan's Expedition*, 308–11; Connelley, comp., *Doniphan's Expedition*, 418–19 n (second quote); Doniphan to Adj. Gen. Jones, March 4, 1847, in *Senate Exec. Doc. No. 1*, Serial 503, 30th Cong., 1st Sess., pp. 500–501.

18. Clark to Doniphan, March 2, 1847, quoted in Edwards, *Campaign in New Mexico*, 175; Edwards, *Marching with the Army*, 264; Hastings Diary, February 28, 1847, Justin Smith Papers, Benson Collection, UT–Austin.

19. Edwards, *Campaign in New Mexico*, 120 (first quote); Clark to Doniphan, March 2, 1847, ibid., 174, 176; Gibson, *Journal of a Soldier*, 346; Hughes, *Doniphan's Expedition*, 307–8; Lt. Robert Todd to Editor William Switzler, March 4, 1847, Columbia *Statesman*, June 4, 1847 (last quote).

20. "bb" [Lt. Kribben] to Editor, March 5, 1847, St. Louis *Republican*, May 19, 1847 (quotes); Robinson, *Journal*, 76; Clark to Doniphan, March 2, 1847, in Edwards, *Campaign in New Mexico*, 176; Jaurrieta, "Batalla de Sacramento," 419.

21. Doniphan to Adj. Gen. Jones, March 4, 1847, in *Senate Exec. Doc. No. 1*, Serial 503, 30th Cong., 1st Sess., p. 500 (first quote); Gibson, *Journal of a Soldier*, 349 (second and third quotes); St. Louis *Daily Union*, June 26, 1847; Edwards, *Campaign in New Mexico*, 115; Edwards, *Marching with the Army*, 264–65.

22. Clark to Doniphan, March 2, 1847, quoted in Edwards, *Campaign in New Mexico*, 176–77 (first and last quotes); Gibson, *Journal of a Soldier*, 349 (second quote); Edwards, *Marching with the Army*, 266. A summary of the action is found in Roger D. Launius, *Alexander William Doniphan, Portrait of a Missouri Moderate* (Columbia, Mo., 1997), 156–57, 159–60.

23. The episode is recounted in Connelley, comp., *Doniphan's Expedition*, 413 n.

24. Hughes to Editor, March 4, 1847, Liberty *Tribune*, May 29, 1847; Hughes, *Doniphan's Expedition*, 313 n; Gibson, *Journal of a Soldier*, 349; Doniphan to Adj. Gen. Jones, March 4, 1847, *Senate Exec. Doc. No. 1*, Serial 503, 30th Cong., 1st Sess., p. 501. These sources varied slightly in giving the American casualty count, but the totals in the text appear to be the most accurate.

25. Robinson, *Journal*, 76 (gives total Mexican casualties between 300 and 500); Hastings Diary, February 28, 1847, (300 killed, 500 wounded, 70 prisoners), Justin Smith Papers, Benson Collection, UT–Austin; Edwards, *Campaign in New Mexico*, 117 (total of 1,100 casualties); soon after the battle John Hughes to Editor, March 4, 1847, Liberty *Tribune*, May 29, 1847, gave 300 killed, 400 wounded, and 60 prisoners, but in his book (Hughes, *Doniphan's Expedition*, 313) Hughes boosted the count to 500 wounded and 70 prisoners. Edwards (*Marching with the Army*, 267) counted 79 prisoners and claimed to have seen 169 Mexicans buried on the battlefield; "bb" [Lt. Kribben] to Editor, March 5, 1847, St. Louis *Republican*, May 19, 1847, also offered the number of 169 Mexican soldiers buried soon after the battle; Kribben's occupation newspaper, the Chihuahua *Anglo Saxon*, March 18, 1847 (Barker/UT–Austin), contended that "the enemy had near three hundred men killed, about the same number wounded and thirty prisoners taken." J. E. D. to brother, March 3, 1847, Mexican War Papers, MHS, St. Louis, put the count at only 40 Mexican prisoners; Kennerly, *Persimmon Hill*, 199.

26. Hastings Diary, February 28, 1847, Justin Smith Papers, Benson Collection, UT–Austin, and Kennerly to Smith, ca. 1900, Kennerly Papers, MHS, St. Louis, described the Black Flag; Gibson, *Journal of a Soldier*, 351; Edwards, *Campaign in New Mexico*, 117–18;

Robinson, *Journal*, 76; Jefferson City *Inquirer*, May 15, 1847; McGroarty, ed., "Richardson's Journal," *MHR* 22 (July 1928), 513; also providing accounting of captured items was Chihuahua *Anglo Saxon*, March 18, 1847, in Barker/UT–Austin; Hughes, *Doniphan's Expedition*, 313.

27. Heredia to Santa Anna, March 2, 1847, in Baltimore *Niles National Register*, May 1, 1847, 132. It is important to recall that one of the Missourians conceded that if the Mexicans had been better led, or better trained, the battle could have taken a different turn and that casualties among the Missourians could have been higher. Lieutenant Gibson related that "had they only fought cooly and directed their musketry well we must have suffered a heavy loss." Gibson, *Journal of a Soldier*, 349.

28. Veteran's quote from Chihuahua *Anglo Saxon*, March 18, 1847, copy at Barker/UT–Austin; McGroarty, ed., "Richardson's Journal," *MHR* (July 1928), 512; Hughes, *Doniphan's Expedition*, 314; Lt. Charles Wooster to Adj. Gen. Jones, March 7, 1847, quoted in Gibson, *Journal of a Soldier*, 346; Lt. Robert Todd to Editor William Switzler, March 4, 1847, Columbia *Statesman*, June 4, 1847.

29. Natchez *Mississippi Free Trader*, May 5, 1847, with other reports on Sacramento in issues of April 14, 21, May 12, 19, 1847; New Orleans *Daily Picayune*, April 10, May 5 (quote), 15 (map), 1847; Indianapolis *Indiana State Sentinel*, May 9, 1847; Cincinnati *Daily Enquirer*, May 2, 1847; Savannah, Ga., *Daily Republican*, May 10, 1847; Baltimore *Daily Republican & Argus*, May 5, 1847; Columbia *Missouri Statesman*, April 23, 1847; Charleston, S.C., *Courier*, May 8, 1847; Tallahassee *Floridian*, April 24, May 15 (quote), 1847; Little Rock *Arkansas State Gazette*, April 24, 1847; Newark *Daily Advertiser*, April 19, 1847; Fayette, Mo., *Boon's Lick Times*, April 24, 1847; St. Louis *Daily Missouri Republican*, April 13, 1847; St. Louis *Weekly Reveille*, May 3, 1847. See also positive reports in Cleveland, Ohio, *Plain Dealer*, April 28, 1847, and St. Louis *Daily Missouri Republican*, May 13, 1847.

30. Baltimore *Niles National Register*, May 8 (quote), May 15, 1847. Other papers with brief reports include Jackson *Mississippian*, May 7, 1847; Augusta, Ga., *Constitutionalist*, May 9, 1847; Richmond, Va., *Enquirer*, May 7, 1847; Frankfort *Weekly Kentucky Yeoman*, April 8, 1847; Milwaukee *Daily Sentinel and Gazette*, May 8, 1847; Springfield *Illinois State Register*, May 7, 1847; Cincinnati *Daily Commercial*, April 21, May 4, 1847; Hartford, Conn., *Weekly Times*, May 15, 1847; New York *Evening Post*, April 22, 1847; New York *Herald*, April 15, 19, May 5, 1847; Philadelphia *North American*, April 17, 19, 1847; Liberty *Weekly Tribune*, April 24, May 22, 1847; Springfield, Mo., *Advertiser*, May 4, 1847; Baltimore *Sun*, May 31, 1847.

31. New York *Tribune*, April 19, 1847; Richmond, Va., *Whig and Public Advertiser*, May 7, 1847; Washington, D.C., *National Era*, May 20 (first quote), May 13 (second quote), 1847.

32. Milo M. Quaife, ed., *The Diary of James K. Polk, 1845–1849*, 4 vols. (Chicago, 1910), entry for May 4, 1847, 3:10.

33. Americans of the 1840s were familiar with other battles having modest forces (5,000 soldiers or fewer on the field) that they nevertheless considered noteworthy. A sampling from the American Revolution includes Bunker Hill (Breed's Hill), Quebec, Trenton, and Cowpens; and from the War of 1812, Queenston Heights, Detroit, York, the Thames River, and Chippewa. For a convenient reference for approximate numbers of troops engaged in these battles, see Vincent J. Esposito, ed., *The West Point Atlas of American Wars*, 2 vols. (New York, 1959), passim.

34. It should be noted that some on the Mexican side marked Buena Vista (La Angostura) as a Mexican victory. Buena Vista was hard fought, with Mexican units several times appear-

ing on the verge of maneuvering in ways to gain the overall advantage over Taylor's American units. Taylor's army suffered losses that rendered it unfit for any offensive operations in support of Scott, though it may have been unlikely that Taylor would have conducted such operations in any event. After all, President Polk had reduced Taylor's army and given units from it to Scott in order to downplay Taylor's status in the war. Quickly calculating the results of the closely contested battle, Santa Anna concluded that he could not risk further attacks at La Angostura; he ordered a retreat, leaving control of the field, and credit for the victory, to Taylor.

35. Before the battle, the Mexicans discussed their intention to regain New Mexico. See Alcaraz et al., *Other Side*, 174. Gibson, *Journal of a Soldier*, 344, implied a link between Sacramento and New Mexico, and the Whigs' Washington *National Era* (April 22, 1847) judged that victory at Sacramento helped protect "the safety of New Mexico."

36. Gibson, *Journal of a Soldier*, 321.

37. Ibid., 344. Doniphan's dealings with the merchants traveling with his column were mentioned by a number of diarists.

38. As George L. Rives asserted, "Doniphan's spectacular success served to confirm Mexican hopelessness." George L. Rives, *The United States and Mexico, 1821–1848*, 2 vols. (New York, 1913), 2:376.

39. New Orleans *Daily Delta*, May 14, 1847; Washington *Daily Union*, April 19, 1847.

Chapter 8. From Chihuahua to the Coast

1. The population estimates varied from the point of view of several soldiers, ranging from 9,000 by George R. Gibson, *Journal of a Soldier under Kearny and Doniphan, 1846–1847*, ed. Ralph P. Bieber (Glendale, Calif., 1935), 355 (quote on 352), to 25,000 by Marcellus B. Edwards, in Abraham R. Johnston, Marcellus B. Edwards, and Philip G. Ferguson, *Marching with the Army of the West, 1846–1848*, ed. Ralph P. Bieber (Glendale, Calif, 1936), 271; and John T. Hughes, *Doniphan's Expedition; Containing an Account of the Conquest of New Mexico . . .* (Cincinnati, 1847; repr., Chicago, 1962), 330. Other population estimates included 12,000 by "bb" [Lt. Christian Kribben] to Editor, March 5, 1847, St. Louis *Daily Missouri Republican* (hereafter St. Louis *Republican*), May 19, 1847; and 15,000 by Frederick A. Wislizenus, *Memoir of a Tour to Northern Mexico Connected with Col. Doniphan's Expedition in 1846 and 1847* (*Senate Misc. Doc. No. 26*, Serial 511, 30th Cong., 1st Sess.; repr., Glorieta, N.M., 1969), 54, 60. Describing the regiment's entry to the city are Jacob S. Robinson, *A Journal of the Santa Fe Expedition under Colonel Doniphan*, ed. Carl L. Cannon (Princeton, 1932), 76–77; William B. McGroarty, ed., "William H. Richardson's Journal of Doniphan's Expedition," *Missouri Historical Review (MHR)* 22 (July 1928), 514; Hughes, *Doniphan's Expedition*, 316; Daniel Hastings Diary, March 2, 1847, in Justin H. Smith Papers, Benson Latin American Collection, University of Texas–Austin (UT–Austin). One of the foreigners who was pleased to see the Doniphan Expedition was Dr. Frederick A. Wislizenus, a physician who had been on an odyssey of his own. After immigrating to the United States from one of the German states in 1835, Wislizenus practiced medicine in Illinois but wanted to see the Great West and catalog its plants and animals. Despite the fact that war had been declared, the doctor set out on travels that took him across the Rocky Mountains and into Mexico. Mexican authorities held him in confinement in Chihuahua, though Wislizenus had no official

rank and, in fact, as a former German citizen and a physician, might have been made welcome. Wislizenus met with Doniphan and offered his services as a regimental surgeon. The colonel was pleased to sign the doctor on in that capacity, and Wislizenus's journal, later published by the federal government, became one of the sources on the latter part of the expedition.

2. Frank S. Edwards, *A Campaign in New Mexico with Colonel Doniphan* (Philadelphia, 1847), 121–23 (quote on 121); Gibson, *Journal of a Soldier,* 353–56 (quote on 353); James J. Webb, *Adventures in the Santa Fe Trade, 1844–1847*, ed. Ralph P. Bieber (Glendale, Calif., 1931), 273; Doniphan to E. M. Ryland, editor of St. Louis *Republican,* March 7, 1847, also printed in Baltimore *Niles National Register,* July 3, 1847; Robinson, *Journal*, 77. See also Hastings Diary, March 2, 1847, Justin Smith Papers, Benson Collection, UT–Austin; Doniphan interview, Santa Fe *Era Southwestern*, August 5, 1880; Hughes, *Doniphan's Expedition*, 329–31.

3. Gibson, *Journal of a Soldier,* 353–54 (quotes); Robinson, *Journal*, 77; Hastings Diary, March 3, 1847, Justin Smith Papers, Benson Collection, UT–Austin; Edwards, *Campaign in New Mexico,* 123–24; Wislizenus, *Memoir of a Tour,* 60; Edwards, *Marching with the Army,* 271; Milledgeville, Ga., *Southern Recorder,* June 29, 1847.

4. Edwards, *Campaign in New Mexico,* 124 (long quote); Gibson, *Journal of a Soldier,* 354; Edwards, *Marching with the Army,* 272–73; Hastings Diary, March 3, 1847, Justin Smith Papers, Benson Collection, UT–Austin.

5. Robinson, *Journal*, 78–79; Gibson, *Journal of a Soldier,* 360.

6. Hughes, *Doniphan's Expedition*, 328; Potts's quote and Doniphan's reply, Hastings Diary, March 4, 1847, Justin Smith Papers, Benson Collection, UT–Austin, with Hastings highlighting Doniphan's personal involvement; Wislizenus, *Memoir of a Tour,* 54, described the soldiers. In a variation of the incident, Edwards, *Campaign in New Mexico,* 129–30, and McGroarty, ed., "Richardson's Journal," *MHR* (July 1928), 515, placed Mitchell in charge of a confrontation with Potts at Governor Trías's personal residence. See also "Hughes Diary," in William E. Connelley, comp., *Doniphan's Expedition and the Conquest of New Mexico and California* (Topeka, 1907) 107; Roger D. Launius, *Alexander William Doniphan, Portrait of a Missouri Moderate* (Columbia, Mo., 1997), 165.

7. Doniphan's Proclamation, in Spanish, in Mexican War Papers, Missouri Historical Society (MHS), St. Louis. The proclamation was widely reported in the United States; for examples see Louisville *Daily Democrat,* May 10, 1847; New York *Weekly Evening Post,* May 13, 1847; New York *Herald,* May 7, 1847; Liberty *Weekly Tribune,* May 22, 1847 (hereafter Liberty *Tribune*). On punishments see also Hughes, *Doniphan's Expedition,* 329, and Edwards, *Campaign in New Mexico,* 143.

8. Chihuahua *Anglo Saxon,* March 18, 1847, American occupation newspaper, copies in New Mexico State Records Center, Santa Fe, and Barker Texas History Center, University of Texas–Austin. See also Gibson, *Journal of a Soldier,* 360 and 360 n, and McGroarty, ed., "Richardson's Journal," *MHR* (July 1928), 516. Exactly how many issues of the *Anglo Saxon* were printed is unknown. See "Hughes Diary," in Connelley, comp., *Doniphan's Expedition*, 107.

9. Montgomery, Ala., *Triweekly Flag & Advertiser,* May 20, 1847; New York *Evening Post,* May 20, 1847; New Orleans, *Daily Picayune,* May 11, 1847; Hartford, Conn., *Weekly Times*, April 17, 1847; Baltimore *Sun*, May 19, 1847; Baltimore *Niles National Register*, June 5, 1847; Gen. Taylor to Adj. Gen. U.S. Army, Washington, D.C., March 20, 1847, in *House Exec.*

Doc. No. 60, Serial 520, 30th Cong., 1st Sess., p. 1120, and a similar report, March 28, 1847, ibid., p. 1125; Sec. of War William L. Marcy to Missouri Gov. John Edwards, March 25, 1847, Secretary of War, Letters Sent by the Secretary of War Relating to Military Affairs, 1800–1889, Microcopy M-6, roll 27, Record Group (RG) 107, National Archives (NA), Washington, D.C.

10. Information on the dispatch of messengers in Gibson, *Journal of a Soldier*, 361 and 361 n; Hughes, *Doniphan's Expedition*, 334–35; Doniphan to Adj. Gen. Roger Jones, March 4, 1847, Adjutant General, Letters Received, 1805–1889, Microcopy M-567, roll 339, RG 94, NA; Doniphan to Editor E. M. Ryland, St. Louis *Republican*, March 7, 1847.

11. Gibson, *Journal of a Soldier*, 356 (quote), 362; Edwards, *Campaign in New Mexico*, 122; Hughes, *Doniphan's Expedition*, 320 n; Edwards, *Marching with the Army*, 276–77; Wislizenus, *Memoir of a Tour*, 61; William C. Kennerly, *Persimmon Hill: A Narrative of Old St. Louis and the Far West* (Norman, Okla., 1948), 201–2.

12. Gibson, *Journal of a Soldier*, 359.

13. Kennerly, *Persimmon Hill*, 200; Wislizenus, *Memoir of a Tour*, 60; Gibson, *Journal of a Soldier*, 357; Hastings Diary, March 5–19, 1847, Justin Smith Papers, Benson Collection, UT–Austin; Hughes, *Doniphan's Expedition*, 330.

14. Hastings Diary, April 1–3, 1847, Justin Smith Papers, Benson Collection, UT–Austin; Robinson, *Journal*, 81; Gibson, *Journal of a Soldier*, 358.

15. Stella M. Drumm, ed., *Down the Santa Fe Trail and into Mexico: The Diary of Susan Shelby Magoffin 1846–1847* (New Haven, Conn., 1926), 228–29.

16. One anonymous soldier's denial is in Hughes, *Doniphan's Expedition*, 350–51; soldiers' attitudes, described by Wislizenus, *Memoir of a Tour*, 61; Doniphan to Editor E. M. Ryland, St. Louis *Republican*, March 7, 1847; Gibson, *Journal of a Soldier*, 358; Doniphan to Brig. Gen. John Wool, March 20, 1847, quoted in Hughes, *Doniphan's Expedition*, 338; Hastings Diary, early April and April 13, 1847, Justin Smith Papers, Benson Collection, UT–Austin.

17. Fayette, Mo., *Boon's Lick Times*, June 19, 1847 (quotes); Hughes to Editor, Liberty *Tribune*, May 28, 1847, in Alvord Collection, Joint Collection, Western Historical Manuscript Collection–State Historical Society of Missouri, University of Missouri–Columbia (hereafter Joint Collection, WHMC–SHSM, UM–Columbia); Mark L. Gardner, ed., *Brothers on the Santa Fe and Chihuahua Trails* (Niwot, Colo., 1993), 114; James Hobbs, *Wild Life in the Far West, Personal Adventures of a Border Mountain Man* (Hartford, Conn., 1873; repr., Glorieta, N.M., 1969), 131; Gibson, *Journal of a Soldier*, 352 (quote).

18. Doniphan to Wool, March 20, 1847, in *House Exec. Doc. No.* 60, Serial 520, 30th Cong., 1st Sess., p. 1129, also in Hughes, *Doniphan's Expedition*, 338. See also Gardner, ed., *Brothers on the Santa Fe and Chihuahua Trails*, 114.

19. Hughes, *Doniphan's Expedition*, 335–36; Doniphan to Wool, March 20, 1847, ibid., 336–37; Edwards, *Marching with the Army*, 276.

20. Hughes, *Doniphan's Expedition*, 349–50, and Connelley, comp., *Doniphan's Expedition*, 464–65 n; "bb" [Lt. Christian Kribben] to Editor, March 5, 1847, St. Louis *Republican*, May 19, 1847; Edwards, *Campaign in New Mexico*, 131, who quoted the colonel as saying "*I'm for going home to Sara* [sic] *and the children*" (emphasis in the original). See also Launius, *Doniphan, Missouri Moderate*, 173.

21. Hastings Diary, April 23, 1847, Justin Smith Papers, Benson Collection, UT–Austin; John Hughes to Robert H. Miller, editor of Liberty *Tribune*, in Hughes, *Doniphan's Expedition*, 339–40. Collins and his express reached Saltillo on April 2. Waiting only long enough for

General Taylor to draft a reply to Doniphan's letter, the messengers, plus a detachment of Arkansas cavalry, departed for Chihuahua on April 9. Ibid., 339–44. Taylor reported receiving the message from Doniphan: Taylor to Adj. Gen. U.S. Army, Washington, D.C., April 4, 1847, *House Exec. Doc. No.* 60, Serial 520, 30th Cong., 1st Sess., p. 1127.

22. Hastings Diary, April 4–5, April 9, 1847 (quote on April 4), Justin Smith Papers, Benson Collection, UT–Austin; Wislizenus, *Memoir of a Tour,* 62; Robinson, *Journal,* 80; Edwards, *Campaign in New Mexico,* 131; Gibson, *Journal of a Soldier,* 362; Edwards, *Marching with the Army,* 277. Hastings seems to imply that Lieutenant Colonel Jackson was concerned about civil unrest in Chihuahua if a Mexican army approached the city (Hastings Diary, April 5–6, 1847). See also Launius, *Doniphan, Missouri Moderate,* 177.

23. Hastings Diary, April 23, 1847, Justin Smith Papers, Benson Collection, UT–Austin; Edwards, *Campaign in New Mexico,* 132; Wislizenus, *Memoir of a Tour,* 62; Edwards, *Marching with the Army,* 279; Robinson, *Journal,* 81–82 (quote on 82). Taylor to Lt. H. L. Scott (Asst. Adj. Gen. for Gen. Winfield Scott), April 16, 1847, in *House Exec. Doc. No.* 60, Serial 520, 30th Cong., 1st Sess., pp. 1170–71. Soon after Taylor issued his order, the New Orleans *Daily Delta* (May 5, 1847) printed an article indicating that the Missouri regiment would be leaving the war zone.

24. Hastings Diary, April 25, 1847, Justin Smith Papers, Benson Collection, UT–Austin; Robinson, *Journal,* 82; Hughes, *Doniphan's Expedition,* 351; Connelley, comp., *Doniphan's Expedition,* 467 and 467–68 n; Hughes to Editor, Liberty *Tribune,* May 28, 1847, Alvord Collection, Joint Collection, WHMC–SHSM, UM–Columbia.

25. Hughes, *Doniphan's Expedition,* 352; *Mitchell v. Harmony* 13 Howard 119–20, 140; Harmony's Petition, *House Report No.* 458, Serial 525, 30th Cong., 1st Sess., pp. 13–14.

26. Hastings Diary, notations for April 25 through early May 1847, Justin Smith Papers, Benson Collection, UT–Austin; Robinson, *Journal,* 82.

27. Kennerly, *Persimmon Hill,* 203; Wislizenus, *Memoir of a Tour,* 63.

28. Edwards, *Campaign in New Mexico,* 134; Robinson, *Journal,* 83; McGroarty, ed., "Richardson's Journal," *MHR* (July 1928), 520; Wislizenus, *Memoir of a Tour,* 64–65; Hughes, *Doniphan's Expedition,* 353.

29. McGroarty, ed., "Richardson's Journal," *MHR* (July 1928), 520; Wislizenus, *Memoir of a Tour,* 65; Hughes, *Doniphan's Expedition,* 353–54; Hughes to Editor, Liberty *Tribune,* May 28, 1847, Alvord Collection, Joint Collection, WHMC–SHSM, UM–Columbia.

30. McGroarty, ed., "Richardson's Journal," *MHR* (July 1928), 521; Hughes, *Doniphan's Expedition,* 355, 356, 358; Wislizenus, *Memoir of a Tour,* 65–66.

31. Wislizenus, *Memoir of a Tour,* 67; Hughes to Editor, Liberty *Tribune,* June 8, 1847, Alvord Collection, Joint Collection, WHMC–SHSM, UM–Columbia.

32. Robinson, *Journal,* 84–87; McGroarty, ed., "Richardson's Journal," *MHR* (July 1928), 521–22; Wislizenus, *Memoir of a Tour,* 68–69; Hughes, *Doniphan's Expedition,* 356–61 (the other two dead soldiers were King and Ferguson, who died of unspecified maladies). For the basic route of the regiment, see also James M. Cutts, *The Conquest of California and New Mexico by the Forces of the United States in the Years 1846 and 1847* (Philadelphia, 1847; repr., Albuquerque, 1965), 87.

33. Edwards, *Campaign in New Mexico,* 95 (emphasis in the original).

34. Ibid., 139; Wislizenus, *Memoir of a Tour,* 71; Kennerly, *Persimmon Hill,* 203.

35. Capt. John Reid to Gen. John Wool, May 21, 1847, in *House Exec. Doc. No.* 60, Serial 520, 30 Cong., 1st Sess., p. 1144; Hughes to Miller, April 4, 1847, in Hughes, *Doniphan's*

Expedition, 342–43; Hughes to Miller, June 9, 1847, Liberty *Tribune*, July 10, 1847; Columbia *Missouri Statesman*, July 2, 1847; Kennerly, *Persimmon Hill*, 203; Wislizenus, *Memoir of a Tour*, 71.

36. Reid to Wool, May 21, 1847, in *House Exec. Doc. No.* 60, Serial 520, 30th Cong., 1st Sess., p. 1144; Hughes to Miller, June 9, 1947, Liberty *Tribune*, July 10, 1847; Wislizenus, *Memoir of a Tour*, 71; Connelley, comp., *Doniphan's Expedition*, 478 n.

37. Reid to Wool, May 21, 1847, in *House Exec. Doc. No.* 60, Serial 520, 30th Cong., 1st Sess., pp. 1144–45; Connelley, comp., *Doniphan's Expedition*, 477 n (first quote), 476 and 476 n (second quote); Wislizenus, *Memoir of a Tour*, 71; Columbia *Statesman*, July 2, 1847; Robinson, *Journal*, 85. See also Launius, *Doniphan, Missouri Moderate*, 184.

38. Wislizenus, *Memoir of a Tour*, 71; New Orleans *Daily Picayune*, June 16, 1847; Kennerly, *Persimmon Hill*, 203–4; Kennerly to Justin H. Smith [n.d.], William C. Kennerly Papers, MHS, St. Louis (quote).

39. Reid to Wool, May 21, 1847, in *House Exec. Doc. No.* 60, Serial 520, 30th Cong., 1st Sess., p. 1144; Columbia *Statesman*, July 2, 1847; Wislizenus, *Memoir of a Tour*, 71; fiesta quote from Kennerly, *Persimmon Hill*, 204; Hughes, *Doniphan's Expedition*, 342, 365.

40. Hughes, *Doniphan's Expedition*, 366 (first quote); Robinson, *Journal*, 86 (second quote), 85 (third quote); McGroarty, ed., "Richardson's Journal," *MHR* (July 1928), 523, (emphasis in the original); Wislizenus, *Memoir of a Tour*, 73.

41. Hughes, *Doniphan's Expedition*, 365–66.

42. No memoir of the expedition gives a full account of this episode, but see Wislizenus, *Memoir of a Tour*, 73; Robinson, *Journal*, 87; Edwards, *Campaign in New Mexico*, 141–42; McGroarty, ed., "Richardson's Journal," *MHR* (July 1928), 523–24; Hughes, *Doniphan's Expedition*, 367, gives the man's name as "Lickenlighter." The *Articles of War*, Article 32, specifies that "every officer commanding . . . on the march, shall keep good order, and . . . redress all abuses or disorders which may be committed by an officer or soldier under his command"; and that commanding officers should take appropriate action against any "officers or soldiers beating or otherwise ill-treating any person." U.S. War Department, *Articles of War* (Washington, D.C., 1824), 12.

43. McGroarty, ed., "Richardson's Journal," *MHR* (July 1928), 524.

44. Hastings Diary, May 18, 1847, Justin Smith Papers, Benson Collection, UT–Austin; Wislizenus, *Memoir of a Tour*, 74–75 (quote on 74); Edwards, *Campaign in New Mexico*, 145; Hughes, *Doniphan's Expedition*, 367–68.

45. Wislizenus, *Memoir of a Tour*, 75; Edwards, *Campaign in New Mexico*, 146–47; McGroarty, ed., "Richardson's Journal," *MHR* (July 1928), 525; Jonathan W. Buhoup, *Narrative of the Central Division, or Army of Chihuahua* (Pittsburgh, 1847), 140; Hobbs, *Wild Life in the Far West*, 157; Order of Gen. Wool, May 22, 1847, quoted in Hughes, *Doniphan's Expedition*, 369; see also Connelley, comp., *Doniphan's Expedition*, 483 and 483–84 n; Launius, *Doniphan, Missouri Moderate*, 185–86.

46. Hughes, *Doniphan's Expedition*, 369; George W. Cullum, *Biographical Register of the Officers and Graduates of the United States Military Academy*, 3 vols. (Boston, 1891), 1:616.

47. Wislizenus, *Memoir of a Tour*, 76–77; Taylor to Adj. Gen., U.S. Army, May 26, 1847, in *House Exec. Doc. No.* 60, Serial 520, 30th Cong., 1st Sess., p. 1143; Edwards, *Campaign in New Mexico*, 149; McGroarty, ed., "Richardson's Journal," *MHR* (July 1928), 526; Isaac George, *Heroes and Incidents of the Mexican War, Containing Doniphan's Expedition* (Greensburg, Pa., 1903), 132; Hughes, *Doniphan's Expedition*, 370.

48. Edwards, *Campaign in New Mexico,* 151 (first quote), 163; Kennerly, *Persimmon Hill,* 204–5 (quote on 204); McGroarty, ed., "Richardson's Journal," *MHR* (July 1928), 526; Taylor's Order in Camp near Monterrey, April 14, 1847, quoted in George, *Heroes and Incidents,* 132–34 (quote on 134); Zachary Taylor/Asst. Adj. Gen. W. W. Bliss to Adj. Gen. Roger Jones, May 26, 1847, Adjutant General, Letters Received, 1845–1889, Microcopy M-567, roll 362, RG 94, NA; Robinson, *Journal,* 89; Wislizenus, *Memoir of a Tour,* 80; Thomas L. Karnes, *William Gilpin, Western Nationalist* (Austin, 1970), 184; Hughes, *Doniphan's Expedition,* 375–76.

49. McGroarty, ed., "Richardson's Journal," *MHR* (July 1928), 526; Edwards, *Campaign in New Mexico,* 152; Wislizenus, *Memoir of a Tour,* 77; Launius, *Doniphan, Missouri Moderate,* 187–88.

50. McGroarty, ed., "Richardson's Journal, *MHR* (July 1928), 526; Wislizenus, *Memoir of a Tour,* 78–79; Kennerly, *Persimmon Hill,* 203; Edwards, *Campaign in New Mexico,* 157.

51. Hughes, *Doniphan's Expedition,* 373 (burial of soldier [Tharp]); McGroarty, ed., "Richardson's Journal," *MHR* (July 1928), 528; Edwards, *Campaign in New Mexico,* 158; Wislizenus, *Memoir of a Tour,* 79.

52. Robinson, *Journal,* 89; Wislizenus, *Memoir of a Tour,* 80; Edwards, *Campaign in New Mexico,* 159; McGroarty, ed., "Richardson's Journal," *MHR* (July 1928), 528; Hughes, *Doniphan's Expedition,* 373–74; U.S. War Department, *Articles of War,* Article 32, committing violence against "any person," and Article 54, regarding destruction of property. *Articles of War,* 12, 17.

53. Wislizenus, *Memoir of a Tour,* 80; Robinson, *Journal,* 89–90.

54. Josiah Gregg, *Diary and Letters of Josiah Gregg,* ed. Maurice G. Fulton, 2 vols. (Norman, Okla., 1944), 2:1438; McGroarty, ed., "Richardson's Journal," *MHR* (July 1928), 528; Matamoros *Flag,* cited in New Orleans *Daily Picayune,* June 15, 1847; Kennerly, *Persimmon Hill,* 205; Edwards, *Campaign in New Mexico,* 164.

55. Wislizenus, *Memoir of a Tour,* 80; McGroarty, ed., "Richardson's Journal," *MHR* (July 1928), 529.

56. Gregg, *Diary and Letters of Josiah Gregg,* 2:149; Claude M. Fuess, *The Life of Caleb Cushing,* 2 vols. (New York, 1923), 2:44; Matamoros *Flag,* quoted in *Niles National Register,* June 26, 1847.

57. McGroarty, ed., "Richardson's Journal," *MHR* (July 1928), 529; Wislizenus, *Memoir of a Tour,* 81; Hughes, *Doniphan's Expedition,* 375.

58. Wislizenus, *Memoir of a Tour,* 81–82 (quote on 82); McGroarty, ed., "Richardson's Journal," *MHR* (July 1928), 530; Wool's Order, May 22, 1847, quoted in Hughes, *Doniphan's Expedition,* 369.

Chapter 9. Coming Home a Hero: "American Xenophon"

1. William B. McGroarty, ed., "William H. Richardson's Journal of Doniphan's Expedition," *Missouri Historical Review (MHR)* 22 (July 1928), 530–32 (quote on 530); New Orleans *Daily Picayune,* June 16, 1847 (hereafter cited as *Picayune,* with all citations to the *Daily Picayune*); New Orleans *Commercial Bulletin,* June 17, 1847 (hereafter cited as *Commercial Bulletin*); Columbia *Missouri Statesman,* July 2, 1847 (hereafter Columbia *Statesman*); John T. Hughes, *Doniphan's Expedition; Containing an Account of the Conquest of New Mexico . . .*

(Cincinnati, 1847; repr., Chicago, 1962), 376–77; Isaac George, *Heroes and Incidents of the Mexican War, Containing Doniphan's Expedition* (Greensburg, Pa., 1903), 141. Hughes gave the name of the second steamer as *Murillo,* but some newspaper reports mentioned the name of another vessel, the *Sovereign*. The Missourians' Gulf voyage was similar to that of other volunteers. See, for examples, Joseph E. Chance, ed., *Mexico under Fire: Being the Diary of Samuel Ryan Curtis . . .* (Fort Worth, Tex., 1994), 207–8; and Allan Peskin, ed., *Volunteers: The Mexican War Journals . . .* (Kent, Ohio, 1991), 313–15.

2. New Orleans *National*, n.d., was given play in the East by being quoted in the Baltimore *Niles National Register,* July 17, 1847, and the same story ran in the Milledgeville, Ga., *Southern Recorder,* June 29, 1847 (hereafter cited as N.O. *National* in *Niles National Register*); *Picayune*, June 16 and 17 (quote), 1847.

3. New Orleans *Bee,* June 16, 1847; New Orleans *Louisiana Courier,* June 16, 1847 (hereinafter cited as *Courier*); Jacob S. Robinson, *A Journal of the Santa Fe Expedition under Colonel Doniphan*, ed. Carl L. Cannon (Princeton, 1932), 91; *Picayune,* June 18, 1847; New Orleans *Daily Delta*, June 26, 1847 (quote), hereafter cited as *Delta*.

4. N.O. *National* in *Niles National Register,* July 17, 1847; *Delta,* June 17 and 18, 1847; *Courier,* June 16, 1847; Lt. Nelson McClanahan, 14th Infantry Regiment, New Orleans, to John R. McClanahan, Jackson, Tennessee, June 19, 1847, in McClanahan and Taylor Family Papers, Southern Historical Collection, University of North Carolina at Chapel Hill. See also Hughes, *Doniphan's Expedition*, 378.

5. N.O. *National* in *Niles National Register,* July 17, 1847.

6. For turning in the rifles see Hughes, *Doniphan's Expedition*, 379. Sargeant William C. Kennerly recalled that they "turned our muskets," not using the word "rifles"; William C. Kennerly, *Persimmon Hill: A Narrative of Old St. Louis and the Far West* (Norman, Okla., 1948), 204–5. For receiving pay see ibid., 206, and Company Muster Rolls, with notations of pay and allowances, Volunteer Organizations, Mexican War, 1st Missouri Mounted Regiment, Records of the U.S. Army Adjutant General's Office, Record Group (RG) 94, National Archives (NA) (copy at Missouri State Archives, Jefferson City); New Orleans *Picayune,* June 27, 1847; George, *Heroes and Incidents*, 142, Thomas D. Tennery, *The Mexican War Diary of Thomas D. Tennery*, ed. D. E. Livingston-Little (Norman, Okla., 1970), 95. Purchasing clothes: Doniphan, *Address in Liberty, Missouri, June 5, 1872; Delta*, June 17, 1847; *Picayune*, June 17, 1847 ("lions" quote). See also *Commercial Bulletin*, June 17, 1847.

7. *Delta*, June 19 (first quote), 20, 27 (other quotes), 1847.

8. For activities around the city and Doniphan's jest about recognizing his soldiers, see James Hobbs, *Wild Life in the Far West, Personal Adventures of a Border Mountain Man* (Hartford, Conn., 1873; repr., Glorieta, N.M., 1969), 167, 170; *Courier,* June 18, 1847; *Delta,* June 17 (quote) and 19, 1847; *Picayune,* June 17, 1847 (paraphrasing Marshall's speech); the report on Lafayette Square is in St. Louis *Weekly Reveille,* June 28, 1847.

9. St. Louis *Weekly Reveille,* July 5, 1847; Columbia *Statesman*, July 2, 1847; Kennerly, *Persimmon Hill*, 207.

10. St. Louis *Weekly Reveille,* July 5, 1847.

11. See Waldo W. Braden, ed., *Oratory in the Old South* (Baton Rouge, La., 1970).

12. The best summary about returning soldiers is found in James M. McCaffrey, *Army of Manifest Destiny: The American Soldier in the Mexican War, 1846–1848* (New York, 1992), 202–3. For some specific examples see Ernest M. Lander Jr., *Reluctant Imperialists: Calhoun, the South Carolinians, and the Mexican War* (Baton Rouge, La., 1980), 140–47; Jack A. Meyer,

South Carolina in the Mexican War: A History of the Palmetto Regiment of Volunteers (Columbia, S.C., 1996), 120–28; Randy W. Hackenburg, *Pennsylvania in the War with Mexico* (Shippensburg, Pa., 1992), 88; Joseph E. Chance, *Jefferson Davis's Mexican War Regiment* (Jackson, Miss., 1991), 128–29; Robert E. May, *John A. Quitman: Old South Crusader* (Baton Rouge, La., 1985), 200–201; John S. Kendall, *History of New Orleans*, 3 vols. (Chicago, 1922), 1:167.

13. J. Thomas Scharf, *History of St. Louis City and County*, 2 vols. (Philadelphia, 1883), 1:379–81; Hughes, *Doniphan's Expedition*, 380; St. Louis *Daily Missouri Republican*, June 23, 1847; St. Louis *Weekly Reveille*, June 28, 1847; St. Louis *Daily Union*, June 26, 1847 (last quote).

14. St. Louis *Daily Union*, July 3, 1847; Scharf, *History of St. Louis*, 1:380–81.

15. St. Louis *Daily Union*, July 3, 1847 (quote); Scharf, *History of St. Louis*, 1:381.

16. Columbia *Statesman*, July 9, 1847; St. Louis *Daily Union*, July 3, 1847; St. Louis *Weekly Reveille*, July 5, 1847; Scharf, *History of St. Louis*, 1:381.

17. Hughes, *Doniphan's Expedition*, 380; St. Louis *Daily Union*, July 3, 1847 (quotes).

18. St. Louis *Daily Union*, July 3, 1847, and Bowlin's speech in Liberty, Mo., *Weekly Tribune* (hereafter Liberty *Tribune*), July 10, 1847.

19. The best description is in St. Louis *Daily Union*, July 3, 1847.

20. For examples of newspaper coverage in Missouri of Benton's speech, see ibid.; St. Louis *Weekly Reveille*, July 5, 1847; Jefferson City *Weekly Inquirer* (hereafter Jefferson City *Inquirer*), July 10, 1847; Columbia *Statesman*, July 9, 1847. For examples outside Missouri, see New Orleans *Daily Picayune*, July 9, 1847; Washington *Daily Union*, July 12, 1847; Baltimore *Niles National Register*, July 17, 1847. Benton's speech was also published as a contemporary broadside, copy in Mexican War Papers, Missouri Historical Society (MHS), St. Louis, and also appeared in contemporary books, such as Hughes, *Doniphan's Expedition*, 380; *Rough and Ready Annual* (New York, 1848), 207–16; James M. Cutts, *The Conquest of California and New Mexico by the Forces of the United States in the Years 1846 and 1847* (Philadelphia, 1847; repr., Albuquerque, 1965), 89–98. The speech is also quoted in Scharf, *History of St. Louis*, 1:382–85. See also note 36, below.

21. Benton/Doniphan broadside, Mexican War Papers, MHS, St. Louis; Liberty, *Tribune*, July 17, 1847; St. Louis *Daily Union*, July 3, 1847; Washington *National Whig*, July 12, 1847. See also Roger D. Launius, *Alexander William Doniphan, Portrait of a Missouri Moderate* (Columbia, Mo., 1997), 191–92.

22. James Glasgow to William Glasgow, July 4, 1847, William C. Lane Collection, MHS, St. Louis; Elizabeth G. Sargent to Mother, July 10, 1847, St. Louis History Papers, MHS, St. Louis; Jefferson City *Inquirer*, July 10, 1847.

23. Liberty *Tribune*, July 17, 24, 1847, reported Atchison's speech, a complete copy of which is in the Alvord Collection, Joint Collection, Western Historical Manuscript Collection–State Historical Society of Missouri, University of Missouri–Columbia; transcripts of toasts, ibid.; lengthy speech welcoming Company H back to Callaway County, comparing the Doniphan Expedition to Hannibal's troops, in Charles Hardin Collection, ibid.; Hughes, *Doniphan's Expedition*, 382–83; Jefferson City *Inquirer*, July 17, 1847; festivities, including dinners, receptions, and a parade, in Glasgow and Fayette reported in Fayette, Mo., *Boon's Lick Times*, July 10, 17, 31, 1847.

24. Reporting on the Gallatin festivities was Volney E. Bragg to Robert H. Miller, editor of the Liberty *Weekly Tribune*, in the paper's issue of August 28, 1847; see also ibid., July 31,

1847, for the Davis and Forbis advertisement. The political speculation came in the Springfield, Mo., *Advertiser*, June 22, 1847, and Columbia *Statesman*, June 4, 1847. See also John V. Mering, *The Whig Party in Missouri* (Columbia, Mo., 1967), 203.

25. May, *John A. Quitman*, esp. 173, 181, 190–93, 199–203, 368; Thomas W. Cutrer, *Ben McCulloch and the Frontier Military Tradition* (Chapel Hill, N.C., 1993), esp. 68–69, 73–74, 88–89. Robert Johannsen concludes that "Doniphan . . . became *the* hero to the citizen-soldiers." Robert W. Johannsen, *To the Halls of the Montezumas: The Mexican War in the American Imagination* (New York, 1985), 123 (Johannsen's emphasis).

26. Another officer with a creditable record but only a few months of service in 1846 was Albert Sidney Johnston (West Point Class of 1826, served on active duty 1826–1834); Charles P. Roland, *Albert Sidney Johnston, Soldier of Three Republics* (Austin, 1964), 127–37. Selected treatments include, for Davis (West Point 1828, served 1828–1835), Chance, *Jefferson Davis's Mexican War Regiment*, esp. 53–54, 98–99, 104; for McKee (West Point 1829, served 1829–1836), see Johannsen, *To the Halls of the Montezumas*, 95; and for McKee and Marshall (West Point 1832, served 1832–1833), see Richard B. Salisbury, "Kentuckians at the Battle of Buena Vista," *Filson Club Quarterly* 61 (January 1987), 34–53; for Hughes (West Point cadet 1823–1827 but not a graduate, served 1827–1847, on active duty when appointed), see Adrian G. Trass, *From the Golden Gate to Mexico City: The U.S. Army Topographical Engineers in the Mexican War* (Washington, D.C., 1993), 201 and passim; for Hamtramck (West Point 1819, served 1819–1822), see Lee A. Wallace Jr., "The First Regiment of Virginia Volunteers, 1846–1848," *Virginia Magazine of History and Biography* 77 (January 1969), 46–77; for Butler (a Regular infantry captain, 1819–1829), see Lander, *Reluctant Imperialists*, 88–121; for Burnett (West Point 1832, served 1832–1836), see Francis B. Heitman, *Historical Register and Dictionary of the United States Army*, 2 vols. (Washington, D.C., 1903), 1:264; and George W. Cullum, *Biographical Register of the Officers and Graduates of the United States Military Academy*, 2 vols. (New York, 1868), 1:405. A listing of former Regular officers serving as volunteer colonels is given in note 11, chapter 2.

27. St. George L. Sioussat, ed., "Mexican War Letters of Col. William Bowen Campbell of Tennessee," *Tennessee Historical Magazine* 1 (June 1915), 129–67. Other colonels rated poorly or ended the war with controversial records, including Archibald Yell of Arkansas (William W. Hughes, *Archibald Yell* [Fayetteville, Ark., 1988]); Henry R. Jackson of Georgia (Wilbur G. Kurtz Jr., "The First Regiment of Georgia Volunteers in the Mexican War," *Georgia Historical Quarterly* 27 [December 1943], 301–23); Joseph Lane and James H. Lane of Indiana (Herman J. Viola, "Zachary Taylor and the Indiana Volunteers," *Southwestern Historical Quarterly* 72 [January 1969], 335–46); and Robert T. Paine of North Carolina (Lee A. Wallace Jr., "Raising a Volunteer Regiment for Mexico, 1846–1847," *North Carolina Historical Review* 35 [January 1958], 20–33).

28. New Orleans *Bee*, June 26, 1847; N.O. *National* in *Niles National Register*, July 17, 1847.

29. *Commercial Bulletin*, June 17, 1847. For an introduction to the matters of parallels, see Carl J. Richard, *The Founders and the Classics: Greece, Rome and the American Enlightenment* (Cambridge, Mass., 1994), passim, and esp. chap. 1, "The Classical Conditioning of the Founders."

30. New Orleans *Courier*, June 16, 1847.

31. Richard, *Founders and the Classics*, refers to Xenophon as a heroic model for Americans,

pp. 53, 56–57. Richard quotes one of the signers of the Constitution, James Wilson, who emphasized, "When some future Xenophon or Thucydides shall arise to do justice to their virtues and their actions, the glory of America will rival—it will outshine the glory of Greece." Ibid., 227. Thucydides was an Athenian general-admiral who stressed the need to maintain a navy to defend Athens.

32. References for this paragraph and the two following include the excellent introduction by Maurice W. Mather and Joseph W. Hewitt, eds., *Xenophon's Anabasis, Books I–IV* (Norman, Okla., 1962), 11–33, W. E. Higgins, *Xenophon the Athenian: The Problem of the Individual in the Society of the Polis* (Albany, N.Y., 1977), passim; H. W. Parke, *Greek Mercenary Soldiers from the Earliest Times to the Battle of Ipsus* (Oxford, 1933), 23–42; and G. B. Nussbaum, *The Ten Thousand: A Study in Social Organization and Action in Xenophon's Anabasis* (Leiden, Netherlands, 1967), esp. 13, 40, 114, 115, 117, 125, 135–39, 144.

33. The contemporary use of the phrase "American Xenophon" appears in an article from the St. Louis *New Era*, n.d., quoted in Baltimore *Niles National Register*, June 12, 1847.

34. New York *Evening Post*, June 25, 1847.

35. *Delta*, May 7 (first quote), May 14, 1847 (second quote).

36. St. Louis *New Era*, n.d., quoted in Baltimore *Niles National Register*, June 12, 1847 (emphasis in the original); Baltimore *Daily Republican & Argus*, May 15, 1847. For Senator Benton's speech, see, for example, St. Louis *Daily Union*, July 3, 1847; St. Louis *Weekly Reveille*, July 5, 1847; Columbia *Statesman*, July 9, 1847; Jefferson City *Inquirer*, July 10, 1847; Baltimore *Niles National Register*, July 17, 1847; New Orleans *Picayune*, July 9, 1847; Washington *Daily Union*, July 12, 1847; Richmond, Va., *Enquirer*, July 3, 13, 1847; Detroit *Free Press*, July 13, 1847; Cleveland *Plain Dealer*, July 10, 1847; Hughes, *Doniphan's Expedition*, 383, 376 (emphasis added), 385; John S. Jenkins, *History of the War between the United States and Mexico from the Commencement of Hostilities to the Ratification of the Treaty of Peace* (New York, 1850), 320; interview with Doniphan in Santa Fe *Era Southwestern*, August 5, 1880. However, for negative commentary on the march by a Regular Army lieutenant, see Roswell S. Ripley, *The War with Mexico*, 2 vols. (New York, 1849), 1:467.

37. Abeil Leonard et al. to James K. Polk, October 23, 1847, in Office of the Secretary of War Applications File, 1846–1848, Box 9, RG 107, NA.

38. *Delta*, June 16 (first quote), June 17, 1847 (second quote); Isaac Smith, *Reminiscences of a Campaign in Mexico: An Account of the Operations of the Indiana Brigade* (Indianapolis, 1848), 57; Hughes, *Doniphan's Expedition*, 387. Confirming the *Delta*'s conclusion, historian Robert Johannsen contends that "aside from Taylor, the commander who most captured the public's esteem and admiration was . . . Doniphan." Johannsen, *To the Halls of the Montezumas*, 123.

39. William L. Marcy to QM Major Samuel McKee (in St. Louis), May 23, 1848, Letters Sent by the Secretary of War Relating to Military Affairs, 1800–1889, Microcopy M-6, roll 28, RG 107, NA. Marcy had complimented Doniphan in a letter to General Kearny, praising his "gallant action and . . . glorious victory at Sacramento." Marcy to Kearny, May 10, 1847, William L. Marcy Papers, Library of Congress.

40. New York *Herald*, June 18, 1848; *Addresses Delivered in the Chapel at West Point before the Officers and Cadets of the United States Military Academy by the Hon. Ashbel Smith, of Texas, and Col. A. W. Doniphan, of Missouri, June 16, 1848* (New York, 1848), 7, copy of pamphlet in the archives, U.S. Military Academy Library.

41. New York *Herald*, June 18, 1848; *Addresses Delivered in the Chapel at West Point*, 16.

Rather than believing that Doniphan was physically ill, Raymond Settle concluded that Doniphan had experienced a severe case of anxiety. See Raymond Settle, "Alexander William Doniphan: Zenophon [*sic*] of the West" (unpublished typescript, Raymond Settle Collection, Charles F. Curry Library, William Jewell College, Liberty, Missouri), 399.

42. New York *Herald*, June 18, 1848 (first quote); *Addresses Delivered in the Chapel at West Point*, 16 (second quote). For analysis of Jefferson's expectations for the Military Academy providing citizen-officers, as well as Regulars, see Stephen E. Ambrose, *Duty, Honor, Country: A History of West Point* (Baltimore, 1966), 85; and Theodore J. Crackel, *Mr. Jefferson's Army: Political and Social Reform of the Military Establishment, 1801–1809* (New York, 1987), 73.

43. *Addresses Delivered in the Chapel at West Point*, 20 (first quote); New York *Herald*, June 18, 1848 (second quote); Philadelphia *Alexander's Pictorial Messenger*, June 28, 1848 (last quote). See also Launius, *Doniphan, Missouri Moderate*, 194, 207.

Chapter 10. The Hero in the Crisis of the Union

1. Doniphan interview, Santa Fe *Era Southwestern*, August 5, 1880; Polk's message of December 5, 1848, in James D. Richardson, *Messages and Papers of the Presidents, 1789–1897*, 10 vols. (Washington, D.C., 1897), 4:631.

2. Otero quoted in Charles A. Hale, *Mexican Liberalism in the Age of Mora, 1821–1853* (New Haven, Conn., 1968), 14; see also ibid., 13, 207–9, 213.

3. Allan Nevins, ed., *The Diary of Philip Hone, 1828–1851*, 2 vols. (New York, 1927), 2:774, entry for October 3, 1846 (emphasis in the original).

4. Of the many works treating the controversy over slavery expansion, see Allan Nevins, *Ordeal of the Union*: vol. 1, *Fruits of Manifest Destiny, 1847–1852* (New York, 1947), esp. 8–9, 21–24, 28–29, 32–33; and Chaplain W. Morrison, *Democratic Politics and Sectionalism: The Wilmot Proviso Controversy* (Chapel Hill, N.C., 1967), 16–20, 34, 37–51. See also Josefina Zoraida Vázquez, *Mexicans and North Americans on the War of 47* [1977], excerpt in Cecil Robinson, ed., *The View from Chapultepec: Mexican Writers on the Mexican-American War* (Tucson, 1989), 196–97. Resolution quoted in Liberty, Mo., *Weekly Tribune*, June 7, 1850 (hereafter cited as Liberty *Tribune*).

5. John V. Mering, *The Whig Party in Missouri* (Columbia, Mo., 1967), 143–44 (Wilson quoted on 143); Doniphan was mentioned as a gubernatorial candidate as early as June 1847: Liberty *Tribune*, June 12, 19, 1847; see also ibid., May 15, August 11, 1848; André P. Duchateau, "Missouri Colossus: Alexander William Doniphan, 1808–1887" (Ed.D. dissertation, Oklahoma State University, 1973), 270–71.

6. On the compromise generally, see Holman Hamilton, *Prologue to Conflict: The Crisis and Compromise of 1850* (Lexington, Ky., 1964); and David M. Potter, *The Impending Crisis, 1848–1861* (New York, 1976), 96–112; and Nevins, *Fruits of Manifest Destiny*, 318–45.

7. John Wilson to James Rollins, July 14, 1847, James S. Rollins Papers, Joint Collection, Western Historical Manuscript Collection–State Historical Society of Missouri Manuscripts, University of Missouri-Columbia (hereafter Joint Collection, WHMC–SHSM, UM–Columbia); Liberty *Tribune*, February 22, 1850 ("Bronchittis" quote), April 30 (Doniphan for governor), May 7, 21, 28, June 11, 1852; Mering, *Whig Party in Missouri*, 182, 208; Duchateau, "Missouri Colossus," 295–96; Robert E. Shalhope, *Sterling Price: Portrait of a Southerner* (Columbia, Mo., 1971), 98.

8. D. C. Allen, *An Address at the Unveiling of the Monument to the Memory of Col. Doniphan, Delivered Oct. 17, 1888* (Liberty, Mo., 1893), 5; Duchateau, "Missouri Colossus," 297, 299–301, 307, 322–24; Roger D. Launius, *Alexander William Doniphan, Portrait of a Missouri Moderate* (Columbia, Mo., 1997), 212–13; Doniphan, at Liberty, Missouri, to Gen. George Gibson, Commissary General, Washington, D.C., February 12, 1856, and endorsement by Mordecai Oliver to Gibson, March 13, 1856, in Records of the Office of the Quartermaster General, Consolidated Correspondence File, 1794–1915, Box 515, Records of the Office of the Quartermaster General, Record Group (RG) 92, National Archives (NA), Washington, D.C.; Doniphan and J. Thompson to Quartermaster Office, December 29, 1856, ibid., Box 262; Liberty *Tribune*, December 17, 1858. A report, ibid., December 17, 1858, indicates that the soldiers finally won reimbursement for their horses lost or killed on the expedition. On the founding of William Jewell College, see Liberty *Tribune*, September 7, 1849.

9. Liberty *Tribune*, May 13, 1853; William E. Connelley, comp., *Doniphan's Expedition and the Conquest of New Mexico and California* (Topeka, 1907), vii; Doniphan made a religious profession to his cousin Emma in an undated letter, found in William B. McGroarty, ed., "Letters from Alexander W. Doniphan," *Missouri Historical Review (MHR)* 24 (October 1929), 39. Doniphan expressed his thanks for his "unchanging and undoubting faith, [giving him] the most implicit confidence of again meeting my loved and lost ones in a brighter world."

10. See generally Potter, *Impending Crisis*, 240, and Mering, *Whig Party in Missouri*, 209. An excellent summary for political developments in Missouri is Perry McCandless, *A History of Missouri*, vol. 2, *1820–1860* (Columbia, Mo., 1972), 251–53, 261, 265–66. Doniphan's support for Scott is noted in Liberty *Tribune*, August 6, 1852. On the postwar competition among high-ranking veterans, see Richard Bruce Winders, *Mr. Polk's Army: The American Military Experience in the Mexican War* (College Station, Tex., 1997), 203.

11. Duchateau, "Missouri Colossus," 304–7; Launius, *Doniphan, Missouri Moderate*, 224–25, 228–29; Mering, *Whig Party in Missouri*, 203, 206–8; William E. Parrish, *David Rice Atchison of Missouri, Border Politician* (Columbia, Mo., 1961), 157–59; Liberty *Tribune*, January 12, February 2, 1855; William N. Chambers, *Old Bullion Benton: Senator from the New West* (Boston, 1956), 409–10. In 1857 the legislature picked former congressman James S. Green, a Democrat, to fill the Senate seat.

12. Potter, *Impending Crisis*, 160–77; Parrish, *Atchison*, 146–51.

13. Liberty *Tribune*, December 8, 1854; Duchateau, "Missouri Colossus," 304; Launius, *Doniphan, Missouri Moderate*, 221–23; McCandless, *History of Missouri*, 273; James A. Rawley, *Race and Politics: "Bleeding Kansas" and the Coming of the Civil War* (Philadelphia, 1969).

14. On the state's growth in the 1850s (from 682,000 to 1,182,000) and the decline of slaves by percent of population, see Edwin C. McReynolds, *Missouri: A History of the Crossroads State* (Norman, Okla., 1962), 159, 163–64. A map of slave population density is included in William E. Parrish et al., *Missouri: The Heart of the Nation* (St. Louis, 1980), 108. According to the Eighth Census of the United States, 1860, Missouri, Slave Population Schedule, Clay County, Microcopy M-653, roll 661, RG 29, NA, Doniphan owned five slaves. Their ages, sexes, and estimated values were a twenty-six-year-old male ($1,100), a twenty-five-year-old male ($1,100), an eighteen-year-old male ($1,100), a twelve-year-old male ($500), and an eighteen-year-old female ($800), for an estimated total of $4,600. See also Harrison A. Tresler, "The Value and the Sale of the Missouri Slave," *MHR* 8 (January

1914), 69, 71–73; and Duchateau, "Missouri Colossus," 332. Owning five slaves made Doniphan a typical Missouri slaveholder, as about 70 percent of those owning slaves held five or fewer in 1860. See the discussion of slavery in William E. Parrish, *A History of Missouri*, vol. 3, *1860–1875* (Columbia, Mo., 1973), 7.

15. Duchateau, "Missouri Colossus," 308, 320; Launius, *Doniphan, Missouri Moderate*, 240; Parrish, *Atchison*, 175–76, 199–203; Shalhope, *Price*, 116–17; Liberty *Tribune*, July 20, 1855, June 13, 1858. See also Floyd C. Shoemaker, "Missouri's Proslavery Fight for Kansas, 1854–1855," *MHR* 48 (July 1954), 335–37.

16. Jay Monaghan, *Civil War on the Western Border, 1854–1865* (Boston, 1955), 53–59; Rawley, *Race and Politics*, 129–34; Parrish, *Atchison*, 199–202; James C. Malin, "LeCompte and the 'Sack of Lawrence,' May 21, 1856," *Kansas Historical Quarterly* 20 (August 1953), 465; Duchateau, "Missouri Colossus," 316; Launius, *Doniphan, Missouri Moderate*, 236–37.

17. Liberty *Tribune*, January 11, 1856, reported that the Jackson, Mississippi, *Southern Mercury* proposed Doniphan's name as presidential nominee of the American party. For mention of Doniphan's speeches and other aspects of the campaign, see Liberty *Tribune*, May 2, 16, 23, 30, July 18, 25, August 1, 1856; Duchateau, "Missouri Colossus," 312–14; Launius, *Doniphan, Missouri Moderate*, 225–26, 235; McCandless, *History of Missouri*, 268–70.

18. Liberty *Tribune*, August 3, 24, 31, November 9 (quote), 1860; Duchateau, "Missouri Colossus," 326–28; Launius, *Doniphan, Missouri Moderate*, 242–43.

19. Paraphrase of Doniphan's speech, quoted in Liberty *Tribune*, November 9, 1860.

20. Summary of election results, ibid. William E. Parrish, *Turbulent Partnership: Missouri and the Union, 1861–1865* (Columbia, Mo., 1963), 5–6; Launius, *Doniphan, Missouri Moderate*, 244.

21. Charles M. Wiltse, ed., *The Papers of Daniel Webster*, series 4, *Speeches and Formal Writings, 1800–1833*, 2 vols. (Hanover, N.H., 1988), 1:347–48, 586.

22. José María Roa Bárcena, *Memories of the North American Invasion* [1902], in Robinson, ed., *View from Chapultepec*, p. 46; see also Robinson's introduction, ibid., 34. Secession dates were Mississippi (January 9), Florida (January 10), Alabama (January 11), Georgia (January 19), and Louisiana (January 26).

23. Liberty *Tribune*, February 1, 1861; Doniphan to nephew John Doniphan, January 28, 1861, Alexander William Doniphan Letters, Joint Collection, WHMC–SHSM, UM–Columbia; Duchateau, "Missouri Colossus," 330–32; Arthur R. Kirkpatrick, "Missouri on the Eve of the Civil War," *MHR* 55 (January 1961), 103.

24. Potter, *Impending Crisis*, 546.

25. *Biographical Directory of the American Congress, 1774–1989* (Washington, D.C., 1989), 687; Theodore C. Pease and James G. Randall, eds., *The Diary of Orville Hickman Browning*, 2 vols. (Springfield, Ill., 1925), 1:xi, xiv, 451. The two men attended Augusta College together from 1825 to 1826. Doniphan graduated in 1826; Browning matriculated from 1825 to 1829 but did not graduate. Maurice G. Baxter, *Orville H. Browning, Lincoln's Friend and Critic* (Bloomington, Ind., 1957), 3–4.

26. Liberty *Tribune*, February 15, 1861; Browning quoted in Pease and Randall, eds., *Browning Diary*, 1:451 (emphasis added).

27. Robert G. Gunderson, *Old Gentlemen's Convention: The Washington Peace Conference of 1861* (Madison, Wis., 1961), 10–12, 105–6, provides lists of delegates. They included more than sixty who had served in their state legislature, nineteen former state governors, fifty who once held seats in the U.S. House of Representatives, and fourteen former U.S. senators. Fessenden and Morrill continued to serve as Republicans in the Senate. Curtis became a

Union general. Future cabinet members included Seddon, secretary of war for the Confederacy, Chase, secretary of the Treasury for the Union, and Smith, secretary of the interior under Lincoln. Zollicoffer was a Confederate general. As a congressman from Massachusetts, Boutwell was a member of the congressional Joint Committee on Reconstruction and one of the managers of President Andrew Johnson's impeachment.

28. Gunderson, *Old Gentlemen's Convention*, 12–13 (Greeley quoted on 12).

29. Ibid., 63, 98–100; James M. McPherson, *Battle Cry of Freedom: The Civil War Era* (New York, 1988), 253. President-elect Abraham Lincoln had been skeptical of what the convention might produce, and he already had indicated that he would not support any compromise that either encouraged the expansion of slavery into the western territories or gave the peculiar institution a permanent place in the nation's life. Lincoln especially opposed the idea reestablishing the old 36°30′ line of the Missouri Compromise because Southern pro-slavery leaders intended to add other territories that would be transformed into future slave states. Thus the divisive issue of slavery would be perpetuated in American society and American politics. See David H. Donald, *Lincoln* (New York, 1995), 268.

30. Lucius E. Chittenden, *A Report of the Debates and Proceedings in the Secret Sessions of the Convention for Proposing Amendments to the Constitution of the United States* (New York, 1864), 312, 378; Gunderson, *Old Gentlemen's Convention*, 47.

31. Gunderson, *Old Gentlemen's Convention*, 62, 87–90, 107–9 (quote on 108); McPherson, *Battle Cry of Freedom*, 256.

32. Doniphan to John Doniphan, February 22, 1861 (emphasis added), Alexander William Doniphan Letters, Joint Collection, WHMC–SHSM, UM–Columbia; McPherson, *Battle Cry of Freedom*, 257. An overview of the Peace Convention is found in Launius, *Doniphan, Missouri Moderate*, 245–48.

33. The Doniphan-Lincoln meeting is described in the Liberty *Tribune*, March 8, 1861. Lincoln's quotations from Roy P. Basler et al., eds., *The Collected Works of Abraham Lincoln*, 9 vols. (New Brunswick, N.J., 1953–1955), 1:420–22, 439; Benjamin P. Thomas, *Abraham Lincoln* (New York, 1952), 118–21 (congressional resolution quoted on 119). See also Donald, *Lincoln*, 123–24, 279.

34. Doniphan to John Doniphan, February 22, 1861, Alexander William Doniphan Letters, Joint Collection, WHMC–SHSM, UM–Columbia.

35. Thomas L. Snead, *The Fight for Missouri, from the Election of Lincoln to the Death of Lyon* (New York, 1886), 54; *History of Clay and Platte Counties, Missouri* (St. Louis, 1885), 192; Walter H. Ryle, *Missouri: Union or Secession* (Nashville, Tenn., 1931), 196; Albert Castel, *General Sterling Price and the Civil War in the West* (Baton Rouge, La., 1968), 10–11; Shalhope, *Price*, 149–51; Duchateau, "Missouri Colossus," 338; Parrish, *Turbulent Partnership*, 10; Parrish, *Missouri, 1860–1875*, 6; McReynolds, *Missouri*, 259.

36. Duchateau, "Missouri Colossus," 338; McReynolds, *Missouri*, 210, 212.

37. *Journal and Proceedings of the Missouri State Convention Held at Jefferson City and St. Louis, March 1861* (St. Louis, 1861), *Journal*, first pagination, 23–24, quotations from *Proceedings*, second pagination, 23–24. See also Liberty *Tribune*, March 15, 1861.

38. Duchateau, "Missouri Colossus," 338; Parrish, *Turbulent Partnership*, 11–14.

39. Doniphan's speech quoted in Liberty *Tribune*, March 29, 1861; also quoted in Ryle, *Missouri: Union or Secession*, 226, and Duchateau, "Missouri Colossus," 339; Launius, *Doniphan, Missouri Moderate*, 251. See also Snead, *Fight for Missouri*, 54; Parrish, *Turbulent Partnership*, 14.

40. Duchateau, "Missouri Colossus," 329–30; Liberty *Tribune*, March 29, 1861. A few

months later, Johnson was in Confederate service. See Ezra J. Warner and W. Buck Yearns, *Biographical Register of the Confederate Congress* (Baton Rouge, La., 1975), 135.

41. Parrish, *Missouri, 1860–1875*, 10–11, 18–22.

42. W. H. Woodson, *History of Clay County, Missouri* (Topeka, 1920), 124; Christopher Phillips, *Damned Yankee: The Life of General Nathaniel Lyon* (Columbia, Mo., 1990), 141–54, 185–99; Castel, *General Sterling Price*, 14–15; Shalhope, *Price*, 156–59; Parrish, *Turbulent Partnership*, 18–24, 26; Parrish, *Missouri, 1860–1875*, 13–17.

43. Liberty *Tribune*, May 24, 1861; Thomas L. Snead, "The First Year of the War in Missouri," in Robert U. Johnson and C. C. Buel, eds., *Battles and Leaders of the Civil War*, 4 vols. (New York, 1887–1888), 1:266 (quote); Snead, *Fight for Missouri*, 184–85, recalls some of the men considered for militia commissions.

44. For the strained circumstances of the temporary "truce," see Castel, *General Sterling Price*, 18–22, and Shalhope, *Price*, 161–65. See also William L. Webb, *Battles and Biographies of Missouri: Or the Civil War Period in Our State* (Kansas City, 1900), 280; Woodson, *History of Clay County*, 125; Duchateau, "Missouri Colossus," 340–41; Launius, *Doniphan, Missouri Moderate*, 252–53.

45. Liberty *Tribune*, May 31, June 7, 1861; Parrish, *Atchison*, 215. For contrasting conclusions about Doniphan's attitudes and motivations, see Duchateau, "Missouri Colossus," 341. William Connelley recounted the traditional story that in the winter of 1861 Doniphan himself brought information to Union colonel James Birch about a Confederate raid on a railroad bridge near Camden, thereby thwarting a plan by John Hughes to destroy the bridge. See Connelley, comp., *Doniphan's Expedition*, 55–57; Webb, *Battles and Biographies of Missourians*, 86; and Duchateau, "Missouri Colossus," 344–45.

46. Doniphan to John Doniphan, June 2, 1861, Alexander William Doniphan Letters, Joint Collection, WHMC–SHSM, UM–Columbia; see also Duchateau, "Missouri Colossus," 342–43.

47. Duchateau, "Missouri Colossus," 343; Parrish, *Missouri, 1860–1875*, 22; Phillips, *Damned Yankee*, 212–14.

48. Duchateau, "Missouri Colossus," 343–44; McReynolds, *Missouri*, 260; Parrish, *Turbulent Partnership*, 33–42; Parrish, *Missouri, 1860–1875*, 24–28, 30.

49. Phillips, *Damned Yankee*, 240–64; Parrish, *Missouri, 1860–1875*, 30–35, 38. Kentucky was the only other state that placed representatives and senators in both congresses.

50. Liberty *Tribune*, April 18, 1862; Duchateau, "Missouri Colossus," 346; Parrish, *Turbulent Partnership*, 87.

51. *History of Clay and Platte Counties*, 195; Duchateau, "Missouri Colossus," 347–49; Parrish, *Turbulent Partnership*, 141–48; Parrish, *Missouri, 1860–1875*, 96; Doniphan to D. C. Allen, June 22, 1863, Doniphan Papers, Missouri Historical Society (MHS), St. Louis.

52. Doniphan's vote and views, probably paraphrased from his address to the State Convention, quoted in Liberty *Tribune*, July 10, 1863.

53. Doniphan to W. H. Jennings, September 2, 1864, Civil War Papers, MHS, St. Louis; Launius, *Doniphan, Missouri Moderate*, 261–62.

After Doniphan's Wars

1. Dwight L. Clarke, *Stephen Watts Kearny, Soldier of the West* (Norman, Okla., 1961), 180–293, passim.

2. George W. Cullum, *Biographical Register of the Officers and Graduates of the United States Military Academy*, 2 vols. (New York, 1868), 1:538–39.

3. Ibid., 1:481; Register of Personnel of Walker's Army in Nicaragua, February 26, 1857, C. I. Fayssoux Collection of William Walker Papers, Box 3, Latin American Library, Tulane University, New Orleans, Louisiana.

4. Ray H. Mattison, "David Dawson Mitchell," in LeRoy R. Hafen, ed., *The Mountain Men and the Fur Trade of the Far West: Biographical Sketches of the Participants*, 10 vols. (Glendale, Calif., 1965–1972), 2:241–46; Roger D. Launius, *Alexander William Doniphan, Portrait of a Missouri Moderate* (Columbia, Mo., 1997), 204–6. See *Harmony v. Mitchell* 1 *Blatchford* 549, 11 Federal Cases 559 [1850], in the Federal District Court for the Southern District of New York, and *Mitchell v. Harmony* 13 *Howard* 115 [1851], in the U.S. Supreme Court, plus the request from Secretary of the Treasury Thomas Corwin to Secretary of War Jefferson Davis, requesting ninety-seven thousand dollars to apply to Harmony's petition and the judgment against Mitchell. *Senate Report No. 53*, Serial 630, 32nd Cong., 1st Sess., p. 2. Congress rescued Mitchell from financial distress by appropriating funds to cover Harmony's losses.

5. William E. Connelley, comp., *Doniphan's Expedition and the Conquest of New Mexico and California* (Topeka, 1907), 362–63 n; *Biographical Directory of the American Congress, 1774–1989* (Washington, D.C., 1989), 2023–24.

6. Connelley, comp., *Doniphan's Expedition*, 46–58.

7. Ezra J. Warner, *Generals in Gray: Lives of the Confederate Commanders* (Baton Rouge, La., 1959), 228–29.

8. Ibid., 246–47; Robert E. Shalhope, *Sterling Price, Portrait of a Southerner* (Columbia, Mo., 1971), passim.

9. J. Thomas Scharf, *History of St. Louis City and County*, 2 vols. (Philadelphia, 1883), 2:1487.

10. Connelley, comp., *Doniphan's Expedition*, 133–34 n.

11. Bruce S. Allardice, *More Generals in Gray* (Baton Rouge, La., 1995), 61–62.

12. *Biographical Directory of the American Congress*, 1704–5.

13. Ibid., 1116; Connelley, comp., *Doniphan's Expedition*, 238–42 n.

14. George W. Cullum, *Biographical Register of the Officers and Graduates of the United States Military Academy*, 3rd ed., 3 vols. (Boston, 1891), 1:728–29.

15. *Biographical Directory of the American Congress*, 1272; Connelley, comp., *Doniphan's Expedition*, 363 n; Ezra J. Warner and W. Buck Yearns, *Biographical Register of the Confederate Congress* (Baton Rouge, La., 1975), 135.

16. William Y. Chalfant, *Dangerous Passage: The Santa Fe Trail and the Mexican War* (Norman, Okla., 1994), 165–84, 188–99; Henry Nash Smith, *Virgin Land: The American West as Symbol and Myth* (Cambridge, Mass., 1957), 35–43, 150. Thomas L. Karnes, *William Gilpin, Western Nationalist* (Austin, 1970), is the complete biography.

17. Ezra J. Warner, *Generals in Blue: Lives of the Union Commanders* (Baton Rouge, La., 1964), 476–77.

18. Individual Service Record of Alexander William Doniphan, Military Pension Records, Record Group 75, National Archives, Washington, D.C.; Duchateau, "Missouri Colossus," 268, 376; Launius, *Doniphan, Missouri Moderate*, 265–83.

BIBLIOGRAPHY

Primary Sources

MANUSCRIPT COLLECTIONS

Beinecke Library, Yale University, New Haven, Connecticut
- Baker, M. L., Letters
- Clark, Meriwether Lewis, Letterbook
- Emory, William H., Papers
- Prince, William E., Letterbook
- Western Americana Manuscripts: Mexican War

Charles F. Curry Library, William Jewell College, Liberty, Missouri
- Moss, O. P., Manuscript
- Settle, Raymond, Collection

Library of Congress, Washington, D.C.
- Marcy, William L., Papers

Missouri Historical Society, St. Louis
- Civil War Papers
- Clemens, Mary C., Collection
- Doniphan, Alexander W., Papers
- Jones, Lewis, Papers
- Kearny, Stephen W., Papers
- Kennerly, William C., Papers
- Kribben, Christian, Letters
- Lackland, James C., Papers
- Lane, William C., Collection
- Mexican War Papers
- Miller, Robert H., Papers
- Ruff, Charles F., Papers
- Stevenson, John D., Papers
- St. Louis History Papers
- Turner, Henry S., Collection

Missouri State Archives, Jefferson City
Muster Rolls of Missouri Volunteers, Mexican War, 1846–1848
Service Records of Missouri Volunteers, Mexican War, 1846–1848
Southern Historical Collection, University of North Carolina at Chapel Hill
McClanahan and Taylor Families, Papers
University of Missouri, Columbia: Joint Collection, Western Historical Manuscript Collection–State Historical Society of Missouri Manuscripts
Alvord Collection, 1760–1972
Colman-Hayter Collection
Doniphan, Alexander William, Letters
Hardin, Charles, Collection
Johnson, Waldo P., Papers
Miscellaneous Manuscripts
Rollins, James S., Papers
Smith, Elizabeth C., Papers
New Mexico State Records Center and Archives, Santa Fe
Getty Family, Papers
Read, Benjamin M., Collection
University of Texas at Austin: Barker Texas History Center
Chihuahua *Anglo-Saxon* Newspaper
University of Texas at Austin: Benson Latin American Collection
Smith, Justin H., Papers

RECORDS IN THE NATIONAL ARCHIVES, WASHINGTON, D.C.

Record Group 29, Federal Population Censuses of the United States
Fifth Census, 1830, Missouri, Population Schedules, St. Louis County and Lafayette County (Microcopy M-19, rolls 72, 73)
Sixth Census, 1840, Missouri, Population Schedules for Clay County (Microcopy M-704, roll 222)
Seventh Census, 1850, Missouri, Free Population Schedules, Clay County; Slave Schedules, Clay County (Microcopy M-432, rolls 396, 422)
Eighth Census, 1860, Missouri, Free Population Schedules, Clay County; Slave Population Schedules, Clay County (Microcopy M-653, rolls 614, 661)
Record Group 75, Military Pension Records
Individual Service Record of Colonel Alexander William Doniphan
Record Group 92, Records of the Office of the Quartermaster General
Consolidated Correspondence File, 1794–1915, Box 515
Record Group 94, Records of the United States Army Adjutant General's Office
Letters Received by the Office of the Adjutant General (Main Series), 1822–1860 (Microcopy M-567, rolls 314, 316, 319, 339, 362, and 373)
Muster Rolls of Volunteer Organizations, Mexican War: Missouri, Mounted Infantry
Orders of Brigadier General Stephen W. Kearny and Brigadier General Sterling Price, Army of the West (Microcopy T-1115, roll 1)
Record Group 107, Records of the United States Secretary of War
Applications File, 1846–1848

Registers of Letters Received (Microcopy M-22, rolls 63 and 64)
Letters Sent by the Secretary of War Relating to Military Affairs, 1800–1889 (Microcopy M-6, rolls 26, 27, and 28)
Record Group 156, Records of the Office of the Chief of Ordnance
Letters, Telegrams, and Endorsements Sent to Ordnance Officers and Military Storekeepers, 1839–1889
Quarterly Summary Statements of Ordnance and Ordnance Stores on Hand at Forts and Batteries, 1838–1853

UNITED STATES GOVERNMENT PUBLICATIONS

29th Congress, 1st Session
Senate Document No. 439, Serial 478 (Secretary of War, Call for Volunteers)
29th Congress, 2nd Session
House Executive Document No. 19, Serial 499 (Occupation of Mexican Territory, Including S. W. Kearny's Civil Appointments and Kearny's "Organic Law of Territory of New Mexico")
House Executive Document No. 42, Serial 499 (Volunteers Received into the Service of the United States)
House Executive Document No. 48, Serial 499 (Terms of Service of Volunteers)
30th Congress, 1st Session
Senate Executive Document No. 1, Serial 503 (Message of President James K. Polk to Congress, with Accompanying Documents and Correspondence, including Correspondence of Missouri Volunteer Officers) [duplicated in *House Executive Document No. 8*, Serial 515, 30th Congress, 1st Session]
Senate Executive Document No. 7, Serial 505 (Lieutenant William H. Emory's "Notes of a Military Reconnoissance [*sic*] from Fort Leavenworth . . . to San Diego . . . ") [duplicated as part of *House Executive Document No. 41*, Serial 517, 30th Congress, 1st Session]
Senate Executive Document No. 23, Serial 506 (Report of Lieutenant James W. Abert, "Examination of New Mexico in the Years 1846–47") [duplicated in House *Executive Document No. 41*, Serial 517, 30th Congress, 1st Session]
Senate Executive Document No. 36, Serial 507 (Adjutant General's Office, Report on Number of Troops in Service)
Senate Miscellaneous Document No. 26, Serial 511 (Dr. [Frederick] A. Wislizenus, "Memoir of a Tour to Northern Mexico Connected with Col. Doniphan's Expedition in 1846 and 1847")
House Executive Document No. 8, Serial 515 (Message of President James K. Polk to Congress, with Accompanying Documents and Correspondence) [duplicated as *Senate Executive Document No. 1*, Serial 503, 30th Congress, 1st Session]
House Executive Document No. 41, Serial 517 (Reports and Journals of U.S. Army Officers: Journal of Captain Abraham R. Johnston, 1st Dragoons; Lieutenant William H. Emory, Topographical Engineers, "Notes of a Military Reconnoissance [*sic*] from Fort Leavenworth . . . to San Diego . . . "; Report of Captain Philip St. George Cooke, "From Santa Fe to San Diego"; Report of Lieutenant James W. Abert, "Examination of New Mexico in the Years 1846–47")

House Executive Document No. 60, Serial 520 (Correspondence and Documents Relating to the War with Mexico, including Material Related to the Occupation of New Mexico) [reprinted in *Senate Doc. No.* 896, Serial 6179, 62nd Congress, 2nd Session]
House Executive Document No. 62, Serial 521 (Regular and Volunteer Soldiers Engaged in the War with Mexico)
House Executive Document No. 70, Serial 521 (Message of President James K. Polk, Documents Referring to Civil Government in New Mexico and California) [duplicated in *Senate Executive Document No. 17*, Serial 573, 31st Congress, 1st Session]
House Executive Document No. 74, Serial 521 (Strength of the U.S. Army at the Close of the Mexican War)
House Executive Document No. 76, Serial 521 (Message of the President Relating to Indians in Oregon, California, and New Mexico)
House Report No. 458, Serial 525 (Report on the Petition of Manual X. Harmony)
30th Congress, 2nd Session
Senate Miscellaneous Document No. 11, Serial 533 (Additional Documents in the Claim of Manuel X. Harmony)
30th Congress, Special Session
Senate Document No. 2, Serial 547 (Report of Lieutenant Colonel Philip St. George Cooke, "From Santa Fe to San Diego") [duplicated in *House Executive Document No. 41*, Serial 517, 30th Congress, 1st Session]
31st Congress, 1st Session
Senate Executive Document No. 17, Serial 573 (Documents Relating to the War with Mexico and Government in California and New Mexico) [duplicated as *House Executive Document No.* 70, Serial 521, 30th Congress, 1st Session]
31st Congress, 2nd Session
House Executive Document No. 23, Serial 599 (War Department Contracts and Purchases)
32nd Congress, 1st Session
Senate Report No. 53, Serial 630 (Memorial for the Relief of Lieutenant Colonel David Mitchell, Relating to the Case of Manuel X. Harmony)
56th Congress, 1st Session
Senate Executive Document No. 442, Serial 3878 (Report of Military Government of New Mexico and California, 1847–1848)
58th Congress, 2nd Session
Senate Document No. 319, Serial 4624 (Charles J. Kappler, comp. and ed., *Indian Affairs. Law and Treaties*)
62nd Congress, 2nd Session
Senate Document No. 896, Serial 6179 (partial reprint of *House Executive Document No.* 60, Serial 520, 30th Congress, 1st Session, Letters and Documents Relating to the Occupation of Mexican Territory)
63rd Congress, 2nd Session
Senate Document No. 698, Serial 6589 (reprint of John T. Hughes, *Doniphan's Expedition* [1847])

Congressional Globe
U.S. War Department. *Articles of War.* Washington, D.C.: E. deKrafft, 1824.

——. *General Regulations for the Army of the United States, 1841*. Washington, D.C.: Gideon, 1841.

——. *General Regulations for the Army of the United States, 1847*. Washington, D.C.: J. and G. S. Gideon, 1847.

——. *System of Exercise and Instruction of Field-Artillery, including Maneuvres for Light or Horse-Artillery*. Boston: Hilliard, Gray, Little and Wilkins, 1829.

Federal Court Cases

Federal Circuit Court, Southern District of New York, 1850

Harmony v. Mitchell, 11 Federal Cases 559, 1 Blatchford 549

U.S. Supreme Court, 1851

Mitchell v. Harmony, 13 Howard 115

WARTIME NEWSPAPERS

Albany, New York, *Evening Journal*
Augusta, Georgia, *Constitutionalist*
Baltimore *Daily Republican & Argus*
Baltimore *Niles National Register*
Baltimore *Sun*
Boston *Evening Transcript*
Boston *Post*
Brooklyn, New York, *Daily Eagle*
Charleston, South Carolina, *Courier*
Charleston, South Carolina, *Mercury*
Chicago *Daily Journal*
Chihuahua *Anglo Saxon*
Cincinnati *Daily Commercial*
Cincinnati *Daily Enquirer*
Cleveland, Ohio, *Plain Dealer*
Columbia *Missouri Statesman*
Detroit *Free Press*
Fayette, Missouri, *Boon's Lick Times*
Frankfort *Weekly Kentucky Yeoman*
Hartford, Connecticut, *Weekly Times*
Houston *Telegraph & Texas Register*
Indianapolis *Indiana State Sentinel*
Jackson *Mississippian*
Jefferson City, Missouri, *Weekly Inquirer*
Liberty, Missouri, *Weekly Tribune*
Little Rock *Arkansas State Gazette*
Louisville, Kentucky, *Daily Democrat*
Milledgeville, Georgia, *Federal Union*
Milledgeville, Georgia, *Southern Recorder*
Milwaukee *Daily Sentinel and Gazette*
Mobile, Alabama, *Daily Register*
Monterrey, Mexico, *American Pioneer*
Montgomery, Alabama, *Triweekly Flag & Advertiser*
Nashville *Republican Banner*
Natchez *Mississippi Free Trader*
New Orleans *Bee*
New Orleans *Commercial Bulletin*
New Orleans *Daily Delta*
New Orleans *Daily Picayune*
New Orleans *Louisiana Courier*
New York *Herald*
New York *Tribune*
New York *Weekly Evening Post*
Newark, New Jersey, *Daily Advertiser*
Philadelphia *Alexander's Pictorial Messenger*
Philadelphia *Gazette*
Philadelphia *North American*
Philadelphia *Public Ledger*
Pittsburgh *Morning Chronicle*
Raleigh *North Carolina Standard*
Richmond, Virginia, *Enquirer*
Richmond, Virginia, *Whig and Public Advertiser*
Saltillo, Mexico, *Picket Guard*
Santa Fe *Republican*
Savannah, Georgia, *Daily Republican*
Springfield *Illinois State Register*
Springfield, Missouri, *Advertiser*
St. Louis *Daily Missouri Republican*
St. Louis *Daily Union*
St. Louis *Weekly Reveille*
Tallahassee *Floridian*

Vicksburg, Mississippi, *Daily Whig*
Washington, D.C., *Daily Union*
Washington, D.C., *National Era*
Washington, D.C., *National Intelligencer*
Washington, D.C., *National Whig*

POSTWAR NEWSPAPERS

Denver *Post*
Kansas City *Star*
Kansas City *Times*
Santa Fe *Era Southwestern*

AUTOBIOGRAPHIES, MEMOIRS, DIARIES, EDITED PAPERS, AND CONTEMPORARY ACCOUNTS

BOOKS

Abert, James W. *Western America in 1846–1847*. Ed. John Galvin. San Francisco: John Howell, 1966.

Addresses Delivered in the Chapel at West Point . . . by the Hon. Ashbel Smith, of Texas, and Col. A. W. Doniphan, of Missouri, June 16, 1848. New York: Burroughs, 1848.

Alcaraz, Ramón, et al. *The Other Side; or Notes for the History of the War between Mexico and the United States*. Trans. Albert C. Ramsey. New York: Wiley, 1850. Repr., New York: Burt Franklin, 1970.

Allen, D. C. *An Address at the Unveiling of the Monument to the Memory of Col. Doniphan, Delivered Oct. 17, 1888*. Liberty, Mo.: Murry Bros., 1893.

———. *A Sketch of the Life and Character of Col. Alexander W. Doniphan*. Liberty, Mo.: Advance Printing, 1897. Reprinted in Allen, "Builders of the Great American West." *Journal of American History* 4 (1910), 511–24.

Anderson, Robert. *An Artillery Officer in the Mexican War, 1846–1847: Letters of Robert Anderson*. New York: Putnam, 1911.

Ballentine, George. *Autobiography of an English Soldier in the United States Army, Comprising Observations and Adventures in the States and Mexico.* New York: Stringer and Townsend, 1853.

Bartlett, John R. *Dictionary of Americanisms: A Glossary of Words and Phrases*. 2nd ed. Boston: Little, Brown, 1859.

Basler, Roy P., et al., eds. *The Collected Works of Abraham Lincoln*. 9 vols. New Brunswick, N.J.: Rutgers University Press, 1953–1955.

Basset, John S., ed. *The Correspondence of Andrew Jackson*. 7 vols. Washington, D.C.: 1926–1935.

Battles of Mexico: Containing an Authentic Account of All the Battles Fought in That Republic from the Commencement of the War until the Capture of the City of Mexico. New York: Martin and Ely, 1847.

Benton, Thomas Hart. *Thirty Years' View; or, A History of the Working of the American Government of Thirty Years, from 1820 to 1850*. New York: Appleton and Co., 1854, 1856.

Berge, Dennis E., ed. *The Mexican Republic, 1847*. El Paso: Texas Western Press, 1975.

Bieber, Ralph P., ed. *Exploring Southwestern Trails, 1846–1854*. Glendale, Calif.: Arthur H. Clark, 1938.

Brooks, Nathan C. *A Complete History of the Mexican War: Its Causes, Conduct and Consequences*. Philadelphia: Grigg, Elliot and Co., 1849. Repr., Chicago: Rio Grande Press, 1965.

Buhoup, Jonathan W. *Narrative of the Central Division, or Army of Chihuahua*. Pittsburgh: M. P. Morse, 1847.

Callan, John F. *The Military Laws of the United States*. Baltimore: Murphy and Co., 1858.

———. *The Military Laws of the United States, Relating to the Army, Volunteers, Militia, and to Bounty Lands and Pensions, from the Foundation of the Government to the Year 1863*. Philadelphia: G. W. Childs, 1863.

Calvin, Ross, ed. *Lieutenant Emory Reports*. Albuquerque: University of New Mexico Press, 1951.

Captain of Volunteers. *The Conquest of Santa Fe and Subjugation of New Mexico*. Philadelphia: Packer and Co., 1847.

Carleton, James H. *The Battle of Buena Vista*. New York: Harper and Bros., 1848.

Chamberlain, Samuel E. *My Confession*. New York: Harper, 1956.

Chance, Joseph E., ed. *Mexico under Fire: Being the Diary of Samuel Ryan Curtis, 3rd Ohio Volunteer Regiment during the American Military Occupation of Northern Mexico, 1846–1847*. Fort Worth: Texas Christian University Press, 1994.

Chittenden, Lucius E. *A Report of the Debates and Proceedings in the Secret Sessions of the Convention for Proposing Amendments to the Constitution of the United States*. New York: Appleton, 1864.

Clarke, Dwight L., ed. *The Original Journals of Henry Smith Turner with Stephen Watts Kearny to New Mexico and California, 1846–1847*. Norman: University of Oklahoma Press, 1966.

Connelley, William E., comp. *Doniphan's Expedition and the Conquest of New Mexico and California*. Topeka, Kans.: By the author, 1907.

Cooke, Philip St. George. *The Conquest of New Mexico and California: An Historical and Personal Narrative*. New York: Putnam, 1878. Repr., Oakland, Calif.: Biobooks, 1942.

Cutts, James M. *The Conquest of California and New Mexico by the Forces of the United States in the Years 1846 and 1847*. Philadelphia: Carey and Hart, 1847. Repr., Albuquerque: Horn & Wallace, 1965.

Doniphan, Alexander W. *Address by Col. Alexander W. Doniphan, Delivered in Liberty, Mo., June 5, 1872*. Liberty, Mo.: Advance Printing, 1883.

Doniphan, Alexander W., and Willard P. Hall. *Organic Laws of the Territory of New Mexico*. Santa Fe: n.p., 1846. Repr., Santa Fe: New Mexico State Historical Society, 1970.

Drumm, Stella M., ed. *Down the Santa Fe Trail and into Mexico: The Diary of Susan Shelby Magoffin 1846–1847*. New Haven, Conn.: Yale University Press, 1926. Repr., Lincoln: University of Nebraska Press, 1982.

Edwards, Frank S. *A Campaign in New Mexico with Colonel Doniphan*. Philadelphia: Carey and Hart, 1847. Repr., Ann Arbor, Mich.: University Microfilms, 1966.

Elliott, Richard S. *Notes Taken in Sixty Years*. St. Louis: R. P. Studley, 1883.

Ferrell, Robert H., ed. *Monterrey Is Ours! The Mexican War Letters of Lt. Dana, 1845–1847*. Lexington: University of Kentucky Press, 1989.

Frazer, Robert W., ed. *New Mexico in 1850: A Military View*. Norman: University of Oklahoma Press, 1968.

Frost, John. *The History of Mexico and Its Wars*. New Orleans: Armand Hawkins, 1882.

———. The Mexican War and Its Warriors: Comprising a Complete History of All the Operations of the American Armies in Mexico . . . New York: Mansfield, 1848.

———. *Pictorial History of Mexico and the Mexican War*. Philadelphia: Thomas Cowperthwait and Co., 1848.

Fuess, Claude M. *The Life of Caleb Cushing*. 2 vols. New York: Harcourt, Brace, and Co., 1923.

Furber, George C. *The Twelve Months Volunteer, or Journal of a Private in the Tennessee Regiment of Cavalry*. Cincinnati: J. A. and U. P. James, 1848.

Gardner, Mark L., ed. *Brothers on the Santa Fe and Chihuahua Trails*. Niwot: University Press of Colorado, 1993.

Gardner, Mark L., and Marc Simmons, eds. *The Mexican War Correspondence of Richard Smith Elliott*. Norman: University of Oklahoma Press, 1997.

Garrard, Lewis. *Wah-to-yah and the Taos Trail*. Philadelphia: W. H. Derby, 1850. Repr., ed. Ralph P. Bieber. Glendale, Calif.: Arthur H. Clark, 1938.

George, Isaac. *Heroes and Incidents of the Mexican War, Containing Doniphan's Expedition*. Greensburg, Pa.: Review Publishing Co., 1903. Repr., Hollywood, Calif.: Sun Dance Press, 1971.

Gibson, George R. *Journal of a Soldier under Kearny and Doniphan, 1846–1847*. Ed. Ralph P. Bieber. Glendale, Calif.: Arthur H. Clark, 1935.

———. *Over the Chihuahua and Santa Fe Trails, 1847–1848*. Ed. Robert W. Frazer. Albuquerque: University of New Mexico Press, 1981.

Gilpin, William. *Mission of the North American People, Geographical, Social, and Political*. Philadelphia: Lippincott, 1893.

Gregg, Josiah. *Commerce of the Prairies*. 2 vols. New York: Langley, 1844.

———. *Diary and Letters of Josiah Gregg*. 2 vols. Ed. Maurice G. Fulton. Norman: University of Oklahoma Press, 1944.

Hafen, LeRoy R., Clyde Porter, and Mae Reed Porter, eds. *Ruxton of the Rockies*. Norman: University of Oklahoma Press, 1950.

Henry, William S. *Campaign Sketches of the War with Mexico*. New York: Harper and Bros., 1847. Repr., New York: Arno, 1973.

Hitchcock, Ethan A. *Fifty Years in Camp and Field: Diary of Major General E. A. Hitchcock, U.S.A.* New York: Putnam's, 1909.

Hobbs, James. *Wild Life in the Far West, Personal Adventures of a Border Mountain Man*. Hartford, Conn.: Wiley, Waterman, and Eaton, 1872. Repr., Glorieta, N.M.: Rio Grande Press, 1969.

Hughes, John T. *Doniphan's Expedition; Containing an Account of the Conquest of New Mexico; General Kearny's Overland Expedition to California; Doniphan's Campaign against the Navajos; His Unparalleled March upon Chihuahua and Durango; and the Operations of General Price at Santa Fé*. Cincinnati: J. A. and U. P. James, 1847. Repr., Chicago: Rio Grande Press, 1962.

Jenkins, John S. *History of the War between the United States and Mexico from the Commencement of Hostilities to the Ratification of the Treaty of Peace*. Auburn, N.Y.: Derby and Miller, 1850.

Johnson, Robert U., and C. C. Buel, eds. *Battles and Leaders of the Civil War*. 4 vols. New York: Century Co., 1887–1888.

Johnston, Abraham R., Marcellus B. Edwards, and Philip G. Ferguson. *Marching with the Army of the West, 1846–1848*. Ed. Ralph P. Bieber. Glendale, Calif.: Arthur H. Clark, 1936.

Journal and Proceedings of the Missouri State Convention Held at Jefferson City and St. Louis, March 1861. St. Louis: George Knapp, 1861.

Kendall, George W. *The War between the United States and Mexico, Illustrated*. New York: Appleton, 1851. Repr., Austin: Texas State Historical Association, 1994.

Kennerly, William C. *Persimmon Hill: A Narrative of Old St. Louis and the Far West*. Norman: University of Oklahoma Press, 1948.

Leopard, Buel, and Floyd C. Shoemaker, eds. *The Messages and Proclamations of the Governors of the State of Missouri*. 2 vols. Columbia: State Historical Society of Missouri, 1922.

Lowe, Percival. *Five Years a Dragoon: ('49 to '54) and Other Adventures on the Great Plains*. Kansas City, Mo.: Franklin-Hudson, 1906. Repr., ed. Don Russell. Norman: University of Oklahoma Press, 1965.

Majors, Alexander. *Seventy Years on the Frontier: Alexander Majors' Memoirs of a Lifetime on the Border*. Chicago: Rand, McNally, 1893. Repr., Columbus, Ohio: Long's College Book Co., 1950.

Mansfield, Edward D. *The Mexican War; History of Its Origin and a Detailed Account of the Victories . . .* New York: A. S. Barnes, 1851.

Maury, Dabney H. *Recollections of a Virginian in the Mexican, Indian and Civil Wars*. New York: Scribner's, 1894.

Mayer, Brantz. *Mexico As It Was and As It Is*. Philadelphia: Zieber, 1847.

McCall, George A. *Letters from the Frontier, Written during a Period of 30 Years' Service in the Army of the United States*. Philadelphia: Lippincott, 1868.

McClellan, George B. *The Mexican War Diary of George B. McClellan*. Ed. William S. Myers. Princeton: Princeton University Press, 1917. Repr., New York: DaCapo Press, 1972.

McDougal, Henry C. *Recollections, 1844–1909*. Kansas City: Franklin Hudson, 1910.

Meade, George G. *The Life and Letters of George Gordon Meade*. 2 vols. New York: Scribner's, 1913.

The Mexican War and Its Heroes: Being a Complete History of the Mexican War . . . Together with Numerous Anecdotes of the War, and Personal Adventures of the Officers. Philadelphia: Lippincott, Grambo, and Co., 1850.

Murphy, Charles J. *Reminiscences of the War of the Rebellion and of the Mexican War*. New York: Ficker, 1882.

Nevins, Allan, ed. *The Diary of Philip Hone, 1828–1851*. 2 vols. New York: Dodd, Mead and Co., 1927.

———. *Polk: The Diary of a President, 1845–1849*. New York: Longmans, Green and Co., 1929.

Pease, Theodore C., and James G. Randall, eds. *The Diary of Orville Hickman Browning*. 2 vols. Springfield: Illinois State Historical Library, 1925.

Perry, Oran, comp. *Indiana in the Mexican War*. Indianapolis: Burford, 1902.

Peskin, Allan, ed. *Volunteers: The Mexican War Journals of Private Richard Coulter and Sergeant Thomas Barclay, Company E, Second Pennsylvania Infantry*. Kent, Ohio: Kent State University Press, 1991.

Peterson, Charles J. *Military Heroes of the War with Mexico*. Philadelphia: Smith and Co., 1858.

Porter, Valentine M. *A History of Battery "A" of St. Louis: With an Account of the Early Artillery Companies from Which It Is Descended*. St. Louis: Missouri Historical Society, 1905.

Quaife, Milo M., ed. *The Diary of James K. Polk, 1845–1849*. 4 vols. Chicago: McClurg, 1910.

Richardson, James D. *Messages and Papers of the Presidents, 1789–1897*. 10 vols. Washington, D.C.: Government Printing Office, 1897.

Richardson, William H. *Journal of William H. Richardson, A Private Soldier in Col. Doniphan's Command*. Baltimore: J. W. Woods, 1848.

Ripley, Roswell S. *The War with Mexico*. 2 vols. New York: Harper and Bros., 1849.

Robinson, Fayette. *An Account of the Organization of the Army of the United States: with Biographies of the Distinguished Officers of All Grades*. Philadelphia: E. H. Butler, 1848.

Robinson, Jacob S. *A Journal of the Santa Fe Expedition under Colonel Doniphan*. Ed. Carl L. Cannon. Princeton: Princeton University Press, 1932. Repr., New York: DaCapo Press, 1972.

Rough and Ready Annual. New York: D. Appleton Co., 1848.

Royce, Josiah. *California from the Conquest in 1846 to the Second Vigilance Committee in San Francisco: A Study of American Character*. Boston: Houghton Mifflin, 1886.

Ruxton, George F. *Adventures in Mexico and the Rocky Mountains*. London: John Murray, 1847; New York: Harper and Bros., 1855. Repr., Glorieta, N.M.: Rio Grande Press, 1973.

Scott, Henry L. *Military Dictionary: Comprising Technical Definitions . . .* New York: Van Nostrand, 1861. Repr., New York: Greenwood Press, 1968.

Scott, Winfield. *Memoirs of Lieutenant General Scott. Written by Himself*. 2 vols. New York: Sheldon, 1864.

Sherman, William T. *Memoirs of General William T. Sherman*. 2 vols. New York: D. Appleton and Co., 1875.

Sierra, Justo. *The Political Evolution of the Mexican People*. Trans. Charles Ramsdell. Austin: University of Texas Press, 1969.

Smith, E. Kirby. *To Mexico with Scott: Letters of Captain E. Kirby Smith to His Wife*. Ed. Emma J. Blackwood. Cambridge, Mass.: Harvard University Press, 1917.

Smith, Isaac. *Reminiscences of a Campaign in Mexico: An Account of the Operations of the Indiana Brigade*. Indianapolis: Chapman and Spann, 1848.

Snead, Thomas L. *The Fight for Missouri, from the Election of Lincoln to the Death of Lyon*. New York: Charles Scribner's Sons, 1886.

Stevens, Hazard. *The Life of Isaac Ingalls Stevens*. 2 vols. Boston: Houghton Mifflin, 1900.

Stevens, Isaac I. *Campaigns of the Rio Grande and of Mexico*. New York: D. Appleton and Co., 1851.

Strong, George T. *The Diary of George Templeton Strong*. 4 vols. Ed. Allan Nevins. New York: Macmillan, 1952.

Tennery, Thomas D. *The Mexican War Diary of Thomas D. Tennery*. Ed. D. E. Livingston-Little. Norman: University of Oklahoma Press, 1970.

Thompson, Waddy. *Recollections of Mexico*. New York: Wiley and Putnam, 1846.

Thorpe, Thomas B. *Our Army on the Rio Grande*. Philadelphia: Carey and Hart, 1846.

Tocqueville, Alexis de. *Democracy in America*. 2 vols. New York: Century Co., 1898.

Turnley, Parmenas T. *Reminiscences of Parmenas Taylor Turnley*. Chicago: Donohue and Henneberry, n.d.

Webb, James J. *Adventures in the Santa Fe Trade, 1844–1847*. Ed. Ralph P. Bieber. Glendale, Calif.: Arthur H. Clark, 1931.

Weber, David J., ed. *Arms, Indians, and the Mismanagement of New Mexico: Donaciano Vigil, 1846*. El Paso: Texas Western Press, 1986.

Wilcox, Cadmus M. *History of the Mexican War*. Washington, D.C.: Church News Press, 1892.

Wiltse, Charles M., ed. *The Papers of Daniel Webster*. Series 4, *Speeches and Formal Writings*. 2 vols. Hanover, N.H.: University Press of New England, 1988.

Wislizenus, Frederick A. *Memoir of a Tour to Northern Mexico Connected with Col. Doniphan's Expedition in 1846 and 1847*. 1848. Repr., Glorieta, N.M.: Rio Grande Press, 1969.

ARTICLES

Bieber, Ralph P., ed. "Letters of James and Robert Aull." *Missouri Historical Society Collections* 5 (1928), 276–310.

Connelley, William E., ed. "The Magoffin Papers." *Publications of the Historical Society of New Mexico,* no. 24 (1921), 42–63.

Cooke, Philip St. George. "A Journal of the Santa Fe Trail." Ed. William E. Connelley. *Mississippi Valley Historical Review* 12 (September 1925), 227–55.

Gallahar, F. M., ed. "Official Report of the Battle of Temascalitos (Brazito)." *New Mexico Historical Review* 3 (October 1928), 381–89.

Jaurrieta, Rómulo. "Batalla de Sacramento 28 de Febrero de 1847." *Boletín de la Sociedad Chihuahuense de Estudios Históricos* 7 (July/August 1950), 413–20.

McGroarty, William B., ed. "Letters from Alexander W. Doniphan." *Missouri Historical Review* 24 (October 1929), 26–39.

———. "William H. Richardson's Journal of Doniphan's Expedition." *Missouri Historical Review* 22 (January 1928), 193–236; (April 1928), 331–60; (July 1928), 511–42.

Moorhead, Max L., ed. "Notes and Documents [Relating to the U.S. Occupation of Santa Fe]." *New Mexico Historical Review* 26 (January 1951), 68–82.

"Origin of the War with Mexico." *Southern Quarterly Review* 15 (April 1849), 83–113.

O'Sullivan, John L. "Annexation." *Democratic Review* 17 (July 1845), 5–10.

Porter, Valentine M. "A History of Battery 'A' of St. Louis: With an Account of the Early Artillery Companies from Which It Is Descended." *Missouri Historical Society Collections* 2 (1905), 1–48.

Rollins, C. B., ed. "Letters of George Caleb Bingham." *Missouri Historical Review* 32 (October 1937), 3–34.

Scott, Jessup W. "The Great West." *DeBow's Review* 15 (July 1853), 50.

Sioussat, St. George L., ed. "Mexican War Letters of Col. William Bowen Campbell of Tennessee." *Tennessee Historical Magazine* 1 (June 1915), 129–67.

Smith, Justin H., ed. "Letters of General Antonio Lopez de Santa Anna Relating to the War between the United States and Mexico, 1846–1848." In *American Historical Association Annual Report for 1917*. 2 vols. Washington, D.C.: Government Printing Office, 1920.

Snead, Thomas L. "Alexander William Doniphan." *Magazine of American History* 13 (February 1885), 187–93.

Secondary Works

BOOKS

Almada, Francisco R. *Resumen de Historia del Estado de Chihuahua*. Mexico City: Libros Mexicanos, 1955.

Ambrose, Stephen E. *Duty, Honor, Country: A History of West Point*. Baltimore: Johns Hopkins University Press, 1966.

Anderson, J. K. *Military Theory and Practice in the Age of Xenophon*. Berkeley: University of California Press, 1970.

Balbontín, Manuel. *Estado Militar de la República Mexicana en 1846*. Mexico City: Tipografía de Ignacio Pombo, 1891.

Bancroft, Hubert H. *History of Arizona and New Mexico, 1530–1888*. San Francisco: The History Company, 1889. Repr., Albuquerque: Horn and Wallace, 1962.

———. *History of the Life of William Gilpin: A Character Study*. San Francisco: The History Company, 1889.

Bauer, K. Jack. *The Mexican War, 1846–1848*. New York: Macmillan, 1974.

Baxter, Maurice G. *Orville H. Browning, Lincoln's Friend and Critic*. Bloomington: Indiana University Press, 1957.

Beck, Warren A. *New Mexico: A History of Four Centuries*. Norman: University of Oklahoma Press, 1962.

Bergeron, Paul H. *The Presidency of James K. Polk*. Lawrence: University Press of Kansas, 1987.

Biggs, Donald C. *Conquer and Colonize: Stevenson's Regiment and California*. San Rafael: Presidio Press, 1977.

Billington, Ray A. *Westward Expansion*. New York: Macmillan, 1949.

Binkley, William C. *The Expansionist Movement in Texas, 1836–1850*. Berkeley: University of California Press, 1925.

Birkhimer, William E. *Military Government and Martial Law*. Washington, D.C.: Chapman, 1892; 2nd ed., Kansas City, Mo.: Franklin Hudson, 1892; 3rd ed., Kansas City, Mo.: Franklin Hudson, 1914.

Blainey, Geoffrey. *The Causes of War*. 3rd ed. New York: Free Press, 1988.

Brack, Gene M. *Mexico Views Manifest Destiny, 1821–1846: An Essay on the Origins of the Mexican War*. Albuquerque: University of New Mexico Press, 1975.

Braden, Waldo W., ed. *Oratory in the Old South*. Baton Rouge: Louisiana State University Press, 1970.

Brown, Thomas. *Politics and Statesmanship: Essays on the American Whig Party*. New York: Columbia University Press, 1985.

Bustamente, Carlos María de. *El Nuevo Bernal Díaz del Castillo o Sea, História de la Invasión de los Anglo-Americanos en México, compuesta en 1847*. 2 vols. Mexico: Secretaria de Educación Pública, 1949.

Carreño, Alberto M., ed. *Jefes del Ejército Mexicano en 1847: Biografías de generales de división y de brigada y de coronelles del ejército Mexicano por fines del año de 1847*. Mexico City: Imprenta y Fototipia de Secretaria de Formento, 1914.

Castel, Albert. *General Sterling Price and the Civil War in the West*. Baton Rouge: Louisiana State University Press, 1968.

Chalfant, William Y. *Dangerous Passage: The Santa Fe Trail and the Mexican War*. Norman: University of Oklahoma Press, 1994.

Chambers, William N. *Old Bullion Benton: Senator from the New West*. Boston: Little Brown, 1956.

Chance, Joseph E. *Jefferson Davis's Mexican War Regiment*. Jackson: University Press of Mississippi, 1991.

Chandler, David G. *The Military Maxims of Napoleon*. London: Greenhill Press, 1987.

Clarke, Dwight L. *Stephen Watts Kearny, Soldier of the West*. Norman: University of Oklahoma Press, 1961.

Clausewitz, Carl von. *On War*. Ed. and trans. Michael Howard and Peter Paret. Princeton: Princeton University Press, 1984.

Coffman, Edward M. *The Old Army: A Portrait of the American Army in Peacetime, 1784–1898*. New York: Oxford University Press, 1986.

Connor, Seymour V., and Odie B. Faulk. *North America Divided: The Mexican War, 1846–1848*. New York: Oxford University Press, 1971.

Connor, Seymour V., and Jimmy M. Skaggs. *Broadcloth and Britches: The Santa Fe Trade.* College Station: Texas A&M University Press, 1977.

Cooper, Jerry. *The Rise of the National Guard: The Evolution of the American Militia, 1865–1920.* Lincoln: University of Nebraska Press, 1997.

Copeland, Fayette. *Kendall of the Picayune.* Norman: University of Oklahoma Press, 1943.

Costeloe, Michael. *The Central Republic in Mexico, 1835–1846.* Cambridge, Mass.: Harvard University Press, 1993.

Cotner, Thomas E. *The Military and Political Career of José Joaquín de Herrera, 1792–1854.* Austin: University of Texas Press, 1949.

Cotner, Thomas E., and Carlos E. Castañeda, eds. *Essays in Mexican History.* Austin: Institute of Latin American Studies, 1958.

Crackel, Theodore J. *Mr. Jefferson's Army: Political and Social Reform of the Military Establishment, 1801–1809.* New York: New York University Press, 1987.

Crouch, Brodie. *Jornada del Muerto: A Pageant of the Desert.* Spokane, Wash.: Arthur H. Clark, 1989.

Cunliffe, Marcus. *Soldiers and Civilians: The Martial Spirit in America, 1775–1865.* Boston: Little, Brown, 1968.

Cutrer, Thomas W. *Ben McCulloch and the Frontier Military Tradition.* Chapel Hill: University of North Carolina Press, 1993.

Daugherty, William E., and Marshall Andrews. *A Review of U.S. Historical Experience with Civil Affairs, 1776–1954.* Bethesda, Md.: Operations Research Office of Johns Hopkins University, 1961.

Delbruck, Hans. *History of the Art of War within the Framework of Political History.* Vol. 1, *Antiquity.* Trans. Walter J. Renfroe Jr. Westport, Conn.: Greenwood Press, 1975.

DePalo, William A., Jr. *The Mexican National Army, 1822–1852.* College Station: Texas A&M University Press, 1997.

DeVoto, Bernard. *The Year of Decision, 1846.* Boston: Little, Brown, 1943.

Donald, David H. *Lincoln.* New York: Scribner's, 1995.

Dufour, Charles L. *The Mexican War: A Compact History, 1846–1848.* New York: Hawthorn Books, 1968.

Edrington, Thomas S., and John Taylor. *The Battle of Glorieta Pass.* Albuquerque: University of New Mexico Press, 1998.

Eisenhower, John S. D. *So Far from God: The U.S. War with Mexico, 1846–1848.* New York: Random House, 1989.

Freehling, William W. *The Road to Disunion: Secessionists at Bay, 1776–1854.* New York: Oxford University Press, 1990.

Fuller, Claud E. *The Breechloader in the Service, 1816–1917.* Topeka, Kans.: Arms Reference Club, 1933.

Fuller, John D. P. *The Movement for the Acquisition of All Mexico, 1846–1848.* Baltimore: Johns Hopkins University Press, 1936.

Garavaglia, Louis, A., and Charles G. Worman. *Firearms of the American West, 1803–1865.* Albuquerque: University of New Mexico Pres, 1984.

García Cantú, Gastón. *Las invasiones norteamericanas en México.* Mexico City: Ediciones Era, 1971.

Goetzmann, William H. *When the Eagle Screamed: The Romantic Horizon in American Diplomacy, 1800–1860.* New York: Wiley, 1966.

Graebner, Norman A. *Empire on the Pacific: A Study in American Continental Expansion*. New York: Ronald Press, 1955. Repr., Santa Barbara, Calif.: ABC Clio, 1983.

Green, Stanley C. *The Mexican Republic: The First Decade, 1823–1832*. Pittsburgh: University of Pittsburgh Press, 1987.

Griswald del Castillo, Richard. *The Treaty of Guadalupe Hidalgo*. Norman: University of Oklahoma Press, 1990.

Grivas, Theodore. *Military Governments in California, 1846–1850*. Glendale, Calif.: Arthur H. Clark, 1963.

Gunderson, Robert G. *Old Gentlemen's Convention: The Washington Peace Conference of 1861*. Madison: University of Wisconsin Press, 1961.

Hackenburg, Randy W. *Pennsylvania in the War with Mexico*. Shippensburg, Pa.: White Mane Publishing, 1992.

Hafen, LeRoy R., ed. *The Mountain Men and the Fur Trade of the Far West: Biographical Sketches of the Participants*. 10 vols. Glendale, Calif.: Arthur H. Clark, 1965–1972.

Hafen, LeRoy R., and William J. Ghent. *Broken Hand: The Life Story of Thomas Fitzpatrick, Chief of the Mountain Men*. Denver: Old West Publishing, 1931.

Hagan, Kenneth J. *This People's Navy: The Making of American* Sea Power. New York: Free Press, 1991.

Hale, Charles A. *Mexican Liberalism in the Age of Mora, 1821–1853*. New Haven, Conn.: Yale University Press, 1968.

Hamilton, Holman. *Prologue to Conflict: The Crisis and Compromise of 1850*. Lexington: University of Kentucky Press, 1964.

Hardin, Stephen L. *Texian Iliad: A Military History of the Texas Revolution*. Austin: University of Texas Press, 1994.

Harlow, Neal. *California Conquered: War and Peace on the Pacific, 1846–1850*. Berkeley: University of California Press, 1982.

Haynes, Sam W. *Soldiers of Misfortune: The Somervell and Mier Expeditions*. Austin: University of Texas Press, 1990.

Haynes, Sam W., and Christopher Morris, eds. *Manifest Destiny and Empire: American Antebellum Expansionism*. College Station: Texas A&M University Press, 1997.

Heller, Charles E., and William A. Stofft, eds. *America's First Battles, 1776–1965*. Lawrence: University Press of Kansas, 1986.

Henry, Robert S. *The Story of the Mexican War*. Indianapolis: Bobbs-Merrill, 1950.

Hietala, Thomas R. *Manifest Design: Anxious Aggrandizement in Late Jacksonian America*. Ithaca, N.Y.: Cornell University Press, 1985.

Higgins, W. E. *Xenophon the Athenian: The Problem of the Individual in the Society of the Polis*. Albany: State University of New York Press, 1977.

History of Callaway County, Missouri. St. Louis: National Historical Co., 1884.

History of Clay and Platte Counties, Missouri. St. Louis: National Historical Co., 1885.

History of Cole, Moniteau, Morgan, Benton, Miller, Maries and Osage Counties, Missouri. Chicago: Goodspeed Publishing Co., 1889.

Holden Reid, Brian. *The Origins of the American Civil War*. London and New York: Longman, 1996.

Horn, Calvin. *New Mexico's Troubled Years: The Story of the Early Territorial Governors*. Albuquerque: Horn and Wallace, 1963.

Horsman, Reginald. *Race and Manifest Destiny: The Origins of American Racial Anglo-Saxonism*. Cambridge, Mass.: Harvard University Press, 1981.
Hughes, Nathaniel C., Jr., and Roy P. Stonesifer Jr. *The Life and Wars of Gideon J. Pillow*. Chapel Hill: University of North Carolina Press, 1993.
Hughes, William W. *Archibald Yell*. Fayetteville: University of Arkansas Press, 1988.
Hunt, Elvid. *History of Fort Leavenworth, 1827–1927*. Fort Leavenworth, Kans.: General Service Schools Press, 1926.
Hyde, William, and Howard L. Conrad, eds. *Encyclopedia of the History of St. Louis*. 4 vols. St. Louis: Southern History Co., 1899.
Johannsen, Robert W. *To the Halls of the Montezumas: The Mexican War in the American Imagination*. New York: Oxford University Press, 1985.
Jomini, Antoine Henri de. *The Art of War*. Trans. G. H. Mendell and W. P. Craighill. Philadelphia: Lippincott, 1862. Repr., Westport, Conn.: Greenwood Press, 1971.
Karnes, Thomas L. *William Gilpin, Western Nationalist*. Austin: University of Texas Press, 1970.
Keleher, William A. *Turmoil in New Mexico, 1846–1848*. Santa Fe: Rydal Press, 1952.
Kelly, M. Margaret Jean. *The Career of Joseph Lane, Frontier Politician*. Washington, D.C.: Catholic University Press, 1942.
Kendall, John S. *History of New Orleans*. 3 vols. Chicago: Lewis Publishing, 1922.
Knoles, George H., ed. *Essays and Assays: California History Reappraised*. San Francisco: California Historical Society, 1973.
Kohn, Hans. *American Nationalism: An Interpretive Essay*. New York: Macmillan, 1957.
Kreidberg, Marvin A., and Merton G. Henry. *History of Military Mobilization in the United States, 1775–1945*. Washington, D.C.: Department of the Army, 1955.
Lamar, Howard R. *The Far Southwest, 1846–1912, A Territorial History*. New Haven, Conn.: Yale University Press, 1966.
Lander, Ernest M., Jr. *Reluctant Imperialists: Calhoun, the South Carolinians, and the Mexican War*. Baton Rouge: Louisiana State University Press, 1980.
Larson, Robert W. *New Mexico's Quest for Statehood, 1848–1912*. Albuquerque: University of New Mexico Press, 1968.
Launius, Roger D. *Alexander William Doniphan, Portrait of a Missouri Moderate*. Columbia: University of Missouri Press, 1997.
Lavender, David. *Bent's Fort*. Garden City, N.Y.: Doubleday, 1954.
———. *Climax at Buena Vista: The American Campaign in Northeastern Mexico*. Philadelphia: Lippincott, 1966.
LeSueur, Stephen C. *The 1838 Mormon War in Missouri*. Columbia: University of Missouri Press, 1987.
Liddell Hart, B. H. *Strategy*. 2nd rev. ed. New York: Praeger, 1967.
Limerick, Patricia N. *The Legacy of Conquest: The Unbroken Past of the American West*. New York: W. W. Norton, 1987.
Linderman, Gerald E. *Embattled Courage: The Experience of Combat in the American Civil War*. New York: Free Press, 1987.
Lister, Florence C., and Robert H. Lister. *Chihuahua, Storehouse of Storms*. Albuquerque: University of New Mexico Press, 1966.
Magoon, Charles E. *Reports on the Law of Civil Government in Territory Subject to Military*

Occupation by the Military Forces of the United States. Washington, D.C.: Government Printing Office, 1903. Repr., Buffalo, N.Y.: Hein and Co., 1972.

Mahon, John K. *History of the Militia and the National Guard*. New York: Macmillan, 1983.

Mary Loyola, Sister. *The American Occupation of New Mexico, 1821–1852*. Albuquerque: University of New Mexico Press, 1939. Repr., New York: Arno Press, 1976.

Mather, Maurice W., and Joseph W. Hewitt, eds. *Xenophon's Anabasis, Books I–IV*. Norman: University of Oklahoma Press, 1962.

May, Robert E. *John A. Quitman, Old South Crusader*. Baton Rouge: Louisiana State University Press, 1985.

McCaffrey, James M. *Army of Manifest Destiny: The American Soldier in the Mexican War, 1846–1848*. New York: New York University Press, 1992.

McCandless, Perry. *A History of Missouri*. Vol. 2, *1820–1860*. Columbia: University of Missouri Press, 1972.

McCoy, Charles A. *Polk and the Presidency*. Austin: University of Texas Press, 1960.

McGaw, William C. *Savage Scene: The Life and Times of James Kirker*. New York: Hastings House, 1972.

McKiernan, F. Mark, and Roger D. Launius, eds. *Missouri Folk Heroes of the Nineteenth Century*. Independence, Mo.: Independence Press, 1989.

McNitt, Frank. *Navajo Wars: Military Campaigns, Slave Raids, and Reprisals*. Albuquerque: University of New Mexico Press, 1972.

McPherson, James M. *Battle Cry of Freedom: The Civil War Era*. New York: Oxford University Press, 1988.

McReynolds, Edwin C. *Missouri: A History of the Crossroads State*. Norman: University of Oklahoma Press, 1962.

Meinig, D. W. *The Shaping of America: A Geographical Perspective on 500 Years of History*. Vol. 2, *Continental America, 1800–1867*. New Haven, Conn.: Yale University Press, 1993.

Mering, John V. *The Whig Party in Missouri*. Columbia: University of Missouri Press, 1967.

Merk, Frederick. *Slavery and the Annexation of Texas*. Cambridge, Mass., Harvard University Press, 1972.

Merk, Frederick, and Lois B. Merk. *Manifest Destiny and Mission in American History: A Reinterpretation*. New York: Alfred A. Knopf, 1963.

———. *The Monroe Doctrine and American Expansionism, 1843–1849*. New York: Alfred A. Knopf, 1966.

Meyer, Jack A. *South Carolina in the Mexican War: A History of the Palmetto Regiment of Volunteers, 1846–1917*. Columbia: South Carolina Department of Archives and History, 1996.

Millett, Allan R., and Peter Maslowski. *For the Common Defense*. Rev. ed. New York: Free Press, 1994.

Mitchell, Reid. *Civil War Soldiers: Their Expectations and Their Experiences*. New York: Viking, 1988.

———. *The Vacant Chair: The Northern Soldier Leaves Home*. New York: Oxford University Press, 1993.

Monaghan, Jay. *Civil War on the Western Border, 1854–1865*. Boston: Little, Brown, 1955.

Moorhead, Max L. *New Mexico's Royal Road: Trade and Travel on the Chihuahua Trail*. Norman: University of Oklahoma Press, 1958.

Morison, Samuel E., Frederick Merk, and Frank Freidel. *Dissent in Three American Wars*. Cambridge, Mass.: Harvard University Press, 1970.

Morrison, Chaplain W. *Democratic Politics and Sectionalism: The Wilmot Proviso Controversy*. Chapel Hill: University of North Carolina Press, 1967.

Morrison, Michael A. *Slavery and the American West: The Eclipse of Manifest Destiny and the Coming of the Civil War*. Chapel Hill: University of North Carolina Press, 1997.

Nagel, Paul C. *One Nation Indivisible: The Union in American Thought*. New York: Oxford University Press, 1964.

Nance, John Milton. *After San Jacinto: The Texas-Mexican Frontier, 1836–1841*. Austin: University of Texas Press, 1963.

Nevin, David. *The Mexican War*. Alexandria, Va.: Time-Life Books, 1978.

Nevins, Allan. *Ordeal of the Union*. Vol. 1, *Fruits of Manifest Destiny, 1847–1852*. New York: Scribner's, 1947.

Nichols, Roy F. *Franklin Pierce: Young Hickory of the Granite Hills*. Philadelphia: University of Pennsylvania Press, 1958.

Nussbaum, G. B. *The Ten Thousand: A Study in Social Organization and Action in Xenophon's Anabasis*. Leiden, Netherlands: E. J. Brill, 1967.

Oberly, James W. *Sixty Million Acres: American Veterans and the Public Lands before the Civil War*. Kent, Ohio: Kent State University Press, 1990.

Officer, James E. *Hispanic Arizona, 1536–1856*. Tucson: University of Arizona Press, 1987.

Oliva, Leo E. *Soldiers on the Santa Fe Trail*. Norman: University of Oklahoma Press, 1967.

Olivera, Ruth R., and Liliane Crété. *Life in Mexico under Santa Anna, 1822–1855*. Norman: University of Oklahoma Press, 1991.

Parke, H. W. *Greek Mercenary Soldiers from the Earliest Times to the Battle of Ipsus*. Oxford: Clarendon Press, 1933.

Parrish, William E. *David Rice Atchison of Missouri, Border Politician*. Columbia: University of Missouri Press, 1961.

———. *A History of Missouri*, Vol. 3, *1860–1875*. Columbia: University of Missouri Press, 1973.

———. *Turbulent Partnership: Missouri and the Union, 1861–1865*. Columbia: University of Missouri Press, 1963.

Parrish, William E., et al. *Missouri: The Heart of the Nation*. St. Louis: Forum Press, 1980.

Paxton, William H. *Annals of Platte County, Missouri*. Kansas City: Hudson-Kimberly Publishing Co., 1897.

Perry, Thomas S., ed. *The Life and Letters of Francis Lieber*. Boston: J. R. Osgood, 1882.

Peterson, Merrill D. *The Great Triumvirate: Webster, Clay, and Calhoun*. New York: Oxford University Press, 1987.

Peterson, Norma Lois. *The Presidencies of William Henry Harrison and John Tyler*. Lawrence: University Press of Kansas, 1989.

Phillips, Christopher. *Damned Yankee: The Life of General Nathaniel Lyon*. Columbia: University of Missouri Press, 1990.

Phillips, Thomas R., ed. *Roots of Strategy*. Harrisburg, Pa.: Military Service Publishing Co., 1940.

Pletcher, David M. *The Diplomacy of Annexation: Texas, Oregon, and the Mexican War*. Columbia: University of Missouri Press, 1973.

Portrait and Biographical Record of Clay, Ray, Carroll, Chariton and Linn Counties, Missouri. Chicago: Chapman Bros., 1893.

Potter, David M. *The Impending Crisis, 1848–1861*. New York: Harper and Row, 1976.

Powell, E. Alexander. *The Road to Glory*. New York: Scribner's, 1915.

Prucha, Francis P. *American Indian Treaties: A History of a Political Anomaly*. Berkeley: University of California Press, 1994.

———. *The Great Father: The United States Government and the American Indians*. 2 vols. Lincoln: University of Nebraska Press, 1984.

Raat, W. Dirk. *Mexico from Independence to Revolution, 1810–1910*. Lincoln: University of Nebraska Press, 1982.

Rawley, James A. *Race and Politics: "Bleeding Kansas" and the Coming of the Civil War*. Philadelphia: Lippincott, 1969.

Remini, Robert V. *Andrew Jackson and the Course of American Empire*. New York: Harper and Row, 1977.

———. *The Life of Andrew Jackson*. New York: Harper and Row, 1988.

Richard, Carl J. *The Founders and the Classics: Greece, Rome and the American Enlightenment*. Cambridge, Mass.: Harvard University Press, 1994.

Ricketts, Norma B. *The Mormon Battalion, U.S. Army of the West, 1846–1848*. Logan: Utah State University Press, 1996.

Rives, George L. *The United States and Mexico, 1821–1848*. 2 vols. New York: Scribner's, 1913.

Roa Bárcena, José María. *Recuerdos de la invasión norteamericana (1846–1848)*. 3 vols. Mexico City: Editorial Porrúa, 1947.

Roberts, Brigham H. *The Mormon Battalion: Its History and Achievements*. Salt Lake City: Deseret News, 1919.

Robinson, Cecil, ed. *The View from Chapultepec: Mexican Writers on the Mexican-American War*. Tucson: University of Arizona Press, 1989.

Roland, Charles P. *Albert Sidney Johnston, Soldier of Three Republics*. Austin: University of Texas Press, 1964.

Rosen, Stephen Peter. *Societies and Military Power: India and Her Armies*. Ithaca, N.Y.: Cornell University Press, 1996.

Russell, Carl P. *Guns on the Early Frontiers*. Berkeley: University of California Press, 1957.

Ryle, Walter H. *Missouri: Union or Secession*. Nashville, Tenn.: George Peabody College, 1931.

Sandweiss, Martha A., et al. *Eyewitness to War: Prints and Daguerreotypes of the Mexican War, 1846–1848*. Washington, D.C.: Smithsonian Institution Press/Fort Worth, Tex.: Amon Carter Museum, 1989.

Santoni, Pedro. *Mexicans at Arms: Puro Federalists and the Politics of War, 1845–1848*. Fort Worth: Texas Christian University Press, 1996.

Scharf, J. Thomas. *History of St. Louis City and County*. 2 vols. Philadelphia: Everts and Co., 1883.

Schlesinger, Arthur M., Jr., ed. *History of American Presidential Elections, 1789–1968*. 4 vols. New York: Chelsea House, 1971.

Schroeder, John H. *Mr. Polk's War: American Opposition and Dissent, 1846–1848*. Madison: University of Wisconsin Press, 1973.

Sellers, Charles. *James K. Polk, Continentalist, 1843–1846*. Princeton: Princeton University Press, 1966.

Settle, Raymond W. *Alexander William Doniphan, Symbol of Pioneer Americanism*. Liberty, Mo.: William Jewell College, 1947.

Shalhope, Robert E. *Sterling Price, Portrait of a Southerner*. Columbia: University of Missouri Press, 1971.

Singletary, Otis A. *The Mexican War*. Chicago: University of Chicago Press, 1960.

Skelton, William B. *An American Profession of Arms: The Army Officer Corps, 1784–1861*. Lawrence: University Press of Kansas, 1992.

Smith, George W., and Charles Judah, eds. *Chronicles of the Gringos: The U.S. Army in the Mexican War, 1846–1848, Accounts of Eyewitnesses and Combatants*. Albuquerque: University of New Mexico Press, 1968.

Smith, Harry A. *Military Government*. Fort Leavenworth, Kans.: General Service School Press, 1920.

Smith, Henry Nash. *Virgin Land: The American West as Symbol and Myth*. Cambridge, Mass.: Harvard University Press, 1957.

Smith, Justin H. *The War with Mexico*. 2 vols. New York: Macmillan, 1919.

Sonnichsen, Charles L. *Pass of the North: Four Centuries on the Rio Grande*. El Paso: Texas Western Press, 1968.

Spencer, Ivor D. *The Victor and the Spoils: A Life of William L. Marcy*. Providence, R.I.: Brown University Press, 1959.

Spicer, Edward H. *Cycles of Conquest: The Impact of Spain, Mexico, and the United States on the Indians of the Southwest, 1533–1960*. Tucson: University of Arizona Press, 1962.

Stephenson, Nathaniel. *Texas and the Mexican War: A Chronicle of the Winning of the Southwest*. New Haven, Conn.: Yale University Press, 1921.

Stevens, Donald F. *Origins of Instability in Early Republican Mexico*. Durham, N.C.: Duke University Press, 1991.

Stevens, Walter B. *Missouri the Center State*. 3 vols. Chicago: S. J. Clarke, 1915.

Stuart, Reginald C. *United States Expansionism and British North America, 1775–1871*. Chapel Hill: University of North Carolina Press, 1988.

Thomas, Benjamin P. *Abraham Lincoln*. New York: Alfred A. Knopf, 1952.

Thomas, David Y. *A History of Military Government in Newly Acquired Territory of the United States*. New York: Columbia University, 1904.

Traas, Adrian G. *From the Golden Gate to Mexico City: The U.S. Army Topographical Engineers in the Mexican War, 1846–1848*. Washington, D.C.: Center of Military History, 1993.

Trennert, Robert A. *Alternative to Extinction: Federal Indian Policy and the Beginnings of the Reservation System, 1846–51*. Philadelphia: Temple University Press, 1975.

Turner, Frederick C. *The Dynamic of Mexican Nationalism*. Chapel Hill: University of North Carolina Press, 1968.

Tuveson, Ernest L. *Redeemer Nation: The Idea of American's Millennial Role*. Chicago: University of Chicago Press, 1968.

Twitchell, Ralph E. *The History of the Military Occupation of the Territory of New Mexico, from 1846 to 1851*. Denver: Smith-Brooks, 1909. Repr., Chicago: Rio Grande Press, 1963.

———. *The Story of the Conquest of Santa Fe, New Mexico, and the Building of Old Fort Marcy*. Albuquerque: New Mexico Historical Society Bulletin No. 24, 1922.

United States Biographical Dictionary and Portrait Gallery of Eminent and Self-Made Men, Missouri Volume. New York: United States Biographical Publishing Co., 1878.

Valadés, José C. *Breve historia de la guerra con los Estados Unidos*. Mexico City: Editorial Patria, 1947; 2nd ed., Mexico City: Editorial Diana, 1980.

Vázquez, Josefina Zoraida, and Lorenzo Meyer. *The United States and Mexico*. Chicago: University of Chicago Press, 1985.

Velasco Márquez, Jesús. *La guerra del 47 y la opinión pública, 1845–1848*. Mexico City: Secretaría de Educación Pública, 1975.

Walker, Henry P. *The Wagonmasters*. Norman: University of Oklahoma Press, 1966.

Wallach, Jehuda L. *The Dogma of the Battle of Annihilation*. Westport, Conn.: Greenwood Press, 1986.

Ward, Adolphus W. *The History of Greece*. 5 vols. London: Bentley and Son, 1869–1873.

Webb, William L. *Battles and Biographies of Missourians, or the Civil War Period in Our State*. Kansas City: Hudson-Kimberly, 1900.

Weber, David J. *Foreigners in Their Native Land*. Albuquerque: University of New Mexico Press, 1973.

———. *The Mexican Frontier, 1821–1846*. Albuquerque: University of New Mexico Press, 1982.

———. *The Taos Traders: The Fur Trade in the Southwest, 1540–1846*. Norman: University of Oklahoma Press, 1970.

Weems, John E. *To Conquer a Peace: The War between the United States and Mexico*. New York: Doubleday, 1974.

Weigley, Russell F. *The American Way of War: A History of United States Military Strategy and Policy*. New York: Macmillan, 1973.

———. *History of the United States Army*. Enl. ed. Bloomington: Indiana University Press, 1984.

Weinberg, Albert K. *Manifest Destiny: A Study of Nationalist Expansionism in American History*. Baltimore: Johns Hopkins University Press, 1935.

Wellman, Paul I. *The House Divides: The Age of Jackson and Lincoln*. Garden City, N.Y.: Doubleday, 1966.

Welter, Rush. *The Mind of America, 1820–1860*. New York: Columbia University Press, 1975.

Williams, T. Harry. *Hayes of the Twenty-third: The Civil War Volunteer Officer*. New York: Alfred A. Knopf, 1965.

Winders, Richard B. *Mr. Polk's Army: The American Military Experience in the Mexican War*. College Station: Texas A&M University Press, 1997.

Winn, Kenneth H. *Exiles in a Land of Liberty: Mormons in America, 1830–1846*. Chapel Hill: University of North Carolina Press, 1989.

Woodson, W. H. *History of Clay County, Missouri*. Topeka: Historical Publishing Co., 1920.

Xenophon. *The Persian Expedition*. Trans. Rex Warner. Baltimore: Penguin, 1949.

Young, Otis E. *The West of Philip St. George Cooke, 1809–1895*. Glendale, Calif.: Arthur H. Clarke, 1955.

Young, William. *Young's History of Lafayette County, Missouri*. 2 vols. Indianapolis: B. F. Brown, 1910.

Zornow, William F. *Kansas: History of the Jayhawk State*. Norman: University of Oklahoma Press, 1957.

ARTICLES

Allen, D. C. "Builders of the Great American West: Remarkable Experiences of Alexander Doniphan." *Journal of American History* 4 (1910), 511–24.

Armstrong, Andrew. "The Brazito Battlefield." *New Mexico Historical Review* 35 (January 1960), 63–74.

Atherton, Lewis E. "Disorganizing Effects of the Mexican War on the Santa Fe Trade." *Kansas Historical Quarterly* 6 (May 1937), 115–23.

———. "James and Robert Aull: A Frontier Missouri Mercantile Firm." *Missouri Historical Review* 30 (October 1935), 3–27.

———. "The Santa Fe Trader as Mercantile Capitalist." *Missouri Historical Review* 77 (October 1982), 1–12.

Bender, Averam B. "Government Explorations in the Territory of New Mexico, 1846–1859." *New Mexico Historical Review* 9 (January 1934), 1–32.

Benjamin, Thomas. "Recent Historiography of the Origins of the Mexican War." *New Mexico Historical Review* 54 (July 1979), 169–81.

Bloom, John P. "Johnny Gringo at the Pass of the North." *Password: The Quarterly Journal of the El Paso County Historical Society* 4 (October 1959), 134–40.

———. "New Mexico as Viewed by Americans, 1846–1849." *New Mexico Historical Review* 34 (July 1959), 165–98.

Bochin, Hal W. "Tom Corwin's Speech against the Mexican War: Courageous but Misunderstood." *Ohio History* 90 (Winter 1981), 33–54.

Brack, Gene M. "Mexican Opinion, American Racism, and the War of 1846." *Western Historical Quarterly* 1 (April 1970), 161–74.

Brown, Robert B. "Doniphan's Expedition: A Problem for Bibliographers." *Historical and Philosophical Society of Ohio Bulletin* 9 (1951), 50–55.

Carrion, Jorge. "Efectos Psicologiocos de la Guerra de 47 en la Hombre de Mexico." *Cuadernos Americanos* 7 (January–February 1948), 116–32.

Clark, Kimball. "The Epic March of Doniphan's Missourians." *Missouri Historical Review* 80 (January 1986), 134–55.

Creel, George. "Doniphan's Volunteers." *Collier's*, September 9, 1933, 22, 45.

Culmer, Frederic A. "A Snapshot of Alexander Doniphan." *Missouri Historical Review* 38 (October 1943), 25–32.

DeVoto, Bernard. "Anabasis in Buckskin: An Exploit of Our War with Mexico." *Harper's*, March 1940, 400–410.

———. "Geopolitics with the Dew on It." *Harper's*, March 1944, 313–23.

Elliott, R. Kenneth. "The Rhetoric of Alexander W. Doniphan." *The Trail Guide* 1 (December 1969), 3–14.

Gilbert, Thomas D. "The U.S. Military Occupation of El Paso del Norte, 1846–1847." *Password: The Quarterly Journal of the El Paso County Historical Society* 40 (Fall 1995), 107–18.

Graebner, Norman A. "Lessons of the Mexican War." *Pacific Historical Review* 47 (August 1978), 325–42.

———. "The Mexican War: A Study in Causation." *Pacific Historical Review* 49 (August 1980), 405–26.

Haecker, Charles M. "Brazito Battlefield: Once Lost, Now Found." *New Mexico Historical Review* 72 (July 1997), 229–38.

Hale, Charles A. "The War with the United States and the Crisis in Mexican Thought." *The Americas* 14 (October 1957), 153–74.

Harstad, Peter T., and Richard W. Resh. "The Causes of the Mexican War: A Note on Changing Interpretations." *Arizona and the West* 6 (Winter 1964), 289–302.

Jones, Oakah L., Jr. "The Pacific Squadron off California." *Journal of the West* 5 (April 1966), 187–202.

Kearful, Jerome. "Doniphan's Artillery." *Field Artillery Journal* 40 (January–February 1950), 70–71.

Keleher, William A. "The Year of Decision." *New Mexico Historical Review* 22 (January 1947), 8–17.

Kirkpatrick, Arthur R. "Missouri on the Eve of the Civil War." *Missouri Historical Review* 55 (January 1961), 99–108.

Kurtz, Wilbur G., Jr. "The First Regiment of Georgia Volunteers in the Mexican War." *Georgia Historical Quarterly* 27 (December 1943), 301–23.

Latham, Frank B. "Doniphan of Missouri: Soldier, Lawyer, and Statesman." *New York Westerners Brandbook* 2, no. 4 (1955), 73, 75–76, 95.

Lecompte, Janet. "Manuel Armijo and the Americans." *Journal of the West* 19 (July 1980), 51–63.

Livingston-Little, D. E. "U.S. Military Forces in California." *Journal of the West* 11 (April 1972), 299–306.

Lofgren, Charles A. "Force and Diplomacy, 1846–1848." *Military Affairs* 31 (Summer 1967), 57–65.

Malin, James C. "LeCompte and the 'Sack of Lawrence,' May 21, 1856." *Kansas Historical Quarterly* 20 (August 1953), 465–94.

Mangum, Neil C. "The Battle of Brazito: Reappraising a Lost and Forgotten Episode in the Mexican-American War." *New Mexico Historical Review* 72 (July 1997), 217–28.

Marshall, Thomas M. "Commercial Aspects of the Texas–Santa Fe Expedition." *Southwestern Historical Quarterly* 20 (January 1917), 242–59.

Mary Loyola, Sister. "The American Occupation of New Mexico, 1821–1852." *New Mexico Historical Review* 14 (January 1939), 34–75; (April 1939), 143–99; (July 1939), 230–86.

Michel, Peter J. "No Mere Holiday Affair: The Capture of Santa Fe in the Mexican War." *Gateway Heritage* 9 (Spring 1989), 12–25.

Miles, Edwin A. "'Fifty-Four Forty or Fight'—An American Political Legend." *Mississippi Valley Historical Review* 44 (September 1957), 291–309.

Millett, Allan R., and Williamson Murray. "Lessons of War." *The National Interest* 14 (Winter 1988), 83–95.

Neely, Mark E. "Lincoln and the Mexican War: An Argument by Analogy." *Civil War History* 24 (March 1978), 5–24.

Noggle, Burl. "Anglo Observers of the Southwest Borderlands, 1825–1890: The Rise of a Concept." *Arizona and the West* 1 (Summer 1959), 105–31.

Perrine, Fred S. "Military Escorts on the Santa Fe Trail." *New Mexico Historical Review* 2 (April 1927), 175–93; (July 1927) 269–304.

Puckett, Fidelia M. "Ramon Ortiz (1813–1896): Priest and Patriot." *New Mexico Historical Review* 25 (October 1950), 265–95.

Ruhlen, George. "The Battle of Brazito: Where Was It Fought?" *Password: The Quarterly Journal of the El Paso County Historical Society* 2 (May 1957), 53–60.

———. "Brazito—The Only Battle in the Southwest between American and Foreign Troops." *Password: The Quarterly Journal of the El Paso County Historical Society* 2 (February 1957), 4–13.

Salisbury, Richard B. "Kentuckians at the Battle of Buena Vista." *Filson Club Quarterly* 61 (January 1987), 34–53.

Santoni, Pedro. "A Fear of the People: The Civic Militia of Mexico in 1845." *Hispanic–American Historical Review* 68 (May 1988), 269–88.

Seematter, Mary E. "Merchants in the Middle: The Glasgow Brothers and the Mexican War." *Gateway Heritage* 9 (Fall 1988), 34–43.

Shoemaker, Floyd C. "Missouri's Proslavery Fight for Kansas, 1854–1855." *Missouri Historical Review* 48 (April 1954), 221–36; (July 1954), 325–40, 49; (October 1954), 41–54.

Smith, Heman C. "The Hero of Sacramento, Alexander W. Doniphan." *Journal of History* 4 (1911), 338–56.

Smith, Ralph A. "The 'King of New Mexico' and the Doniphan Expedition." *New Mexico Historical Review* 38 (January 1963), 29–55.

Spell, Lota M. "The Anglo-Saxon Press in Mexico, 1846–1848." *American Historical Review* 38 (October 1932), 20–31.

Sunseri, Alvin R. "Revolt in Taos, 1846–47: Resistance to U.S. Occupation." *El Palacio* 96 (Fall 1990), 38–47.

Taylor, Mendell L. "The Western Services of Stephen Watts Kearny, 1815–1848." *New Mexico Historical Review* 21 (July 1946), 169–84.

Tresler, Harrison A. "The Value and the Sale of the Missouri Slave." *Missouri Historical Review* 8 (January 1914), 69–85.

Tucker, Phillip T. "Above and Beyond: African-American Missourians of Colonel Alexander Doniphan's Expedition." *Password: The Quarterly Journal of the El Paso County Historical Society* 35 (Fall 1990), 133–37.

———. "The Missourians and the Battle of the Brazito, Christmas Day, 1846." *Password: The Quarterly Journal of the El Paso County Historical Society* 34 (Winter 1989), 159–70.

Tyler, Daniel. "Governor Armijo's Moment of Truth." *Journal of the West* 11 (April 1972), 307–16.

———. "Gringo Views of Governor Manuel Armijo." *New Mexico Historical Review* 45 (January 1970), 23–46.

Vázquez, Josefina Zoraida. "The Texas Question in Mexican Politics, 1836–1845." *Southwestern Historical Quarterly* 89 (January 1986), 309–44.

Viola, Herman J. "Zachary Taylor and the Indiana Volunteers." *Southwestern Historical Quarterly* 72 (January 1969), 335–46.

Wallace, Lee A., Jr. "The First Regiment of Virginia Volunteers, 1846–1848." *Virginia Magazine of History and Biography* 77 (January 1969), 46–77.

———. "Raising a Volunteer Regiment for Mexico, 1846–1847." *North Carolina Historical Review* 35 (January 1958), 20–33.

Welter, Rush. "The Frontier West as Image of American Society: Conservative Attitudes before the Civil War." *Mississippi Valley Historical Review* 46 (March 1960), 593–614.

Williamson, Hugh P. "Colonel Alexander W. Doniphan, Soldier, Lawyer, and Statesman." *Journal of the Missouri Bar* 8 (October 1952), 180–85.

Wilson, Major L. "The Concept of Time and the Political Dialogue in the United States, 1828–1848." *American Quarterly* 19 (Winter 1967), 619–44.

Wyman, Walker D. "The Military Phase of Santa Fe Freighting, 1846–1865." *Kansas Historical Quarterly* 1 (November 1931), 17–27.

THESES, DISSERTATIONS, AND UNPUBLISHED TYPESCRIPTS

Banta, Byron B. "The Military Occupation of New Mexico, 1846–1851." M.A. thesis, Washington University, 1947.

Bloom, John P. "With the American Army into Mexico, 1846–1848." Ph.D. dissertation, Emory University, 1956.

DePalo, William A., Jr. "Praetorians and Patriots: The Mexican National Army, 1822–1852." Ph.D. dissertation, University of New Mexico, 1994.

Duchateau, André P. "Missouri Colossus: Alexander William Doniphan, 1808–1887." Ed.D. dissertation, Oklahoma State University, 1973.

Grivas, Theodore. "General Stephen Watts Kearny and the Army of the West." M.A. thesis, University of Southern California, 1953.

Maynard, Gregory P. "Alexander William Doniphan: The Forgotten Man from Missouri." M.A. thesis, Brigham Young University, 1968.

Minge, Ward Alan. "Frontier Problems in New Mexico Preceding the Mexican War, 1840–1846." Ph.D. dissertation, University of New Mexico, 1965.

Samponaro, F. N. "The Political Role of the Army in Mexico, 1821–1848." Ph.D. dissertation, State University of New York at Stony Brook, 1974.

Settle, Raymond. "Alexander William Doniphan: Zenophon [*sic*] of the West." Unpublished typescript, Raymond Settle Collection, Charles F. Curry Library, William Jewell College, Liberty, Missouri.

Sunseri, Alvin R. "New Mexico in the Aftermath of the Anglo-American Conquest, 1846–1861." Ph.D. dissertation, Louisiana State University, 1973.

REFERENCE WORKS

Allardice, Bruce S. *More Generals in Gray*. Baton Rouge: Louisiana State University Press, 1995.

Biographical Directory of the American Congress, 1774–1989. Washington, D.C.: Government Printing Office, 1989.

Cullum, George W. *Biographical Register of the Officers and Graduates of the United States Military Academy*. 2 vols. New York: Appleton, 1868.

———. *Biographical Register of the Officers and Graduates of the United States Military Academy*. 3rd ed., 3 vols. Boston: Houghton Mifflin, 1891.

DeConde, Alexander, ed. *Encyclopedia of American Foreign Policy*. 3 vols. New York: Scribner's, 1978.

Diccionario Porrua: De históría, biografía y geografía de México. Mexico, D.F.: Editorial Porrua, 1964.

Esposito, Vincent J., ed. *The West Point Atlas of American Wars*. 2 vols. New York: Praeger, 1959.

Frazier, Donald S., ed. *The United States and Mexico at War: Nineteenth-Century Expansionism and Conflict*. New York: Macmillan, 1998.

Gardner, Charles K. *A Dictionary of All Officers Who Have Been Commissioned, or Have Been Appointed and Served, in the Army of the United States* . . . New York: G. P. Putnam and Co., 1853.

Heitman, Francis B. *Historical Register and Dictionary of the United States Army*. 2 vols. Washington, D.C.: Government Printing Office, 1903.

Warner, Ezra J. *Generals in Blue: Lives of the Union Commanders*. Baton Rouge: Louisiana State University Press, 1964.

———. *Generals in Gray: Lives of the Confederate Commanders*. Baton Rouge: Louisiana State University Press, 1959.

Warner, Ezra J., and W. Buck Yearns. *Biographical Register of the Confederate Congress*. Baton Rouge: Louisiana State University Press, 1975.

INDEX